# *Frommer's®*

# Atlanta

## *11th Edition*

## by Karen K. Snyder

## Here's what the critics say about Frommer's:

"Amazingly easy to use. Very portable, very complete."
—**BOOKLIST**

"Detailed, accurate, and easy-to-read information
for all price ranges."
—**GLAMOUR MAGAZINE**

"Hotel information is close to encyclopedic."
—**DES MOINES SUNDAY REGISTER**

"Frommer's Guides have a way of giving you a
real feel for a place."
—**KNIGHT RIDDER NEWSPAPERS**

Wiley Publishing, Inc.

## ABOUT THE AUTHOR

K.K. Snyder admits that she had trepidations about moving to the South, but quickly fell in love with the region and its people and has lived there for the past 27 years. A freelance writer who lives to travel and travels to live, she writes for a number of publications from Chicago to Miami and places in between.

Published by:

## WILEY PUBLISHING, INC.

111 River St.
Hoboken, NJ 07030-5774

ISBN 978-0-470-38526-5

Editor: Shelley W. Bance with Jamie Ehrlich
Production Editor: Lindsay Conner
Cartographer: Andrew Dolan
Photo Editor: Richard Fox
Production by Wiley Indianapolis Composition Services

Front cover photo: Centennial Olympic Park lit up
Back cover photo: Martin Luther King foundation for peace, portrait of the Reverend King, woman and child admiring portrait

# CONTENTS

ATLANTA

CONTENTS

## 9 SHOPPING 193

## 10 ATLANTA AFTER DARK 208

## APPENDIX: FAST FACTS, TOLL-FREE NUMBERS & WEBSITES 219

## INDEX 231

# LIST OF MAPS

*For my mother, Carol Kay Randle Lee, who fought the battle with dignity, courage, and laughter, reminding us that every day is a treasure just waiting to be discovered.*

## ACKNOWLEDGMENTS

This project would not be possible without the help and support I receive from tourism and public relations professionals in the great city of Atlanta, especially those of the Atlanta Convention and Visitors Bureau. In addition, the enthusiasm of the fine people of Atlanta helps this city live up to the gracious Southern hospitality expectations of those who visit here.

## AN INVITATION TO THE READER

In researching this book, we discovered many wonderful places—hotels, restaurants, shops, and more. We're sure you'll find others. Please tell us about them, so we can share the information with your fellow travelers in upcoming editions. If you were disappointed with a recommendation, we'd love to know that, too. Please write to:

*Frommer's Atlanta,* 11th Edition
Wiley Publishing, Inc. • 111 River St. • Hoboken, NJ 07030-5774

## AN ADDITIONAL NOTE

Please be advised that travel information is subject to change at any time—and this is especially true of prices. We therefore suggest that you write or call ahead for confirmation when making your travel plans. The authors, editors, and publisher cannot be held responsible for the experiences of readers while traveling. Your safety is important to us, however, so we encourage you to stay alert and be aware of your surroundings. Keep a close eye on cameras, purses, and wallets, all favorite targets of thieves and pickpockets.

---

### Other Great Guides for Your Trip:

*Frommer's Carolinas & Georgia*
*Frommer's Portable Savannah*
*Frommer's USA*

# FROMMER'S STAR RATINGS, ICONS & ABBREVIATIONS

Every hotel, restaurant, and attraction listing in this guide has been ranked for quality, value, service, amenities, and special features using a **star-rating system.** In country, state, and regional guides, we also rate towns and regions to help you narrow down your choices and budget your time accordingly. Hotels and restaurants are rated on a scale of zero (recommended) to three stars (exceptional). Attractions, shopping, nightlife, towns, and regions are rated according to the following scale: zero stars (recommended), one star (highly recommended), two stars (very highly recommended), and three stars (must-see).

In addition to the star-rating system, we also use seven feature icons that point you to the great deals, in-the-know advice, and unique experiences that separate travelers from tourists. Throughout the book, look for:

| | |
|---|---|
| **(Finds)** | Special finds—those places only insiders know about |
| **(Fun Facts)** | Fun facts—details that make travelers more informed and their trips more fun |
| **(Kids)** | Best bets for kids, and advice for the whole family |
| **(Moments)** | Special moments—those experiences that memories are made of |
| **(Overrated)** | Places or experiences not worth your time or money |
| **(Tips)** | Insider tips—great ways to save time and money |
| **(Value)** | Great values—where to get the best deals |

The following **abbreviations** are used for credit cards:

| | | | | | |
|---|---|---|---|---|---|
| **AE** | American Express | **DISC** | Discover | **V** | Visa |
| **DC** | Diners Club | **MC** | MasterCard | | |

# FROMMERS.COM

Now that you have this guidebook to help you plan a great trip, visit our website at **www.frommers.com** for additional travel information on more than 4,000 destinations. We update features regularly to give you instant access to the most current trip-planning information available. At Frommers.com, you'll find scoops on the best airfares, lodging rates, and car rental bargains. You can even book your travel online through our reliable travel booking partners. Other popular features include:

- Online updates to our most popular guidebooks
- Vacation sweepstakes and contest giveaways
- Newsletter highlighting the hottest travel trends
- Podcasts, interactive maps, and up-to-the-minute events listings
- Opinionated blog entries by Arthur Frommer himself
- Online travel message boards with featured travel discussions

# What's New in Atlanta

Atlanta is a city constantly rein-venting itself, from reigning as the nation's conventions capital, to hosting the 1996 Summer Olympic Games, to emerging as one of the hottest new vacation spots in the South. Today, visitors to this fine city are greeted by a new landmark structure: the Millennium Gate. Though it didn't rise into the sky until several years after the turn of the new century, the city's 73-foot-tall Millennium Gate was constructed in honor of Atlanta's many philanthropic families. Unveiled July 4, 2008 near the popular Atlantic Station retail wonder-land, the arch has been compared to the Washington Arch in New York, the Wel-lington Arch in London, the Carrousel Arch in Paris, and the Siegestor Arch in Munich. Perhaps it gives Atlanta a bit of cosmopolitan flavor, but you can decide for yourself.

**WHERE TO STAY & DINE**   Evidently, developers willing to take a gamble on Atlanta have learned that if they build it, the people will come. With more than 90,000 hotel rooms in the metro area, finding a place to rest your weary feet after a full day of fun and frolic is an easy task. In addition, Atlanta is home to 8,000-plus restaurants that continue to redefine the Southern palate, serving cuisine from every ethnic corner of the world.

Most recently, W Hotels have taken the city by storm, opening three new lodgings in the past year, including **W Atlanta Midtown,** 188 14th St. NE (© **404/892-6000**), where the former Sheraton Colony Square Hotel has been transformed into a sleek, ultra-modern, 466-room hotel with exclusive service (p. 82). The property includes the first Bliss Spa in Georgia and **Spice Market,** the famous restaurant of that famous celebrity chef, Jean-Georges Vongerichten (p. 106). W Hotels are also open in Buckhead and Downtown, bring-ing the total number located here to four.

Not your mama's 1950s motor court hotel and with a much-anticipated debut, the **Mansion on Peachtree,** 3376 Peach-tree Rd. (© **404/995-7500**), has rede-fined luxury accommodations in Atlanta. This exclusive 127-room hotel features private butler service for each and every guest (p. 86). If you can drag yourself away from your finely appointed guest room, make dinner reservations at either of the two on-site restaurants: **NEO,** a contemporary Italian dining experience (p. 118), or the newest, **Craft Atlanta,** the latest foray of Tom Colicchio, which opened in December 2008. Contact the Mansion's concierge for reservations at either restaurant.

And this is just the beginning. By the end of 2009, Atlanta will have added a $100-million Palomar Hotel in Midtown and an ultra-luxurious 26-story St. Regis hotel in Buckhead. By 2010, visitors will also have the option of staying at a new Mandarin Oriental Hotel or the Loews Atlanta Hotel, both coming to Midtown.

**ATTRACTIONS**   If you get bored in the busy city of Hotlanta, well shame on you! The city has lauded the more than

$6 billion spent since 2005 on new and expanded attractions and facilities, including the new World of Coca-Cola, the Georgia Aquarium, Atlantic Station, and the Woodruff Arts Center, as well as major improvements to the Hartsfield-Jackson International Airport. There's always something new to see, even if you've been here many times before.

Among the latest attractions is the Sky Hike at **Stone Mountain Park,** U.S. hwy. 78 E., Stone Mountain (© **800/317-2006**). Adults and kids who dare can traverse the treetops on the family adventure course, featuring suspended bridges, high ropes, and vertical nets, some as high as 40 feet in the air. An overhead safety system keeps visitors safe while allowing them to see the park from a whole new angle.

Also new since 2008 is the relocation of the **National Museum of Patriotism** to the Lobby of the Hilton Garden Inn Downtown, 275-B Baker St. (© **877/276-1692**). In addition to the museum's extensive World War II patriotic sweetheart jewelry and collectibles, as well as interactive, educational displays honoring the U.S. armed forces, the facility houses Georgia's only exhibit on the September 11, 2001 terrorist attacks.

A 2010 expansion will double the size of the **Center for Puppetry Arts,** 1404 Spring St. (© **404/873-3391**), making room for, among other things, the center's recent acquisition of more than 500 of the late Jim Henson's Muppets, as well as props, videos, and memorabilia from such classics as "The Muppet Show" and "Sesame Street." The collection will be housed in a Jim Henson Wing when the expansion is completed. Until then, a number of Henson puppets are currently on display.

# The Best of Atlanta

"How do I get to Tara?"
"Where are Scarlett and Rhett buried?"
"Why do you put sugar in iced tea but not on grits?"
"Just what is a grit anyway?"

Some visitors come to Atlanta looking for Old South stereotypes—white-columned mansions surrounded by magnolias, owned by slow-moving folks with accents as thick as molasses. Instead, they discover a region that's more cosmopolitan and a heck of a lot more interesting than what they'd expected.

When General William Sherman burned Atlanta to the ground in 1864, the city rose from those smoldering bitter ashes and has not looked back since. Instead, it has spent the last 145 years building what's been described as the Capital of the New South and the Next Great International City. Atlanta's heritage may be Southern, but the current dynamic is brashly Sunbelt, and straight-up economic vitality now drives this city's engines.

Atlanta is and always has been a city on the move. Longtime mayor William B. Hartsfield called it the city "too busy to hate," and the spirit of Atlanta is one of working together to get the job done. The dramatic downtown skyline, with its gleaming skyscrapers, is testimony to Atlanta's inability to sit still—even for a minute. And its role as host for the Centennial Olympic Games in 1996 finally convinced the rest of the world that Atlanta is a force to be reckoned with—and a great place to visit. Recent projects have only reinforced that notion. These ventures include the new World of Coca-Cola, bigger and better than ever, the addition of the Atlanta Dream, the city's first venture into women's professional basketball, and the onslaught of new hotels and restaurants that call Atlanta home.

Consistently ranked as one of the best cities in the world in which to do business, Atlanta is headquarters for hundreds of corporations, including Coca-Cola, Delta Air Lines, UPS, Holiday Inn, Georgia-Pacific, Home Depot, BellSouth, and Cox Enterprises, and it has become a magnet for many Internet-related companies. A major convention city and a crossroads where three interstate highways converge, it's home to the country's busiest airport. And all those convention-goers certainly find many places to spend money—Atlanta is considered the shopping capital of the Southeast. Although the city limits are only 131 square miles, the metro area is vast and sprawling. With a population that recently broke 5 million (and still counting), there seems to be no limit to its growth.

But commerce and development are not the only things that characterize this bustling metropolis. Its success is due in no small part to its quality of life, which is hard to beat. Atlanta is often called the City of Trees, and the streets are indeed filled with dogwoods and azaleas. The city has a small-town quality to it, with dozens of neighborhoods and parks. A temperate climate makes Atlanta a magnet for anyone who enjoys the outdoors, and the city's Southern roots ensure graciousness and hospitality. As Atlanta has grown in stature, it has attracted residents from across the continent and around the world, further enriching the city's social fabric. You'll still hear gentle Southern accents here, but at least half of Atlanta's citizens were born outside the South. Interestingly, many of these transplants find themselves bending to the local customs, saying "please" and "ma'am" and holding doors open for one another.

When H. L. Mencken came south earlier in the century, he branded Atlanta a cultural wasteland. He should visit now. Media mogul Ted Turner inaugurated CNN here in 1980, and subsequently launched Superstation TBS, Headline News, and TNT. Also in 1980, the revitalized black neighborhood of Sweet Auburn became a national historic district, with 10 blocks of notable sites including Martin Luther King, Jr.'s, boyhood home, his crypt, the church where he preached, a museum, and the Martin Luther King, Jr., Center for Nonviolent Social Change. It is probably *the* major black historical attraction in the country, and in the last several years it has undergone a major revitalization and restoration.

Atlanta is home to major art, science, nature, and archaeology museums; a vibrant theater community; an outstanding symphony orchestra; a well-regarded ballet company; opera, blues, and jazz performances; Broadway musicals; a presidential library; Confederate and African-American heritage sites; and dozens of art galleries. To those leisure options, add such attractions as Stone Mountain Park, a regional theme park, a botanical garden, and professional sports teams, and you have the makings of a lively and sophisticated city. The culinary spectrum here ranges from grits and biscuits to caviar and sushi. Sure, you can still feast on fried chicken and barbecued beef, but Atlanta also serves up cuisine from across the globe.

Of great significance is the ongoing development downtown. For years, city leaders have tried to encourage central city living, and it's finally taken hold as developers renovate old buildings into attractive apartments and lofts. The mark of a great city is an appealing and vital downtown area where people live as well as work, and Atlanta finally appears to be living the dream.

Atlanta now has Shirley Franklin, the first African-American female elected as mayor of this busy city. Her vision for this heart of the New South is expansive, and she's not too shy to tell you all about it. So if you've set your heart on hoop skirts and plantations, go on down to your local bookstore and pick up a copy of *Gone with the Wind*. But if you want to visit a vibrant, energetic city that's rich in heritage, culture, fine cuisine, entertainment, and commerce, Atlanta runs right up there with the big dogs.

## 1  FROMMER'S FAVORITE ATLANTA EXPERIENCES

- **Stepping Back in Time at the Atlanta History Center:** A re-created farm (with original buildings from the 1840s) shows how rural Southern folks really lived before the Civil War, and the beautifully restored 1928 Swan House, an estate on the property, gives a fascinating glimpse into the lifestyle enjoyed by upper-crust Atlantans in the early–20th century. Kids will love the hands-on discovery

areas at the history museum. Explore the walking trails after you take in the exhibits. It all adds up to a great look at the rich tapestry of Atlanta's past and present. See p. 140.

- **Frolicking in the Fountain:** The biggest attraction at Centennial Olympic Park is the Fountain of Rings, where young and old can get delightfully soaked on warm days. The fountain is a

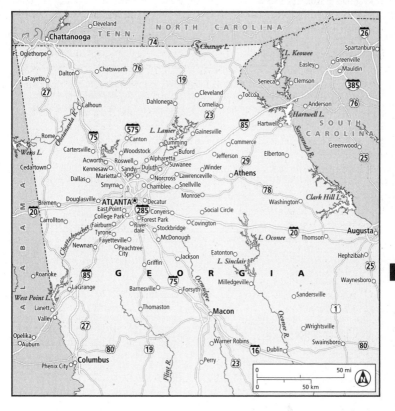

simple but ingenious design on the plaza floor, consisting of 251 water jets in the shape of the five Olympic rings. Take a deep breath and zip in and around the 12-foot water bursts, or just sit and watch the timed light-and-sound-effects show, when the water bursts 35 feet into the air. See p. 142.

- **Touring the CNN Studios:** The network that started round-the-clock television news lets you take a peek behind the scenes to see how it's all done. You can even have a videotape made of yourself reading the day's top stories from behind a CNN anchor desk. See p. 143.

- **Time-Traveling at Fernbank Museum of Natural History:** Check out the 45-foot-long model of a *Giganotosaurus,* then travel back 15 billion years and experience the Big Bang that jump-started the formation of the universe. The museum's stunning architecture is notable. IMAX films are shown here, too. See p. 144.

- **Discovering the Fox Theatre:** This Moorish-Egyptian palace exemplifies the glamorous movie-theater architecture of the 1920s, complete with onion domes, minarets, and a twinkling starlit sky over the auditorium. See p. 145.

(Tips) **Cheers to the New World of Coca-Cola**

With downtown revitalization at the top of the list for Atlanta leaders and developers, the proposal for a new and improved World of Coca-Cola right next to the well-attended Georgia Aquarium was well received. The new cola museum further focuses on the timeless values of Coca-Cola, while also celebrating consumer connections with the brand in new and exciting ways. State-of-the-art technology and story-telling techniques make the guest experience interactive and engaging.

This completed project, along with the Georgia Aquarium, Imagine It! Children's Museum, the CNN Center, Philips Arena, and the Tabernacle—the latter two being popular entertainment venues—has proved to be a much-needed shot in the arm for the downtown residential and commercial markets. These developments no doubt make the downtown area *the* place to be in this city, for visitors, residents, and convention-goers alike.

- **Marveling at the Creatures in the Georgia Aquarium:** Even if you have only a day or two to spend in the city, this is a must-see. The Georgia Aquarium, the largest in the country, continues to draw mind-boggling numbers of visitors every day. The highlights include giant whale sharks and unforgettable exhibits in five major categories, from river life to sea life in foreign waters around the planet. A 4-D movie, numerous opportunities for dining and shopping, and amazing play spaces for the little ones provide a full day of fun at this hot spot. Plan to order advance tickets online, as huge crowds usually converge on this attraction. See p. 146.

- **Exploring the King Center:** It's an inspiring experience to visit this living memorial to a true American hero. You'll see lots of memorabilia for Dr. Martin Luther King, Jr., and a film on his life and works. Especially moving is Freedom Plaza, where he's buried. The tomb is inscribed with his words: "Free at Last. Free at Last. Thank God Almighty I'm Free at Last." See p. 149.

- **Strolling around Oakland Cemetery:** This 88-acre cemetery is a peaceful

place, and its Victorian graves are of aesthetic, historic, and symbolic interest. The guided tour is recommended. Bring a picnic lunch; even your dog is welcome to hang out here (on a leash). See p. 156.

- **Relaxing in Stone Mountain Park:** Hike to the top of the big granite rock or spend a leisurely day taking in the diverse attractions, from a paddlewheel cruise to a living museum of Southern history. You can also choose from an array of activities—golf, tennis, swimming, hiking, boating, and more. See p. 157.

- **Touring the World of Coca-Cola:** Atlanta is Coke's hometown, so it's only fitting that there's a museum dedicated to the world's most renowned beverage. Come see the gigantic collection of memorabilia, explore the interactive exhibits, and sample Coke products from around the world—some not so refreshing to most Americans' taste buds. See p. 160.

- **Hanging Out at the Zoo:** Ever since the giant pandas, Yang Yang and Lun Lun, arrived at Zoo Atlanta, this has been one of the hottest tickets in town.

It's been even more popular since the arrival of two baby pandas, Mei Lan in 2006 and Xi Lan in 2008. You don't have to be a kid to be fascinated by these adorable creatures. See p. 175.

- **Getting a Breath of Fresh Air in Piedmont Park:** Atlanta's favorite public park is fun and funky and a terrific place to watch the world go by. Take your in-line skates or pack a lunch and find a shady spot for a picnic. See p. 179.
- **Spending a Day at the Ballpark:** Pack up the kids and take them out to the old ballgame. Even if there isn't an Atlanta Braves game scheduled, you can take a tour of Turner Field, play in Tooner Field playground, and visit the museum. The ballpark served as the Olympic Stadium for the 1996 Olympic Games. See p. 184.
- **Trekking through Virginia Highland:** Atlanta's version of New York's Greenwich Village or SoHo, this trendy neighborhood is full of coffee bars, galleries, cafes, and funky little boutiques. It all makes for a pleasant stroll on a sunny afternoon. For some of the shopping highlights, see p. 199.

- **Shopping at Lenox Square:** One of the most popular malls in the Southeast, Lenox Square is a mecca for affluent shoppers. It's hard to visit every store, even if you spend the whole day, but many visitors think it's a worthy goal. You'll enjoy good restaurants and great people-watching, too. See p. 201.
- **Spending the Morning at the Market:** Atlanta is home to two gigantic indoor farmers' markets, both jammed with locals who are shopping in earnest and visitors who have a hard time keeping their eyes from bugging out. Choose from the DeKalb Farmers' Market, which has an international flavor, and Harry's, which is a little more upscale. Each has loads of gourmet goodies you can take home or consume on the spot. See p. 205.
- **Taking in a Chastain Park Amphitheatre Concert:** Big-name entertainers perform under the stars, and everyone brings elaborate picnic fare (some people even bring tablecloths and candelabra for the picnic table). Even the entertainers seem dazzled by the setting. See p. 211.

## 2 BEST HOTEL BETS

- **Best for Business Travelers:** All the major downtown megahotels—which cater largely to a business and convention clientele—are fully equipped to meet your business needs. The finest is the **Ritz-Carlton Atlanta,** 181 Peachtree St. NE (✆ **800/241-3333**), which combines a full business center and a can-do concierge with superb service. See p. 74.
- **Best for Families:** The **Residence Inn by Marriott Buckhead,** 2960 Piedmont Rd. NE (✆ **800/331-3131**), offers accommodations large enough to ensure privacy for all, plus fully equipped kitchens, washers and dryers,

indoor and outdoor swimming pools, barbecue grills, and basketball, volley-ball, and paddle tennis courts. Many rooms even have fireplaces. See p. 91.
- **Best for a Romantic Getaway:** You'll fall for each other all over again at the luxurious **Four Seasons Hotel,** 75 14th St. (✆ **800/819-5053**), an elegant choice with lavish guest rooms, luxurious marble tubs, and impeccable service. See p. 80.
- **Best Moderately Priced Hotel:** It's hard to beat the **Residence Inn by Marriott Downtown,** 134 Peachtree St. NW (✆ **800/331-3131**). It offers a convenient location, large rooms, and a

bundle of amenities for a very reasonable price. See p. 78.

- **Best Inexpensive Accommodations:** It's nothing fancy, but the convenient Buckhead location of the **Country Inn and Suites Buckhead,** 800 Sidney Marcus Blvd. (© **888/236-2427**), makes this a good deal. See p. 92.

- **Best Location:** Buckhead is one of the loveliest—and busiest—parts of town, offering exceptional nightlife, dining, and shopping. There are two MARTA stations (Buckhead and Lenox) where you can connect to other parts of the city, and any hotel within walking distance of either of those stations is a sure bet. A good example is the **J. W. Marriott Hotel Buckhead,** 3300 Lenox Rd. NE (© **800/613-2051**), adjacent to the upscale Lenox Square mall. See p. 86.

- **Best Service:** The **Mansion on Peachtree,** new in 2008, takes the cake when it comes to guest service, employing three staff members to every overnight guest. Where else does a private butler come with every hotel room? The **Ritz-Carlton Atlanta,** 181 Peachtree St. NE (© **800/241-3333**), and the **Ritz-Carlton Buckhead,** 3434 Peachtree Rd. NE (© **800/241-3333**), are tied for a close second. See p. 86, 74, and 88 for each hotel, respectively.

- **Best _Architectural Digest_ Interior:** The towering **Grand Hyatt Atlanta,** 3300 Peachtree Rd. (© **800/233-1234**), offers a stunning combination of 18th-century American architecture and Japanese attention to aesthetic detail. A 9,000-square-foot garden features waterfalls viewable from the lobby overlook. See p. 85.

- **Best Trendy Hotel:** Atlanta's four W Hotels (more than any other city outside New York) are trendy, but the **W Atlanta Midtown,** 188 14th St. (© **404/892-6000**), which opened in 2008 with its popular lobby bar, is definitely the trendiest. The **Westin Buckhead Atlanta,** 3391 Peachtree Rd. NE (© **404/365-0065**), with its clean Euro-modern style, is a favorite among visiting celebrities.

- **Best for Travelers with Disabilities:** The **Embassy Suites Atlanta Buckhead,** 3285 Peachtree Rd. NW (© **800/ 362-2779**), is fully accessible, with 10 suites completely equipped for visitors with disabilities (some with roll-in showers, too). The hotel is just a block away from the Buckhead MARTA station. See p. 89.

- **Best for Pets:** Some hotels get downright snooty if you try to check in with your pooch, but not the trendy **Hotel Indigo,** 683 Peachtree St. (© **404/874-9200**). All pets are welcome—no fees, no weight limit. If you're in town on Tuesdays, don't miss Canine Cocktail Hour in the bar. See p. 83.

---

## 3 BEST DINING BETS

- **Best Spot for a Business Lunch:** Power brokers head for steaks at **Bone's,** 3130 Piedmont Rd. NE (© **404/237-2663**), in Buckhead, where the food is serious and the service is impeccable and unobtrusive. See p. 116.

- **Best Spot for a Romantic Dinner:** There's no better spot than the tree-shaded terrace at **Horseradish Grill,** 4320 Powers Ferry Rd. (© **404/255-7277**). See p. 121.

- **Best Spot for a Celebration:** Why not pick one of the most sought-after tables in town? That would be at **Bacchanalia,** 1198 Howell Mill Rd. (© **404/365-0410**). See p. 105.

- **Best Newcomer: Straits,** 793 Juniper St. NE (© **404/877-1283**), is the new

## (Fun Facts) **The Importance of P.C.**

P.C. is a big priority in Atlanta. No, no—not *P.C.*, as in political correctness. P.C., as in pimento cheese. And let's get the pronunciation down right off the bat. It's puh-*men*-uh cheese, an utterly simple but delightful mixture, usually consisting of just three main ingredients—canned pimentos, cheese, and some sort of binder, probably mayonnaise—slapped between two pieces of white bread. Southern cooks have hot debates over the fine points. Cheddar or Monterey Jack? Sharp or extra-sharp? Duke's mayonnaise or Hellmann's? Is onion okay? How about red-pepper flakes?

Regardless of the mixture, a pimento-cheese sandwich is right up there with grits as one of the ultimate Southern comfort foods. It's usually a home-made concoction, not found on many restaurant menus. But Scott Peacock, renowned executive chef of Watershed (p. 134) in Decatur, has seen fit to include it among his lunch *and* dinner offerings. Here's his take on the venerable Southern classic. I recommend adding a little more mayonnaise.

**Watershed's Pimento Cheese**

2 1/2 cups (10 oz.) extra-sharp cheddar cheese, grated
1/8 teaspoon cayenne pepper, or to taste
salt to taste, if needed
5 or 6 grinds of black pepper
3/4 cup homemade mayonnaise
3 tablespoons finely chopped pimento

In a mixing bowl, stir together all of the ingredients until well mixed and creamy. Taste carefully for seasoning and adjust as needed. Cover and keep refrigerated until ready to use. Makes about 2 cups.

Atlanta food venture of rapper/actor Chris "Ludacris" Bridges, and restaurateur Chris Yeo. Straits's menu features a fusion of Yeo's Asian culinary roots with local ingredients.

- **Best View: Canoe,** 4199 Paces Ferry Rd. NW, in Vinings (© **770/432-2663**), is perched on the north side of the Chattahoochee River. Ask for a table on the large, canopied patio, surrounded by landscaped gardens, and watch the river go by. See p. 132.
- **Best Wine List: The Dining Room** at the Ritz-Carlton Buckhead, 3434 Peachtree Rd. NE (© **404/237-2700**), is Atlanta's premier dining venue, and

its cuisine is complemented by a vast wine cellar. See p. 117.
- **Best Italian Cuisine:** It's noisy as the devil, but **Sotto Sotto,** 313 N. Highland Ave. (© **404/523-6678**), gets my vote for its inspired Northern Italian cuisine. See p. 128.
- **Best Italian on a Budget: Pasta da Pulcinella,** 1123 Peachtree Walk (© **404/876-1114**), serves gourmet pasta for next to nothing. See p. 111.
- **Best Seafood:** The **Atlanta Fish Market,** 265 Pharr Rd. (© **404/262-3165**), is the ticket, with an enormous selection of fresh seafood dishes that are done to perfection. See p. 120.

- **Best New Southern Cuisine:** The competition is stiff, but the **Horseradish Grill** (see "Best Spot for a Romantic Dinner," above) wins by a hair. See p. 121.

- **Best Traditional Southern Cuisine:** It's a tie between **Colonnade,** 1879 Cheshire Bridge Rd. NE (☎ **404/874-5642**), keeper of the best heirloom recipes; and **Mary Mac's Tea Room,** 224 Ponce de Leon Ave. NE (☎ **404/876-1800**), a legend in this city for more than 60 years. See p. 112 and 110, respectively.

- **Best Southwestern Cuisine: Nava,** 3060 Peachtree Rd. (☎ **404/240-1984**), is a stunning restaurant with food to match. See p. 122.

- **Best Steakhouse:** There's quite a turf war going on, but **Bone's** (see "Best Spot for a Business Lunch," above), that powerhouse for powerbrokers, gets my vote. See p. 116.

- **Best Fried Chicken:** There are lots of New Southern restaurants trying to invent newfangled ways to cook fried chicken. Well, they should just cut it out. And you should head to the **Colonnade** (see "Best Traditional Southern Cuisine," above) for some of the best fried chicken you've ever tasted. This establishment has been turning it out for years, and they know what they're doing. See p. 112.

- **Best Brunch:** The winner of this category can be none other than **Murphy's,** 997 Virginia Ave. NE (☎ **404/872-0904**), where the serving of American and Continental cuisine has transitioned right along with this funky neighborhood. See p. 128.

- **Best Breakfast:** The fun and funky **Flying Biscuit Cafe,** 1655 McLendon Ave. (☎ **404/687-8888**), fulfills all the usual breakfast expectations, and also has a great selection of offbeat specialties. See p. 132.

- **Best Afternoon Tea:** Fresh-baked scones with Devonshire cream, finger sandwiches, pastries, and tea are served every afternoon in the posh lobby lounge of the **Ritz-Carlton Buckhead,** 3434 Peachtree Rd. NE (☎ **800/241-3333**). See p. 88.

- **Best Desserts: Bacchanalia** (see "Best Spot for a Celebration," above) takes this category with its warm Valrhona chocolate cake with vanilla-bean ice cream—a flourless confection with a sinful, gooey center. They tried to take it off the menu once, but the public outcry was too great. See p. 105.

- **Best Late-Night Dining:** Head to the 24/7 **R. Thomas Deluxe Grill,** 1812 Peachtree St. NW (☎ **404/872-2942**), where you can eat some of the healthiest fare in town at any hour of the day. See p. 111.

- **Best Decor: Bluepointe,** 3455 Peachtree Rd. NE (☎ **404/237-9070**), is an energy-filled multilevel restaurant in a soaring contemporary space. Its dramatic decor feels very of-the-moment and classy. See p. 114.

- **Best People-Watching:** Famous beefeaters flock to **Bone's** (see "Best Spot for a Business Lunch," above), which has welcomed the likes of Bob Hope, George Bush, and the Atlanta Braves. See p. 116.

- **Best Pre- and Post-Theater Dining:** If you're attending a show at the Woodruff Arts Center—Atlanta's major performance facility—dine at **Veni Vidi Vici,** 41 14th St. (☎ **404/875-8424**), which opens early enough to have a relaxing meal. For post-theater noshing, try **South City Kitchen,** 1144 Crescent Ave. (☎ **404/873-7358**). See p. 112 and 105, respectively.

# Atlanta in Depth

**Atlanta continues to polish its edges as the gateway to the New South** and has certainly come a long way since it burned to the ground during General William Tecumseh Sherman's "March to the Sea" in 1864. This is the city from which Martin Luther King, Jr., launched his social revolution, and the city where Ted Turner launched his media empire. It is home to many of America's largest corporations and is one of the top convention destinations in the country.

Atlanta may be best known, however, for hosting the 1996 Summer Olympics. The city went all out in its preparations for the 1996 Games, with new parks, hotels, and sports venues. In the center of downtown is Woodruff Park, which was spruced up to the tune of $5 million. The Olympic Village, erected just north of the central business district, now provides housing for Georgia State University students. South of Olympic Village, and stretching to the CNN Center, is the 21-acre Centennial Olympic Park—a major gathering place during the Olympics, with lawns, gardens, and the dramatic (and hot-weather fun) Fountain of Rings. The park regularly hosts concerts, street festivals, and other cultural events, and anchors the city's efforts to revitalize commercial and residential development in this once-neglected corner of downtown. The Olympic Stadium, site of the opening and closing ceremonies, as well as track and field events, has been reincarnated as Turner Field, home of the Atlanta Braves baseball team.

Since the Olympics, Atlantans have had some time to think about their future and how to shape it. They've always been an optimistic bunch, but the breakneck development that began with the Olympics and still continues has many local citizens wondering if they have too much of a good thing. Atlanta has had big-city problems like crime, urban blight, and clogged freeways for some time now, but the overall quality of life remains high. Currently, the spotlight is not on growth and how to encourage it, but on growth and how to manage it. Of great concern is traffic—horrendous by any standards—and the accompanying decline in air quality. Everyone is rethinking the role that the automobile plays—even more so now that gas prices have seen record highs—and there's a lot of discussion about how to improve public transportation and make the metro area more pedestrian-friendly. Of great significance is the recent development downtown. For years, city leaders have tried to encourage "in-town" living, but it's quickly taken hold as developers remake old buildings into attractive apartments and lofts, and home buyers are breathing new life into the city's old neighborhoods. The mark of a great city is an attractive and vital downtown area where people live as well as work, and Atlanta continues to head quickly in that direction, with in-town addresses among the most desirable of residences.

## 1 ATLANTA TODAY

For Atlanta, a new century means a new effort to spruce up its image, especially that of the downtown area, which for years was a seedy section of town where not even the locals ventured after dark. Today, attractions such as the Georgia Aquarium,

Centennial Olympic Park, the CNN Studio, and the new World of Coca-Cola are drawing scores of residents and visitors to a shiny new downtown area that sprouts new offerings with great frequency—and much success. In 2004, Atlanta was named the number-one city for African Americans by *Black Enterprise* magazine. Mayor Shirley Franklin—an African-American female—has been highly active in the quest to pitch Atlanta as a tourist destination: In 2006, the city branded itself with a spirally red "ATL" logo and the slogan

"Every day is opening day." The campaign drew criticism early on, but has begun to grow on folks. Regardless, the number of visitors to this heart of the South continues to increase, averaging 37 million a year, nearly double what it was just 10 years ago. National recognition of Atlanta also continues to improve, including being named by *Forbes* magazine in 2008 as the "Best City for Singles," citing a hopping nightlife, high number of singles, and sizzling job growth among its many assets.

## 2 LOOKING BACK AT ATLANTA

It is most fitting that Atlanta in the 21st century is an international gateway and transportation hub. The city was conceived as a rail crossroads for travel north, south, east, and west, and its role as a strategic junction has always figured largely in its destiny. It all began with a peach tree.

In 1826, surveyors first suggested this area of Georgia as a practical spot for a railroad connecting the state with northern markets. This was not yet the heyday of railroads, and the report was more or less ignored for a decade. But in 1837, the state legislature approved an act establishing the Western & Atlantic Railroad here. Look for the marker known as Zero Milepost when you visit Underground Atlanta;

this marks the W & A Railroad site around which the city grew. The new town was unimaginatively dubbed "Terminus," but future governor Alexander H. Stephens, visiting what was still dense forest in 1839, predicted that "a magnificent inland city will at no distant date be built here."

### THE TRAIL OF TEARS

One aspect of the city's inception, however, was far from magnificent. In the early 1800s, most of Georgia was still Native American territory. White settlers coveted the Cherokee and Creek lands because they wanted to expedite the building of the railroad and further expand their

### DATELINE

- **1782** Explorers discover Cherokee village of Standing Peachtree.
- **1820s** Cherokee and Creek leaders cede millions of acres to white settlers in hopes of keeping peace.
- **1837** The town, newly named Terminus, is selected as the site of a railroad terminus connecting Georgia with the Tennessee River.

The same year, 17,000 Native Americans are forced to march westward on a "Trail of Tears."
- **1843** Terminus is renamed Marthasville.
- **1845** The first locomotive chugs into town. The city is renamed Atlanta.
- **1851** Georgia secedes from the Union, the Civil War begins, and Atlanta becomes a major Confederate supply depot and medical center.

- **1864** Union forces under General Sherman burn Atlanta.
- **1865** Civil War ends.
- **1877** Atlanta becomes the capital of Georgia.
- **1886** Newspaper editor Henry Grady inspires readers with vision of a "New South." John S. Pemberton introduces Coca-Cola.
- **1900** Atlanta University professor W. E. B. Du Bois founds the NAACP.

> **(Fun Facts)  The Standing Peachtree**
>
> Today, just about everything in Atlanta is called "Peachtree" something, but the first Peachtree reference dates back to 1782, when explorers discovered a Cherokee village on the Chattahoochee River called Standing Peachtree. Since peach trees are not native to the region, some historians maintain the village was actually named for a towering "pitch" tree (a resinous pine). Nevertheless, the Indian village became the location of Fort Peachtree, a tiny frontier outpost, during the War of 1812; a Peachtree Road connecting Fort Peachtree to Fort Daniel (in Gwinnett County) was completed by 1813.

settlements. Throughout the 1820s, in order to keep the peace, Native American leaders signed numerous treaties ceding millions of acres. They adopted a democratic form of government similar to the white man's, complete with a constitution and Supreme Court; erected schools and shops; built farms; and accepted Christianity. But the white frontiers-people cared little whether the Native Americans adapted—they wanted them to leave.

With President Andrew Jackson's support, Congress passed a bill in 1830 forcing all Southern tribes to move to lands hundreds of miles away on the other side of the Mississippi River. When the U.S. Supreme Court ruled against the order, Jackson ignored the ruling and backed the Georgia settlers. In 1832, the state gave away Cherokee farms in a land lottery, and the white settlers used guns to force the Cherokee off their land. In 1837, 17,000 Native Americans were rounded up by federal soldiers, herded into camps, and forced on a cruel westward march called the "Trail of Tears." Some 4,000 died on the 800-mile journey to Oklahoma, and those who survived suffered bitterly from cold, hunger, and disease. Terminus and its surroundings were now firmly in the hands of the white settlers.

## A CITY GROWS

Terminus soon began its evolution from a sleepy rural hamlet to a thriving city, a meeting point of major rail lines. In 1843, the town was renamed Marthasville, for ex-governor Wilson Lumpkin's daughter Martha. No one in Marthasville took note in 1844 when a 23-year-old army lieutenant, William Tecumseh Sherman, was

- **1904** Piedmont Park designed.
- **1917** Fire destroys 73 square blocks of the city.
- **1929** Atlanta's first airport opens; Delta Air Lines takes to the skies and becomes Atlanta's home carrier.
- **1936** Margaret Mitchell's blockbuster novel, *Gone with the Wind,* is published.
- **1939** The movie version of *Gone with the Wind* premieres in Atlanta.

- **1952** The city of Atlanta incorporates surrounding areas, increasing its population by 100,000, and its size from 37 to 118 square miles.
- **1960** Sit-ins and boycotts protesting segregation begin. The million-square-foot Merchandise Mart is erected.
- **1961** Ivan Allen, Jr., defeats segregationist Lester Maddox in mayoral election. Atlanta's public schools and

the Georgia Institute of Technology are peacefully desegregated.
- **1964** Atlanta native Martin Luther King, Jr., wins Nobel Peace Prize.
- **1965** A plane crash at Orly Airport in Paris kills 106 of Atlanta's civic and cultural leaders. Atlanta Fulton County Stadium is built.
- **1966** Baseball's Braves move from Milwaukee and

· *continues*

stationed for 2 months in their area, but the knowledge he gained of local geography would vitally affect the city's history 2 decades later. The first locomotive, the *Kentucky*, chugged into town in 1845, and shortly thereafter, the name Marthasville was deemed too provincial for a burgeoning metropolis. J. Edgar Thomson, the railroad's chief engineer, suggested Atlanta (a feminized form of Atlantic).

In 1848, the newly incorporated city held its first mayoral election, an event marked by dozens of street brawls. Moses W. Formwalt, a maker of stills and member of the Free and Rowdy Party, was elected over temperance candidate John Norcross. But if Atlanta was a bit of a wild frontier town, it also had civic pride. An 1849 newspaper overstated things poetically:

> *Atlanta, the greatest spot in all the nation, The greatest place for legislation, Or any other occupation, The very center of creation.*

## STORM CLOUDS GATHER: ANTEBELLUM ATLANTA

By the middle of the 19th century, the 31-state nation was in the throes of a westward expansion, and the institution of slavery was the major issue of the day. In his 1858 debate with Stephen Douglas, Abraham Lincoln declared, "This government cannot endure permanently half slave and half free." A year later it was obvious that only a war would resolve the issue. In 1861 (a year that began dramatically in Atlanta—with an earthquake), Georgia legislators voted for secession and joined the Confederacy.

In peacetime, the railroads had fashioned Atlanta into a center of commerce. In wartime, this transportation hub would emerge as a major Confederate military post and supply center—the vital link between Confederate forces in Tennessee and Virginia. Atlanta made the following ridiculous bid to become the capital of the Confederacy: "The city has good railroad connections, is free from yellow fever, and can supply the most wholesome foods and, as for 'goobers,' an indispensable article for a Southern legislator, we have them all the time." The lure of plentiful peanuts notwithstanding, the Confederacy chose Richmond, Virginia, as its capital. However, from early on, Federal forces saw Atlanta's destruction as essential to Northern victory.

## A CITY BURNS

Atlanta served as not only a major Southern supply depot, but also the medical center of the Confederacy. Throughout the city, buildings were hastily converted into makeshift hospitals and clinics, and trains pulled into town daily to disgorge sick and wounded soldiers. By 1862, close

the Falcons become a new NFL expansion team. The Beatles perform in Atlanta.
- **1968** Martin Luther King, Jr., is assassinated in Memphis.
- **1974** Atlanta's first black mayor, Maynard Jackson, is inaugurated. Atlanta Braves's Hank Aaron hits his record-breaking 715th home run.
- **1976** Georgian Jimmy Carter elected president. Georgia World Congress Center, the nation's largest

single-floor exhibit space, is completed.
- **1979** MARTA rapid-transit train system opens.
- **1980** New Hartsfield International Airport dedicated.
- **1983** Martin Luther King, Jr.'s birthday becomes national holiday.
- **1988** Atlanta hosts Democratic National Convention.
- **1989** Underground Atlanta reopens with great fanfare.

- **1992** Atlanta completes the new 70,500-seat Georgia Dome.
- **1994** Atlanta hosts Super Bowl XXVIII at the Georgia Dome.
- **1995** On their third try, the Atlanta Braves win the World Series.
- **1996** Atlanta completes the 85,000-seat Olympic Stadium and hosts the Centennial Olympic Games.

## Impressions

*I want to say to General Sherman, who is an able man . . . though some people think he is kind of careless about fire, that from the ashes he left us in 1864, we have raised a brave and beautiful city; that we have caught the sunshine in our homes and built therein not one ignoble prejudice or memory.*

—Henry Grady, *Atlanta Constitution* editor, 1886

to 4,000 soldiers were convalescing here, and the medical crisis was further aggravated by a smallpox epidemic.

That same year, Union spy James J. Andrews and a group of Northern soldiers disguised as civilians seized a locomotive called the *General,* with the aim of blocking supply lines by destroying tracks and bridges behind them. A wild train chase ensued, and the raiders were caught and punished (most, including Andrews, were executed). The episode came to be known as the "Great Locomotive Chase," one of the stirring stories of the Civil War and the subject of two subsequent movies. Today, you can see the *General* on display at the Southern Museum of Civil War and Locomotive History (p. 168).

The locomotive chase was an Atlanta victory, but the Northern desire to destroy the Confederacy's supply link remained intact. In 1864, General Ulysses S. Grant ordered Major General William T. Sherman to "move against Johnston's army to

break it up, and get into the interior of the enemy's country as far as you can, inflicting all the damage you can against their resources." Georgians had great faith that the able and experienced General Joseph E. Johnston, whom they called "Old Joe," would repel the Yankees. As Sherman's Georgia campaign got underway, an overly optimistic editorial in the *Intelligencer* scoffed at the notion of Federal conquest, claiming "we have no fear of the results, for General Johnston and his great and invincible satellites are working out the problem of battle and victory at the great chess board at the front." Johnston himself was not as sanguine. Sherman had 100,000 men to Johnston's 60,000, and the Union troops were better armed.

By July, Sherman was forcing the Confederate troops back, and Atlanta's fall seemed a foregone conclusion; Johnston informed Confederate President Jefferson Davis that he was outnumbered almost two to one and was in a defensive position.

- **1997** Atlanta reopens Olympic Stadium as the new Turner Field, home of the Atlanta Braves baseball team.
- **1998** A renovated Centennial Olympic Park opens as a major city gathering spot and a lasting legacy of the Centennial Olympic Games.
- **1999** Atlanta completes the Philips Arena, home to the Atlanta Hawks basketball

team and the Atlanta Thrashers hockey team.
- **2000** The city hosts Super Bowl XXXIV.
- **2003** The $95-million Georgia International Convention Center—featuring a 40,000-square-foot ballroom—opens for business.
- **2005** The 5-million-gallon Georgia Aquarium opens in the middle of revitalized downtown Atlanta.

- **2007** The all-new, bigger and better World of Coca-Cola opens downtown next to the Georgia Aquarium.
- **2009** Atlanta's population continues to climb, having recently bypassed the five million milestone.

> **Impressions**
>
> *No one goes anywhere without passing through Atlanta.*
> —Francis C. Lawley, *London Times* reporter, 1861

His candid assessment was not appreciated, and Davis removed him from command, replacing him with the pugnacious 32-year-old General John Bell Hood. The change of leadership only further demoralized the ranks, and Sherman openly rejoiced when he heard the news.

Some disgruntled Confederate soldiers deserted. Hood abandoned the defensive tactics of Johnston, aggressively assaulting his opponent. His policy cost thousands of troops and gained nothing. In the Battle of Peachtree Creek on July 20, 1864, Union casualties totaled 1,710; Confederate, 4,796. Throughout the summer, the city suffered a full-scale artillery assault. More than 8,000 Confederates perished in the Battle of Atlanta on July 22, while Union deaths totaled just 3,722. The Confederates lost another 5,000 men during hours of fierce fighting on July 28, while the Yankees lost just 600. The Yankees further paralyzed the city by ripping up train rails, heating them over huge bonfires, and twisting them around trees into useless spirals of mangled iron that came to be known as "Sherman's neckties." The most devastating bombardment came on August 9—"that red day . . . when all the fires of hell, and all the thunders of the universe, seemed to be blazing and roaring over Atlanta."

By September 1, when Hood's troops pulled out of the area, first setting fire to vast stores of ammunition (and anything else that might benefit the Yankees), the town was in turmoil. Its roads were crowded with evacuees, and its hospitals, hotels, and private residences were flooded with wounded men. Crime and looting were rife, and food was almost unavailable;

the price of a ham-and-eggs breakfast with coffee soared to $25. Rooftops were ripped off houses and buildings, there were huge craters in the streets, and many civilians were dead. The railroads were in Sherman's hands.

On September 2, Mayor James M. Calhoun, carrying a white flag to the nearest Federal unit, officially surrendered the city. The U.S. Army entered and occupied Atlanta, raising the Stars and Stripes at city hall for the first time in 4 years. Claiming he needed the city for military purposes, Sherman ordered all residents to evacuate. Atlantans piled their household goods on wagons, abandoned their homes and businesses, and became refugees. Before departing Atlanta in November, Union troops leveled railroad facilities and burned the city, leaving it a wasteland—defunct as a military center and practically uninhabitable. The Yankees marched out of the city to the strains of "The Battle Hymn of the Republic."

As of January 1865, there was $1.64 in the treasury, the railroad system was destroyed, and most of the city was burned to the ground.

## A CITY REBUILDS

Slowly, exiled citizens began to trickle back into Atlanta. Confederate money had become worthless. At the inauguration of his second term in 1865, Lincoln pledged "malice toward none, charity for all"—but after his assassination later that year, this policy was replaced with one of harsh Republican vengeance. It wasn't until 1876 that Federal troops were withdrawn and Atlanta was freed from military occupation.

Still, the city was making a remarkable recovery. Like the ever-resilient Scarlett O'Hara ("It takes more than Yankees or a burning to keep me down"), Atlanta rolled up its sleeves and began rebuilding. A Northern newspaper reported, "From all this ruin and devastation a new city is springing up . . . the streets are alive from morning till night with drays and carts and hand-barrows and wagons . . . with loads of lumber and loads of brick."

In the years after the war, Atlanta was filled with carpetbaggers (Northern adventurers and politicians who went south to take advantage of the unsettled postwar conditions) and other adventurers hoping to turn a quick buck, and with them came gambling houses, brothels, and saloons. But the city also boasted hundreds of new stores and businesses, churches, schools, banks, hotels, theaters, and a new newspaper, the *Atlanta Constitution*. The railroads began operating again. In 1867, African Americans chartered Atlanta University, today the world's largest predominantly black institution of higher learning. Newspaper editor Henry Grady, Atlanta's biggest civic booster, inspired readers with his vision of an industrialized and culturally advanced "New South." A new constitution in 1877 made Atlanta the permanent capital of the state of Georgia. Two years later, General Sherman visited the city he had destroyed and was welcomed with a ball and, lest he get any funny ideas, a grand military review.

In 1886, a new headache cure was introduced to the city—a syrup made from the coca leaf and the kola nut, which would become the world's most renowned beverage, Coca-Cola. Atlanta adopted the symbol of a phoenix rising from the ashes for its official seal in 1888 and, the following year, dedicated the gold-domed state capitol and opened a zoo in Grant Park. Piedmont Park was built in 1904 as the site of the Cotton States and International Exposition—a

$2.5-million world's fair–like extravaganza with entertainment ranging from Buffalo Bill and His Wild West Show to reconstructed "international villages." Former slave Booker T. Washington gave a landmark address, and John Philip Sousa composed the "King Cotton March" to mark the event.

## THE 20TH CENTURY

At the turn of the 20th century, Atlanta's population was 90,000, a figure that more than doubled 2 decades later. Though a massive fire destroyed almost 2,000 buildings in 1917, the city was on a course of rapid growth. In 1929, Atlanta opened its first airport on the site of today's Hartsfield International, presaging the growth of a major air-travel industry. The same year, Delta Air Lines took to the skies and became Atlanta's home carrier.

Margaret Mitchell's blockbuster Civil War epic, *Gone with the Wind,* which went on to become the world's second-bestselling book (after the Bible) and the basis for domestically the biggest-grossing picture of all time (when adjusted for inflation), was published in 1936. Louis B. Mayer turned down a chance to make the film version for MGM, because "no Civil War picture ever made a nickel."

A grimmer legacy of the Civil War and the institution of slavery was racial strife, and the early years of the 20th century were marked by violent race riots. Atlanta University professor W. E. B. Du Bois founded the National Association for the Advancement of Colored People, or NAACP, in 1900. In 1939, black cast members were unable to attend the glamorous premiere of *Gone with the Wind* because the theater was segregated. And as late as 1960, segregation in Atlanta (as everywhere in the South) was still firmly entrenched and backed by state law. Unlike much of the South, though, the city adopted a progressive attitude regarding race relations. Even before the civil rights movement, there were hints of tolerance—the hiring of black police officers, the election of a black professional to the Atlanta Board of Education, the desegregation of a public golf course in 1955, and, in 1959, the desegregation of public transit. Mayor Bill Hartsfield (who held office for almost 3 decades) called Atlanta "a city too busy to hate." And his successor, Mayor Ivan Allen, Jr., called on Atlantans to face race problems "and seek the answers in an atmosphere of decency and dignity."

Atlanta peacefully desegregated its public schools and the Georgia Institute of Technology in 1961. Atlanta native Dr. Martin Luther King, Jr., headquartered his Southern Christian Leadership Conference here and made Ebenezer Baptist Church, where he was a co-pastor with his father, a hub of the civil rights movement. In 1974, Atlanta inaugurated its first black mayor, Maynard Jackson, and, following a term by another black mayor, Andrew Young, Jackson was reelected.

In 1966, Atlanta went big league when the Braves and the Falcons came to town. And Atlantans went wild in 1974, when Hank Aaron broke Babe Ruth's home-run record here.

## ALL ABOUT ATLANTA

There's so much to learn about this gateway city and so many ways to do it. For an overview, start with the **Atlanta History Center,** which includes the Atlanta History Museum and a new wing dedicated to the 1996 Olympic Games.

Or schedule a tour of the **Georgia State Capitol,** which was modeled after the nation's Capitol, another neoclassical edifice atop a "crowning hill." Its 75-foot dome, covered in gold leaf and topped by a Statue of Freedom, is a major Atlanta landmark. The building is fronted by a massive four-story portico with a pediment supported by six Corinthian columns set on large stone piers. In the rotunda, with its soaring 237-foot ceiling,

are busts of famous Georgians, including signers of the Declaration of Independence and the Constitution. The governor's office is off the main hall. The capitol building's public spaces have been restored to their 1889 grandeur. The fourth floor houses legislative galleries and the Georgia Capitol Museum, with exhibits on cotton, peach, and peanut growing; cases of mounted birds, fish, deer, insects, and other species native to Georgia; rocks and minerals; American Indian artifacts; and more. Note, too, the museum displays on the first floor.

You'd be surprised by how many folks come to Atlanta expecting to tour the *Gone with the Wind* mansion or see where Scarlett and Rhett are buried—no joke. But the story is so much a part of the fiber of Atlanta that you really should plan to visit the **Margaret Mitchell House & Museum,** "the dump" she lived in while crafting the famous tale of the South. The museum contains movie memorabilia and chronicles the making of the movie, its premiere in Atlanta, and the impact of the book and movie on society. The tour concludes in the museum shop, which features a variety of *GWTW* collectibles. If you finish your tour around mealtime and you're ready for a real change of pace, walk a few blocks south on Peachtree to the Vortex, a rowdy burger joint and bar that serves some of the best burgers in town.

The **Atlanta Preservation Society** offers a number of guided historic walking tours throughout the city, including the fabulous Fox Theatre, Piedmont Park, downtown Atlanta, Grant Hill, Inman Park, and the Sweet Auburn/Martin Luther King, Jr., historic district. All of these tours provide insight to the history of Atlanta and the people and places that make this city what it is today.

## CIVIL WAR TRAIL

Atlanta was obviously in the midst of the action throughout the Civil War, and many opportunities exist to learn about what many here still refer to—with tongue in cheek—as "the war of Northern aggression." Begin with a visit to the **Atlanta Cyclorama & Civil War Museum,** in Grant Park. The building that houses the Cyclorama also contains a museum of related artifacts, the most important being the steam locomotive *Texas* from the 1862 Great Locomotive Chase. Other exhibits include displays of Civil War arms and artillery, Civil War–themed paintings, portraits of Confederate and Union leaders, "life in camp" artifacts and photographs, and uniforms.

Next, venture northwest to the **Kennesaw Mountain/National Battlefield Park,** a 2,884-acre park established in 1917 on the site of a crucial Civil War battle in the Atlanta campaign of 1864. Some 2 million visitors come annually to explore the Confederate entrenchments and earthworks, some of them featuring Civil War artillery. Located in the same vicinity is the **Southern Museum of Civil War and Locomotive History,** operated in association with the Smithsonian Institute, which means that Civil War and transportation objects from the Smithsonian are incorporated into the exhibits here. It was here that the wild adventure known as the Great Locomotive Chase began. The museum, occupying a building that was once the Frey cotton gin, houses the *General* locomotive; a walk-through caboose; exhibits of Civil War artifacts, memorabilia, and photographs (including those relating to the chase and its participants); and exhibits on railroads. You can view a 20-minute narrated video about the chase, but if you really want the full story, pick up the Disney movie *The Great Locomotive Chase,* starring Fess Parker, available in the museum gift shop.

Even **Oakland Cemetery** is ripe with Civil War history, as Confederate and Union soldiers, including five Southern generals, are among the more than 48,000 people buried here. Listed on the National Register of Historic Places, this outstanding 88-acre Victorian cemetery was founded in 1850. Two monuments honor the Confederate war dead. Standing at the marker that commemorates the Great Locomotive Chase, you can see the trees from which the Yankee raiders were hanged; the Confederate train conductor Capt. William Fuller is buried nearby.

## AFRICAN-AMERICAN HISTORY

Atlanta is ripe with ties to the rich history of African Americans and the civil rights movement. After all, this is the birthplace of Martin Luther King, Jr. And all of the sites are full of learning opportunities, so bring the whole family along this sightseeing trail, beginning with the **APEX (African-American Panoramic Experience) Museum** in the Sweet Auburn district. Featuring exhibits on the history of Sweet Auburn and the African-American experience, the museum includes a children's gallery with interactive displays.

Leaving the APEX, follow the walking tour for **Sweet Auburn** (p. 188), which includes the **King Center,** Dr. King's final resting place, where late wife Coretta Scott King will soon join him in Freedom Plaza. Next, the **Birth Home of Martin Luther King, Jr.,** is open for half-hour guided tours. Though the tour is free, you must get tickets at the National Park Service Visitor Center on Auburn Avenue. Don't miss **Ebenezer Baptist Church** or the **Herndon Building,** named for an ex-slave who went on to found the Atlanta Life Insurance Company, the second-largest black insurance company in the country. Built in the early 1900s, the **Butler Street YMCA** was a popular meeting place for civil rights leaders. And the **Sweet Auburn Curb Market** offers fare not often enjoyed outside of the South.

For answers about African-American history, visit the **Auburn Avenue Research Library on African-American Culture**

**and History.** Several churches along the avenue, such as **Big Bethel AME** and **First Congregational,** helped build and maintain the heritage of the street. The **Royal** **Peacock Club** provided an elegant setting where many African Americans could perform and bring the changing styles of black popular music to Atlanta.

## 3 ATLANTA IN POPULAR CULTURE: BOOKS, FILM, MUSIC

**BOOKS** Many books have been written—both fiction and nonfiction—about this beloved city. And while most nonfiction can be taken for fact, many natives will tell you that a lot of the fiction holds nearly as many truths (and some not-so-secret skeletons) about Atlanta and the folks who've lived here through the decades.

*Archival Atlanta: Forgotten Facts and Well-Kept Secrets from Our City's Past,* by Perry Buffington and Kim Underwood, is a light read, packed with fascinating historical tidbits—some of which are sure to surprise even the most knowledgeable Atlanta history buff. The book includes its share of humorous anecdotes.

For those more interested in looking at pictures than reading, Andy Ambrose, deputy director of the Atlanta History Center, compiled *Atlanta: An Illustrated History,* filled with images from Atlanta's archives. From the days of saloons and brothels in the early 1800s to the city's renaissance beginning in the 1960s, this account explores everything from Atlanta's troubling racial past to the celebrated, historically rich neighborhoods of Ansley Park and Buckhead.

Michael Rose's *Atlanta Then and Now* delivers an illustrated juxtaposition of Atlanta's past and present. The photos allow first-time visitors as well as old friends to see just how far this southern city has come in the past century.

For an account of some of the down-and-dirty backroom dealings that brought Atlanta to the forefront as an international city, many readers swear by Frederick Allen's *Atlanta Rising: The Invention of an International City 1946–1996.* This mostly objective account of Atlanta's dealings over the past 50 years describes the relationships among the city's decision-makers as various events unfold.

Of course, Margaret Mitchell's novel *Gone with the Wind* is a given for those who wish to take in a Civil War–era depiction of this area.

Author Fred Willard has a big following, which began with his Atlanta-based satirical mystery, *Down on Ponce,* and continued with *Princess Naughty and the Voodoo Cadillac.* Those folks who know the area intimately will swear to the authenticity of the Deep South social outcasts who inhabit a side of Atlanta that most residents would rather keep quiet.

Anne Rivers Siddons was reared just 20 miles from the big city, and *Hills Town, King's Oak,* and *Homeplace* are all set in Georgia. Her *Peachtree Road* is a dark, hypnotic tale of Buckhead high society in the mid–20th century, when money and civil rights were the fuel on which the city ran. Her *Downtown* depicts Atlanta's last years of innocence: "Atlanta in the autumn of 1966 was a city being born, and the energy and promise of that lying-in sent out subterranean vibrations all over the just-stirring South, like underground shock waves—a call to those who could hear it best, the young. And they came, they came in droves, from small, sleeping towns and large, drowsing universities, from farms and industrial suburbs and backwaters so still that even the building firestorm of the civil rights movement had not yet rippled the surface."

And while he doesn't live in Atlanta, Tom Wolfe ruffled more than a few feathers with his 1998 tome *A Man in Full.* As Wolfe states in the book, Atlanta is a place "where your 'honor' *is* the thing you possess." More critics than not thought his depiction of the slums and socialites of Atlanta might do more harm than good in boosting the tourism economy here.

**FILM** Atlanta's biggest connection to film is, of course, **Gone with the Wind,** taken from the Pulitzer Prize–winning novel of the same name written in 1936 by Margaret Mitchell of Atlanta. The 1939 Academy Award–winning film depicted Atlanta and the Old South during the Civil War as seen from the viewpoint of a rebellious Southern belle, Scarlett O'Hara, whose home, a plantation called Tara, is taken over by the northern opposition. The movie premiere was held in the ballroom of Atlanta's Georgian Terrace, still a grand working hotel today on Peachtree Street, across from the Fox Theatre. In attendance were actors from the film, including Vivienne Leigh as Scarlett and Clark Gable as Rhett Butler.

Atlanta playwright Alfred Uhry penned a play from which the movie **Driving Miss Daisy** was adapted. The plot follows a 72-year-old Atlanta widow, Miss Daisy Werthan, in 1948 as she deals with issues of aging, race relations (she is white and Jewish, her son hires an African-American chauffeur after she has a fender bender), religion, fear, and relationships. Miss Daisy was played by Jessica Tandy and Morgan Freeman starred as Hoke Colburn, the chauffeur. She's initially embarrassed—because of age or her fear of appearing too rich—to be driven around, and even walks to the grocery store in defiance. Once she accepts the fact that she is unable to drive herself, she and Colburn warm up to one another and she teaches him to read. On a

trip out of town for a family occasion, Miss Daisy is awakened to the prejudicial treatment her new friend encounters. When her synagogue is bombed, she realizes that she, too, is subjected to racism as a Jew. The elderly lady eventually goes into a retirement home, to be visited frequently by Colburn, the two having become best friends. The film took four awards from nine nominations at the 62nd Academy Awards in 1989. It is the only film based on an off-Broadway production ever to win an Academy Award for Best Picture. At age 80, Tandy was the oldest winner in the Best Actress category.

Also an Atlanta-related film is Disney's **The Great Locomotive Chase,** starring Fess Parker as the dashing Union spy James J. Andrews. The movie tells how the story of the wild adventure known as the "Great Locomotive Chase" began. The Civil War had been underway for a year on April 12, 1862, when Andrews and a group of 21 Northern soldiers disguised as civilians boarded a locomotive called the *General* in Marietta, buying tickets for diverse destinations to avert suspicion. When the train made a breakfast stop at the Lacy Hotel in Big Shanty, they seized the locomotive and several boxcars and fled northward to Chattanooga. The goal of these daring raiders was to destroy tracks, telegraph wires, and bridges behind them, thus cutting off the Confederate supply route between Virginia and Mississippi.

Conductor William A. Fuller, his breakfast interrupted by the sound of the *General* chugging out of the station, gave chase on foot, then grabbed a platform car and poled along the tracks. With him were a railroad superintendent and the *General's* engineer. At the Etowah River, Fuller and crew commandeered a small locomotive called the *Yonah* and made better progress. Meanwhile, the raiders tore up track behind them, and when the pursuers got close, the raiders slowed them down by throwing ties and firewood onto the tracks.

Andrews, a very smooth talker, managed to convince station attendants en route that he was on an emergency mission running ammunition to Confederate General Beauregard in Mississippi.

Fuller's chances of catching the *General* improved when he seized the southbound *Texas* and began running it backward toward the raiders, picking up reinforcements along the way and eventually managing to get a telegraph message through to General Danville Leadbetter, commander at Chattanooga. The chase went on, with Andrews sending uncoupled boxcars careening back toward Fuller as obstructions. Fuller, who was running in reverse, merely attached the rolling boxcars to his engine and kept on. At the covered Oostanaula Bridge, the raiders detached a boxcar and set it on fire in hopes of finally creating an impassable obstacle—a burning bridge behind them. But the *Texas* was able to push the flaming car off the bridge. It soon burned out, and Fuller tossed it off the track and continued.

By this time the *General* was running low on fuel and water, the *Texas* was hot on its heels, and the raiders realized that all was lost. Andrews gave his final command: "Jump off and scatter! Every man for himself!" All were captured and imprisoned within a few days. Some escaped, others were exchanged for Confederate prisoners of war, and the rest were hanged in Atlanta, most of them at a site near Oakland Cemetery. Though the mission failed, the raiders, some of them posthumously, received the newly created Medal of Honor for their valor.

Today, Atlanta is a hopping scene in the film industry, with such homegrown film products as *The Lady from Sockholm, Last Goodbye, Freez'er, The Adventures of Ociee Nash,* and *No Witness.* Of greatest note is *Last Goodbye,* starring David Carradine and Faye Dunaway among others. The movie brings six very different individuals together on a hot summer day in Atlanta. Carradine, as a whacked-out Bible salesman, and Dunaway, as a film director, play the role of saviors to some needy younger people.

In addition, Tyler Perry, whose numerous stage plays continue to be reborn as movies, also lives in Atlanta, where his talent as a playwright first wowed audiences. In 2005, Perry opened at the top of the box office with his instant hit *Diary of a Mad Black Woman,* which he wrote, produced, and starred in. That success was followed by additional movies adapted from his plays, including *Meet the Browns, Why Did I Get Married, Daddy's Little Girls, Madea's Family Reunion, The Family That Preys,* and *Madea Goes to Jail,* scheduled for a spring 2009 release. His Tyler Perry Studios, the first independent studio of its size to open in Georgia, is located in Atlanta.

**MUSIC** Atlanta seems to be a magnet for talented musicians and a long list of singers, musicians, and entire bands hail from the city. Among the most popular are Atlanta Rhythm Section, Mother's Finest, Indigo Girls, Black Crowes, Georgia Satellites, SOS Band, Heart to Heart, and Mose Davis.

Today, Atlanta is a mecca for rap and hip-hop artists, with major recording studios based here, such as Jermaine Dupri's So So Def. Among the artists hailing from Atlanta or now calling the city home are Lil Jon, Outkast, Ludacris, Ying Yang Twins, Young Jeezy, and Jermaine Dupri.

The country music scene is also well tied to Atlanta, including Trisha Yearwood, who frequents the city but wasn't born here, and Sugarland, the darling duo of Jennifer Nettles and Kristian Bush, both of whom now call the city home. In 2008, they recorded their number one album, *Love on the Inside,* here at Southern Tracks, a studio with a long Atlanta history and an even longer client list of all the top musicians, from the '50s through today. Musicians of all genres have recorded here at one time or another, including Pearl Jam, Aerosmith, Creed, Third Day, Newsong, Gladys Knight, Collective Soul, Keith Sweat, and Bruce Springsteen. The original studio was founded by music producer Bill Lowery in the mid–1950s. He's best known for discovering such jewels as "Be Bop a Lula," "I Never Promised You a Rose Garden," and "Games People Play."

## 4 EATING & DRINKING IN ATLANTA

Atlanta runs right up there with the big dogs when it comes to fine dining. With cuisine from nearly every ethnic group in the universe, the city isn't just about sweet tea and fried chicken—though you can certainly get your fill of authentic Southern cooking here as well. But when you've tired of turnip greens, fried okra, and cheese grits (p. 108 for the scoop on this Southern staple), prepare to dazzle your taste buds with fare ranging from Russian and Indian to Moroccan and Greek. Whatever you choose to dine on, you can always wash it down with one of many local brews, including the most popular, Sweetwater 420 Extra Pale Ale. A number of brewpubs in Atlanta serve their own house brews, so take a taste drive at 55 Seasons, Park Tavern Brewery, or Max Lager's American Grill & Brewery.

In addition, some of the country's top chefs operate successful restaurants here, including Richard Blais (a former competitor on *Iron Chef America*), who always has a new venture in the works (his latest is FLIP Burger Boutique, a modern hamburger joint concept for which Blais serves as creative director). The legendary Anne Quatrano and Clifford Harrison—the wife/husband team and owners of Bacchanalia, Quinones, Floataway Café, and Star Provisions—were recently jointly named the James Beard Foundation's "Best Chef in the Southeast."

**DINING LIKE A TRUE SOUTHERNER**
In the South, we call our first meal of the day breakfast, like the rest of the country, but the water gets murky after that. What most of the country calls "lunch," Southerners often refer to as "dinner." And to differentiate between it and the evening meal, we typically refer to "dinner" as "supper." But don't worry, even Atlanta's Southern cuisine eateries use the standard breakfast, lunch, and dinner references.

It's no surprise that many folks visiting Atlanta and/or the South for the first time have some curiosity about Southern or "country" cooking, and visitors here won't be disappointed. While many establishments serve what they consider Southern dishes, many of them miss the mark. But that reliable handful of seasoned cooks (and some are true chefs) serving up authentic, "down home" cooking do us all proud. One anomaly for many unfamiliar with Southern fare is **grits.** There's really no mystery here, folks; grits are ground corn, similar to what our northern counterparts do with wheat and call "cream of wheat." Now, what you do with grits is a whole 'nother story. While the traditional style is hot grits topped with butter, salt and pepper, cheese grits is another tasty option, especially popular as a side to fried fish. However, even cheese grits have taken on a new spin, with chefs constantly trying to find some fancy cheese to mix in rather than sticking to the Velveeta upon which most Southern cooks rely for flavoring. Today's cooks are liable to do all manner of dishes with grits, including the popular **shrimp and grits,** quail and grits, and even baked garlic cheese grits. Many chefs use grits much like others

ATLANTA IN DEPTH

2

EATING & DRINKING IN ATLANTA

would use polenta, and the taste isn't terribly different. Transplants to the South have been known to eat their grits with sugar, much to the dismay of natives, of course. But even locals add a twist to their grits on occasion, such as cream cheese, ham, or **red eye gravy,** not really a gravy at all, but rather a thin sauce made from the drippings of country ham and coffee (it tastes much better than it sounds—trust me).

While among us dwells a small percentage of vegetarians, most Southerners do like their meat, especially if it's fried, like fried chicken, fried pork chops, and country fried steak. Wild game is typically easy to come by and includes venison, wild hog, quail, turkey, dove, and even alligator and rattlesnake for the most daring amongst us. Barbecued meat of all types is another Southern favorite, and if you're going to eat it, you've got to have **Brunswick Stew,** for which the most traditional recipe calls for cooking down a hog's head (or even squirrel). Whatever meat is used—pork, chicken, beef—is combined with corn, tomatoes, potatoes, and a wide variety of ingredients, depending on who's cooking. We're also fond of fried seafood, especially catfish and **mullet** (it's got to be fresh to be good).

Another large sector of Southern food is fresh vegetables, including black-eyed peas, **collard, turnip or mustard greens,** okra (fried or stewed with tomatoes are favored among Southerners), fried green tomatoes, and squash, most tasty when baked into a casserole with cheese and cracker crumbs. Other Southern sides include pear salad (a canned pear half topped with a dollop of mayonnaise and sprinkled with shredded cheddar cheese) and sweet potato soufflé, both of which are almost dessertlike. Speaking of desserts, Southerners will charm you with pecan pie, **red velvet cake** (the cake really is red, thanks to food coloring, and then topped with rich cream cheese frosting),

slap-yo-mama it's so good banana pudding, peanut butter pie, and 12-layer caramel cake.

In between meals, you might try some Southern snacks, such as fried pork skins in any variety of flavors, **boiled peanuts** (a truly acquired taste—I think it's the texture that throws first-timers), or **cheese straws,** a cheesy crumbly cracker and a staple at any respectable shower, tea, reception, or other such event that calls for Southern hospitality.

Bread is on the table for all Southern meals, from morning to night. But what we consider "bread" in the South takes on a wide definition, including your standard grocery store loaf of white bread, or **"light bread"** as we are known to call it. It also includes such high-carb treats as buttermilk biscuits, thick slabs of cornbread, and **lace hoecake cornbread**—a thin, lacy bread fried in a cast-iron skillet. There's nothing better with any Southern meal than a good ol' **cat head biscuit,** so called because they are as big as a cat's head. And don't be surprised if you see one of us dipping (or sopping, as it's known here) our biscuit in the gravy or drowning it in cane syrup, blackstrap molasses, Tupelo honey, Mayhaw jelly, or any number of sweet concoctions.

Wash it all down with a tall glass of **sweet tea,** that Southern nectar that leaves Northerners scratching their heads when we try to order it in a restaurant north of the Mason-Dixon line (Mary Macs, a Southern dining tradition in Atlanta, refers to sweet tea as "the table wine of the South"). RC (Royal Crown) Cola and, of course, **Coca-Cola** (pronounced co-cola by Southerners) are other staples. And many old-timers still belly up to the bar for a nice cold glass of fresh buttermilk.

If you're looking for something a little stronger in the drink category, Atlanta is home to many brewpubs, bubbling up their own beers, among the most popular of which is Sweetwater 420. Of course, some folks do still drink their **mint juleps,** but not with the frequency that outsiders might think. This stereotypical libation is a strong combination of whiskey, sugar, mint, and crushed ice, and it'll knock your socks off.

## 5  FAMOUS ATLANTANS

**Henry Louis "Hank" Aaron** (b. 1934) An outfielder with the Milwaukee (later Atlanta) Braves, Aaron broke Babe Ruth's record in 1974 with his 715th home run, in Atlanta–Fulton County Stadium. He remained cool and dignified in the face of the media frenzy surrounding his pursuit of the record, despite receiving countless death threats and bags of hate mail from bigots who felt that Ruth's achievement should never be surpassed by a black man. He retired in 1976 with 755 homers.

**Henry W. Grady** (1850–89)  Managing editor of the *Atlanta Constitution,* Grady preached post–Civil War reconciliation, and worked passionately to draw Northern capital and diversified industry to the agrarian South. His name is synonymous with the phrase "The New South."

**Joel Chandler Harris** (1848–1908) Called "Georgia's Aesop," he created Uncle Remus, the wise black raconteur of children's fables. His tales of Br'er Rabbit and Br'er Fox were the basis for Disney's delightful animated feature, *Song of the South.*

**Robert Tyre "Bobby" Jones** (1902–71)  The founder of the Masters tournament, Jones won golf's Grand Slam at age 28 and has been called the world's greatest golfer. He also held academic degrees in engineering, law, and English literature.

**Martin Luther King, Jr.** (1929–68) Civil rights leader, minister, orator, and winner of the Nobel Peace Prize, King preached Gandhi's doctrine of passive resistance.

**Margaret Mitchell** (1900–49)  Originally a journalist, Mitchell was the author of the definitive Southern blockbuster novel, *Gone with the Wind.* She began writing "the book" in 1926 when a severe ankle injury forced her to give up reporting. GWTW is still one of the world's best-selling books.

**John C. Portman** (b. 1924)  An architect/developer who revolutionized hotel design in the United States with his lofty atrium-lobby concept, Portman almost single-handedly designed Atlanta's skyline in the 1960s. He has been called "Atlanta's one-man urban-renewal program."

**Robert Edward "Ted" Turner III** (b. 1938)  Dubbed "the mouth of the South," America's most dynamic media mogul, Ted Turner, created 24-hour cable news networks CNN and Headline News,

### Impressions

*It stinks, I don't know why I bother with it, but I've got to have something to do with my time.*

—Margaret Mitchell, author of *Gone with the Wind*

Gone with the Wind *is very possibly the greatest American novel.*

—*Publishers Weekly*

along with entertainment networks Super-station TBS and TNT. Turner is vice chairman of Time Warner, Inc., and owns a portion of MGM, the Atlanta Braves, and the Atlanta Hawks.

**Alfred Uhry** (b. 1936)   One of the most winning present-day playwrights (an Oscar, a Tony, and a Pulitzer Prize), Uhry, who was born and reared in Atlanta and spent much of his adult life here, has since moved away from the city. But he still has Atlanta on his mind: Many of his plays, the most notable of which are *Driving Miss Daisy* and *The Last Night of Ballyhoo,* take place in this city. Uhry's early scripts were produced when he was a student at Druid Hills High School in the mid–1950s, including one about rural life that was upstaged by a boisterous live chicken.

**Robert W. Woodruff** (1889–1985) Woodruff was the Coca-Cola Company president, a philanthropist, and a leading Atlanta citizen for over half a century. He put Coca-Cola on the map worldwide; promoted civil rights; and gave over $400 million to educational, artistic, civil, and medical projects in Atlanta, such as Emory University, the Woodruff Arts Center, and the High Museum.

# Planning Your Trip to Atlanta

In the pages that follow, you'll find practical information that will help you make travel arrangements, pick a time to visit, find local resources for specialized needs, and even access tons of useful information on the Internet.

For additional help in planning your trip and for more on-the-ground resources in Atlanta, see the "Fast Facts, Toll-Free Numbers & Websites" appendix on p. 219.

## 1 VISITOR INFORMATION

As soon as you know you're going to Atlanta, write or call the **Atlanta Convention & Visitors Bureau (ACVB),** 233 Peachtree St. NE, Ste. 2000, Atlanta, GA 30303 (© **800/ATLANTA [285-2682]** or 404/222-6688). They'll send you a copy of *Atlanta Heritage Guide,* a visitors' guide, a book of discount coupons, a *Metro Atlanta Map and Attractions Guide,* and a 2-month calendar of events; they can also advise you on anything from Atlanta's hotel and restaurant scene to the best tour packages available. Visit the ACVB website at **www.atlanta.net** for lots of information.

You can also learn a lot about the city and its latest happenings by visiting **www.Access Atlanta.com,** a website whose partners include the *Atlanta Journal-Constitution* and WSB-TV and radio. There, you'll find current local news, a 5-day weather forecast, street maps, and up-to-date information about special events, the arts, entertainment, sports, recreation, restaurants, shopping, and more. There's even a link to the Atlanta Yellow Pages.

Another site worth checking out is **www.Atlanta.Citysearch.com.** Although it's not as complete as www.AccessAtlanta. com, it still has lots of useful information about the arts, entertainment, attractions, restaurants, shopping, and hotels. Finally, **Creative Loafing (www.cln.com)** features loads of entertainment information and great restaurant reviews.

## 2 ENTRY REQUIREMENTS

### PASSPORTS

New regulations issued by the Department of Homeland Security now require virtually every air traveler entering the U.S. to show a passport. As of January 23, 2007, all persons, including U.S. citizens, traveling by air between the United States and Canada, Mexico, Central and South America, the Caribbean, and Bermuda are required to present a valid passport. As of January 31, 2008, U.S. and Canadian citizens entering the U. S. at land and sea ports of entry from within the Western Hemisphere will need to present government-issued proof of citizenship, such as a birth certificate, along with a government-issued photo ID, such as a driver's license. A passport is not required for U.S. or

## Cut to the Front of the Airport Security Line as a Registered Traveler

In 2003, the **Transportation Security Administration** (**TSA;** www.tsa.gov) approved a pilot program to help ease the time spent in line for airport security screenings. In exchange for information and a fee, persons can be pre-screened as registered travelers, granting them a front-of-the-line position when they fly. The program is run through private firms—the largest and most well-known is Steven Brill's **Clear** (www.flyclear.com), and it works like this: Travelers complete an online application providing specific points of personal information including name, addresses for the previous 5 years, birth date, social security number, driver's license number, and a valid credit card (you're not charged the **$99 fee** until your application is approved). Print out the completed form and take it, along with proper ID, with you to an "enrollment station" (this can be found in over 20 participating airports and in a growing number of American Express offices around the country, for example). It's at this point where it gets seemingly sci-fi. At the enrollment station, a Clear representative will record your biometrics necessary for clearance; in this case, your fingerprints and your irises will be digitally recorded.

Once your application has been screened against no-fly lists, outstanding warrants, and other security measures, you'll be issued a clear plastic card that holds a chip containing your information. Each time you fly through participating airports (and the numbers are steadily growing), go to the Clear Pass station located next to the standard TSA screening line. Here you'll insert your card into a slot and place your finger on a scanner to read your print—when the information matches up, you're cleared to cut to the front of the security line. You'll still have to follow all the procedures of the day like removing your shoes and walking through the x-ray machine, but Clear promises to cut 30 minutes off your wait time at the airport.

On a personal note: Each time I've used my Clear Pass, my travel companions are still waiting to go through security while I'm already sitting down, reading the paper, and sipping my overpriced smoothie. Granted, registered traveler programs are not for the infrequent traveler, but for those of us who fly on a regular basis, it's a perk I'm willing to pay for.

—David A. Lytle

Canadian citizens entering by land or sea, but it is highly encouraged to carry one.

For information on how to obtain a passport, go to **"Passports"** in the **"Fast Facts"** appendix (p. 224).

## VISAS

The U.S. State Department has a **Visa Waiver Program** (**VWP**) allowing citizens of the following countries to enter the United States without a visa for stays of up to 90 days: Andorra, Australia, Austria, Belgium, Brunei, Denmark, Finland, France, Germany, Iceland, Ireland, Italy, Japan, Liechtenstein, Luxembourg, Monaco, the Netherlands, New Zealand, Norway, Portugal, San Marino, Singapore,

Slovenia, Spain, Sweden, Switzerland, and the United Kingdom. (*Note:* This list was accurate at press time; for the most up-to-date list of countries in the VWP, consult www.travel.state.gov/visa). Even though a visa isn't necessary, in an effort to help U.S. officials check travelers against terror watch lists before they arrive at U.S. borders, as of January 12, 2009, visitors from VWP countries must register online before boarding a plane or a boat to the U.S. Travelers will complete an electronic application providing basic personal and travel eligibility information. The Department of Homeland Security recommends filling out the form at least 3 days before traveling. Authorizations will be valid for up to 2 years or until the traveler's passport expires, whichever comes first. Currently, there is no fee for the online application. Canadian citizens may enter the United States without visas; they will need to show passports (if traveling by air) and proof of residence, however. *Note:* Any passport issued on or after October 26, 2006, by a VWP country must be an **e-Passport** for VWP travelers to be eligible to enter the U.S. without a visa. Citizens of these nations also need to present a round-trip air or cruise ticket upon arrival. e-Passports contain computer chips capable of storing biometric information, such as the required digital photograph of the holder. (You can identify an e-Passport by the symbol on the bottom center cover of your passport.) If your passport doesn't have this feature, you can still travel without a visa if it is a valid passport issued before October 26, 2005, and includes a machine-readable zone, or between October 26, 2005, and October 25, 2006, and includes a digital photograph. For more information, go to **www.travel.state. gov/visa**.

Citizens of all other countries must have (1) a valid passport that expires at least 6 months later than the scheduled end of their visit to the U.S., and (2) a

tourist visa. To obtain a visa, applicants must schedule an appointment with a U.S. consulate or embassy, fill out the application forms (available from www. travel.state.gov/visa), and pay a $131 fee. Wait times can be lengthy, so it's best to initiate the process as soon as possible.

As of January 2004, many international visitors traveling on visas to the United States will be photographed and fingerprinted on arrival at Customs in airports and on cruise ships in a program created by the Department of Homeland Security called **US-VISIT.** Exempt from the extra scrutiny are visitors entering by land or those (mostly in Europe; see above) that don't require a visa for short-term visits. For more information, go to the Homeland Security website at **www.dhs.gov/ dhspublic**.

For specifics on how to get a visa, see **"Visas"** in the **"Fast Facts"** appendix (p. 226).

## MEDICAL REQUIREMENTS

Unless you're arriving from an area known to be suffering from an epidemic (particularly cholera or yellow fever), inoculations or vaccinations are not required for entry into the United States.

## CUSTOMS
### What You Can Bring into the U.S.

Every visitor more than 21 years of age may bring in, free of duty, the following: (1) 1 liter of wine or hard liquor; (2) 200 cigarettes, 100 cigars (but not from Cuba), or 3 pounds of smoking tobacco; and (3) $100 worth of gifts. These exemptions are offered to travelers who spend at least 72 hours in the United States and who have not claimed them within the preceding 6 months. It is forbidden to bring into the country almost any meat products (including canned, fresh, and dried meat products such as bouillon, soup mixes, and the like). Generally, condiments including vinegars, oils, spices, coffee, tea, and some cheeses and baked goods are permitted. Avoid rice products, as rice can often harbor insects. Bringing fruits and vegetables is not advised, though not prohibited. Customs will allow produce depending on where you got it and where you're going after you arrive in the U.S. Foreign tourists may carry in or out up to $10,000 in U.S. or foreign currency with no formalities; larger sums must be declared to U.S. Customs on entering or leaving, which includes filing form CM 4790. For details regarding U.S. Customs and Border Protection, consult your nearest U.S. embassy or consulate, or **U.S. Customs** (www.cbp.gov).

## What You Can Take Home from Atlanta

**Canadian Citizens:** For a clear summary of Canadian rules, write for the booklet *I Declare,* issued by the Canada Border Services Agency (© **800/461-9999** in Canada, or 204/983-3500; www.cbsa-asfc. gc.ca).

**U.K. Citizens:** For information, contact **HM Customs & Excise** at © **0845/ 010-9000** (from outside the U.K., 020/ 8929-0152), or consult their website at **www.hmrc.gov.uk**.

**Australian Citizens:** A helpful brochure available from Australian consulates or Customs offices is *Know Before You Go.* For more information, call the **Australian Customs Service** at © **1300/363-263,** or log on to **www.customs.gov.au**.

**New Zealand Citizens:** Most questions are answered in a free pamphlet available at New Zealand consulates and Customs offices: *New Zealand Customs Guide for Travellers, Notice no. 4.* For more information, contact **New Zealand Customs,** The Customhouse, 17–21 Whitmore St., Box 2218, Wellington (© **04/473-6099** or 0800/428-786; **www.customs.govt.nz**).

# 3  WHEN TO GO

Although there is no high season for tourism here, Atlanta is a major convention and trade-show destination. Before choosing travel dates, it's wise to ask the Atlanta Convention & Visitors Bureau (ACVB; p. 27) or your travel agent what major events will be taking place in Atlanta when you plan to visit. Large conventions can mean an increase in hotel prices and longer waits at popular restaurants. Among the largest conventions that occupy a high percentage of Atlanta hotels each year are the twice-a-year Atlanta International Gift and Home Furnishings Markets, with 93,000 attendees in early to mid-January and 72,000 attendees in mid-July, as well as the Cheer Sport gathering of about 70,000 attendees in the third week of February. With more than 93,000 hotel rooms, Atlanta can accommodate both convention goers and tourists, the first of

which tend to rely on the MARTA public transportation system rather than clogging up already congested roadways.

Spring and autumn are long seasons, and in terms of natural beauty and moderate temperatures, they're ideal times to visit. April, when the dogwoods and azaleas put on a brilliant, colorful display, is especially lovely, but May and October are excellent months here, too.

If you come during July and August, when Atlanta gets a little steamy, you may find some hotels offering summer discounts. Almost all accommodations offer reduced rates during the Christmas holiday season.

## THE WEATHER

Atlanta's climate is mostly temperate year-round. The city enjoys four distinct seasons, but the variations are less extreme than in other parts of the United States.

It does get cold here in winter. The mercury dips below freezing—usually at night—an average of 50 days a year, and at least once a year there's a snowfall or an ice storm. (Northern transplants think it's pretty hilarious the way an inch or two of snow can paralyze the city.) But for the most part, winter days are mild, and it's often possible to enjoy the parks and even the outdoor restaurants in the middle of January or February.

Don't let the low average daytime temperatures for July, August, and early September fool you. Summers can be hot and humid, with daytime highs reaching into the 90s, although the really stifling spells usually last just a few days at a time. Annual rainfall is about 48 inches, and the wettest months are December through April, plus July.

**Atlanta's Average Daytime Temperature & Rainfall**

|  | Jan | Feb | Mar | Apr | May | June | July | Aug | Sept | Oct | Nov | Dec |
|---|---|---|---|---|---|---|---|---|---|---|---|---|
| Temp. °F/°C | 52/11 | 57/14 | 65/18 | 73/23 | 80/27 | 87/31 | 89/32 | 88/31 | 82/28 | 73/23 | 63/17 | 55/13 |
| Rainfall (in.) | 5.0 | 4.7 | 5.4 | 3.6 | 4.0 | 3.6 | 5.1 | 3.7 | 4.0 | 3.1 | 4.1 | 3.8 |

# ATLANTA CALENDAR OF EVENTS

**Note:** Some events, such as the Georgia Renaissance Festival and the Georgia Shakespeare Festival, begin in 1 month and continue for several months thereafter. These are listed under the month in which they start, so do look back and ahead a few months for information on ongoing events. The ACVB's website (www.atlanta.net) also has a terrific calendar of events.

For an exhaustive list of events beyond those listed here, check http://events.frommers.com, where you'll find a searchable, up-to-the-minute roster of what's happening in cities all over the world.

## JANUARY

**Martin Luther King, Jr., Weekend.** This major event begins with an interfaith service and includes musical tributes, seminars, awards dinners, and speeches by notables. There are also concerts by major performers (in past years, Stevie Wonder and the Neville Brothers, among others, have performed). For details, contact the **King Center** (© **404/526-8900;** www.thekingcenter.org). Second weekend of January.

**Cathedral Antiques Show.** For 4 days, 30 to 35 high-quality antiques dealers display their wares at the Cathedral of St. Philip, 2744 Peachtree Rd. (at W. Wesley Rd.). The merchandise ranges from 18th- and 19th-century furnishings to vintage jewelry and Oriental rugs. Admission is $15 per day. On the first day of the show, a tour of homes and mansions in Buckhead is offered for an additional $25. For details, call © **404/365-1000.** Last week in January.

## FEBRUARY

**Southeastern Flower Show.** One of the South's premier gardening events, the flower show takes place for 5 days toward the beginning of the month at Cobb Galleria Centre, 2 Galleria Pkwy. You'll find nearly 4 acres of stunning landscapes and gardens displaying both flowers and plants. Garden-related products are sold at the 90-vendor marketplace; there are also events for children and demonstrations of gardening techniques. Admission is $12 in advance, $16 at the door, with discounts for seniors and children. For information, directions, and tickets, call © **404/351-1074** or visit www.flowershow.org. Five days in late January/early February.

**Lasershow Spectacular.** This 45-minute extravaganza of laser lights and fireworks, held for the past 25 years at Stone Mountain Park, is choreographed to popular, patriotic, country, and classical music. Admission is free, but you must pay $8 for a parking permit to the park. For details, call ✆ **770/498-5690** or visit www.stonemountainpark.com. Beginning in March, the show is held on Saturdays at 8:30pm. From Memorial Day weekend through Labor Day, the show takes place nightly at 9:30pm. After Labor Day, it resumes its Saturday 8:30pm schedule through October.

**International Auto Show.** Held at the Georgia World Congress Center, this annual showcase features over 500 current-year import and domestic cars, light trucks, vans, and SUVs. Special attractions include concept cars, exotics, and next year's intros. Tickets are $8 for adults and $5 for children. For details, call ✆ **770/916-1741** or visit www.ajcautoshow.com. Mid-March.

APRIL

**Easter Sunrise Services.** This service is held at the top and the base of Stone Mountain at 30 minutes before sunrise. Park gates open at 4am, and the skylift begins operating at 5am. For details, call ✆ **770/498-5690** or visit www.stonemountainpark.com. Easter Sunday.

**Atlanta Dogwood Festival.** Held in Piedmont Park, this huge festival features concerts, food booths, kite-flying contests, children's activities, a juried arts-and-crafts show, the National Disc-Dog Championship (a canine Frisbee tournament), and an exciting display of hot-air balloons. For details, call ✆ **404/329-0501** or visit www.dogwood.org. Three days in mid-April.

**Atlanta Film Festival.** The IMAGE (Independent Media Artists of Georgia Etc.) Film & Video Center, 535 Means St., features hundreds of films by some of the country's most important independent media artists. Admission averages $10 per movie, and films are shown at several venues around the city, including some newly added outdoor ones. For details, call ✆ **404/352-4225** or visit www.atlantafilmfestival.com. Ten days in mid-April.

**Georgia Renaissance Festival.** This re-creation of a 16th-century English county fair (held in Fairburn—8 miles south of the airport on I-85, Exit 61) boasts a 30-acre "village," a juried crafts show and marketplace with over 100 craftspeople (many of them demonstrating 16th-c. skills), continuous entertainment on 12 stages (there are more than 100 shows each day), period foods, a birds-of-prey show, and a cast of costumed characters including jousting knights, jugglers, storytellers, giant stilt-walkers, minstrels, magicians, and choral groups. King Henry VIII and one of his wives oversee the festivities. Admission is $20 for adults, $18 for seniors, $9 for kids 6 to 12. For details, call ✆ **770/964-8575** or visit www.garenfest.com. Saturdays and Sundays, mid-April to early June (plus Memorial Day).

**Inman Park Spring Festival.** This Atlanta suburb (the city's oldest) is noted for its gorgeous turn-of-the-20th-century Victorian mansions and Crafts-man-style cottages. Activities include a tour of homes, live entertainment (theater, jazz bands, cloggers, Irish music, country music, and more), an arts-and-crafts festival/flea market, a parade, and food vendors. Tickets to the tour of homes are $10 in advance, $12 on the day of the tour. All other events are free. For more information, call ✆ **770/635-3711** or visit www.inmanparkfestival.org. Last weekend in April.

**Gardens for Connoisseurs Tour.** Gardening buffs will enjoy this excellent tour, which allows a peek into several outstanding private gardens. Tickets, which benefit the Atlanta Botanical Garden, are $20 for all the gardens or $10 for an individual garden. For details, call ☎ **404/876-5859** or visit www.atlantabotanicalgarden.org. Mother's Day weekend.

**Decatur Arts Festival and Garden Tour.** This 3-day event features an art show on the south lawn of the Old Courthouse in Decatur, various juried shows nearby, garden tours, mimes, jugglers, puppet shows, clowns, children's art activities, great food, and performances by music, dance, and theater groups. The literary arts are celebrated with storytelling, readings, and book signings. Events are free. For details, call ☎ **404/371-8386.** Memorial Day weekend, but most events take place on Saturday and Sunday.

**Atlanta Jazz Festival.** This is a week of jazz in different venues around the city, beginning the week before Memorial Day and continuing through the holiday weekend. Past concerts have included such major stars as Wynton Marsalis, Nancy Wilson, Shirley Horn, Cyrus Chestnut, Max Roach, and Sonny Rollins. Admission is charged to most events, but concerts in Piedmont Park on Memorial Day weekend are free. The celebration in the park also includes artists' booths and food vendors. For details, call ☎ **404/853-4234** or visit www.atlantafestivals.com. Week before Memorial Day through Memorial Day.

JUNE

**Virginia-Highland Summerfest.** This weekend neighborhood arts and music festival takes place along Virginia Avenue near the intersection of North Highland Avenue. There's a juried arts-and-crafts show, an artists' market, food booths, and plenty of free entertainment in John Howell Park. Afterward, take a stroll through Virginia Highland, which has lots of galleries and shops. All events are free. For more information, call ☎ **404/898-8986,** or visit www.vahi.org. Weekend in early June.

**Georgia Shakespeare Festival.** Five productions are presented from mid-June through November on the campus of Oglethorpe University, 4484 Peachtree Rd., in the intimate 510-seat Conant Performing Arts Center. Before the summer performances, audiences enjoy farcical vignettes on the lawn. Everyone brings a pre-performance picnic or arranges in advance to purchase it on the premises. The company, made up of Actors Equity pros for the most part, offers both traditional and innovative Shakespearean productions as well as other classics. Picnic grounds open $1\frac{1}{2}$ hours before summer performances, and the pre-show begins 1 hour before curtain time. There are both matinees and evening performances. Admission is $15 to $40 for adults. Call for tickets as far in advance as possible, especially for weekend performances. For information about tickets or picnic lunches, call ☎ **404/264-0020** or visit www.gashakespeare.org. Mid-June through November.

**Stone Mountain Village Annual Arts & Crafts Festival.** This family-oriented festival has something for everyone. More than 125 Southeastern craftspeople display their wares in a juried show, and entertainment (cloggers, clowns, country music, and more) is offered continually in the Village. There are food booths and lots of activities for kids, too. Admission is free. For details, call ☎ **770/879-4971.** Father's Day weekend.

## Impressions

*We're going to ride these buses desegregated in Atlanta, Georgia, or we're going to ride a chariot in heaven or push a wheelbarrow in hell.*

—Rev. William Holmes Borders, civil rights leader, 1957

*Atlanta is like Los Angeles was before it went bad.*

—Jane Fonda, activist, 1996

### JULY

**Independence Day.** If you're willing to get up early on July 4th, you can start the day's celebrations by watching 55,000 runners pound the pavement in the **Peachtree Road Race,** a 10K run down Peachtree Road from Lenox Square to Piedmont Park. For details, call ✆ **404/231-9064.**

Later in the afternoon, take in Atlanta's star-spangled **Salute 2 America Parade.** The floats, marching bands, and giant helium-filled balloons start their marching, rolling, and floating at Peachtree and Ralph McGill at 1pm, winding up at Centennial Olympic Park. For information, call ✆ **404/897-7855.** Afterward, there's more free entertainment and music in Centennial Olympic Park; the best part is the stunning fireworks display at night. For information, call ✆ **404/222-7275.**

An old-fashioned **Fourth of July Parade,** complete with floats, bands, baton twirlers, cloggers, and more, takes place in **Stone Mountain Village,** traveling from Mountain Street at the foot of the west gate of Stone Mountain Park along Main Street through the Village shopping area. The stores are open, and when the parade's over, there's free watermelon for everyone at the visitor center. The parade begins at 10am, preceded by a 5K run at 7am. For details, call ✆ **770/879-4971.** The biggest attraction at Stone Mountain Park's **Fantastic Fourth Celebration** is the extravagant fireworks display after the star-spangled laser show. Many people make a day of it, coming early for the race and parade, picnicking in the park, and staying through the grand finale of the fireworks. For details, call ✆ **770/498-5690** or visit www.stonemountain park.com.

**National Black Arts Festival.** More than 150 events (most of them free) take place throughout the city during this festival. Billed as "a celebration of the sights, sounds, and expressions of the African Diaspora," it features concerts (including such big names as Gladys Knight and Wynton Marsalis), theater, film, dance, storytelling, poetry readings, performance art, art and folk-art exhibitions, children's activities, workshops, African puppet shows, and more. For details, call ✆ **404/730-7315** or visit www.nbaf.org. A 10-day affair in mid-July.

**Asian Cultural Experience.** The Gwinnet Center, 6400 Sugarloaf Pkwy., Duluth, celebrates Asian culture with demonstrations of crafts, musical performances, children's activities, an art show, and dancing, among other offerings. Admission is $10 for adults, $8 for seniors, and $5 for students. For details, call ✆ **770/998-8375** or visit www. asianculturalexperienceinga.com. Weekend in late July.

### AUGUST

**Decatur Book Festival.** Held in and around the downtown Decatur Square, the Decatur Book Festival brings more than 200 authors to town for readings, talks, and panel discussions. Authors include Pulitzer Prize winners and best-sellers of fiction in many genres and nonfiction on diverse topics. The event also includes writing workshops, a street fair with many vendor booths, arts performances, cooking demonstrations, activities for children, and opportunities to meet the writers. Events are free. For details, call ℂ **404/370-4100** or visit www.decaturbookfestival.com. Three days at the end of August.

### SEPTEMBER

**Art in the Park.** This Labor Day weekend art show, on the historic square in Marietta (just northwest of Atlanta), offers fine art by more than 120 artists, plus food and antiques. Admission is free. Call ℂ **770/429-1115** for details. Labor Day weekend.

**Yellow Daisy Festival.** Stone Mountain Park hosts a vast outdoor arts-and-crafts show (more than 400 exhibitors) with musical entertainment, a flower show, great food, clogging, and storytellers. About 200,000 people attend each year. For details, call ℂ **770/498-5690** or visit www.stonemountainpark.com. Weekend after Labor Day.

### OCTOBER

**Annual Scottish Festival and Highland Games.** This gathering of the clans at Stone Mountain comprises 2 days of Highland dancing, pipe and drum concerts, Scottish harping and fiddling, sword dancing, reel dancing, lilting, and athletic events such as the hammer throw and caber toss. Fee is $15 for adults and $4 for children. For details, call ℂ **770/498-5690** or visit www.stonemountain park.com. Mid-October.

**Sunday in the Park at Oakland Cemetery.** On an October Sunday every year, this graveyard party is attended by several thousand visitors and features storytellers, historians, guided tours, a hat and costume contest, turn-of-the-20th-century music, and Victorian

boutiques. Admission is free. For a small charge, you can reserve a picnic lunch. Call ℂ **404/688-2107** or visit www.oaklandcemetery.com for details. One Sunday in October.

### NOVEMBER

**Veterans Day Parade.** Atlanta mounts an impressive version of this parade each year, with floats, drill teams, marching bands, clowns, color guards, and more. The parade begins at 11am at West Peachtree Street and proceeds to Centennial Olympic Park. Visit www.gavetsdayparade.org for details. Veterans Day.

**An Olde-Fashioned Christmas.** The holiday season kicks off with an array of events at Stone Mountain Park from mid-November to December 30 (daily 6–10pm, except for Dec 24–25). Tour the authentically decorated Antebellum Plantation, where you'll find a five-story poinsettia Christmas tree, crafters, carolers, storytellers, and a live nativity scene. The open-air Scenic Railroad is decorated to the hilt, too, and travels through a spectacular array of Christmas-light displays as it makes its way around the base of Stone Mountain. Santa Claus is here, and there's also a Polar Express 4D attraction. Crossroads features over two million lights and "snow" is abundant. Admission is $20 for adults and $17 for children 3 to 11, in addition to the $8 parking charge. For details, call ℂ **770/498-5690** or visit www.stonemountainpark.org. Mid-November through December 30.

**Stone Mountain Village Candlelight Shopping.** This charming village lures holiday shoppers with candlelight and the aroma of mulled cider. A jolly St. Nick, strolling carolers, gaily lighted trees, and carriage rides are part of the fun. Admission is free. The Village also hosts the **Sugar Plum Festival,** a breakfast with Santa Claus from 7 to 11am on the first Saturday of December. The

$5 admission includes breakfast and a photograph with Santa. Call (C) 770/879-4971 or visit www.stonemountainvillage.com for details. Every Thursday and Friday night, beginning the Thursday before Thanksgiving and continuing until Christmas.

**Ride the Pink Pig.** From its 1953 debut as a children's ride at the downtown Richs department store to a brief stint at the Festival of Trees, the Pink Pig has found a new holiday home at Macy's in Lenox Square on Peachtree Road NE. Four generations have heralded in the holiday season with a ride on the pig. Fee is $3 per child with proceeds benefiting Children's Healthcare of Atlanta. Ride open daily from late November through New Year's Day. For information, call (C) 404/231-2800.

**Holidays in the Garden.** The Atlanta Botanical Garden is beautifully decorated, and highlights of the month-long list of events include a dog parade, a holiday train, photos with St. Nick, puppet shows, a moonlight event, high tea, and holiday greenery displays. For details, call (C) 404/876-5859 or visit www.atlantabotanicalgarden.org. Events run from late November through early January.

### DECEMBER

**Children's Healthcare of Atlanta Christmas Parade and Festival of Trees.** The parade is a major to-do, with award-winning bands, lavish holiday-themed floats, helium-balloon cartoon characters, and, of course, Santa Claus. It kicks off the 9-day Festival of Trees at the Georgia World Congress Center, for which Atlanta artists and designers lavishly decorate more than 200 trees, wreaths, and other holiday ornaments, which are exhibited and auctioned off to benefit Children's Healthcare of Atlanta. The festival also features live entertainment, cooking demonstrations, an antique carousel, a roller coaster, a giant slide, a balloon ride, international holiday displays, and more. Admission to the festival is $8 for adults, $5 for seniors and children 2 to 12. The parade begins at 10:30am, and the festival follows. For information, call (C) 404/325-NOEL [6635] or visit www.choa.org/festival. First Saturday in December.

**Peach Bowl Game.** This exciting football game is held annually at the Georgia Dome. Tickets are hard to come by; reserve well in advance. Call (C) 404/586-8496 or visit www.peachbowl.com for information. Sometime between Christmas and New Year's Eve (occasionally in early Jan).

**New Year's Eve.** The Big Peach that rings in Atlanta's New Year is dropped at the stroke of midnight from the 138-foot light tower at Underground Atlanta. Festivities begin earlier (about noon) with children's activities, followed later by live music for dancing in the streets, a pyrotechnic display and laser show, balloons, and usually a marching band. Call (C) 404/523-2311 or visit www.peachdrop.com for details.

## 4 GETTING THERE & GETTING AROUND

### GETTING TO ATLANTA
#### By Plane
**Hartsfield-Jackson Atlanta International Airport** ((C) 404/530-7300; www.atlanta-airport.com; airport code: ATL), 10 miles south of downtown, is the world's largest and busiest passenger airport and transfer hub, accommodating 78 million passengers a year. It provides 186 U.S. cities with nonstop service.

Delta Air Lines (© **800/221-1212;** www.delta.com), which is based at Hartsfield-Jackson, is the major carrier to Atlanta, connecting the city to the rest of the U.S. as well as 62 countries internationally. It carries 80% of the air passengers who come into Atlanta and serves more than 350 international cities.

Other major carriers include **AirTran** (© 800/247-8726; www.airtran.com), **American Airlines** (© 800/433-7300; www.aa.com), **British Airways** (© 800/247-9297; www.british-airways.com), **Continental** (© 800/525-0280; www.continental. com), **Japan Airlines** (© 800/525-3663; www.jal.com), **Lufthansa** (© 800/645-3880; www.lufthansa-usa.com), **Northwest/ KLM** (© 800/225-2525; www.nwa.com), **United Airlines** (© 800/241-6522; www. united.com), and **US Airways** (© 800/428-4322; www.usairways.com). For more information, see the appendix.

## Getting Through the Airport

With the federalization of airport security, security procedures at U.S. airports are more stable and consistent than ever. Generally, you'll be fine if you arrive at the airport **1 hour** before a domestic flight and **2 hours** before an international flight; if you show up late, tell an airline employee and she'll probably whisk you to the front of the line.

Bring a **current, government-issued photo ID** such as a driver's license or passport. Keep your ID at the ready to present at check-in, the security checkpoint, and sometimes even the gate. (Children 17 and under do not need government-issued photo IDs for domestic flights, but they do for international flights to most countries.)

The Transportation Security Administration (TSA) has phased out **gate check-in** at all U.S. airports. But passengers with e-tickets, which have made paper tickets nearly obsolete, can beat the ticket-counter lines by using airport **electronic kiosks** or even **online check-in** from their home computers. Online check-in involves logging on to your airline's website, accessing your reservation, and printing out your boarding pass—and the airline may even offer you bonus miles to do so! If you're using a kiosk at the airport, bring the credit card you used to book the ticket or your frequent-flier card. Print out your boarding pass from the kiosk and simply proceed to the security checkpoint with your pass and a photo ID. If you're checking bags or looking to snag an exit-row seat, you will be able to do so using most airline kiosks. Even the smaller airlines are employing the kiosk system, but call your airline to make sure these alternatives are available. **Curbside check-in** is also a good way to avoid lines, although a few airlines still don't allow it; call before you go.

Security lines remain, particularly during periods of high security alerts. If you have trouble standing for long periods of time, tell an airline employee; the airline will provide a wheelchair. Speed up security by **not wearing metal objects** such as big belt buckles. If you've got metallic body parts, a note from your doctor can prevent a long chat with the security screeners. Keep in mind that only **ticketed passengers** are allowed past security, except for folks escorting passengers with disabilities or children.

Federalization has stabilized **what you can carry on** and **what you can't.** The general rule is that sharp things are out, but nail clippers are okay. Bring food in your carry-on rather than checking it, as explosive-detection machines used on checked luggage have been known to mistake food (especially chocolate, for some reason) for bombs. Travelers in the U.S. are allowed one carry-on bag, plus a "personal item" such as a purse, briefcase, or laptop bag. Carry-on hoarders can stuff all sorts of things into a laptop bag; as long as it has a laptop in it, it's still considered a personal item. The TSA has issued a list of restricted items; check www.tsa.gov/311/index.shtm for the most up-to-date details.

**(Tips)** **Prepare to Be Fingerprinted**

Many international visitors traveling on visas to the United States will be photographed and fingerprinted at Customs, thanks to a new Department of Homeland Security program called **US-VISIT.** Non-U.S. citizens arriving at airports and on cruise ships must undergo an instant background check as part of the government's efforts to deter terrorism by verifying the identity of incoming and outgoing visitors. Exempt from the extra scrutiny are visitors entering by land or those who don't require a visa for short-term visits (p. 28 for a list of Visa Waiver Program countries). For more information, go to the Homeland Security website at **www.dhs.gov/dhspublic**.

Airport screeners may decide that your checked luggage warrants a hand search. You can now purchase luggage locks that allow screeners to open and relock a checked bag if hand searching is necessary. Look for Travel Sentry certified locks at luggage or travel shops and Brookstone stores (www.brookstone.com). Luggage inspectors can open these TSA-approved locks with a special code or key—rather than having to cut them off the suitcase, as they normally do to conduct a hand search. For more information on the locks, visit **www.travelsentry.org**.

**IMMIGRATION & CUSTOMS** International visitors arriving by air, no matter what the port of entry, should cultivate patience and resignation before setting foot on U.S. soil. U.S. airports have considerably beefed up security clearances in the years since the September 11, 2001, terrorist attacks, and clearing Customs and Immigration can take as long as 2 hours.

### Getting into Town from the Airport

Those flying into Atlanta have several options for getting from the airport to the downtown area. Most large hotels offer their guests shuttle service, accessible through a courtesy phone located near baggage claim at Hartsfield-Jackson Atlanta International Airport. Other options include taxi, MARTA rapid-rail or

bus service, and rental cars. See p. 40 for details on getting from the airport to your destination.

### Long-haul Flights: How to Stay Comfortable

- Your choice of airline and airplane will definitely affect your legroom. Find more details about U.S. airlines at **www.seatguru.com**. For international airlines, the research firm Skytrax has posted a list of average seat pitches at **www.airlinequality.com**.

- Emergency exit seats and bulkhead seats typically have the most legroom. Emergency exit seats are usually left unassigned until the day of a flight (to ensure that someone able-bodied fills the seats); it's worth checking in online at home (if the airline offers that option) or getting to the ticket counter early to snag one of these spots for a long flight. Many passengers find that bulkhead seating offers more legroom, but keep in mind that bulkhead seats have no storage space on the floor in front of you.

- To have two seats for yourself in a three-seat row, try for an aisle seat in a center section toward the back of coach. If you're traveling with a companion, book an aisle and a window seat. Middle seats are usually booked last, so chances are good you'll end up with three seats to yourselves. And in the

## (Tips) Coping with Jet Lag

Jet lag is a pitfall of traveling across time zones. If you're flying north–south and you feel sluggish when you touch down, your symptoms will be the result of dehydration and the general stress of air travel. When you travel east–west or vice versa, your body becomes confused about what time it is, and everything from your digestive system to your brain is knocked for a loop. Traveling east is more difficult on your internal clock than traveling west because most people's bodies are more inclined to stay up late than to fall asleep early.

Here are some tips for combating jet lag:

- **Reset your watch** to your destination time before you board the plane.
- **Drink lots of water** before, during, and after your flight. Avoid alcohol.
- **Exercise and sleep well** for a few days before your trip.
- If you have trouble sleeping on planes, **fly eastward on morning flights.**
- **Daylight** is the key to resetting your body clock. At the website for **Outside In** (www.bodyclock.com), you can get a customized plan of when to seek and avoid light.

event that a third passenger is assigned the middle seat, he or she will probably be more than happy to trade for a window or an aisle.

- To sleep, avoid the last row of any section or the row in front of an emergency exit, as these seats are the least likely to recline. Avoid seats near highly trafficked toilet areas. Avoid seats in the back of many jets—these can be narrower than those in the rest of coach. Or reserve a window seat so you can rest your head and avoid being bumped in the aisle.
- Get up, walk around, and stretch every 60 to 90 minutes to keep your blood flowing. This helps avoid **deep vein thrombosis,** or "economy-class syndrome." See the box "Avoiding 'Economy Class Syndrome,'" p. 47.
- Drink water before, during, and after your flight to combat the lack of humidity in airplane cabins. Avoid caffeine and alcohol, which will dehydrate you.

## By Car

Navigating Atlanta by car can be freeing or terrifying, depending on your approach to major traffic. While city and state officials

continue to stumble around improvements to traffic flow, there is much to be said for having your own ride in this sprawling metropolis. Of course, the use of Global Positioning System (GPS) makes navigation much easier, though frequent and ongoing road construction can result in it leading you to a dead-end or blocked road. Three major interstate highways (**I-20, I-75,** and **I-85**) converge near the center of downtown Atlanta.

Below is a list of approximate mileage from other major cities in the region:

Birmingham, Ala.: 148
Charleston, S.C.: 320
Charlotte, N.C.: 240
Jacksonville, Fla.: 346
Louisville, Ky.: 417
Nashville, Tenn.: 244
New Orleans, La.: 473
Norfolk, Va.: 555
Orlando, Fla.: 441
Savannah, Ga.: 252
Tampa, Fla.: 458

## By Train

**Amtrak** operates the *Crescent* daily between Atlanta and New York, with stops in

Washington, D.C., Philadelphia, and other intermediate points. Travel time between New York and Atlanta is approximately 18$^1$/$_2$ hours. The *Crescent* also goes beyond Atlanta to many points south each day, terminating in New Orleans. Other Amtrak trains connect with most of the country. To find out if your city connects via rail with Atlanta, call ✆ **800/USA-RAIL [872-7245]** or check www.amtrak.com.

Like the airlines, Amtrak offers discount fares, and though not all are based on advance purchase, reserving early may pay off.

Contact **Amtrak Vacations** (✆ **800/ 321-8684;** www.amtrak.com) to inquire about money-saving packages that include hotel accommodations and attraction tickets with your train fare.

Trains arrive in Atlanta at 1688 Peachtree St., just off I-85. From this central location, you can take a taxi to your hotel or to the nearest MARTA station (Arts Center). For information, call ✆ **800/USA-RAIL [872-7245]** or 404/ 881-3060.

International visitors can buy a **USA Rail Pass,** good for 15 or 30 days of unlimited travel on **Amtrak** (✆ **800/USA-RAIL [872-7245];** www.amtrak.com). The pass is available online or through many overseas travel agents. See Amtrak's website for the cost of travel within the western, eastern, or northwestern United States. Reservations are generally required and should be made as early as possible. Regional rail passes are also available.

## By Bus

Bus travel is often the most economical form of public transit for short hops between U.S. cities, but it's certainly not an option for everyone (particularly when Amtrak, which is far more luxurious, offers similar rates). **Greyhound** (✆ **800/ 231-2222;** www.greyhound.com) is the sole nationwide bus line and connects the entire country with Atlanta via bus.

The bus terminal is located at 232 Forsyth St., at the Garnett Street MARTA station, one stop south of Five Points (the main MARTA station downtown). Taxis are available, but it's both convenient and inexpensive to take MARTA into the central city.

The fare structure on buses is complex and not always based on distance traveled. The good news is that when you call Greyhound, you'll always get the lowest-fare options. Once again, advance-purchase fares booked 3 to 21 days prior to travel can garner big savings.

International visitors can obtain information about the **Greyhound North American Discovery Pass.** The pass can be obtained from foreign travel agents or through www.discoverypass.com for unlimited travel and stopovers in the U.S. and Canada.

## GETTING AROUND
### By Car

Traffic can be a nightmare in Atlanta, and the region's leaders are working hard to figure out what to do about it. Rush hours—roughly 6:30 to 9am and 3:30 to 6:30 or 7pm—can be vicious, especially when traveling into town in the morning or out of town in the afternoon on any of the interstates. The Downtown Connector (where I-75 and I-85 become one) is almost always congested, even during non-rush times, mostly because travelers on their way to points north, south, east, and west join the locals trying to make their way through the city. The area looks a lot like a pig trying to pass through a python. Atlanta drivers are generally courteous, but they tend to travel at breakneck speeds well above the posted limit, so it's wise to stay off the interstates during peak hours. I-285, which circles the city and supports a lot of truck traffic, should be avoided if at all possible. It's possible to reach most major Atlanta sights via the transit system (MARTA); public transportation is usually the best bet during sporting and entertainment events and conventions.

Even if you're here for just a few days, you'll get a pretty good feel for the layout of the city. Just remember that the main drag is **Peachtree Street** (becoming Peachtree Rd. to the north), and use it to get your bearings. Just don't fall prey to the confusion created by dozens of streets with "Peachtree" in their name.

Georgia law requires the driver and front-seat passengers to wear seat belts while the car is in motion. Children 4 and under must be buckled into safety seats in the rear; those 5 to 12 must sit in the rear seat if the car is equipped with air bags.

Gas stations and public parking lots are plentiful and toll roads are nearly nonexistent. That being said, while parking isn't a problem in Atlanta's outlying areas, it's getting to be a headache downtown and in some commercial areas of Midtown and Buckhead. It can be especially scarce and expensive downtown during conventions and other major events. If you can't find a spot close to your destination, there's often parking available a block or two away, and it's likely to be cheaper.

If you're visiting from abroad and plan to rent a car in the United States, keep in mind that foreign driver's licenses are usually recognized in the U.S., but you should get an international one if your home license is not in English.

Check out **Breezenet.com**, which offers domestic car-rental discounts with some of the most competitive rates around. Also worth visiting are Orbitz, Hotwire, Travelocity, and Priceline, all of which offer competitive online car-rental rates. For additional car rental agencies, see the appendix, p. 219.

## Renting a Car

Renting a car in Atlanta will not be a problem. All of the major rental agencies maintain branch offices in the city. In addition, **Atlanta Rent-A-Car** (© **800/542-8278;** www.atlantarac.com), a local independently owned company, has been serving the area for over 25 years and its rates are often lower than most. It has 20 metro locations, including one close to the airport, and provides free courtesy pickup anywhere in metro Atlanta.

If you pick up your rental car at Hartsfield-Jackson Atlanta International Airport, expect to pay a 10% government tax (which includes a 7% local sales tax) and a 10% airport tax. Elsewhere in the metro area, car rentals incur only the local sales tax, which can range from 5% to 7%.

**SAVING MONEY**  Car-rental rates vary even more than airline fares. The price you pay will depend on the size of the car, where and when you pick it up and drop it off, the length of the rental period, where and how far you drive it, whether you purchase insurance, and a host of other factors. A few key questions could save you hundreds of dollars. Here are some things to ask:

- Are weekend rates lower than weekday rates? Ask if the rate is the same for pickup Friday morning, for instance, as it is for Thursday night.
- Is a weekly rate cheaper than the daily rate? Even if you need the car for only 4 days, it may be cheaper to keep it for 5.
- Does the agency assess a drop-off charge if you don't return the car to the same location where you picked it up? Is it cheaper to pick up the car at the airport compared to a downtown location?
- Are special promotional rates available? If you see an advertised price in your local newspaper, be sure to ask for that specific rate; otherwise, you may be charged the standard cost. Terms change constantly.
- Are discounts available for members of AARP, AAA, frequent-flier programs, or trade unions? If you belong to any of these organizations, you may be entitled to discounts of up to 30%.
- How much tax will be added to the rental bill? Local tax? State use tax?

- What is the cost of adding an additional driver's name to the contract?
- How many free miles are included in the price? Free mileage is often negotiable, depending on the length of your rental.
- How much does the rental company charge to refill your gas tank if you return with the tank less than full? Though most agencies claim these prices are "competitive," fuel is almost always cheaper in town. Try to allow enough time to refuel the car yourself before returning it. Some companies offer "refueling packages," in which you pay for an entire tank of gas upfront. The price is usually fairly competitive with local gas prices, but you don't get credit for any gas remaining in the tank. If a stop at a gas station on the way to the airport will make you miss your plane, then by all means take advantage of the fuel purchase option. Otherwise, skip it.

**ONLINE RENTALS** Internet resources make comparison shopping easier. **Expedia** (www.expedia.com) and **Travelocity** (www.travelocity.com) can help you compare prices and locate car-rental bargains from various companies nationwide. They will even make the reservation for you once you've found the best deal.

**PACKAGE DEALS** Many packages are available that include airfare, accommodations, and a rental car with unlimited mileage. Compare the price of the package with the cost of booking airline tickets and renting a car separately to see if the offer is a good deal. See p. 53 for more on package deals.

**DEMYSTIFYING RENTERS INSURANCE** Before you drive off in a rental car, be sure you're insured. Hasty assumptions about your personal auto insurance or a rental agency's additional coverage could end up costing you tens of thousands of dollars—even if you are involved in an accident that was clearly the fault of another driver.

If you already hold a **private auto insurance** policy, you are most likely covered in the United States for loss of or damage to a rental car, and liability in case of injury to any other party involved in an accident. Be sure to find out whether you are covered in the area you are visiting, whether your policy extends to all persons who will be driving the rental car, how much liability is covered in case an outside party is injured in an accident, and whether the type of vehicle you are renting is included under your contract. (Rental trucks, SUVs, and luxury vehicles such as Jaguars may not be covered.)

Most **major credit cards** provide some degree of coverage as well—provided they were used to pay for the rental. Terms vary widely, however, so be sure to call your credit card company directly before you rent. Most American Express Optima cards, for instance, do not provide any insurance. In addition, American Express does not cover vehicles valued at over $50,000 when new, or luxury vehicles such as Porsches, or vehicles built on a truck chassis. MasterCard does not provide coverage for loss, theft, or fire damage, and only covers collision if the rental period does not exceed 15 days. Call ahead of time for details; you may also be able to purchase additional coverage from your credit card company.

If you are **uninsured,** your credit card may provide primary coverage as long as you decline the rental agency's insurance. This means that the credit card will cover damage or theft of a rental car for the full cost of the vehicle. If you already have insurance, your credit card will provide secondary coverage—which basically covers your deductible. **Credit cards will not cover liability,** or the cost of injury to an outside party and/or damage to an outside party's vehicle. If you do not hold an insurance policy, you may seriously want to consider purchasing additional liability insurance from your rental company. Be sure to check the terms: Some rental agencies cover liability only if the renter is not at fault, and even then, the rental company's obligation varies from state to state.

The basic insurance coverage offered by most car-rental agencies, known as the **Loss/Damage Waiver (LDW)** or **Collision Damage Waiver (CDW),** can cost as much as $20 per day. It usually covers the full value of the vehicle with no deductible if an outside party causes an accident or other damage to the rental car. In all states but California, you will probably be covered in case of theft as well. Liability coverage varies according to company policy and state law, but the minimum is usually at least $15,000. If you are at fault in an accident, however, you will be covered for the full replacement value of the car but not for liability. Some states allow you to buy additional liability coverage in case of such accidents. Most rental companies will require a police report in order to process any claims you file, but your private insurer will not be notified of the accident.

## BY TAXI

Atlanta is not New York. It's not possible to step outside and hail a cab at all times, though there are always cabs waiting outside the airport, major hotels, Underground Atlanta, and most MARTA stations, except those found downtown. If a cab is not waiting at your MARTA rail stop, use the white assistance phone in the station and MARTA will call one for you.

Taxi fares are a bit complicated in Atlanta. Within the Downtown Zone, you pay a flat rate of $5 for one passenger, $1 for each additional rider. That's fine if you're going from one end of this extensive zone to the other; unfortunately, though, you pay the same rate even if you go just a block. Rates and rules are the same in Buckhead.

There's also a flat rate for rides between downtown and the airport: $30 for one passenger, plus $2 for each additional passenger. Between the airport and Midtown,

the rate is $32 for one passenger, $2 for each additional. Between the airport and Buckhead, the rate is $38 for one, $2 for each additional.

Outside these specified zones, Atlanta cabs charge a minimum $1.50 for the meter drop and first $^1/_6$ mile, 20¢ for each additional $^1/_6$ mile for the first passenger, and a flat rate of $1 for each additional passenger, adult or child. Waiting time is $15 per hour.

There are many taxi companies in town. If you need to call a taxi, try **Atlanta Lenox Taxi** (✆ 404/872-2600), **Yellow Cabs** (✆ 404/521-0200), **Checker Cabs** (✆ 404/351-1111), or **Buckhead Safety Cab** (✆ 404/875-3777). If your destination lies outside of the zone system (which applies flat rates to trips within each zone), the meter won't start running until you get into the cab. Some of these companies accept credit cards.

If you have a complaint about taxi service, call the **Taxi Bureau** (✆ **404/658-7600**).

## BY PUBLIC TRANSPORTATION

The **Metropolitan Atlanta Rapid Transit Authority (MARTA)** operates a rail (subway) and bus network, making it possible, though not always convenient, to reach just about any part of town by public transportation. While the system is fairly extensive within the city limits, outside the city (except for areas in DeKalb, Fulton, and Clayton counties) the service is quite limited. Even in some areas served by bus and rail lines, it's often necessary to walk a bit to a station or stop.

Cobb County, a suburban county that includes the city of Marietta, operates a bus system separate from MARTA. **Cobb Community Transit (CCT)** has five local routes and express routes that operate between Cobb and the Arts Center, Dunwoody, and H. E. Holmes MARTA stations. Transfers are free between CCT and MARTA. Call ✆ **770/427-4444** for information.

The **Buckhead Area Transportation Management Association (BATMA)** operates "the buc," free shuttle buses that run every 8 to 15 minutes between the two MARTA rail stations in the area—Lenox and Buckhead—and the hotels, malls, and other businesses along Piedmont and Peachtree roads. The buses operate Monday through Friday from 7am to 7pm, Saturday from 10am to 9pm. For more information, inquire at your hotel or go to www.bucride.com.

## MARTA Rapid Rail

MARTA's rapid-rail (subway) system has been running since 1979. The stations are clean and modern, and the service is reliable. Although MARTA has a good safety record, there is the perception here—as in many big cities—that subway travel is unsafe. MARTA moves more than half a million people every day, and regular riders seem to have more confidence in the security of the trains and stations than infrequent riders do. Visitors should find the subway most pleasant during the day and during early-evening hours, when usage is heavy.

The major problem with MARTA is that not enough parts of the city are served by rail (which is much faster overall than the bus). MARTA will eventually have 45 stations, but the system currently includes only 40 stations. There are two lines: south–north trains (**orange lines** on the MARTA maps) that travel between the airport and Doraville and North Springs; and east–west trains (**blue lines** on the maps) that travel between Indian Creek (east of Decatur) and Hamilton E. Holmes. They intersect at **Five Points Station** in downtown Atlanta, where you can transfer to another train for free. The system's two newest station additions—Sandy Springs and North Springs—were added in late 2000 to the north line that parallels Georgia Highway 400.

The fare is $1.75 for any ride, and passengers must purchase the new Breeze Card from the station vending machines

to ride. Multi-trip passes, as well as 7- and 30-day passes, are also available.

MARTA trains generally arrive and depart every 8 to 10 minutes, 7 days a week, from 5am to 1am. Free transfers between bus and rail are available when you board a bus or enter a rail station. Parking is free but limited at about half the rail stations. If you wish to park overnight, you must use the long-term secured parking available at the stations of Doraville, Dunwoody, Medical Center, Lenox, Brookhaven, Lindbergh, North Springs, Sandy Springs, and College Park. Cost is $3 per day.

For MARTA schedule and route information, go to **www.itsmarta.com** or call ✆ **404/848-4711** Monday through Friday from 6am to midnight, Saturday and Sunday from 8am to 10pm. Printed schedules are available from racks at Five Points and several other stations; instructions are printed in English, French, Japanese, German, and Spanish. All stations and rail cars are fully accessible to passengers with disabilities.

## MARTA Buses

It's possible, but not always efficient, to get anywhere within the city limits by bus. The routes will deliver you to most major attractions and sightseeing stops, but travel can be slow, with long wait times between buses. MARTA buses operate on a 1,550-mile network of 150 routes, and the fare system is the same as described above for rail service. To find out what bus to take, call ✆ **404/ 848-4711** for route information (same hours as listed above for rail information). You must have exact change ($1.75) or a Breeze Card. Special shuttle buses operate from downtown in conjunction with major stadium sports events and conventions; call the above number for details.

## BY PLANE

Overseas visitors can take advantage of the APEX (Advance Purchase Excursion) reductions offered by all major U.S. and

European carriers. In addition, some large airlines offer transatlantic or transpacific passengers special discount tickets under the name **Visit USA,** which allows mostly one-way travel from one U.S. destination to another at very low prices. Unavailable in the U.S., these discount tickets must be purchased abroad in conjunction with your international fare. This system is the easiest, fastest, cheapest way to see the country.

## 5 MONEY & COSTS

Atlanta is a reasonably priced city, whether you live there or just visit. While there are plenty of high dollar hotels and restaurants for those who don't mind spending money, there are an equal number of options for the more money-conscious spenders. On average, a standard hotel room will run about $120 a night, though rates vary depending on the day of the week and any special events in town. Taxis and public transportation costs are in line with other metro areas and when it comes to shopping, well, the sky's the limit.

Nearly every store, hotel, and restaurant in the city will accept all major credit cards and bank debit cards. ATMs are easily accessed anywhere in the city, and rates for using one not tied to your own bank can range from $2 to $4, plus whatever fee your bank charges for withdrawing money from an outside source.

### ATMS

Nationwide, the easiest and best way to get cash away from home is from an ATM (automated teller machine), sometimes referred to as a "cash machine" or "cashpoint." The **Cirrus** (℡ 800/424-7787; www.mastercard.com) and **PLUS** (℡ 800/843-7587; www.visa.com) networks span the country; you can find them even in remote regions. Look at the back of your bank card to see which network you're in; then call or check online for ATM locations at your destination. Be sure you know your personal identification number (PIN) and daily withdrawal limit before you depart. *Note:* Remember that many banks impose a fee every time you use a card at another bank's ATM, and that fee can be higher for international transactions (up to $5 or more) than for domestic ones (where they're rarely more than $2). In addition, the bank from which you withdraw cash may charge its own fee. To compare banks' ATM fees within the U.S., use **www.bankrate.com**. For international withdrawal fees, ask your bank.

### CREDIT CARDS & DEBIT CARDS

The most widely used form of payment in the United States is credit cards: **Visa** (Barclaycard in Britain), **MasterCard** (Euro-Card in Europe, Access in Britain, Chargex in Canada), **American Express, Diners Club,** and **Discover.**

| What Things Cost in Atlanta | U.S.$ | U.K.£ |
|---|---|---|
| Cup of coffee (straight up, nothing fancy) | 2.00 | 1.30 |
| Taxi from the airport (to downtown) | 32.00 | 20.80 |
| Night in a standard hotel room | 120.00 | 78.00 |
| Bus/MARTA fare (one-way) | 1.75 | 1.13 |
| Moderate three-course meal for one (without alcohol) | 35.00 | 22.75 |

It's highly recommended that you travel with at least one major credit card. You must have one to rent a car, and hotels and airlines usually require a credit card imprint as a deposit against expenses. Credit cards also provide a convenient record of all your expenses, and they generally offer relatively good exchange rates. You can withdraw cash advances from your credit cards at banks or ATMs, provided you know your PIN.

Visitors from outside the U.S. should inquire whether their bank assesses a 1% to 3% fee on charges incurred abroad.

ATM cards with major credit card backing, known as **debit cards,** are now a commonly accepted form of payment in most stores and restaurants. Debit cards draw money directly from your checking account. Some stores enable you to receive "cash back" on your debit card purchases as well. The same is true at most U.S. post offices.

## TRAVELER'S CHECKS

Traveler's checks are something of an anachronism from the days before the ATM made cash accessible at any time. Traveler's checks used to be the only sound alternative to traveling with dangerously large amounts of cash. They were as reliable as currency, but, unlike cash, could be replaced if lost or stolen.

These days, traveler's checks are less necessary because most cities have 24-hour ATMs that allow you to withdraw small amounts of cash as needed. However, keep in mind that you will likely be charged an ATM withdrawal fee if the bank is not your own, so if you're withdrawing money every day, you might be better off with traveler's checks—provided that you don't mind showing identification every time you want to cash one.

You can get traveler's checks at almost any bank. **American Express** offers denominations of $20, $50, $100, $500, and (for cardholders only) $1,000. You'll pay a service charge ranging from 1% to 4%. You can also get American Express traveler's checks over the phone by calling ✆ **800/221-7282;** AmEx gold and platinum cardholders who use this number are exempt from the 1% fee.

**Visa** offers traveler's checks at Citibank locations nationwide, as well as at several other banks. The service charge ranges between 1.5% and 2%; checks come in denominations of $20, $50, $100, $500, and $1,000. Call ✆ **800/732-1322** for information. AAA members can obtain Visa checks without a fee at most AAA offices or by calling ✆ **866/339-3378.**

**MasterCard** also offers traveler's checks. Call ✆ **800/223-9920** for a location near you.

If you choose to carry traveler's checks, be sure to keep a record of their serial numbers separate from your checks in the event that they are stolen or lost. You'll get a refund faster if you know the numbers.

For visitors from outside the U.S. who choose to use cash, the American money system is fairly simple to grasp. The most common bills are the $1 (a "buck"), $5, $10, and $20 denominations. There are also $2 bills (seldom encountered), $50 bills, and $100 bills (the last two are usually not welcome as payment for small purchases).

Coins come in seven denominations: 1¢ (1 cent, or a penny); 5¢ (5 cents, or a nickel); 10¢ (10 cents, or a dime); 25¢ (25 cents, or a quarter); 50¢ (50 cents, or a half dollar); the gold-colored Sacagawea coin, worth $1; and the rare silver dollar.

# 6 HEALTH

## STAYING HEALTHY

The **U.S. Centers for Disease Control and Prevention** (✆ **800/311-3435;** www.

cdc.gov) provides up-to-date information on health hazards by region or country and offers tips on food safety. If you suffer from

## Avoiding "Economy Class Syndrome"

**Deep vein thrombosis,** or as it's know in the world of flying, "economy-class syndrome," is a blood clot that develops in a deep vein. It's a potentially deadly condition that can be caused by sitting in cramped conditions—such as an airplane cabin—for too long. During a flight (especially a long-haul flight), get up, walk around, and stretch your legs every 60 to 90 minutes to keep your blood flowing. Other preventative measures include frequent flexing of the legs while sitting, drinking lots of water, and avoiding alcohol and sleeping pills. If you have a history of deep vein thrombosis, heart disease, or another condition that puts you at high risk, some experts recommend wearing compression stockings or taking anticoagulants when you fly; always ask your physician about the best course for you. Symptoms of deep vein thrombosis include leg pain or swelling, or even shortness of breath.

a chronic illness, consult your doctor before your departure. For conditions like epilepsy, diabetes, or heart problems, wear a **MedicAlert identification tag** (✆ 888/633-4298; www.medicalert.org), which will immediately alert doctors to your condition and give them access to your records through MedicAlert's 24-hour hot line.

Pack **prescription medications** in your carry-on luggage, and carry them in their original containers with pharmacy labels affixed—otherwise they won't make it through airport security. Also bring along copies of your prescriptions in case you lose your pills or run out. Don't forget an extra pair of contact lenses or prescription glasses.

## WHAT TO DO IF YOU GET SICK AWAY FROM HOME

Should you fall ill during your visit to Atlanta, a number of options are available, including hospitals and emergency rooms throughout the city. Among them are

**Piedmont Hospital,** 1968 Peachtree Rd., just above Collier Road (✆ **404/605-3297**), which offers 24-hour full emergency-room service, and **Grady Health Systems,** 35 Butler St., downtown (✆ **404/616-6200**). For life-threatening medical emergencies, dial ✆ **911.**

For domestic trips, most reliable health care plans provide coverage if you get sick away from home. Whether you will pay as a walk-in for a hospital visit will be determined by your health insurance carrier, if applicable, and the policy of the hospital you visit.

In addition, the city has a number of 24-hour pharmacies for getting over-the-counter meds or for filling prescriptions. Among them are the supermarket chain **Kroger** (✆ **800/576-4377**), which operates several pharmacies that are open 24 hours. Call for the nearest location.

See **additional emergency numbers** in the "Fast Facts" appendix, p. 219.

## 7 SAFETY

Atlanta's neighborhoods are relatively safe, but it's wise to exercise caution at night near Underground Atlanta, as well as around the major venues for sporting events. Most of the central city is primarily a business district that closes up after dark,

so it's a good idea to stay within the downtown hotel and entertainment district, which is likely to be much busier.

Buckhead, a major restaurant and bar scene, is safe as long as the crowds are out. Recently, however, a few square blocks of

Buckhead's entertainment district—where most of the bars are located—have been plagued by overly rowdy behavior and incidents of violent crime. Much of the undesirable activity takes place after midnight or in the wee hours as the bars are winding down, so be alert.

Avoid carrying valuables with you on the street, and don't display expensive cameras or electronic equipment. If you are using a map, consult it inconspicuously—or better yet, try to study it before you leave your hotel. Hold onto your pocketbook, and place your billfold in an inside pocket. In theaters, restaurants, and other public places, keep your possessions in sight.

Remember also that hotels are open to the public, and in a large hotel, security may not be able to screen everyone entering. Always lock your room door—don't assume that once inside your hotel you are automatically safe and no longer need to be aware of your surroundings.

## DRIVING SAFETY

Question your rental agency about personal safety and ask for a traveler-safety brochure when you pick up your car.

Obtain written directions—or a map with the route clearly marked—from the agency showing how to get to your destination. (Many agencies now offer the option of renting a cellphone for the duration of your car rental; check with the rental agent when you pick up the car.)

Recently, more and more crime has involved cars and drivers. If you drive off a highway into a doubtful neighborhood, leave the area as quickly as possible. If you have an accident, even on the highway, stay in your car with the doors locked until you assess the situation or until the police arrive. If you're bumped from behind on the street or are involved in a minor accident with no injuries and the situation appears to be suspicious, motion to the other driver to follow you. Never get out of your car in such situations. Go directly to the nearest police precinct, well-lit service station, or 24-hour store.

Always try to park in well-lit and well-traveled areas if possible. Never leave any packages or valuables in sight. If someone attempts to rob you or steal your car, don't try to resist the thief/carjacker, but immediately report the incident to the police department by calling ✆ **911.**

# 8 SPECIALIZED TRAVEL RESOURCES

## TRAVELERS WITH DISABILITIES

Most disabilities shouldn't stop anyone from traveling in the U.S. Thanks to provisions in the Americans with Disabilities Act, most public places are required to comply with disability-friendly regulations. Almost all public establishments (including hotels, restaurants, museums, and so on, but not including certain National Historic Landmarks), and at least some modes of public transportation provide accessible entrances and other facilities for those with disabilities.

Before planning a trip to Atlanta, travelers with disabilities should request *A Guide to Atlanta for People with Disabilities,* available from the Shepherd Center, a nationally renowned Atlanta hospital specializing in the treatment of spinal-cord injuries and diseases. The guide rates the accessibility of local museums, parks, restaurants, hotels, theaters, sports venues, and other popular tourist stops. Accessibility is assessed in several categories, including restrooms, parking, main entrances, and telephones. The booklet also lists services and other information of interest to travelers with disabilities. For a free copy, contact the **Noble Learning Resource Center, Shepherd Center,** 2020 Peachtree Rd. NW, Atlanta, GA 30309 (© **404/350-7473**). The guide is also available at www.shepherd.org.

Many travel agencies offer customized tours and itineraries for travelers with disabilities. **Flying Wheels Travel** (© **507/451-5005;** www.flyingwheelstravel.com) provides escorted tours and cruises that emphasize sports, as well as private tours in minivans with lifts. **Access-Able Travel Source** (© **303/232-2979;** www.access-able.com) offers extensive access information and advice for traveling around the world with disabilities. **Accessible Journeys** (© **800/846-4537** or 610/521-0339; www.disabilitytravel.com) caters specifically to slow walkers and wheelchair travelers and their families and friends.

**Avis Rent a Car** has an "Avis Access" program that offers such services as a dedicated 24-hour toll-free number (© **888/879-4273**) for customers with special travel needs; special car features such as swivel seats, spinner knobs, and hand controls; and accessible bus service.

Organizations that provide assistance to travelers with disabilities include **MossRehab** (www.mossresourcenet.org), which provides a library of accessible-travel resources online; **SATH** (Society for Accessible Travel & Hospitality) (© **212/447-7284;** www.sath.org; annual membership fees: $45 adults, $30 seniors and students), which offers a wealth of travel resources for all types of disabilities and informed recommendations on destinations, access guides, travel agents, tour operators, vehicle rentals, and companion services; and the **American Foundation for the Blind** (AFB) (© **800/232-5463;** www.afb.org), a referral resource for the blind and visually impaired, which includes information on traveling with Seeing Eye dogs.

For more information specifically targeted to travelers with disabilities, check out the magazines *Emerging Horizons*

($15 per year, $20 outside the U.S.; www.emerginghorizons.com) and *Open World* ($13 per year, $21 outside the U.S.; published by SATH, described above).

For more on organizations that offer resources to travelers with disabilities, go to www.frommers.com/planning.

## GAY & LESBIAN TRAVELERS

Atlanta has a large gay community. You'll want to check out *Southern Voice,* a newspaper that covers gay issues across the Southeast. Call © **404/876-1819** for information or go to www.southernvoice.com for a comprehensive online edition, including information on distribution points near your hotel.

Once you arrive, you might want to visit **Outwrite Bookstore & Coffeehouse,** 991 Piedmont Ave., at 10th Street (© **404/607-0082;** www.outwritebooks.com). It's a popular Midtown gathering spot for gay men and lesbians, and a sort of unofficial clearinghouse for information on local gay and lesbian resources, events, and issues.

**Gay.com Travel** (© **800/929-2268** or 415/644-8044; www.gay.com/travel or www.outandabout.com), is an excellent online successor to the popular *Out & About* print magazine. It provides regularly updated information about gay-owned, gay-oriented, and gay-friendly lodging, dining, sightseeing, nightlife, and shopping establishments in every important destination worldwide. It also offers trip-planning information for gay and lesbian travelers for more than 50 destinations, along various themes, ranging from Sex & Travel to Vacations for Couples.

The **International Gay and Lesbian Travel Association (IGLTA)** (© **800/448-8550** or 954/776-2626; www.iglta.org), the trade association for the gay and lesbian travel industry, offers an online directory of gay- and lesbian-friendly travel businesses; go to its website and click on "Members."

The following guides are available at most travel bookstores and gay and lesbian bookstores, or you can order them online or from **Giovanni's Room,** 1145 Pine St., Philadelphia, PA 19107 (© **215/923-2960;** www.giovannisroom.com): *Out and About* (© **800/929-2268;** www.outandabout.com), which offers guidebooks and a newsletter ($20 per year; 10 issues) packed with solid information on the global gay and lesbian scene; *Spartacus International Gay Guide* (Bruno Gmünder Verlag; www.spartacusworld.com/gayguide) and *Odysseus: The International Gay Travel Planner* (Odysseus Enterprises Ltd.), both good, annual English-language guidebooks focused on gay men; the *Damron* guides (www.damron.com), with separate, annual books for gay men and lesbians; and *Gay Travel A to Z: The World of Gay & Lesbian Travel Options at Your Fingertips,* by Marianne Ferrari (Ferrari International; Box 35575, Phoenix, AZ 85069), a very good gay and lesbian guidebook series.

For more gay and lesbian travel resources, visit www.frommers.com/planning.

## SENIOR TRAVEL

Mention the fact that you're a senior when you make your travel reservations. Although all of the major U.S. airlines except America West have canceled their senior discount programs, many hotels still offer discounts for seniors. In most cities, those age 60 and over qualify for reduced admission to theaters, museums, and other attractions, as well as discounted fares on public transportation.

Members of **AARP** (formerly known as the American Association of Retired Persons), 601 E St. NW, Washington, D.C. 20049 (© **888/687-2277;** www.aarp.org), get discounts on hotels, airfares, and car rentals. AARP offers members a wide range of benefits, including *AARP The Magazine* and a monthly newsletter. Anyone over 50 can join.

Many reliable agencies and organizations target the 50-plus market. **Elderhostel** (© **877/426-8056;** www.elderhostel.org) arranges study programs for those 55 and over (and a spouse or companion of any age) in the U.S. and in more than 80 countries around the world. Most courses last 5 to 7 days in the U.S. (2–4 weeks abroad), and many include airfare, accommodations in university dormitories or modest inns, meals, and tuition. Elderhostel has a number of Atlanta programs, including those that focus on the city's history, culture, fine arts, and homes and gardens. Atlanta trips range from 3 to 8 nights.

Recommended publications offering travel resources and discounts for seniors include the quarterly magazine *Travel 50 & Beyond* (www.travel50andbeyond.com); *Travel Unlimited: Uncommon Adventures for the Mature Traveler* (Avalon); *101 Tips for Mature Travelers,* available from Grand Circle Travel (© **800/221-2610** or 617/350-7500; www.gct.com); and *Unbelievably Good Deals and Great Adventures That You Absolutely Can't Get Unless You're Over 50* (McGraw-Hill).

For more information and resources on travel for seniors, see www.frommers.com/planning.

## FAMILY TRAVEL

If you have enough trouble just getting your children out of the house in the morning, it may seem like an insurmountable challenge to drag them hundreds of miles away. But as any veteran family vacationer will assure you, a trip with the kids can be among the most pleasurable and rewarding times of your life. See p. 171 for some of Atlanta's best attractions for families. See a list of kid-friendly hotels on p. 79 and a list of restaurants that kids will love on p. 104.

**Familyhostel** (© **800/733-9753**) takes the whole family, including kids 8 to 15, on moderately priced domestic and international learning vacations. Lectures, field trips, and sightseeing are guided by a team of academics.

Recommended family-travel websites include **Family Travel Forum** (www.familytravelforum.com), a comprehensive resource that offers customized trip planning; **Family Travel Network** (www.familytravelnetwork.com), an award-winning site that offers travel features, deals, and tips; and **Family Travel Files** (www.thefamilytravelfiles.com), which offers an online magazine and a directory of off-the-beaten-path tours and tour operators for families.

*Frommer's Unofficial Guide to the Southeast with Kids* (Wiley Publishing, Inc.) also includes information on kid-friendly attractions in and around Atlanta.

To locate accommodations, restaurants, and attractions that are particularly kid-friendly, refer to the "Kids" icon throughout this guide.

For a list of more family-friendly travel resources, visit www.frommers.com/planning.

## AFRICAN-AMERICAN TRAVELERS

Agencies and organizations that provide resources for black travelers in particular include **Rodgers Travel** (© 800/825-1775; www.rodgerstravel.com) and the **African American Association of Innkeepers International** (© 877/422-5777; www.africanamericaninns.com).

**Black Travel Online** (www.blacktravelonline.com) posts news on upcoming events and includes links to articles and travel-booking sites. **Soul of America** (www.soulofamerica.com) is a comprehensive website with travel tips, event information, family-reunion postings, and sections on historically black beach resorts and active vacations.

For more information, check out the following collections and guides: *Go Girl: The Black Woman's Guide to Travel & Adventure* (Eighth Mountain Press), a compilation of travel essays by writers including Jill Nelson and Audre Lorde; *The African American Travel Guide,* by Wayne Robinson (Hunter Publishing; www.hunterpublishing.com); *Steppin' Out,* by Carla Labat (Avalon); and *Pathfinders Magazine* (© 877/977-PATH [7284]; www.pathfinderstravel.com), which includes articles on everything from Rio de Janeiro to Ghana as well as information on upcoming ski, diving, golf, and tennis trips.

## 9 SUSTAINABLE TOURISM

**Sustainable tourism** is conscientious travel. It means being careful with the environments you explore, and respecting the communities you visit. Two overlapping components of sustainable travel are **ecotourism** and **ethical tourism.** The **International Ecotourism Society (TIES)** defines ecotourism as responsible travel to natural areas that conserves the environment and improves the well-being of local people. TIES suggests that ecotourists follow these principles:

• Minimize environmental impact.
• Build environmental and cultural awareness and respect.

• Provide positive experiences for both visitors and hosts.
• Provide direct financial benefits for conservation and for local people.
• Raise sensitivity to host countries' political, environmental, and social climates.
• Support international human rights and labor agreements.

You can find some eco-friendly travel tips and statistics, as well as touring companies and associations—listed by destination under "Travel Choice"—at the **TIES** website, www.ecotourism.org. Also check out **Ecotravel.com**, which lets you search

# 3

## (Tips) It's Easy Being Green

Here are a few simple ways you can help conserve fuel and energy when you travel:

- Each time you take a flight or drive a car, greenhouse gases release into the atmosphere. You can help neutralize this danger to the planet through "carbon offsetting"—paying someone to invest your money in programs that reduce your greenhouse gas emissions by the same amount you've added. Before buying carbon offset credits, just make sure that you're using a reputable company, one with a proven program that invests in renewable energy. Reliable carbon offset companies include **Carbonfund** (www.carbon fund.org), **TerraPass** (www.terrapass.org), and **Carbon Neutral** (www.carbonneutral.org).

- Whenever possible, choose nonstop flights; they generally require less fuel than indirect flights that stop and take off again. Try to fly during the day—some scientists estimate that nighttime flights are twice as harmful to the environment. And pack light—each 15 pounds of luggage on a 5,000-mile flight adds up to 50 pounds of carbon dioxide emitted.

- Where you stay during your travels can have a major environmental impact. To determine the green credentials of a property, ask about trash disposal and recycling, water conservation, and energy use; also question if sustainable materials were used in the construction of the property. The website **www.greenhotels.com** recommends green-rated member hotels around the world that fulfill the company's stringent environmental requirements. Also consult **www.environmentallyfriendlyhotels.com** for more green accommodations ratings.

- At hotels, request that your sheets and towels not be changed daily. (Many hotels already have programs like this in place.) Turn off the lights and air-conditioner (or heater) when you leave your room.

- Use public transport where possible—trains, buses and even taxis are more energy-efficient forms of transport than driving. Even better is to walk or cycle; you'll produce zero emissions and stay fit and healthy on your travels.

- If renting a car is necessary, ask the rental agent for a hybrid, or rent the most fuel-efficient car available. You'll use less gas and save money at the tank.

- Eat at locally owned and operated restaurants that use produce grown in the area. This contributes to the local economy and cuts down on greenhouse gas emissions by supporting restaurants where the food is not flown or trucked in across long distances. Visit **Sustain Lane** (www.sustainlane.org) to find sustainable eating and drinking choices around the U.S.; also check out **www.eatwellguide.org** for tips on eating sustainably in the U.S. and Canada.

for sustainable touring companies in several categories (water-based, land-based, spiritually oriented, and so on).

While much of the focus of eco-tourism is about reducing impacts on the natural environment, ethical tourism concentrates on ways to preserve and enhance local economies and communities, regardless of location. You can embrace ethical tourism by staying at a locally owned hotel or shopping at a store that employs local workers and sells locally produced goods.

**Responsible Travel** (www.responsible travel.com) is a great source of sustainable travel ideas; the site is run by a spokesperson for ethical tourism in the travel industry. **Sustainable Travel International** (www. sustainabletravelinternational.org) promotes ethical tourism practices, and manages an extensive directory of sustainable properties and tour operators around the world.

In the U.K., **Tourism Concern** (www. tourismconcern.org.uk) works to reduce social and environmental problems connected to tourism. The **Association of Independent Tour Operators (AITO)** (www.aito.co.uk) is a group of specialist operators leading the field in making holidays sustainable.

**Volunteer travel** has become increasingly popular among those who want to venture beyond the standard group-tour experience to learn languages, interact with locals, and make a positive difference while on vacation. Volunteer travel usually doesn't require special skills—just a willingness to work hard—and programs vary in length from a few days to a number of weeks. Some programs provide free housing and food, but many require volunteers to pay for travel expenses, which can add up quickly.

For general info on volunteer travel, visit **www.volunteerabroad.org** and **www. idealist.org**.

Before you commit to a volunteer program, it's important to make sure any money you're giving is truly going back to the local community, and that the work you'll be doing will be a good fit for you. **Volunteer International** (www.volunteer international.org) has a helpful list of questions to ask to determine the intentions and the nature of a volunteer program.

# 10 PACKAGES FOR THE INDEPENDENT TRAVELER

Before you start your search for the lowest airfare, you may want to consider booking your flight as part of a travel package. Package tours are not the same thing as escorted tours. They are simply a way to buy the airfare, accommodations, and other elements of your trip (such as car rentals, airport transfers, and sometimes even activities) at the same time and often at discounted prices.

One good source of package deals is the airlines themselves. Most major airlines offer air/land packages, including **American Airlines Vacations** (© 800/321-2121; www.aavacations.com), **Continental Airlines Vacations** (© 800/301-3800; www. covacations.com), **Delta Vacations** (© 800/ 221-6666; www.deltavacations.com), and

**United Vacations** (© 888/854-3899; www.unitedvacations.com). Several big **online travel agencies**—Expedia, Travelocity, Orbitz, and LastMinuteTravel.com— also do a brisk business in packages.

Travel packages are also listed in the travel section of your local Sunday newspaper. Or check ads in the national travel magazines such as *Arthur Frommer's Budget Travel, Travel + Leisure, National Geographic Traveler,* and *Condé Nast Traveler.*

Before you invest in a package tour, get some answers. Find out about the **cancellation policy:** Can you get your money back? Is a deposit required? Ask about the **accommodations choices** and prices for each. Then look up the hotels' reviews in a Frommer's guide and check rates online

# Frommers.com: The Complete Travel Resource

Planning a trip or just returned? Head to **Frommers.com**, voted Best Travel Site by *PC Magazine*. We think you'll find our site indispensable before, during and after your travels—with expert advice and tips; independent reviews of hotels, restaurants, attractions, and preferred shopping and nightlife venues; vacation giveaways; and an online booking tool. We publish the complete contents of over 135 travel guides in our **Destinations** section, covering over 4,000 places worldwide. Each weekday, we publish original articles that report on **Deals and News** via our free **Frommers.com Newsletters.** What's more, **Arthur Frommer** himself blogs 5 days a week, with cutting opinions about the state of travel in the modern world. We're betting you'll find our **Events** listings an invaluable resource; it's an up-to-the-minute roster of what's happening in cities everywhere—including concerts, festivals, lectures, and more. We've also added weekly **podcasts, interactive maps,** and hundreds of new images across the site. Finally, don't forget to visit our **Message Boards,** where you can join in conversations with thousands of fellow Frommer's travelers and post your trip report once you return.

for your specific dates of travel. Also find out what types of rooms are offered. Finally, look for **hidden expenses.** Ask whether airport departure fees and taxes, for example, are included in the total cost—they rarely are.

For more information on Package Tours and for tips on booking your trip, see www.frommers.com/planning.

## 11 ESCORTED GENERAL-INTEREST TOURS

Escorted tours are structured group tours, with a group leader. The price usually includes everything from airfare to hotels, meals, tours, admission costs, and local transportation.

Among the companies currently offering escorted tours to Atlanta is **Trafalgar Tours** (© 866/544-4434; www.trafalgartours. com/georgia). Atlanta is just one of the stops on Trafalgar's Southern Coast and Great Smoky Mountains tour, and visitors get a brief overview of the city and its history. **Maupintour** (© 800/255-4266; www.maupintour.com) has a 7-day Georgia Christmas escorted tour that includes 4 nights in Atlanta, during which travelers take in some of the top attractions and

performing arts in the city. In addition, **Cosmos Vacations** (© 800/276-1241; www.cosmos.com) offers an 11-day Southern Journey tour, including 3 nights and sightseeing in Atlanta.

**TO TOUR OR NOT TO TOUR?** Many people derive a certain ease and security from escorted trips. Escorted tours—whether by bus, train, or boat—let travelers sit back and enjoy their trip without having to spend lots of time behind the wheel or worrying about details. You know your costs upfront, and there are few surprises. Escorted tours can take you to the maximum number of sights in the minimum amount of time with the least amount of hassle—you don't have to sweat over the plotting and planning of a vacation schedule. They're particularly convenient for people with limited mobility. They can also be a great way to make new friends.

On the downside, an escorted tour often requires a big deposit upfront, and lodging and dining choices are predetermined. You'll get little opportunity for serendipitous interactions with locals. The tours can be jam-packed with activities, leaving little room for individual sightseeing, whim, or adventure—plus they often focus only on the heavily touristed sites, so you miss out on the lesser-known gems.

Before you invest in an escorted tour, request a complete **schedule** of the trip to find out how much sightseeing is planned and whether you'll have enough time to relax or wander solo. Also ask about the **cancellation policy:** Is a deposit required? Can they cancel the trip if they don't get enough people? Do you get a refund if they cancel? If *you* cancel? How late can you cancel if you are unable to go? When do you pay in full? *Note:* If you choose an escorted tour, think strongly about purchasing trip-cancellation insurance,

especially if the tour operator asks you to pay in advance. See the section on "Travel Insurance" (appendix, p. 221) for details.

The **size** of the group is also important to know upfront. Generally, the smaller the group, the more flexible the itinerary, and the less time you'll spend waiting for people to get on and off the bus. Find out the **demographics** of the group as well. What is the age range? What is the gender breakdown? Is this mostly a trip for couples or singles?

Discuss what is included in the **price.** You may have to pay for transportation to and from the airport. A box lunch may be included in an excursion, but drinks might cost extra. Tips may not be included. Find out if you will be charged if you decide to opt out of certain activities or meals. Finally, if you plan to travel alone, you'll need to know if you'll be charged a **single supplement** or if the company can match you up with a roommate.

For more information on Escorted General-Interest Tours, including questions to ask before booking your trip, see www.frommers.com/planning.

## 12  SPECIAL-INTEREST TRIPS

Whatever your personal interests may be, Atlanta has enough to keep you busy on mini-tours you create yourself. Got a hankering for some history, Southern-style? Get started at the Atlanta History Center for a primer on the birth of this grand city and the events that followed, including Sherman's visit during the Civil War that left Atlanta in ashes. The on-site Atlanta History Museum provides a great overview and permanent exhibits, including one on Georgia golfing legend Bobby Jones. The center recently opened a new $10-million wing highlighting the 1996 Olympic Games hosted in this city. Other exhibits include those on Southern folk art and the Civil War. A number of historic homes on the property are also available to tour,

including the restored Swan House, offering a glimpse of southern gentry of the 1930s.

Civil War interests are easy to satisfy in Atlanta. From the Cyclorama's 42-foot-high cylindrical oil painting depicting the Battle of Atlanta to the scores of Confederate and Union soldiers buried at Oakland Cemetery, Atlanta has done well to preserve history from that period of time. While not everyone who visits Atlanta is a *Gone with the Wind* fan, those who are will have no trouble filling their days perusing memorabilia and walking in the footsteps of the infamous novel's author, Margaret Mitchell. What you won't find is Tara—it didn't actually exist—or the gravesites of Scarlett and Rhett—they didn't either. But what did exist, and still does, is "the dump," Mitchell's apartment where she wrote the book, now adjacent to the Margaret Mitchell House & Museum. See chapter 4 for more Civil War tour suggestions.

Atlanta is brimming with sights tied to African-American history, the civil rights movement, and Martin Luther King, Jr. From the Sweet Auburn neighborhood and King's childhood home to the Ebenezer Baptist Church, where King was ordained at age 18, you can spend a lot of time tracing Atlanta's role in this turning point in American history. Coretta Scott King was recently interred alongside her husband in a marble crypt in the center of a reflecting pool at the King Center. And King's papers will soon be available for the public to view, as they are now the property of Atlanta's Morehouse College. See chapter 4 for more sightseeing tips on this subject.

## 13 STAYING CONNECTED

### TELEPHONES

Generally, hotel surcharges on long-distance and local calls are astronomical, so you're better off using your **cellphone** or a **public pay telephone.** Many convenience groceries and packaging services sell **pre-paid calling cards** in denominations up to $50; for international visitors, these can be the least expensive way to call home. Many public phones at airports now accept American Express, MasterCard, and Visa. **Local calls** made from public pay phones in most locales cost either 25¢ or 35¢. Pay phones do not accept pennies, and few will take anything larger than a quarter.

Most long-distance and international calls can be dialed directly from any phone. **For calls within the United States and to Canada,** dial 1 followed by the area code and the seven-digit number. **For other international calls,** dial 011 followed by the country code, city code, and the number you are calling.

Calls to area codes **800, 888, 877,** and **866** are toll-free. However, calls to area codes **700** and **900** (chat lines, bulletin boards, "dating" services, and so on) can be very expensive—usually a charge of 95¢ to $3 or more per minute, and they sometimes have minimum charges that can run as high as $15 or more.

**For reversed-charge or collect calls,** and for person-to-person calls, dial the number 0, then the area code and number;

an operator will come on the line, and you should specify whether you are calling collect, person-to-person, or both. If your operator-assisted call is international, ask for the overseas operator.

**For local directory assistance** ("information"), dial ℂ **411;** for long-distance information, dial 1, then the appropriate area code and 555-1212.

### CELLPHONES

Just because your cellphone works at home doesn't mean it'll work everywhere in the U.S. (thanks to our nation's fragmented cellphone system). It's a good bet that your phone will work in major cities, including Atlanta, but take a look at your wireless company's coverage map on its website before heading out; T-Mobile, Sprint, and Nextel are particularly weak in rural areas, but service is available in metro Atlanta from those companies, as well as Verizon, Tracfone, Virgin Mobile, and AT&T. If you need to stay in touch at a destination where you know your phone won't work, rent a phone that does from **InTouch USA** (ℂ **800/872-7626;** www.intouchglobal.com) or a rental-car location, but be aware that you'll pay $1 a minute or more for airtime.

If you're not from the U.S., you'll be appalled at the poor reach of the **GSM (Global System for Mobile Communications) wireless network,** which is used by much of the rest of the world. While your phone will work in Atlanta, it definitely won't work in many rural areas. To see where GSM phones work in the U.S., check out www.t-mobile.com/coverage. And you may or may not be able to send SMS (text messaging) home. Assume nothing—call your wireless provider and get the full scoop.

In a worst-case scenario, you can always rent a phone. InTouch USA delivers to hotels, and **Rent-A-Cellular** kiosks are located throughout the Hartsfield-Jackson Atlanta International Airport.

## VOICE-OVER INTERNET PROTOCOL (VOIP)

If you have Web access while traveling, consider a broadband-based telephone service (in technical terms, **Voice-over Internet Protocol,** or **VoIP**) such as Skype (www.skype.com) or Vonage (www.vonage.com), which allow you to make free international calls from your laptop or in a cybercafe. Neither service requires the people you're calling to also have that service (though there are fees if they do not). Check the websites for details.

## INTERNET & E-MAIL
### With Your Own Computer

More and more hotels, cafes, and retailers are signing on as Wi-Fi (wireless fidelity) "hotspots." **T-Mobile Hotspot** (www.t-mobile.com/hotspot) serves up wireless connections at more than 1,000 Starbucks coffee shops nationwide. **Boingo** (www.boingo.com) and **Wayport** (www.wayport.com) have set up networks in airports and high-class hotel lobbies. To find public Wi-Fi hotspots around Atlanta, go to **www.jiwire.com**; its Hotspot Finder holds the world's largest directory of public wireless hotspots. iPass providers (see below) also give you access to a few hundred wireless hotel-lobby setups. To locate other hotspots that provide free wireless networks in cities around the world, go to **www.personaltelco.net/index.cgi/WirelessCommunities**.

Most business-class hotels in the U.S. offer dataports for laptop dial-up modems, and many hotels now offer free high-speed Internet access using an Ethernet network cable. You can bring your own cables, but most hotels rent them for around $10. Call your hotel in advance to see what your options are.

In addition, major ISPs have **local access numbers** around the world, allowing you to go online by placing a local call. Check your ISP's website or call its toll-free number and ask how you can use your current account away from home, and how much it will cost.

The **iPass** network also has dial-up numbers around the world. You'll have to

---

(Tips) **Hey, Google, Did You Get My Text Message?**

It's bound to happen: The day you leave this guidebook back at the hotel for an unencumbered stroll through Buckhead, you'll forget the address of the lunch spot you had earmarked. If you're traveling with a mobile device, send a text message to ℂ **46645 (GOOGL)** for a lightning-fast response. For instance, type "carnegie deli new york" and within 10 seconds you'll receive a text message with the address and phone number. This nifty trick works in a range of search categories: Look up weather ("weather philadelphia"), language translations ("translate goodbye in spanish"), currency conversions ("10 usd in pounds"), movie times ("harry potter 60605"), and more. If your search results are off, be more specific ("the abbey gay bar west hollywood"). For more tips and search options, see www.google.com/intl/en_us/mobile/sms/. Regular text message charges apply.

sign up with an iPass provider, who will then tell you how to set up your computer for your destination(s). For a list of iPass providers, go to www.ipass.com and click on "Individuals Buy Now." One solid provider is **i2roam** (www.i2roam.com; ✆ **866/811-6209** or 920/235-0475).

Wherever you go, bring a **connection kit** of the right power and phone adapters, a spare phone cord, and a spare Ethernet network cable—or find out whether your hotel supplies them to guests.

For information on electrical currency conversions, see "Electricity" in the "Fast Facts" appendix, p. 220.

## Without Your Own Computer

Most major airports have **Internet kiosks** that provide basic Web access for a per-minute fee that's usually higher than cybercafe prices. Check out copy shops like **Kinko's** (FedEx Office), which offers computer stations with fully loaded software (as well as Wi-Fi).

## Online Traveler's Toolbox

Veteran travelers usually carry some essential items to make their trips easier. Following is a selection of handy online tools to bookmark and use.

- **Airplane Seating and Food.** Find out which seats to reserve and which to avoid (and more) on all major domestic airlines at www.seatguru.com. And check out the type of meal (with photos) you'll likely be served on airlines around the world at www.airlinemeals.net.
- **ATM Locators.** Go to www.visa.com for locations of PLUS ATMs worldwide. Point your browser to www.mastercard.com for locations of Cirrus ATMs worldwide.
- **Club Bookings** for Atlanta's favorite nightspots can be found in the online version of Creative Loafing (www.creativeloafing.com).
- **Mapquest** (www.mapquest.com). This mapping site lets you choose a specific address or destination; in seconds, it will return a map and detailed directions.
- **Restaurant Reviews.** Find the latest reviews on metro Atlanta dining in a number of resources, including the *Atlanta Journal-Constitution* (www.ajc.com) and *Atlanta* magazine (www.atlantamagazine.com).
- **Tickets** to Atlanta concerts, lectures, stage performances, and other entertainment are available through Ticketmaster (www.ticketmaster).
- **Time and Date** (www.timeanddate.com). See what time (and day) it is anywhere in the world.
- **Universal Currency Converter** (www.xe.com/ucc). See what your dollar or pound is worth in more than 100 other countries.
- **Weather** (www.intellicast.com and www.weather.com). Get weather forecasts for all 50 states and for cities around the world.
- **Weather** (www.intellicast.com and www.weather.com).
- **Weekly Events** can be found in the online version of Creative Loafing (www.creativeloafing.com) as well as the *Atlanta Journal-Constitution* (www.ajc.com).

For help locating cybercafes and other establishments where you can go for Internet access, please see "Internet Access" in the **"Fast Facts"** appendix (p. 222).

## 14 TIPS ON ACCOMMODATIONS

### SAVING ON YOUR HOTEL ROOM

The **rack rate** is the maximum rate that a hotel charges for a room. Hardly anybody pays this price, however, except in high season or on holidays. To lower the cost of your room:

- **Ask about special rates or other discounts.** You may qualify for corporate, student, military, senior, frequent-flier, trade union, or other discounts.
- **Dial direct.** When booking a room in a chain hotel, you'll often get a better deal by calling the individual hotel's reservations desk rather than the chain's main number.
- **Book online.** Many hotels offer Internet-only discounts, or supply rooms to Priceline, Hotwire, or Expedia at rates much lower than the ones you can get through the hotel itself. Shop around.
- **Remember the law of supply and demand.** Resort hotels are most crowded and therefore most expensive on weekends, so discounts are usually available for midweek stays. Business hotels in downtown locations are busiest during the week, so you can expect big discounts over the weekend. Many hotels have high-season and low-season prices, and booking even 1 day after "high season" ends can mean big discounts.
- **Look into group or long-stay discounts.** If you come as part of a large group, you should be able to negotiate a bargain rate, since the hotel can then guarantee occupancy in a number of rooms. Likewise, if you're planning a long stay (at least 5 days), you might qualify for a discount. As a general rule, expect 1 night free after a 7-night stay.

- **Avoid excess charges and hidden costs.** When you book a room, ask whether the hotel charges for parking. Use your own cellphone, pay phones, or pre-paid phone cards instead of dialing direct from hotel-room phones, which usually have exorbitant rates. And don't be tempted by the room's minibar offerings: Most hotels charge through the nose for drinks and snacks. Finally, ask about local taxes and service charges, which can increase the cost of a room by 15% or more.
- **Book an efficiency.** A room with a kitchenette allows you to shop for groceries and cook your own meals. This is a big money saver, especially for families on long stays.
- **Consider enrolling in hotel "frequent-stay" programs,** which are upping the ante lately to win the loyalty of repeat customers. Frequent guests can now accumulate points or credits to earn free hotel nights, airline miles, in-room amenities, merchandise, tickets to concerts and events, discounts on sporting facilities—and even credit toward stock in the participating hotel, in the case of the Jameson Inn hotel group. Perks are awarded not only by many chain hotels and motels (Hilton HHonors, Marriott Rewards, Wyndham ByRequest, to name a few), but also by individual inns and B&Bs. Many chain hotels partner with other hotels, car-rental firms, airlines, and credit card companies to give consumers additional incentive to do repeat business with them.

### LANDING THE BEST ROOM

Somebody has to get the best room in the house. It might as well be you. You can

## House-Swapping

House-swapping is becoming a more popular and viable means of travel; you stay in their place, they stay in yours, and you both get an authentic and personal view of the area, the opposite of the escapist retreat that many hotels offer. Try **HomeLink International** (www.homelink.org), the largest and oldest home-swapping organization, founded in 1952, with over 11,000 listings worldwide ($75 for a yearly membership). **HomeExchange.org** ($49.95 for 6,000 listings) and **InterVac.com** ($68.88 for over 10,000 listings) are also reliable. Many travelers find great housing swaps on Craigslist (www.craigslist.org), too, though the offerings cannot be vetted or vouched for.

start by joining the hotel's frequent-guest program, which may make you eligible for upgrades. A hotel-branded credit card usually gives its owner "silver" or "gold" status in frequent-guest programs. Always ask about a corner room—they're often larger and quieter, with more windows and light, and they often cost the same as standard rooms. Ask for a room that has been most recently renovated or redecorated; if the hotel is renovating, request a room away from the construction. Ask about non-smoking rooms, rooms with views, and rooms with twin, queen- or king-size beds. If you're a light sleeper, request a quiet room away from vending machines, elevators, restaurants, bars, and clubs.

If you aren't happy with your room when you arrive, ask for another one. Most lodgings will be willing to accommodate you.

Like all major cities, Atlanta has its share of major chain hotels, including Marriott, which offers a large number of different hotel products throughout the city. Courtyard, the newly renovated Marriott Marquis, and Marriott Suites Midtown are among the offerings. Sheraton also has a strong presence in Atlanta. Those visitors who wish to stay near the airport should consider Sheraton Gateway, while those who want to be in the heart of the upscale bustle might choose the Sheraton Buckhead. Embassy Suites is also represented here, with convenient locations at Centennial Olympic Park and in Buckhead. And last but not least, Hilton hotels are plentiful here as well. In addition to its downtown and airport facilities, a new Hilton Garden Inn near Centennial Olympic Park was added to the mix in 2008.

For tips on surfing for hotel deals online, visit www.frommers.com/planning.

## 15 TIPS ON DINING

Atlantans love to dine out and they love to see and be seen, so dining is often as much a social event as it is an appreciation of fine food. Most of the best restaurants require advance reservations, so plan ahead if you don't want to miss out on a fantastic culinary experience.

Dining hours vary greatly in the city, with some restaurants open for dinner only and others, including many that aren't dives, staying open 24 hours a day. Tipping here is just like anywhere else, with a standard of 15% to 20% to service staff and 10% to 15% for bartenders, $1 per garment to the checkroom attendant, and the same per car for valet-parking attendants. Because of the congestion and crowded parking lots, many restaurants offer valet parking, and some even offer it for free.

# 4

# Suggested Atlanta Itineraries

Whether it's your first visit or your 10th, a trip to Atlanta is always a new experience as the city keeps evolving and providing visitors with more to see each year. This chapter will provide you with essential information, helpful tips, and advice for creating the perfect itinerary for your upcoming trip to "the ATL."

## NEIGHBORHOODS IN BRIEF

You can't really get the feel of a city until you understand the characteristics of its neighborhoods. Here's a brief rundown of Atlanta's diverse districts.

**Downtown** Unlike some big cities, Atlanta has been slower to draw a large population living in the downtown area, though that has changed drastically in the past few years. In-town living is gradually becoming quite popular. Currently, downtown consists primarily of businesses, hotels, restaurants, and sports venues, and is slowly gaining that round-the-clock big-city excitement found in places like New York.

Atlanta's financial and business hub, this area of sleek skyscrapers includes the Peachtree Center hotel/convention center/trade mart/office-tower complex. Here, too: Underground Atlanta, a mix of shops, restaurants, and nightclubs fronted by a 138-foot light tower; the mammoth Georgia World Congress Center, one of the largest meeting and exhibition halls in the nation; the 71,500-seat Georgia Dome, home of the Atlanta Falcons and site of Super Bowl XXXIV; Philips Arena, home of the Atlanta Hawks and Atlanta Thrashers; CNN Center; Georgia State University; the golden-domed, century-old State Capitol, a major landmark; the 21-acre Centennial Olympic Park, the city's newest gathering place; and Woodruff Park.

Just south of downtown is Turner Field, home of the Atlanta Braves. Also in the general area are Oakland Cemetery (it's mentioned in *Gone with the Wind,* and Margaret Mitchell is one of the many notables buried here), Grant Park, Zoo Atlanta, and Cyclorama.

People are beginning to move into newly renovated lofts and other buildings downtown, but there's still not a lot of activity after business hours. For that reason, visitors should stick to the hotel district and the sports venues in the evening.

**Sweet Auburn** This traditionally African-American neighborhood, also called the **Martin Luther King, Jr., Historic District,** is just below downtown's central area. In 1980, under the auspices of the National Park Service, the neighborhood was designated a park to honor King, whose boyhood home, crypt, and church are located here. In spite of the yoke of segregation, affluent black businesspeople and professionals flourished here from the early part of the 20th century through the 1950s. Recently revitalized, Sweet Auburn is one of Atlanta's major sightseeing draws.

**Midtown** Though its boundaries have never been definitively decided, Midtown basically encompasses the area north of downtown from about Ponce de Leon Avenue to I-85. It includes Piedmont Park, the central city's major recreation area; the Woodruff Arts Center, home of the Atlanta Symphony Orchestra, the Alliance Theatre, and the High Museum of Art; the famed Fox Theatre, a 1920s Moorish-motif movie palace; the Atlanta Botanical Garden; Ansley Park, a 230-acre residential greenbelt area, designed at the turn of the 20th century by Frederick Law Olmsted (of New York's Central Park fame); and Colony Square, an office/hotel/retail complex. AT&T, IBM, Bank of America, and BellSouth maintain corporate offices in Midtown.

**Buckhead** Named for an 1838 tavern called the Buck's Head, this is Atlanta's silk-stocking district—one of America's most beautiful and affluent communities. It begins about 6 miles north of downtown, just above I-85. You'll find tree-shaded residential areas filled with magnificent mansions that are surrounded by verdant acreage, as well as many smaller middle-class homes. Shops and boutiques (Lenox Square and Phipps Plaza, two exclusive shopping malls, are here), superb restaurants, and first-class hotels abound. On weekends, the bars and clubs in the center of Buckhead attract crowds of revelers.

Buckhead is also a burgeoning business area, with high-rise office buildings concentrated near Peachtree and Lenox roads. The area's major sightseeing attraction is the Atlanta History Center, with a Palladian villa designed by noted architect Phillip Schutze, and surrounded by 32 woodland acres. The Greek Revival Governor's Mansion is also in Buckhead.

**Virginia Highland** Every major American city has a district that claims kinship (however slight) with New York's Greenwich Village. In Atlanta, it's the Virginia-Highland section (so named for its central avenues), located northeast of downtown. Here you'll find ethnic restaurants, antiques shops, bookstores, sidewalk cafes, art galleries, lively bars and bistros, and shops selling everything from gourmet gadgets and woodworking tools to ecologically correct clothing. The surrounding area is full of tree-lined streets with charming little cottages, many of them recently renovated.

**Little Five Points** Just below Virginia Highland—and a funkier offshoot of it—Little Five Points offers an offbeat ambience, attracting young and old members of the tie-dyed and pierced set. The neighborhood is home to the Jimmy Carter Library/Carter Presidential Center, which opened in 1986 to house the correspondence and memorabilia of this Georgia-born president. The area's many Victorian homes make for an architecturally interesting stroll. The neighborhood is centered at the junction of Euclid and Moreland avenues. Don't confuse this area with **Five Points,** which is a major downtown intersection.

**West End & Cascade Road** Southwest of town lies a booming area populated by well-to-do African-American singles and families. The historic West End, Atlanta's oldest neighborhood, is full of lovely Victorian homes and is the gateway to the Cascade Road area. This is where you'll find the Wren's Nest, the former home of writer Joel Chandler Harris.

**Decatur** Founded in 1823 by Commodore Stephen Decatur, a dashing naval hero of the War of 1812 who died in a duel, this charming suburb centers on an old courthouse square and has become a new favorite destination for residents and visitors alike. About a 15-minute drive east of downtown, Decatur is the scene of numerous annual events, festivals, and concerts, and houses the sprawling DeKalb Farmers' Market, an international food market that must be seen to be believed. Like Virginia Highland and Little Five Points, Decatur weaves a splash of funky color and texture into Atlanta's tapestry of neighborhoods.

**Duluth** Duluth, located in Gwinnett County just north of the city, is a bustling town with shopping, dining, and entertainment. Major roadways here include Buford Highway and its incredible list of ethnic restaurants; Pleasant Hill Road, home to many of the retail opportunities; and Peachtree Industrial Boulevard, which offers a little of everything for visitors—dining, lodging, theater, shopping, and more. Every summer, the town hosts the "Flicks on the Bricks" outdoor family film festival and the SummerStage concert series, enjoyed by residents and visitors alike.

# 1 THE BEST OF ATLANTA IN 1 DAY

If your travels to Atlanta allow you just 1 day to take in the sights, you might feel overwhelmed trying to decide how to make the most of your time. However, you certainly don't want to miss a special handful of attractions among the many worthwhile ones in this city. Plan your day accordingly and, by the end of it, you'll have a strong feel for what this city is all about. Build your schedule around enjoying lunch at the Atlanta History Center's Swan House before leaving the premises. Not only will you dine in a historic setting, but you'll also save valuable travel time by not having to find a restaurant. Whether you choose to drive yourself or use public transportation to navigate the city, a full day of touring can be satisfying; it also might encourage you to return to see what you couldn't squeeze in during a 1-day visit. **Start:** *Atlanta History Center (drive or MARTA to Lenox station).*

If driving, take I-75 N. to Exit 252A Northside Dr. and turn right; right on Arden Rd.; right on W Paces Ferry Rd. NW. Or take MARTA to the Lenox Station; bus 23 to Peachtree St. and W. Paces Ferry Rd.; then walk 3 blocks west on the latter.

### ❶ Atlanta History Center ★★★

Grab your coffee and head up to Buckhead to tour the Atlanta History Center for a good overview of the city's history—it will make the rest of your visit a richer experience. The new 20,000-square-foot addition houses a permanent exhibition about the 1996 Centennial Olympic Games hosted by the city of Atlanta. Another highlight of the center is the beautifully restored Swan House. House-tour tickets are limited and can be purchased only on the day of your visit, so arrive early to avoid disappointment. Enjoy lunch at the on-site restaurant, the Swan Coach House, where lunch is served from 11am to 2:30pm, Monday through Saturday. Get in on the early seating so you won't be pressed for time at your next stop. Consider choosing the signature chicken salad, served in delicate handmade timbales. No reservations are required for dining. See p. 140.

It's about a 15-minute drive back downtown via I-75 S. to the Williams St. exit; right on Baker St., right on Luckie St.; and park in the Pemberton Place deck on the right. Or take MARTA from the Lindbergh station to either Peachtree Center or Omni/Dome/GWCC station and walk a couple of blocks to Baker St.

## ❷ Georgia Aquarium ★★★

While the main attraction in Atlanta these days is the Georgia Aquarium, the world's largest indoor aquarium, it takes about 3 hours to see and enjoy it all, so head here quickly after an early lunch at the Swan House. Order tickets online first and you'll be able to choose an entrance window that helps cut down on bottlenecking at the front gate. Of course, weekends are extremely busy, and you may find yourself shoulder to shoulder trying to nudge your way up close to see the fantastic exhibits. There's also a 4-D movie that shows every half-hour. When you enter the aquarium, decide what time to check out the show, and then work in your exhibits before and after. There are areas designed specifically for the little kids, too, so if they get antsy, they can run around and let off steam in the special playroom. See p. 146.

From the aquarium exit, walk west on Baker St. and turn left on Marietta St. NW and continue walking until you reach:

## ❸ CNN Studio Tour ★★★

Spend the next hour enjoying a CNN Studio Tour, the last one scheduled for 5pm daily. To save precious time, you can purchase tickets online in advance, securing your spot when you arrive for the 55-minute guided walking tour that takes you behind the scenes of this international newsroom. Don't miss the gift shop, where visitors can don news-announcer garb and

record themselves "reporting" the news. Buy your recording and take it home to share with friends and family. See p. 143.

From the main entrance to the CNN Center, walk across the street to:

## ❹ Centennial Olympic Park ★★★

This park was the main gathering place during the 1996 Olympic Games. Kids love to splash in the Fountain of Rings here, especially during a hot Georgia afternoon. The park often plays host to live entertainment, activities for children, art festivals, and other fun events, so check the online calendar to see what's going on during your visit. See p. 142.

From the parking deck, drive east on Baker St.; right on Centennial Olympic Park Dr.; left on Harris St. NW; left on Piedmont Rd. NE; right on Ponce de Leon Ave. NE; and left on Monroe to reach the Virginia-Highland neighborhood. Or take MARTA from Peachtree Center or Omni/Dome/GWCC station to North Avenue station.

## ❺ Virginia Highland

Early in the evening, visit the shops and galleries in the very popular Virginia-Highland neighborhood. You've had a full day and have probably worked up a voracious appetite, so treat yourself to a great dinner at one of the many restaurants. Later, enjoy a nightcap or coffee and dessert in a bar or cafe along North Highland Avenue, where the nightlife is always jumping. See the Virginia-Highland sections of the dining and shopping chapters of this guide.

# 2 THE BEST OF ATLANTA IN 2 DAYS

Follow the suggestions above for your first day in town. On your second day, get up early, go over to Auburn Avenue (p. 188 for the walking tour), and visit the many sites operated by the National Parks Service, a touching tribute to Martin Luther King, Jr. and Atlanta's rich African-American history. Depending on how much energy you're willing to put into day 2, you may decide to skip a site or two, opting to stay longer at one or more of the others. You could while away many hours at most of these sightseeing options. *Start: Martin Luther King, Jr. National Historic Site (drive or MARTA to Five Points station).*

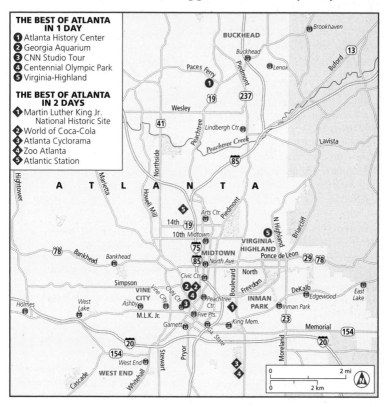

THE BEST OF ATLANTA
IN 1 DAY
1 Atlanta History Center
2 Georgia Aquarium
3 CNN Studio Tour
4 Centennial Olympic Park
5 Virginia-Highland

THE BEST OF ATLANTA
IN 2 DAYS
1 Martin Luther King Jr.
  National Historic Site
2 World of Coca-Cola
3 Atlanta Cyclorama
4 Zoo Atlanta
5 Atlantic Station

If driving, take I-75/85 north- or south-bound, then exit 248C Freedom Pkwy.; right on Boulevard NE; right at next light on John Wesley Dobbs Ave.; parking on left. Or take MARTA bus 3 to Five Points station:

### 1 Martin Luther King, Jr. National Historic Site

Start your morning in the Auburn district early as the entire neighborhood is packed full of historic treasures, starting with the Martin Luther King, Jr. National Historic Site. Designated a national historic site, these blocks include the Birth Home of Martin Luther King, Jr., and the Ebenezer Baptist Church, where King's father and grandfather were ministers and King served as a co-pastor. In the area, you'll also find the King Center, where King is buried, and the APEX Museum. See p. 153.

Drive west on Auburn Ave. NE; right at Fort St. NE; take ramp to I-75/85 N. for exit 249D Spring St.; right on Spring St. NW; left at Centennial Olympic Park Dr., and right at Baker St. NW. Park in Pemberton Place deck. Or from Five Points station, take MARTA to Peachtree Center or Omni/Dome/GWCC station to:

### 2 World of Coca-Cola

It's all new and better than ever at the World of Coca-Cola, where you can meet the Coke polar bear, mingle in the Pop Culture Gallery, and drink free carbonated beverages from around the world until your head spins from the sugar and caffeine buzz. Memorabilia galore awaits those interested in the history of this popular beverage invented right here in Atlanta. A short film in the Happiness Factory Theater allows visitors a behind-the-scenes look at the bottling process, which they later see at the actual in-house bottling line. See p. 160.

**Drive east on Baker St. and turn right on Centennial Olympic Park Dr.; left on Marietta St. NW; continue on Decatur St. SE; right on Hill St. SE; left at Memorial Dr. SE; and right onto Cherokee Ave. Take MARTA bus 97 to Cherokee Ave.**

### ❸ Atlanta Cyclorama

Located in Grant Park next to Zoo Atlanta, the Atlanta Cyclorama features a 42-foot-high rotating cylindrical oil painting, depicting the events of the Battle of Atlanta on July 22, 1864, in meticulous detail. The total program here lasts just 35 minutes, but packs a historic wallop. See p. 139.

**Exit the Cyclorama and turn left to find the Zoo Atlanta ticket booths just yards away.**

### ❹ Zoo Atlanta

Among the highlights in this world-class zoo are the giant pandas. The happy couple welcomed their second baby in 2008, named Xi Lan, after the traditional 100-day waiting period for naming baby pandas. Cute as she is though, the new panda isn't the only draw; the 40-acre Zoo Atlanta features some 200 species of animals from around the world. See p. 175.

**From I-75/85 N., take exit 250 10th/14th sts.; merge onto Williams St.; right on 10th St. NW; left on W. Peachtree St. NW; left on 17th St. NW. Or take MARTA to Arts Center station and hop the free shuttle to:**

### ❺ Atlantic Station

You might be too tired for shopping at this point, but you've got to eat, right? Atlantic Station, a mixed-use development packed with your favorite stores, from Ann Taylor Loft to IKEA, also has a wide variety of dining options. And who knows, once you refuel, you just might be ready to hit the shops before calling it a day. See p. 193.

## 3 THE BEST OF ATLANTA IN 3 DAYS

On your first 2 days, see as many of the sights described above as a comfortable pace allows. While many of your sightseeing decisions may be based on the weather—Atlanta summers can be scorching, making indoor attractions more appealing—you certainly won't want to miss Stone Mountain Park on day 3. You can, however, pass an entire day here, taking in all the activities and dining on-site. ***Start:*** *Stone Mountain Park (drive).*

**Take I-85 N. to I-285 E.; then exit 39B for U.S. Hwy. 78 E.; and exit 8 for Stone Mountain Park. There is no public transportation from the city to Stone Mountain Park.**

### ❶ Stone Mountain Park

Georgia's number one tourist attraction, Stone Mountain Park has lots of things to do, including visiting Crossroads, a re-created 1870s southern town, with costumed characters, craft demonstrations, and diversions for kids, including the Treehouse Challenge and the Great Barn. New since 2008 is the park's Sky Hike attraction, a family-friendly adventure course that allows visitors to "walk" through the treetops.

There are also an Antique Car and Treasure Museum and cruises on the *Scarlett O'Hara* paddlewheel riverboat. In summer, be sure to stay late and see the laser show—it's truly one of a kind. See p. 157.

**From the park, take U.S. Hwy. 78 W. for 15 miles; left at Boulevard NE; left on Freedom Pkwy. Using MARTA from downtown, take train to Five Points station and a Noble bus 16 to:**

### ❷ Jimmy Carter Library & Museum

If you opt out on a morning in the park, or even if you don't, plan to tour the Jimmy Carter Library & Museum. Here, you'll find an impressive collection of some 27 million pages of documents,

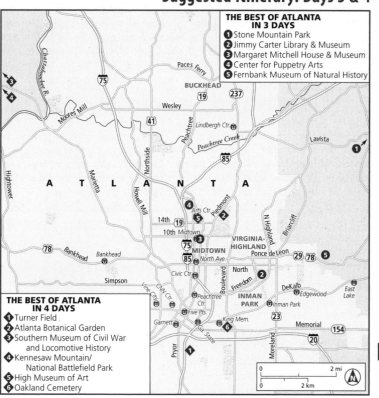

THE BEST OF ATLANTA
IN 3 DAYS
❶ Stone Mountain Park
❷ Jimmy Carter Library & Museum
❸ Margaret Mitchell House & Museum
❹ Center for Puppetry Arts
❺ Fernbank Museum of Natural History

THE BEST OF ATLANTA
IN 4 DAYS
❶ Turner Field
❷ Atlanta Botanical Garden
❸ Southern Museum of Civil War
   and Locomotive History
❹ Kennesaw Mountain/
   National Battlefield Park
❺ High Museum of Art
❻ Oakland Cemetery

memoranda, and correspondence, as well as 1.5 million photographs from Carter's White House years. See p. 149.

Head north on Freedom Pkwy.; left on Ponce de Leon Ave.; right on Peachtree St. Or take MARTA to the Midtown station and walk 1 block east to:

### ❸ Margaret Mitchell House & Museum

Affectionately referred to as "the dump" by *Gone with the Wind* author Margaret Mitchell, her former residence and adjoining museum give great insight into this intriguing author who met with an early demise. Guided tours of 60 and 90 minutes are scheduled throughout the day. See p. 152.

Head north on Peachtree St. and take a left on Spring St. NW to:

### ❹ Center for Puppetry Arts

If you're traveling with kids, you may choose to forgo the Carter Library and Mitchell House Museum and instead spend the afternoon at the Center for Puppetry Arts. In addition to its permanent exhibits and regular performances, this attraction now displays a number of Jim Henson's Muppets, part of the collection of more than 500 Henson puppets and scenes from "The Muppet Show" and "Sesame Street," which were recently acquired by the museum. See p. 171.

Head south on Spring St. NW; turn left on 17th St. NW; turn right on Peachtree St. NE; turn left on Ponce de Leon Ave. NE; left on Clifton Rd. On MARTA, take the train to the North Avenue station, then board bus 2 for Ponce de Leon Ave. Ask the driver to drop you at the corner of Clifton Rd. Walk down Clifton Rd. to:

**❺ Fernbank Museum of Natural History**

Adults don't have to have a kid in tow to enjoy all the Fernbank Museum of Natural History has to offer, including an IMAX theater and a complete mounted skeleton of the largest dinosaur ever found, the *Argentinosaurus.* A number of permanent exhibits include one highlighting Georgia's landscape, from the Piedmont Plateau to the Okefenokee Swamp. See p. 144.

---

# 4 THE BEST OF ATLANTA IN 4 DAYS

---

You're in the home stretch now, so take it easy. Over the busy first 3 days, juggle the above suggestions as you see fit. Enjoy your fourth and final day in the city by taking in the home of the Atlanta Braves baseball team, some Civil War history, and the beautiful collections of the Atlanta Botanical Garden and the High Museum of Art. *Start:* Turner Field (drive or MARTA to Georgia State University station).

---

Take I-75/85 to exit 246 Fulton St./Turner Field; left on Fulton St.; right on Capitol Ave./Hank Aaron Dr. Using MARTA, take train to Georgia State University station and less than a mile on Capitol Ave. to:

**❶ Turner Field**

Even if it isn't game day in Atlanta, Turner Field has a lot to offer visitors year-round, including stadium tours, a Braves Museum and Hall of Fame, and Cartoon Network's Tooner Field playground for kids. See p. 186.

Take I-75/85 N. to exit 250 10th/14th sts.; merge onto Williams St. NW and turn right on 10th St. NW; left on Charles Allen Dr. NE; slight left at Park Dr. NE and gardens are on the right. For MARTA, take train to Arts Center station and bus 36 (bus 27 from Monroe or Lindbergh stations on Sun) to:

**❷ Atlanta Botanical Garden**

Occupying 30 acres in the heart of the city, Atlanta Botanical Garden is home to the 25,000-square-foot Fuqua Orchid Center, a must-see at this attraction. Other highlights include the misty Tropical Rotunda with its exhibit of Central and South American poison dart frogs in colors and patterns you'd never imagine on such a creature. An English herb knot garden and the children's garden are also big draws. See p. 138.

It's a good 45-minute drive to the next stop, depending on traffic. Take I-75 N. to exit 273 for Wade Green Rd.; left on Wade Green Rd. and continue on Cherokee St. NW to destination. There is no public transportation from Atlanta to:

**❸ Southern Museum of Civil War and Locomotive History**

Operated in association with the Smithsonian Institute, the museum marks the site where the wild adventure known as the Great Locomotive Chase began during the Civil War. The museum is located in a former cotton gin and houses the *General,* the locomotive from the aforementioned chase, as well as Civil War artifacts, memorabilia, and photographs. See p. 168.

Head west on Cherokee St. NW; left on S. Main St./Old Hwy. 41 and continue to intersection with Stilesboro Rd. NW. Follow entrance signs to park. No public transportation available to:

**❹ Kennesaw Mountain/National Battlefield Park**

Established in 1917 on the site of a crucial Civil War battle in the Atlanta campaign of 1864, Kennesaw Mountain covers nearly 3,000 acres, including a visitor center, which is where your visit should begin. Start with the 20-minute film about the battle and view Civil War artifact exhibits before hiking the trails to see actual Confederate entrenchments and earthworks. See p. 166.

Take I-75 S. toward Atlanta; exit 250 16th St.; right at 16th St.; right at Market St. NW; right at 17th St. NW; and right on Peachtree St. NE. Or take MARTA to the Arts Center station and a covered walkway to:

## ❺ High Museum of Art

Atlanta's finest art museum, the High is home to extensive permanent exhibits featuring 19th- and 20th-century American paintings, a collection of American Decorative Arts, and Italian paintings and sculpture from the 14th through the 18th centuries. The High is also host to major traveling exhibitions each year, such as a recent 3-year exhibit of pieces on loan from the Louvre. See p. 148.

Take I-75/85 S. to exit 248A MLK Dr.; keep right and merge onto Butler St.; right on Decatur St. SE; right at Grant St. SE; left at Biggers St. SE, which veers right and turns into Oakland Ave. SE. Or take MARTA to the King Memorial station near:

## ❻ Oakland Cemetery

For a cool visit at anytime of day, Oakland Cemetery is especially intriguing in the evening light. If you're visiting during the long light hours of summer, consider picking up a meal from the nearby aptly named Six Feet Under restaurant or other eateries in the vicinity. It might seem weird, but folks frequently enjoy picnic meals on the grounds, surrounded by both the dead and the exquisite monuments to life in this Victorian cemetery on the National Register of Historic Places. See p. 156.

---

# 5 ITINERARIES BY INTEREST

---

## BEAT THE HEAT

The Georgia heat can be relentless, but not to worry: If you can't take the heat, the city has options for fun days in air-conditioned facilities, with everything from museums and shopping to sea life and live entertainment. For a couple of days out of the elements, start with a trip to the world's largest aquarium, the **Georgia Aquarium,** with 100,000 animals from more than 500 species in 80 million gallons of fresh and marine water. You'll be amazed at the massive whale sharks that swim overhead in the glass tunnel as you walk through or glide along on the moving sidewalk. These gentle beasts can grow to be as large as a school bus. Beluga whales, jellyfish, penguins—they're all here in amazing habitats.

Next, make a visit to the **World of Coca-Cola** to browse the world's largest collection of memorabilia celebrating this popular beverage, created right here in Atlanta in 1886. While Coca-Cola was first served at a small pharmacy soda fountain near Underground Atlanta, it is now served over 1 billion times a day and is enjoyed in more than 200 countries across the globe. Come discover the history of this global brand and sample Coca-Cola products from around the world. Some will leave you longing for another sip, while others are worse than castor oil. For big fans of Coke, the Everything Coca-Cola gift shop is an outstanding outlet for memorabilia and literally can't be missed, as you have to pass through it to exit the facility. The museum is open from 9am to 5pm most days, though it may open later or close earlier on certain Sundays.

Plan ahead and schedule a **CNN Studio Tour,** just across the street from the World of Coca-Cola and the Georgia Aquarium. The 55-minute guided walking tour allows a look at one of the world's most trusted names in news, as well as the inventor of 24-hour news. You'll get to journey into the heart of CNN Worldwide and enjoy an up-close, in-depth look at global news in the making. There are a number of behind-the-scenes demonstrations: In the special-effects room, you'll learn just how they make images—like weather maps—appear behind the anchors and correspondents. At the interactive-exhibit area, you can view video clips of the top 100 news stories that CNN has covered during the past 20 years, test your knowledge with the journalism ethics display, and trace the growth of CNN as it parallels world events. The gift shop features a faux newsroom setup where visitors can deliver the news from behind the anchor person's desk, then purchase the tape for themselves.

If you like to spend money while staying cool, Atlanta has no shortage of retail opportunities. **Lenox Square** and **Phipps Plaza** are two of the poshest, most exclusive malls in the city. And Atlanta's newest shopping destination is **Atlantic Station,** a mixed-use community being recognized as a national model for smart growth and sustainable development. Tenants here include the Southeast's first IKEA, a full-day adventure in itself—and its restaurant is the company's first to serve grits and sweet tea. Or dine outside at one of the dozens of eateries in the complex. You'll also find a movie theater here if the weather warrants an afternoon in the dark watching one of the latest flicks. Shopping options include American Eagle Outfitters, Ann Taylor and Ann Taylor Loft, City Sports, Express, the Gap, Nine West, Old Navy, West Elm, and Z Gallerie.

## THE GREAT OUTDOORS

One of the best things about visiting the South is that much of the year can be enjoyed out-of-doors. Start with a day at **Stone Mountain Park.** A monolithic gray-granite outcropping (the world's largest) carved with a massive monument to the Confederacy, Stone Mountain is a distinctive landmark on Atlanta's horizon and the focal point of its major recreation area, which includes 3,200 acres of lakes and beautiful wooded parkland. It's Georgia's number-one tourist attraction, and one of the 10 most-visited paid attractions in the United States. Although the best view of the mountain is from below, the vistas from the top are spectacular. Visitors with lots of energy and lung capacity can take the walking trail up and down the moss-covered slopes, especially lovely in spring when they're blanketed in wildflowers. The trail is 1.3 miles each way. Or you can ride the Skyride cable car to the top, where you'll have an incredible view of the city and the Appalachian Mountains. The best approach is to take the cable car up, and then walk back down.

For a different perspective, check out the park from onboard a World War II amphibious vehicle—the park's new Ride the Ducks Tour is a 40-minute adventure that moves from the land into the waters of Stone Mountain Lake. End your day at the park with Stone Mountain's Lasershow Spectacular, an astonishing display of laser lights and fireworks with animation and music. The brilliant laser beams are projected on the mountain's north face, a natural 1-million-square-foot screen. Bring a picnic supper and arrive early to get a good spot on the lawn at the base of the mountain. Shows are free with park admission.

**Zoo Atlanta** is another popular outdoor venue, with all the excitement these days surrounding the newest addition: another baby panda born in captivity to giant pandas Lun Lun and Yang Yang. Although the pandas' rowdiest period is in the afternoon, the two put on quite a show most of the day: munching bamboo, tussling with each other, playing on their log swing, or climbing on the swinging ladder. When Lun Lun has had enough of Yang Yang's roughhousing, she heads for the water. In the summer, the two can be especially entertaining; if it's really sweltering, zoo officials give each of them a huge block of ice to help them cool off. Of course, there's much more to see at the zoo—you can easily spend a full day here.

Baseball fan? The spectacular 50,000-seat Atlanta Braves stadium at **Turner Field** is a popular spot. The ballpark started life as an 80,000-seat stadium built to host the Centennial Olympic Games in 1996. Don't miss the Braves Museum and Hall of Fame, featuring memorabilia commemorating legendary stars and key moments in Braves history (take a gander at the bat Hank Aaron used to hit his 715th home run). Scouts Alley is designed to teach fans about the fine art of scouting. Fans can test their hitting and throwing skills, call up scouting reports on former and current Braves, play a trivia game, call a play-by-play inning of a game, learn about Hank Aaron's "hot" spot, and much more. Add to that a number of restaurants, the Cartoon Network's Tooner Field playground for kids, and lots of souvenir shopping opportunities, and you'll see that the stadium has something for every member of the family—not to mention a great game of baseball. Stay for the fireworks displays that follow every Friday-night home game.

The delightful **Atlanta Botanical Garden,** occupying 30 acres in Piedmont Park, includes the 25,000-square-foot Fuqua Orchid Center, a children's garden, an education center, and the Dorothy Chapman Fuqua Conservatory. In the Fuqua Orchid Center, a collection of rare high-elevation orchids, which flourish on cool, wet mountains in South America, are being grown in the warm Southeast. Typically, one would have to go to San Francisco or Seattle to see such plants. An "Olympic" olive tree presented by Greece in honor of the 1996 Centennial Olympic Games in Atlanta resides in the botanical garden as well. There are flower shows throughout the year, along with lectures and other activities. Call or check the website to find out what's scheduled during your stay (www.atlantabotanicalgarden.org).

If you want to add thrills and excitement to your trip, Atlanta has a number of amusement parks, including **Six Flags Over Georgia,** the **White Water** water park, and **American Adventures,** a theme park that caters to younger children and families.

# Where to Stay

Don't fight it—you'll have to sleep eventually.

As a major convention city, metro Atlanta is capable of accommodating hordes of visitors. It has more than 92,000 rooms at 749 properties, including budget digs, bed-and-breakfast lodgings, and bastions of luxury. The choices listed below—offering good value in several different price brackets—are in the parts of the city that travelers frequent most often. If you have trouble finding a vacancy at the places listed here, look to the suburbs, where nearly every chain is represented. If you have a car and you're near one of the major interstates, getting into the city from the suburbs should be relatively simple, especially if you avoid rush hours, which last from around 6:30 to 9:30am and 4 to 7:30pm.

Although 100% occupancy is a rarity in Atlanta, this is a major convention city; booking well in advance assures you of a room in the hotel of your choice. Many accommodations, especially those downtown hotels that cater to business travelers, are at full capacity during the standard Monday-through-Friday business week, with more open beds and reduced rates offered over the weekend.

**RATES** The hotels reviewed below are classified first by area, then by price, using the following categories: **Very Expensive:** more than $200 per night; **Expensive:** $150 to $200; **Moderate:** $100 to $150; **Inexpensive:** less than $100. All rates are for double occupancy (two people in one room) and are subject to change.

The prices listed in this book are "rack rates"—the highest that the hotel will charge. If you ask about discounts and packages, or if you book through a travel agent, you can often do better than these posted rates. Reduced-price packages may include extras such as meals, parking, theater tickets, and golf fees, and lower rates are often available for seniors, families, and active-duty military personnel. Preferential rates are also often available when you reserve via toll-free reservation numbers or the Internet. Websites and toll-free telephone information are supplied in all applicable listings below.

Any extras included in the rates (for example, breakfast or other meals) are listed for each property. A 14% tax will be added onto your hotel or motel bill within the city of Atlanta and Fulton County (7% sales tax plus 7% room tax); the rates listed below do not include that tax. If you have a car, be sure to consider the price of parking in the hotel garage at an average of $22 per overnight. Finally, keep in mind that hotel rates often increase during special events.

**BED & BREAKFASTS** Bed & Breakfast Atlanta, 790 North Ave. (© 800/967-3224 or 404/875-0525; www.bedand breakfastatlanta.com), is a free reservations service that has been carefully screening facilities in the Atlanta area since 1979. Its list comprises more than 100 homes and inns; all accommodations have private bathrooms. Among the offerings are a turreted Queen Anne–style Victorian home with nine fireplaces, located near the Carter Library; a delightful honeymoon cottage with a Jacuzzi in Druid Hills; and an elegant 1920s Tudor-style home in Buckhead. The company even has kosher homes on its roster. All rates include continental breakfast, in many cases with more than the usual pastry and coffee. To make sure that you get a room in your top B&B choice, make sure you reserve as early as possible. Call during office hours, which are Monday through Friday from 9am to 5pm.

B&B rates run the gamut from $60 to $240 (the latter for a luxurious Buckhead guest cottage, on a 4-acre estate, that accommodates four people). Rates during special events may be higher. Weekly and monthly rates are available (in guesthouses and apartments) for long-term visitors.

American Express, Diners Club, Master-Card, and Visa are accepted. *Important note:* If you want to book your own B&Bs, be sure to ask if they are licensed and for how many rooms. There are only two licensed B&Bs currently operating in Fulton County (Atlanta proper)—Shell-mont Inn and Beverly Hills Inn—so all others are technically "home stays," and may end up being less than acceptable for some travelers.

# 1 DOWNTOWN

Downtown hotels primarily cater to the business/convention traveler, but there's plenty for leisure travelers here, too: the Georgia Aquarium, the new World of Coca-Cola, the CNN Center, Centennial Olympic Park, Imagine It! Children's Museum of Atlanta, and the Georgia Dome.

## VERY EXPENSIVE

**Glenn Hotel ★★**   The Atlanta lodging scene has never seen anything like this before. The seductive Glenn Hotel, with its wispy-sheer drapery, wraparound lounging sofas, and erotic art, is all about pleasure and was downtown Atlanta's first boutique hotel. Guests can shower in small bathrooms with all-glass stalls that open onto the bedroom, or enjoy a soaking tub for two in one of the 13 roomy and stylish suites. Need a bedtime story? You'll find a pop-up book version of the sensual *Kama Sutra* on the coffee table. This is luxury boutique lodging at its finest.

110 Marietta St. NW, Atlanta, GA 30303. ✆ **404/521-2250.** www.glennhotel.com. 109 units. $209–$269 double; $349 suite. AE, DC, MC, V. Valet parking $25. MARTA: Dome/GWCC/Philips Arena/CNN Center. **Amenities:** Restaurant; bar; concierge; room service. *In room:* A/C, TV, dataport, minibar, coffeemaker, hair dryer, CD player, Wi-Fi.

**Marriott Downtown ★**   This small, upscale property with warmth and charm boasts a central downtown location. The hotel is close to Peachtree Center and a short walk from the Georgia Aquarium, Centennial Olympic Park, the new World of Coca-Cola, Philips Arena, the CNN Center, and the Georgia World Congress Center. The rooms, decorated with traditional quiet prints, dark woods, and overstuffed chairs, are not huge, but they're nicely appointed. Marble floors and counters in the bathrooms lend a handsome touch. The oversize tubs are nice, though not whirlpool tubs. Some units have views of Centennial Olympic Park, and 12 are accessible to travelers with disabilities.

160 Spring St. (at International Blvd.), Atlanta, GA 30303. ✆ **866/316-5959** or 404/688-8600. www.marriott.com. 312 units. $200–$389 double; $290 suite; penthouse suites also available. Children 17 and under stay free in parent's room. Weekend rates often available; higher rates during special events. AE, DC, DISC, MC, V. Valet parking $25. MARTA: Peachtree Center. **Amenities:** Restaurant; bar; large outdoor heated pool; health club; concierge; business center; limited room service; massage; babysitting; laundry service; dry cleaning. *In room:* A/C, TV, dataport, coffeemaker, hair dryer, iron/ironing board, high-speed Internet access.

**Marriott Marquis ★★★**   A dramatic downtown landmark, the Marriott Marquis is a first-class megahotel designed by Atlanta's John Portman, who also designed the Hyatt

Regency Atlanta (reviewed below). Fronted by a vast fountain that looks like a flying saucer, the hotel has a 50-story atrium lobby that is said to be the largest in the Southeast. A total renovation to the tune of $138 million has put this hotel at the top of the list for downtown lodging, with an ultra-contemporary lobby bar as the main attraction. However, the lobby level is so open and attractive that event receptions are often held here and, while they are typically held early in the evening, the noise from a large gathering funnels straight up the atrium and into the rooms. The rooms are attractively decorated in a contemporary style. Guest rooms and bathrooms are of average size. Forty-two rooms are wheelchair-accessible. The Marriott is connected by a covered walkway to shops in the Peachtree Center mall.

265 Peachtree Center Ave. (btw. Baker and Harris sts.), Atlanta, GA 30303. ℂ **888/855-5701** or 404/521-0000. Fax 404/586-6299. www.marriott.com. 1,675 units. $289–$389 double; $489 king suite. Extra person $20. Children 11 and under stay free in parent's room. Packages available. AE, DC, DISC, MC, V. Valet parking $26. MARTA: Peachtree Center. **Amenities:** 2 restaurants; 2 bars; large indoor/outdoor swimming pool; fitness center; Jacuzzi; concierge; airport shuttle; salon; room service. *In room:* A/C, TV, fridge, coffeemaker, hair dryer, safe, high-speed Internet access.

**Ritz-Carlton Atlanta** ★★★   A 2008 renovation glamorized the lounge, guest rooms and suites, and revamped the technology. The impeccable service you'd expect from a Ritz property harkens back to another, more gracious era; you'll be pampered as never before (for instance, housekeeping stops by twice daily). Elegant, spacious rooms, many with bay windows, are furnished with dark hickory bachelor's chests and ostrich-patterned leather headboards. Ample marble and granite bathrooms have rain shower heads. Four rooms have been modified to be accessible to travelers with disabilities.

Overlooking all the action along Peachtree Street, Atlanta Grill features the culinary flair of the widely acclaimed young chef, Bennett Hollberg, serving steaks, chops, and seafood as well as Southern favorites. Diners can count on a warm, clublike atmosphere, accompanied by the soothing sounds of live jazz every night. The Atlanta Grill is a popular Atlanta dining choice with both guests and nonguests.

181 Peachtree St. NE (main entrance on Ellis St.), Atlanta, GA 30303. ℂ **800/241-3333** or 404/659-0400. Fax 404/688-0400. www.ritzcarlton.com. 444 units. $209 double; $259–$679 suite. AE, DC, DISC, MC, V. Valet parking $27. MARTA: Peachtree Center. **Amenities:** Restaurant; fitness center; concierge; car-rental desk; limo; business center; room service; babysitting; laundry service. *In room:* A/C, TV/VCR, fax, dataport, minibar, coffeemaker, hair dryer, high-speed Internet access.

**Westin Peachtree Plaza** ★★   You wouldn't expect a 73-story, 1,000-room hotel to be described as cozy, but that fits here. The 300-square-foot rooms are both elegant and intimate, and floor-to-ceiling windows provide dramatic views of the city. The Westin's "Heavenly Beds"—boasting a custom-designed pillow-top mattress set, a down blanket, three luxury-brand sheets, a comforter, a duvet, and five of the softest

---

Ⓣⓘⓟⓢ   **Rooms and a View**

For a bird's-eye view of the city, take a trip up to the top of the **Westin Peachtree Plaza.** You'll ride up 72 stories in a glass elevator to a viewing area with telescopes where you can get a 360-degree look at Atlanta and the surrounding area. On a clear day, you can see the foothills of the Appalachian Mountains. Open from 10am to 11pm daily; the cost is $5 for adults, $3 for children. Call ℂ **404/659-1400** for details.

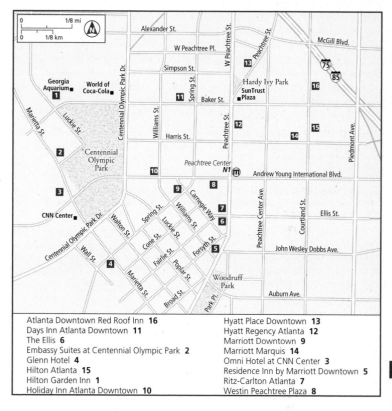

0 1/8 mi
0 1/8 km

Alexander St.
W Peachtree Pl.
McGill Blvd.
Simpson St.
**13**
**75**
**85**
Georgia Aquarium ■ **1**
World of Coca-Cola ■
Hardy Ivy Park
SunTrust Plaza ■
**16**
Spring St.
**11**
Baker St.
Centennial Olympic Park Dr.
Williams St.
Harris St.
Peachtree St.
**12**
**14**
**15**
Piedmont Ave.
Marietta St.
Luckie St.
**2**
Centennial Olympic Park
Peachtree Center
N1 Ⓜ
Andrew Young International Blvd.
**10**
**3**
CNN Center ■
**9**
**8**
Carnegie Way
Williams St.
**7**
**6**
Peachtree Center Ave.
Courtland St.
Ellis St.
Centennial Olympic Park Dr.
Walton St.
Spring St.
Luckie St.
Cone St.
Wall St.
Fairlie St.
Poplar St.
Forsyth St.
**5**
John Wesley Dobbs Ave.
**4**
Marietta St.
Broad St.
Park Pl.
Woodruff Park
Auburn Ave.

| | |
|---|---|
| Atlanta Downtown Red Roof Inn **16** | Hyatt Place Downtown **13** |
| Days Inn Atlanta Downtown **11** | Hyatt Regency Atlanta **12** |
| The Ellis **6** | Marriott Downtown **9** |
| Embassy Suites at Centennial Olympic Park **2** | Marriott Marquis **14** |
| Glenn Hotel **4** | Omni Hotel at CNN Center **3** |
| Hilton Atlanta **15** | Residence Inn by Marriott Downtown **5** |
| Hilton Garden Inn **1** | Ritz-Carlton Atlanta **7** |
| Holiday Inn Atlanta Downtown **10** | Westin Peachtree Plaza **8** |

pillows ever—guarantee you a good night's sleep. Baths are of average size. The revolving Sun Dial Restaurant, on the 71st floor, serves sophisticated American fare and has an impressive 360-degree view of the city skyline. The revolving Sun Dial bar, on the 72nd floor, is a good spot for cocktails and light fare. The Cafe restaurant, located in the atrium lobby, serves buffet and a la carte breakfasts. The Starbucks Coffee Bar is open daily for coffee, sandwiches, and pastries. There's also the Lobby Bar and the adjoining cafe. Twenty-eight rooms are accessible to travelers with disabilities.

210 Peachtree St. NW (at International Blvd.), Atlanta, GA 30303. ⓒ **800/228-3000** or 404/659-1400. Fax 404/589-7424. www.westin.com. 1,068 units. $239–$270 double; $385–$1,450 suite. Extra person $20. Children 17 and under stay free in parent's room. Package rates available. AE, DC, DISC, MC, V. Valet parking $23; self-parking $19. MARTA: Peachtree Center. **Amenities:** 2 restaurants; 2 bars; large indoor/outdoor pool; fitness center; concierge; business center; shopping gallery; room service; laundry service. *In room:* A/C, TV, coffeemaker, hair dryer, iron/ironing board, safe, high-speed Internet access.

## EXPENSIVE

**The Ellis**  The Ellis on Peachtree is downtown Atlanta's newest boutique hotel, but with a historical perspective. Formerly the Winecoff Hotel, destroyed by fire in 1946, the Ellis is the result of a $28-million investment and a vision for returning this grand old landmark to the bustling hotel of former years. The rooms are quite small, but nicely appointed, as are the bathrooms. Unusual is the hotel's "female only" floor, with keyed-entry, a throwback to earlier times, but comforting for women traveling alone who like the added privacy and security. Dining at the **e Street Grille** is a treat, especially if you're looking to add something "Southern" to your Atlanta experience. If adult libations are on your "to do" list, you've got to try the Georgia Sweet Tea cocktail, a blend of peach vodka, sweet tea, and lemon. Fried green tomatoes and Southern-style corn cakes are a "can't miss."

176 Peachtree St. NW, Atlanta, GA 30303. ℭ **404/523-5155.** www.ellishotel.com. 127 units. $159 double. AE, DC, MC, V. Valet parking $22. MARTA: Peachtree Center. **Amenities:** Restaurant; lounge; concierge; business center; room service. *In room:* A/C, TV, dataport, minibar, coffeemaker, hair dryer, CD player, Wi-Fi.

### Embassy Suites at Centennial Olympic Park ★ (Kids)   This Centennial Olympic Park location is a good bet for tourists, conventioneers, and sports fans, since the hotel is just across the street from the Georgia Aquarium, the new World of Coca-Cola, and the Georgia World Congress Center, and within walking distance of MARTA, the CNN Center, Philips Arena, and the Georgia Dome. Kids will immediately spot the fountains at Centennial Park, designed to allow visitors to run through them and get soaked from head to foot.

Each two-room standard suite is decorated with contemporary furniture and includes a pullout sofa in the living room. Bathrooms, with Jacuzzi tubs and separate showers, are spacious and luxurious. Ask for a parkside room, which has a nice view of the park and the city skyline; there's no extra charge. Complimentary cooked-to-order breakfasts and an evening reception will keep a few bucks in your pocket. Seventeen suites are accessible to travelers with disabilities.

267 Marietta St., Atlanta, GA 30313. ℭ **404/223-2300.** Fax 404/223-0925. www.embassysuites.com. 321 units. $230–$270 suite. Children 17 and under stay free in parent's room. Rates include full breakfast. Packages and weekend rates available; higher rates during special events. AE, DC, DISC, MC, V. Valet parking $24. MARTA: Omni/Dome/GWCC. **Amenities:** Restaurant; large outdoor pool; health club w/sauna and Jacuzzi; concierge; airport shuttle; business center; limited room service; laundry service; dry cleaning. *In room:* A/C, TV, dataport, fridge, coffeemaker, hair dryer, iron/ironing board, safe, microwave, Play Station, high-speed Internet access.

### Hilton Atlanta ★★   If you want to stay in one of the downtown megahotels, this is a good choice. One of Atlanta's top convention hotels—with 104,000 square feet of meeting and exhibit space—the Hilton is surprisingly upscale for a chain lodging. Renovations to the executive level lounge, the entrance, and lobby took place in late 2008. The guest rooms and bathrooms are very nice and quite large. Some of the suites have Murphy beds for extra guests.

The Hilton's premier restaurant is **Nikolai's Roof,** a 30th-floor dining room with spectacular skyline vistas, which recently celebrated 30 years in Atlanta. Multicourse prix-fixe French and Russian dinners are the specialty, as are the flavored vodkas steeped in-house. Adjacent to Nikolai's Roof is A Point of View bar. Trader Vic's, a South Seas–Polynesian restaurant found at numerous Hiltons, provides its signature setting of palm trees and tiki torches, plus potent rum drinks.

255 Courtland St. (btw. Baker and Harris sts.), Atlanta, GA 30303. ℭ **800/HILTONS [445-8667]** or 404/659-2000. Fax 404/524-0111. www.hilton.com. 1,224 units. Mon–Thurs $179 double, Fri–Sun $159 double, depending on season. Executive floor: Mon–Thurs $219 double, Fri–Sun $199 double. Extra person $25. Children stay free in parent's room. AE, DC, DISC, MC, V. Valet parking $24; self-parking $17. MARTA: Peachtree Center. **Amenities:** 4 restaurants; 2 bars; outdoor pool; 4 outdoor tennis courts; 2 basketball courts; fitness center w/jogging track; Jacuzzi; sauna; concierge; airport shuttle; business center; room service. *In room:* A/C, TV, dataport, minibar, coffeemaker, hair dryer.

**Hilton Garden Inn** (Kids)  New in 2008, the Hilton Garden Inn provides one more option for staying near the mix of attractions in downtown Atlanta. In walking distance to Centennial Olympic Park, the Georgia Aquarium, the World of Coca-Cola, and Imagine It! Children's Museum, this is a great place for families to use as headquarters during a trip to the city. The hotel has a video arcade and playground, as well as special activities to keep the little ones busy. Rooms are welcoming but pretty basic and of average size, as are the bathrooms; ask for one with a city view for a more interesting stay. Suites have a separate living room so parents can relax after putting the kids to bed. Rooms include a refrigerator and microwave, another plus if you're traveling with children.

275 Baker St., Atlanta, GA 30303. © **800/HILTONS [445-8667]** or 404/577-2001. Fax 404/577-2002. www.hilton.com. 273 units. $190–$200 double; $494 suite. Children stay free in parent's room. AE, DC, DISC, MC, V. Valet parking $24; self-parking $18. MARTA: Peachtree Center. **Amenities:** Restaurant; bar; pool; fitness center; coin-op washers and dryers; concierge; airport shuttle; business center; room service. *In room:* A/C, TV, dataport, fridge, coffeemaker, iron/ironing board, microwave, Internet access.

**Hyatt Place Downtown**  Formerly AmeriSuites, this place got a fresh start under new ownership and now features the double-plus Hyatt Grand Beds and 42-inch flat-panel HD televisions. Still ideal for the business traveler as it's just a few blocks from downtown, Hyatt Place offers a lot, including free Wi-Fi. Leave your car in the parking lot and don't even worry about fighting the Atlanta rush-hour traffic—the hotel offers a free shuttle to and from local offices. Rooms are large and nicely furnished, making them particularly appealing for business travelers on extended stays. Bathrooms are of standard size. Five units are accessible to travelers with disabilities. A complimentary deluxe continental breakfast buffet is served each morning. Don't miss the guest reception every Tuesday evening.

330 Peachtree St. NE (btw. Baker St. and Ralph McGill Blvd.), Atlanta, GA 30308. © **888/492-8847** or 404/577-1980. Fax 404/688-3706. www.hyatt.com. 94 units. $169–$299 double. Children 16 and under stay free in parent's room. Packages available. AE, DC, DISC, MC, V. Self-parking $20. MARTA: Peachtree Center or Civic Center. **Amenities:** Restaurant; fitness center; business center; laundry service; dry cleaning. *In room:* A/C, TV, dataport, minibar, fridge, coffeemaker, hair dryer, iron/ironing board, microwave.

**Hyatt Regency Atlanta** ★★  One of the city's major convention hotels, this Hyatt was designed in 1967 by famed Atlanta architect John Portman. With its innovative 23-story atrium lobby, it created quite a stir. Rooms have a contemporary flavor and feature the Hyatt's "premium bedding" concept—beds are graced with pillow-top mattresses, high-thread-count sheets, and feather blankets. Rooms and baths are of average size. The main building's 22nd floor houses the Regency Club accommodations, featuring a private concierge, lounge, continental breakfast, evening hors d'oeuvres, and plush robes. Business Plan rooms are on the 21st floor. Business Plan guests get free local calls and other perks. The hotel is connected to the Peachtree Center mall by a covered walkway.

Accommodations, rates, and service at the Hyatt are comparable to those at the Hilton, thus any preference is usually based on habit. The Hilton is, however, the more suitable property for large conventions.

265 Peachtree St. NE (btw. Baker and Harris sts.), Atlanta, GA 30303. © **800/233-1234** or 404/577-1234. Fax 404/588-4137. www.hyatt.com. 1,260 units. $189–$239 double. Extra person $25. Children 17 and under stay free in parent's room. Packages and promotional rates available. AE, DC, DISC, MC, V. Valet parking $24. MARTA: Peachtree Center. **Amenities:** 3 restaurants; bar; large outdoor pool; fitness center; concierge; business center; room service; laundry service. *In room:* A/C, TV/VCR, dataport, minibar, coffeemaker, hair dryer, iron/ironing board, safe, high-speed Internet access.

**Omni Hotel at CNN Center** ★★ (Kids)  The Omni has an excellent location—especially if you're attending a sporting event. It adjoins the Georgia World Congress Center, Philips Arena, the Georgia Dome, and the CNN Center, and is across from the

WHERE TO STAY

5

DOWNTOWN

Georgia Aquarium, the new World of Coca-Cola, Centennial Olympic Park, and Imagine It! Children's Museum of Atlanta. Be sure to request a room with a view of Centennial Olympic Park or the downtown skyline. Onsite, the Natural Body Spa can be a treat at the end of a busy day.

Standard rooms and bathrooms are of average size, but the suites here include huge living/dining areas with wet bars. If you don't have a problem dropping a few grand a night, ask for the two-level Omni Suite extraordinaire. Eleven rooms have been modified for visitors with disabilities. Digs are comparable to the Embassy Suites across the street, but the service here is better. If you're traveling with kids, ask about the Omni Kids program.

100 CNN Center (at Marietta St. and International Blvd.), Atlanta, GA 30335. (🕐 **800/THE-OMNI [843-6664]** or 404/659-0000. Fax 404/525-5050. www.omnihotels.com. 1,067 units. $179–$209 double; $359–$1,200 suite. Children 17 and under stay free in parent's room. Weekend packages sometimes available; higher rates during special events. AE, DISC, MC, V. Valet parking $30. MARTA: Omni/Dome/GWCC. **Amenities:** Restaurant; health club; concierge; business center; salon; room service; laundry service. *In room:* A/C, TV, dataport, minibar, hair dryer, high speed Internet access.

### Residence Inn by Marriott Downtown ★★ (Value)

This is the best deal downtown: It's close to all the action; the accommodations are quiet, nicely appointed studios or suites; and it's incredibly well priced—especially for an extended stay. The building itself was constructed in 1928 and is listed on the National Register of Historic Places. The ceiling in the marble lobby was painted by European artists when the building was new, and it has been restored to its original splendor. The most recent renovations were completed in late 2008. The rooms, which are like small apartments, have queen-size beds and kitchens outfitted with all the necessary equipment. Bathrooms are of standard size. High ceilings lend a feeling of spaciousness. For a nice view of downtown, ask for one of the suites on the higher floors. In addition to a complimentary breakfast, the hotel provides a light supper with beer and wine from Monday through Thursday.

134 Peachtree St. NW (1 block north of Woodruff Park), Atlanta, GA 30303. (🕐 **800/331-3131** or 404/522-0950. Fax 404/577-3235. www.residenceinnatlanta.com. 160 units. $159–$219 studio; $179–$229 1-bedroom suite. Higher rates during special events. Children 17 and under stay free in parent's room. AE, DC, DISC, MC, V. Valet parking $19. MARTA: Peachtree Center. **Amenities:** Fitness center; room service; coin-op washers and dryers; same-day dry cleaning; grocery shopping. *In room:* A/C, TV, dataport, kitchen/kitchenette, hair dryer.

## MODERATE

### Days Inn Atlanta Downtown

In a great central location, this Days Inn has balcony rooms on floors three to 10, with views toward Midtown. Although you don't get all the luxury-hotel frills here, the accommodations are still just fine. Guest rooms are large and comfortable. All units boast slim-design televisions. Bathrooms, with tub/shower combinations, are separate from the vanity area, a plus for those traveling in packs and trying to get ready for dinner all at the same time. Six rooms are wheelchair-accessible.

The athletic center and large outdoor pool are other highlights. In-house conference rooms and a location in the heart of the business district make this hotel a great choice for folks in town on official business; the rooms and facilities are quite suitable for families as well. This place is also conveniently located for those who want to enjoy all those downtown attractions or take in a game at the Dome.

300 Spring St. (at Baker St.), Atlanta, GA 30308. (🕐 **800/DAYS-INN [329-7466]** or 404/523-1144. Fax 404/577-8495. www.daysinn.com. 263 units. $109–$135 double. Extra person $10. Special weekend rates available. Children 17 and under stay free in parent's room. AE, DC, DISC, MC, V. Self-parking $15. MARTA: Peachtree Center. **Amenities:** Large outdoor pool; exercise room; laundry service. *In room:* A/C, TV, fridge, microwave, coffeemaker, hair dryer, iron/ironing board, safe.

# (Kids) Family-Friendly Hotels

**Embassy Suites at Centennial Olympic Park** (p. 76)   Children will love this location, just yards away from Centennial Park, which is home to festivals, art markets, and concerts—plus fountains that invite playing and splashing.

**Four Seasons Hotel** (p. 80)   Kids enjoy a special program here that includes cookies and milk upon check-in, a toiletries box with baby shampoo and a rubber duck, chocolates at nightly turndown, board games, and children's movies and video games.

**Holiday Inn Express Hotel & Suites** (p. 93)   All-suite hotels are almost always the most economical way to travel as a family, and this one has an excellent location to boot. Rates include deluxe continental breakfast, and each suite has a fully equipped kitchen and a VCR. On-site are a lovely pool and a patio with barbecue grill. You'll find a city park with a playground down the street.

**Marriott Evergreen Conference Resort** (p. 95)   Kids will love this "castle" nestled in a pine forest. The location is excellent for families who want to take advantage of all of Stone Mountain Park's activities.

**Omni Hotel at CNN Center** (p. 77)   The Omni's fabulous central location puts the family-friendly attractions of the city at your fingertips. Kids receive a welcome gift here, too.

**Residence Inn by Marriott Buckhead** (p. 91)   This place not only has a swimming pool, but also boasts fully equipped kitchens—a potential money-saver for families. Rates here include breakfast, and there are barbecue grills and picnic tables on the premises. It's like having your own Atlanta apartment, with parking at your door. The property also offers basketball, volleyball, and paddle-tennis courts, and guests can rent movies at the front desk.

**Serenbe Southern Country Inn** (p. 98)   Kids will love the open spaces and farm animals here, not to mention activities that range from playing in a treehouse to roasting marshmallows around a bonfire.

**Stone Mountain Inn** (p. 95)   Located in Stone Mountain Park, this lovely inn is the perfect spot for families who want to take full advantage of the park's recreational opportunities. Fishing, boating, miniature golfing, bicycling, hiking, and more are at your doorstep, and the inn features an outdoor pool as well.

**Holiday Inn Atlanta Downtown** ★   This 11-story property offers appealing rooms and one of the better locations for business accommodations, including full conference facilities and services, at a rate that won't break you or your expense account. The hotel is adjacent to the Gift, Apparel, and Merchandise Marts, the Georgia Aquarium, the new World of Coca-Cola, and Centennial Olympic Park, and it's 2 blocks from the CNN Center, Philips Arena, and the Georgia World Congress Center. Guest rooms are of average size, as are the bathrooms with amenities by Bath & Body Works. Sixteen rooms are accessible to travelers with disabilities, eight of them with roll-in shower stalls.

101 International Blvd. (at Williams St.), Atlanta, GA 30303. ℂ **800/972-2404** or 404/524-5555. Fax 404/221-0702. www.hidowntownatlanta.com. 260 units. $102–$149 double. Rates can go up to $250 a night during major conventions. Children 18 and under stay free in parent's room; children 12 and under eat free. AE, DISC, MC, V. Valet parking $20. MARTA: Peachtree Center. **Amenities:** Restaurant; bar; outdoor pool; fitness center; Jacuzzi; concierge; business center; room service; laundry service; dry cleaning. *In room:* A/C, TV, coffeemaker, hair dryer, iron/ironing board, Wi-Fi.

## INEXPENSIVE

**Atlanta Downtown Red Roof Inn** ⟨**Value**⟩    Formerly a family-owned Travelodge, the Downtown Red Roof Inn still provides an inexpensive alternative in the heart of downtown. All rooms are off an interior corridor and sport typical chain decor—nice, but nothing out of the ordinary. The same goes for the bathrooms. Business services include voice mail, modem hookups, and faxing and copying services. Three rooms are accessible to travelers with disabilities.

311 Courtland St. NE (btw. Baker St. and Ralph McGill Blvd.), Atlanta, GA 30303. ℂ **800/733-7663** or 404/659-4545. Fax 404/659-5934. www.redroof.com. 71 units. $80–$95 double. Children 16 and under stay free in parent's room. Rates include continental breakfast. AE, DC, DISC, MC, V. Free parking. MARTA: Peachtree Center. **Amenities:** Outdoor pool. *In room:* A/C, TV, fridge (available upon request), coffeemaker, hair dryer, Wi-Fi.

---

# 2  MIDTOWN

Travelers interested in the cultural highlights of Atlanta will appreciate the hotel choices in Midtown, an area that's home to the Woodruff Arts Center, the High Museum of Art, the Fox Theatre, and the Margaret Mitchell House. Joggers and other outdoor enthusiasts will enjoy the proximity to Piedmont Park and the Atlanta Botanical Garden.

## VERY EXPENSIVE

**Four Seasons Hotel** ★★★ ⟨**Kids**⟩    This elegant hotel is the one to choose if you're looking for luxurious surroundings and impeccable service in the heart of Atlanta's cultural area. Accommodations are lavish and sophisticated, with large windows, upholstered lounge chairs and sofas, and handsome Beidermeier-style furnishings. The gorgeous, large marble bathrooms have huge tubs perfect for soaking, and some have separate showers as well. Thirteen of the rooms have been modified to accommodate travelers with disabilities.

New in 2007, the Spa at Four Seasons offers a wide variety of treatments, many available in-room. The hotel provides several amenities for children, including a gift upon arrival, board and video games, movies, and books. For older kids, trips can be arranged to nearby kid-friendly attractions.

The **Park 75** restaurant, open all day, serves New American cuisine, featuring the freshest goods from local markets combined in incredibly creative contemporary dishes by Chef Robert Gerstenecker.

75 14th St. (btw. Peachtree and West Peachtree sts.), Atlanta, GA 30309. ℂ **800/819-5053** or 404/881-9898. Fax 404/873-4692. www.fourseasons.com. 244 units. $475 double; $875 suite; $4,000 presidential suite. Children 17 and under stay free in parent's room. Weekend cultural packages available. AE, DC, DISC, MC, V. Valet parking $30. MARTA: Arts Center. Pets under 15 lb. accepted. **Amenities:** Restaurant; bar; Olympic-size indoor pool; health club and full-service spa; Jacuzzi; sauna; concierge; business center w/secretarial and translation service; room service; laundry service, dry cleaning/pressing; computers. *In room:* A/C, TV, dataport, minibar, hair dryer, safe.

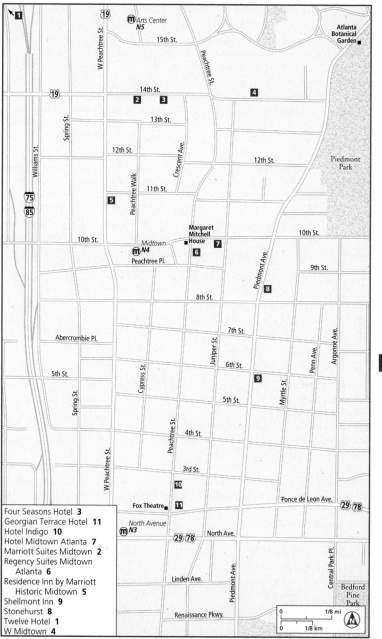

WHERE TO STAY

5

MIDTOWN

Atlanta Botanical Garden
Piedmont Park
Bedford Pine Park

Four Seasons Hotel **3**
Georgian Terrace Hotel **11**
Hotel Indigo **10**
Hotel Midtown Atlanta **7**
Marriott Suites Midtown **2**
Regency Suites Midtown Atlanta **6**
Residence Inn by Marriott Historic Midtown **5**
Shellmont Inn **9**
Stonehurst **8**
Twelve Hotel **1**
W Midtown **4**

**Stonehurst Place** ★★ A one-of-a-kind EarthCraft House, built in 1896 and on the National Register of Historic Places, Stonehurst was extensively renovated in 2008. Its two guest rooms and three suites are all finely appointed. A true "green lodging," Stonehurst emphasizes recycling, rainwater reclamation, air purification, and solar energy. Lovely gardens and porches are great for unwinding at the end of a busy day. It's a convenient walk to Midtown restaurants and MARTA. Beds boast 1,000-thread-count Egyptian cotton bedding. Multiple shower heads and heated Carrara marble floors are available in some bathrooms. Four units have working fireplaces. A full gourmet breakfast is served, along with complimentary refreshments throughout the day.

923 Piedmont Ave. NE, Atlanta, GA 30309. ✆ 404/881-0722. www.stonehurstplace.com. 5 units. $249–$329 double; $349–$499 suite. AE, MC, V. Free parking. MARTA: Midtown. Pets accepted. **Amenities:** Computers; in-room massage. *In room:* A/C, TV/DVD/CD player, dataport, high-speed Internet access, Wi-Fi, MP3 docking.

**W Atlanta Midtown** ★ This former Sheraton underwent a major transformation and the sleek new W Atlanta Midtown now rivals the Glenn boutique hotel as Hotlanta's sexiest hotel. From the thumping dance music that (very loudly) greets you in the lobby and the Living Room Bar to the ultramodern, slightly above-average-size rooms appointed in black and silver and oh-so-hip decor, W has put this address back on the Midtown map. Bathrooms are attractive and of average size. At the W, where staff promises to meet requests with its signature "Whatever/Whenever" service, the attention to detail is hard to beat. Whether it's the miniature martini shaker with all the makings available in-room or the "Intimacy Kit" in the hanging minibar, there isn't much you'd want for in this hot spot.

What's more, the W is home to Bliss, the hotel's signature spa, featuring hot R&B music instead of nature tunes and a brownie buffet (who said you had to be on a diet to enjoy pampering?).

188 14th St. NE (at Peachtree St.), Atlanta, GA 30361. ✆ 877/822-0000 or 404/892-6000. Fax 404/872-9192. www.Whotels.com/Atlanta. 467 units. $285–$309 double; $675 suite. AE, DC, DISC, MC, V. Valet parking $28; self-parking $16. MARTA: Arts Center. **Amenities:** Restaurant; 2 bars; large outdoor pool; fitness center; spa; concierge; business services; room service. *In room:* A/C, TV/DVD, dataport, minibar, coffeemaker, hair dryer, iron/ironing board, safe.

## EXPENSIVE

**Georgian Terrace Hotel** ★★ (Finds) Listed on the National Register of Historic Places, the Georgian Terrace opened in 1911 as a luxury hotel. Clark Gable and Vivien Leigh stayed here in 1939 and attended the premiere party of *Gone with the Wind*. The marble floors, soaring columns, and dramatic French windows hark back to the opulence and grandeur of a bygone era, though the rooms are thoroughly modern. The hotel has studios and one-, two-, and three-bedroom suites, with large bathrooms, and is convenient to all that Midtown has to offer. Bathrooms are large. The Fox Theatre is right across the street. If you'd like a view of Stone Mountain, ask for a suite on the east side of the hotel. Breakfast is served in the original hotel lobby, while cocktails are served in the parlor.

*Note:* Although the suites have full-size kitchens, they lack pots and pans and have only enough dinnerware for two people. Call the front desk for additional accouterments.

659 Peachtree St. (just north of Ponce de Leon Ave.), Atlanta, GA 30308. ✆ 800/651-2316 or 404/897-1991. Fax 404/724-9116. www.thegeorgianterrace.com. 317 units. $169–$189 double; $209 1-bedroom suite; $239–$289 2-bedroom suite. Weekend packages available; reduced rates for stays of more than 30 days. AE, DC, DISC, MC, V. Valet parking $25; self-parking $22. MARTA: North Ave. **Amenities:** Restaurant; heated junior Olympic swimming pool; fitness center; concierge; business center; room service; laundry service; limo (3-mile radius). *In room:* A/C, TV, dataport, kitchen, coffeemaker, hair dryer, iron/ironing board.

> ## (Tips) Hot Enough for You?
>
> Maybe you need to sip a mojito at Midtown's Four Seasons Hotel. The Park 75 Lounge serves up an icy concoction of rum, sugar, mint, lime, and tonic that's the perfect antidote to a steamy summer evening. Okay, it costs about 10 bucks, a price that may make you sweat a bit at first . . . but you'll cool down by the time you finish the last of this classy beverage.

**Hotel Indigo ★★ (Finds)**   This fun boutique hotel opened in 2004 in a space that formerly housed the Days Inn Peachtree. Guest rooms have a welcoming foyer, hardwood floors, and beds with oversize pillows in funky color combinations. Also oversize are the Adirondack lobby chairs in each unit. The spa-style showers are the perfect treat after a long day of sightseeing, though the bathrooms themselves are tiny (and only two have tubs). Dog owners, take note: This is Atlanta's number-one pet-friendly hotel—with no weight limit and no fee. During Tuesday night's Canine Cocktail Hour, guests and locals bring their dogs to the lobby and bar, where the dogs are served special treats and water from a silver pitcher, while their owners socialize. The restaurant serves great seasonal entrees, and the hotel is right across the street from the Fox Theatre, so you can just roll into bed after attending a performance.

683 Peachtree St. (btw. Third St. and Ponce de Leon Ave.), Atlanta, GA 30308. (C) **404/874-9200.** www. hotelindigo.com. 139 units. $169–$204 double. Rates may be higher during conventions and special events. AE, DC, DISC, MC, V. Self-parking $18. MARTA: North Ave. Pets accepted. **Amenities:** Restaurant; business center; coin-op washers and dryers. *In room:* A/C, TV, coffeemaker, hair dryer, high-speed Internet access.

**Hotel Midtown Atlanta ★**   This 11-story red brick hotel is close to many Midtown cultural attractions, including Piedmont Park and the Margaret Mitchell House and Museum. It's also convenient to Georgia Tech, making it a favorite among visitors to the campus. The nicely appointed rooms include a comfy armchair for enjoying a relaxing read. Suites feature separate sitting areas with sofas, extra TVs and phones, and refrigerators. Eight rooms are accessible to travelers with disabilities.

125 10th St. NE (just east of Peachtree St.), Atlanta, GA 30309. (C) **877/999-3223** or 404/873-4800. Fax 404/870-1530. www.hotelmidtownatlanta.com. 191 units. $155–$175 double. AE, DC, DISC, MC, V. Valet parking $20; self-parking $15. MARTA: Midtown. **Amenities:** Restaurant; large heated indoor pool; state-of-the-art fitness center; Jacuzzi; business services; room service. *In room:* A/C, TV, dataport, coffeemaker, hair dryer, iron/ironing board.

**Marriott Suites Midtown ★**   Located in the heart of Midtown, this all-suite hotel is a perfect choice for culture buffs, and its proximity to MARTA makes it easy to get to the rest of the city's attractions, too. Each spacious suite, attractively decorated in a warm, homey style, offers a king-size bed and a full living room with a convertible sofa. Bedrooms are set off from living-room areas by lace-curtained French doors. Large marble bathrooms have a separate shower. Twelve units are accessible to travelers with disabilities.

35 14th St. NE (btw. Peachtree and W. Peachtree sts.), Atlanta, GA 30309. (C) **888/855-5701** or 404/876-8888. Fax 404/876-7727. www.marriott.com. 254 units. $199–$249 double; $274–$319 suite. Discounted rates and packages available through toll-free number. AE, DC, DISC, MC, V. Valet parking $22; self-parking $18. MARTA: Arts Center. **Amenities:** Restaurant; bar; indoor/outdoor swimming pools; fitness center; Jacuzzi; concierge; room service; coin-op washers and dryers; laundry service. *In room:* A/C, TV, dataport, fridge, coffeemaker, hair dryer, iron/ironing board.

**Regency Suites Midtown Atlanta**   This all-suite property is ideally located right in the midst of Midtown activity. The latest renovation enhanced guest suites with new granite counters, marble flooring, and pillow-top mattresses. Regency Suites is ideal for business travelers, who are drawn to the complimentary continental breakfast and the full dinner for two served on Monday through Thursday nights when booked direct. Suites and bathrooms are of average size. If you choose to venture out for meals, numerous restaurants are within walking distance—as is the Fox Theatre, if you're in town to catch a performance. Accommodations include fully equipped kitchenettes with standard appliances and table service for four. Additionally, all units have noise-reduction windows in case the Midtown partying scene goes on too late for your comfort.

975 W. Peachtree St. NE, Atlanta, GA 30309. ✆ **404/876-5003.** Fax 404/817-7511. www.regencysuites. com. 96 units. $209–$249 suite. AE, MC, V. Valet parking $12. MARTA: Midtown. **Amenities:** Fitness center; business center; coin-op washers and dryers; laundry service. *In room:* A/C, TV, kitchenette, coffeemaker, hair dryer, iron/ironing board, high-speed Internet access, Wi-Fi.

**Residence Inn by Marriott Historic Midtown ★**   The complimentary evening reception offered Monday through Thursday sets this inn apart from others in the area. If the free food doesn't tempt your taste buds, you can opt for the complimentary gro-cery-shopping service from Monday through Friday. The studios and spacious suites here boast handsome oak or mahogany furnishings—mostly antique reproductions, including Chippendale-style beds. Most rooms have balconies with French doors. Ten rooms are accessible to travelers with disabilities. There aren't many attractions nearby, but you're not far from a MARTA station. The inn provides hot tea and coffee all day in the lobby.

1041 W. Peachtree St. (at 11th St.), Atlanta, GA 30309. ✆ **404/872-8885.** Fax 404/724-9218. www. marriott.com. 78 units. $169–$249 double. Rates include hot breakfast buffet. Higher rates during special events; reduced rates on weekends and for stays of several nights. AE, DC, DISC, MC, V. Parking $15. MARTA: Midtown. Pets accepted with $100 nonrefundable fee. **Amenities:** Restaurant; exercise room; Jacuzzi; laundry service; coin-op washers and dryers. *In room:* A/C, TV, kitchen (w/fridge, microwave, stove, oven, dishwasher), hair dryer, high-speed Internet access.

**Shellmont Inn ★**   This charming two-story Victorian mansion looks like a fairy-tale house, its exterior embellished with ribbons, bows, garlands, and shells. The building, which dates to 1891, is on the National Register of Historic Places and is a city landmark. Innkeepers Ed and Debbie McCord have done a superb job of restoring the place, meticulously researching original paint colors, stencil designs, woodwork, and period furnishings, and reproducing them with 100% accuracy. Upstairs are the four guest rooms, which can be reserved individually or in pairs (as two-room units). On your way up, be sure to stop on the landing to check out the five-paneled stained-glass window, believed to be an authentic Tiffany. Rooms have elegant queen-size beds, leaded-glass or bay windows, and Oriental rugs on pine floors. Three rooms have whirlpool baths. The carriage house has a luxurious master bedroom, a modern bathroom with steam shower, a fully equipped kitchen, a living room, and a dressing area.

821 Piedmont Ave. NE (at Sixth St.), Atlanta, GA 30308. ✆ **404/872-9290.** Fax 404/872-5379. www. shellmont.com. 4 units, plus carriage house. $160 single; $185–$225 double; $215–$250 whirlpool suite; $245–$275 carriage house. Rates include full breakfast. Children 12 and under allowed in carriage house only. AE, DC, DISC, MC, V. Free parking. MARTA: Midtown. **Amenities:** Innkeepers/concierge services. *In room:* A/C, TV/DVD, Wi-Fi.

**Twelve Hotel ★★**   This posh, all-suite boutique hotel in Atlantic Station, the South-east's largest live/work/play community, will leave guests wishing they could move in for good. While the use of high ceilings and concrete in the large rooms lends an industrial feel, the creature comforts—including track lighting, in-room computers, and beautiful marble counters—will make you feel right at home. The property's high-tech system, known as GHOST (Guest Hotel Operating System Terminal), allows guests to order room service, make specific housekeeping requests, contact the concierge, request their car from valet, and more. Suites include full kitchens and large bathrooms.

Don't miss the opportunity to dine at the on-site restaurant, **Lobby at Twelve** (✆ **404/961-7370**), where diners can choose from an extensive wine list, including some rare vintages. Even breakfast is a treat—try the ricotta, fried egg, and arugula wrap cooked in the wood oven. See p. 109 for more details.

361 17th St., Atlanta, GA 30363. ✆ **404/961-1212.** Fax 404/961-1221. www.twelvehotels.com. 102 units. $209–$229 1-bedroom suite; $289–$389 2-bedroom suite. AE, MC, V. Valet parking $24. MARTA: Arts Station, then free shuttle to Atlantic Station. **Amenities:** Restaurant; bar; outdoor pool; fitness center; concierge; business center; room service; laundry service; dry cleaning. *In room:* A/C, TV, kitchen, coffeemaker, hair dryer, iron/ironing board, safe, computer w/high-speed Internet access.

---

## 3 BUCKHEAD

---

There's something for everyone in Buckhead—shoppers, foodies, history buffs, business travelers, and night owls will all find their niche. The neighborhood's offerings and the ease of getting around (a free community shuttle allows access to popular Buckhead hotels, shopping malls, and restaurants) make Buckhead the ideal place to stay. A word about dining: There are so many fine restaurants and nightspots in Buckhead that it's foolish to limit yourself to hotel fare. There are four notable exceptions, however—the Westin Buckhead Atlanta, Ritz-Carlton Buckhead, The Mansion on Peachtree, and InterContinental Buckhead all have outstanding restaurants. You'll find these establishments reviewed in chapter 6.

### VERY EXPENSIVE

**Doubletree Hotel Atlanta Buckhead ★**    Located within the Tower Place complex and designed with the business traveler in mind, this is also a good choice for leisure travelers, as it's so convenient to both Lenox Mall and Phipps Plaza. You'll be welcomed with Doubletree's signature freshly baked chocolate-chip cookies before you go up to your comfortable guest room, outfitted with an ergonomic work area and a large desk. All standard rooms come with a rich marble bathroom and an armchair with ottoman— perfect for putting your feet up after you've shopped, explored, or worked all day. The large units with king-size beds are especially desirable; other units are of average size, as are bathrooms. Suites offer parlor rooms with spacious sitting areas, leather couches, and a full dining-room ensemble for eight.

3342 Peachtree Rd. NE (btw. Lenox and Piedmont rds.), Atlanta, GA 30326. ✆ **800/833-TREE [8733]** or 404/231-1234. Fax 404/231-5236. www.doubletree1.hilton.com. 230 units. $209–$229 double. AE, DC, DISC, MC, V. Valet parking $25; self-parking $20. MARTA: Buckhead. **Amenities:** Restaurant; bar; access to nearby fitness center; airport shuttle; shuttle service (3-mile radius); room service. *In room:* A/C, TV, dataport, coffeemaker, hair dryer, iron, Wi-Fi.

**Grand Hyatt Atlanta ★**    The towering Grand Hyatt Atlanta offers a winning combination of 18th-century American architecture and Japanese flavor. The lobby overlooks a 9,000-square-foot garden with traditional Japanese plantings, rock formations, and splashing waterfalls created by noted Kyoto landscape architects. A collection of museum-quality Japanese art, spanning 4 centuries, is displayed throughout the hotel.

Guest rooms are furnished with 18th-century mahogany reproductions; the Japanese aesthetic appears in the form of crane-motif headboards, fresh orchids, and Japanese prints in black-lacquer frames. Both the rooms and bathrooms are spacious. Every luxury imaginable is provided at this plush establishment—you'll even find an umbrella in your closet.

3300 Peachtree Rd. (just east of Piedmont Rd.), Atlanta, GA 30305. ⑦ **800/233-1234** or 404/365-8100. Fax 404/233-5686. www.grandatlanta.hyatt.com. 438 units. $299–$324 double; Regency Club floor $349 double. AE, DC, DISC, MC, V. Valet parking $26; self-parking $19. MARTA: Buckhead. **Amenities:** 2 restaurants; bar; seasonal outdoor heated pool; fitness center; children's programs; sauna; concierge; airport shuttle; shuttle service (2-mile radius); business center; room service; massage; babysitting. *In room:* A/C, TV, fax, dataport, hair dryer, high-speed Internet access, Wi-Fi.

### InterContinental Buckhead ★★
An elegant luxury hotel designed to cater to the most discriminating guests, the $115-million InterContinental Buckhead is one of the hottest properties in Atlanta. Large luxury bathrooms feature soaking tubs and separate showers. This is a great choice if you're in town to take advantage of the city's high-end shopping at Phipps Plaza and Lenox Mall, both just a couple of blocks away. The Inter-Continental is also home to the fabulous 24-hour **Au Pied de Cochon** European brasserie (p. 120), with an extensive raw seafood bar and sinful desserts. The adjoining XO bar specializes in cognac and has live jazz Tuesday through Saturday evenings. A sushi lounge is available Monday through Saturday nights. The bar crowd can get rather rowdy late in the evening, as Buckhead is a hot spot for party-goers, so dine early if you're not up for the action, as the noise from the bar can get pretty intense.

3315 Peachtree Rd., Atlanta, GA 30326. ⑦ **404/946-9000.** Fax 404/946-9001. www.intercontinental. com. 422 units. $219–$389 double; $3,000 presidential suite. AE, DC, MC, V. Valet parking $26; self-parking $17. MARTA: Buckhead. **Amenities:** 24-hr. restaurant; bar; outdoor pool; health club; spa; Jacuzzi; concierge; business center; room service, same-day dry cleaning. *In room:* A/C, TV, fax, dataport, minibar, coffeemaker, hair dryer, iron/ironing board, safe, Wi-Fi.

### J. W. Marriott Hotel Buckhead ★
This luxurious Marriott property has an excellent location. Connected to the Lenox Square mall, it's across the street from MARTA and within walking distance of the posh Phipps Plaza mall and many good restaurants. It's popular with business travelers and die-hard shoppers alike. Rooms are charmingly furnished with Chippendale-style mahogany pieces; the picture windows afford great views of Buckhead or the downtown skyline. Lavish marble bathrooms are equipped with scales, terry-cloth robes, and hair dryers. Deluxe rooms have separate showers and bathtubs. Nineteen units have been modified for travelers with disabilities.

3300 Lenox Rd. NE (a few blocks east of Peachtree Rd. at E. Paces Ferry Rd.), Atlanta, GA 30326. ⑦ **800/613-2051** or 404/262-3344. Fax 404/262-8689. www.marriott.com. 371 units. From $289–$339 double. Weekend packages. AE, DC, DISC, MC, V. Valet parking $26; self-parking $19. MARTA: Lenox. **Amenities:** Restaurant; large indoor pool; health club w/Jacuzzi, steam room, and sauna; concierge; car-rental desk; airport shuttle; business center; room service; laundry service; same-day dry cleaning. *In room:* A/C, TV/VCR, minibar, fridge, coffeemaker, hair dryer, iron/ironing board, high-speed Internet access.

### The Mansion on Peachtree ★★★
Designed by noted American architect Robert A.M. Stern, the Mansion opened in 2008, offering travelers a whole new level of luxury and service (you even get your own butler!). Coffee and tea are delivered to your room upon request each morning. Rooms have $9^{1}/_{2}$-foot ceilings and are lush, with neutral velvets and satins. An LCD television is hidden behind a framed piece of art that retracts at the touch of a button to reveal the TV screen. All 31 suites have balconies.

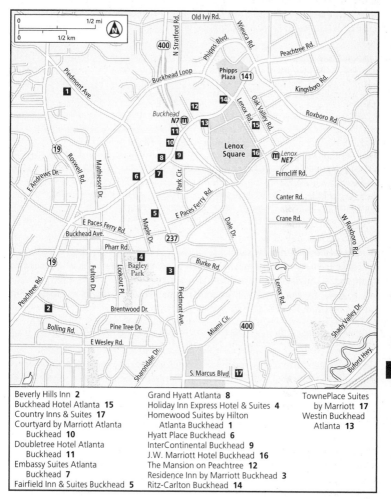

| | | |
|---|---|---|
| Beverly Hills Inn **2** | Grand Hyatt Atlanta **8** | TownePlace Suites |
| Buckhead Hotel Atlanta **15** | Holiday Inn Express Hotel & Suites **4** | by Marriott **17** |
| Country Inns & Suites **17** | Homewood Suites by Hilton | Westin Buckhead |
| Courtyard by Marriott Atlanta | Atlanta Buckhead **1** | Atlanta **13** |
| Buckhead **10** | Hyatt Place Buckhead **6** | |
| Doubletree Hotel Atlanta | InterContinental Buckhead **9** | |
| Buckhead **11** | J.W. Marriott Hotel Buckhead **16** | |
| Embassy Suites Atlanta | The Mansion on Peachtree **12** | |
| Buckhead **7** | Residence Inn by Marriott Buckhead **3** | |
| Fairfield Inn & Suites Buckhead **5** | Ritz-Carlton Buckhead **14** | |

Luxury extends to the spacious bathrooms, where you can soak in a deep tub or enjoy a marble steam shower. The hotel has two excellent restaurants, Tom Colicchio's **Craft Atlanta** and **NEO,** with a contemporary Italian-inspired menu (don't miss the foie gras at NEO). Onsite **29 Spa** by Lydia Mondavi offers exclusive treatments with grapeseed antioxidant products.

3376 Peachtree Rd., Atlanta, GA 30326. ℂ **888/767-3966** or 404/995-7500. Fax 404/995-7501. www. rwmansiononpeachtree.com. 127 units. $495 superior double; $695 executive suite; $4,200 presidential suite. AE, DC, DISC, MC, V. Valet parking $28. MARTA: Lenox. **Amenities:** 2 restaurants; bar; state-of-the-art health club and spa; large indoor pool; concierge; limo/shuttle service; business center; room service; laundry service; dry cleaning. *In room:* A/C, TV/DVD, dataport, minibar, hair dryer, safe, CD player, Internet access, Wi-Fi.

**Ritz-Carlton Buckhead** ★★★   The Ritz-Carlton Buckhead is the Rolls-Royce of Atlanta hotels. Every inch of this hotel oozes luxury, from the lobby to the public areas, now saturated in a color palette representative of a Southern garden. A $38-million renovation, completed in late 2008, brought the hotel to the next level, as well as doubled the number of suites. The rooms, all with large bay windows, are exquisitely decorated with armoires, luxuriously upholstered sofas or armchairs, and marble-topped desks. Bathrooms are roomy and contain the amenities you'd expect in a posh hotel. Twelve units are accessible to travelers with disabilities. Club Level guests can enjoy the comfortable Club Lounge, which serves complimentary meals, snacks, and cocktails.

**The Dining Room,** with Arnaud Berthelier as executive chef, is one of Atlanta's premier restaurants (p. 117) and is consistently rated among the finest in the country. The Lobby Lounge is the setting for afternoon English-style teas.

3434 Peachtree Rd. NE (at Lenox Rd.), Atlanta, GA 30326. ✆ **800/241-3333** or 404/237-2700. Fax 404/239-0078. www.ritzcarlton.com. 517 units. $369–$439 double; $469–$2,400 suite. Rollaway bed $30. Children 11 and under stay free in parent's room. Packages available. AE, MC, V. Valet parking $22; self-parking $15. Pets under 30 lbs. accepted with $250 nonrefundable deposit. MARTA: Buckhead or Lenox. **Amenities:** 3 restaurants; indoor pool; fitness center; Jacuzzi; sauna; concierge; business services; limo; airport shuttle; mall shuttle business center; room service; babysitting; laundry service; dry cleaning/pressing. *In room:* A/C, TV/DVD, minibar, coffeemaker, safe, high-speed Internet access, Wi-Fi.

**W Atlanta** ★★   Pampering the modern business or leisure traveler is the goal of the helpful staff at this boutique hotel. Though it's 20 minutes away from the shopping, dining, and nightlife of the famed Buckhead area, the W Atlanta is conveniently located to attractions such as Fernbank Museum of Natural History. Minimalist and very chic, the W's signature is its "Whatever/Whenever" service—and it provides just that. Where to dine in Buckhead? Any Braves tickets left for the game tonight? Ask and you shall receive—anything—just try it.

Guest rooms stand up well against the pricier Buckhead options; they feature sleek blond-wood furniture and chrome accents. Bathrooms are of average size. Visitors planning an extended stay might want to request a room with a full kitchen. *Note:* Perhaps the staff was in a partying mood during my visit, but the elevators were dark and noisy with loud, booming dance music. Corridors were also darkly lit.

111 Perimeter Center W, Atlanta, GA 30346. ✆ **770/396-6800.** Fax 770/399-5514. www.Whotels.com/Atlanta. 275 units. $285–$309 double; $675 suite. AE, DC, DISC, MC, V. Valet parking $15; self-parking $10. MARTA: Dunwoody. **Amenities:** 2 restaurants; bar; outdoor pool; health club; sauna; concierge; business center; room service; in-room massage; laundry service. *In room:* A/C, TV/VCR, hair dryer, iron/ironing board, safe, high-speed Internet access.

**Westin Buckhead Atlanta** ★★   If the Ritz-Carlton is the Rolls-Royce of Atlanta hotels, the Westin is the Ferrari. Its fresh Euro-modern design makes it a favorite among trendsetters visiting the city. In the heart of Buckhead between Lenox Square and the Atlanta Financial Center, it's a top choice among business travelers and serious shoppers.

The Westin Buckhead boasts postmodern European architecture, including a pristine white-tile exterior with a graceful curve. Interior spaces employ minimalist Bauhaus design elements and feature original works by renowned contemporary artists, including Warhol, Rauschenberg, Chagall, Schnabel, and Stella. Rooms are sleekly furnished with Beidermeier-style maple pieces with black lacquer accents, oversize desks with plug-ins for laptop computers, and ergonomic chairs. The Westin's signature "Heavenly Beds" are so cushy, you might miss breakfast. The corner king rooms are especially luxurious. Bathrooms are spacious.

The superb **Palm** restaurant serves one of the best lobster dinners in town (p. 119).

3391 Peachtree Rd. NE (btw. Lenox and Piedmont rds.), Atlanta, GA 30326. ℂ **404/365-0065.** Fax 404/365-8787. www.westin.com. 365 units. From $341–$411 double. Weekend rates. AE, DC, MC, V. Valet parking $28. MARTA: Buckhead. **Amenities:** Restaurant; large indoor pool; small, well-equipped health club and spa; sauna; concierge; shuttle service (2-mile radius); business center; salon; room service; massage. *In room:* A/C, TV/DVD, dataport, minibar, fridge, coffeemaker, hair dryer, iron/ironing board, safe, CD player, Wi-Fi.

# EXPENSIVE

**Buckhead Hotel Atlanta** ★   This former Sheraton has abundant services and facilities, plus a great location that's close to MARTA, Lenox Square, Phipps Plaza, and many restaurants. It's not quite as fancy as other hotels in the area, but it's still very stylish. Rooms are furnished with French country and 18th-century-reproduction mahogany pieces; some have four-poster or brass beds. Several units have balconies, and those with king-size beds have plush armchairs with ottomans as well. Eleven rooms are accessible to travelers with disabilities.

3405 Lenox Rd. NE (btw. Peachtree and E. Paces Ferry rds.), Atlanta, GA 30326. ℂ **800/241-8260** or 404/261-9250. Fax 404/848-7391. www.buckheadhotelatlanta.com. 369 units. $167 double. Extra person $20. Children 16 and under stay free in parent's room. AE, DC, DISC, MC, V. Self-parking $12. MARTA: Lenox. **Amenities:** Restaurant; bar; outdoor swimming pool; health club; concierge; shuttle service (3-mile radius); room service. *In room:* A/C, TV, dataport, coffeemaker, hair dryer, iron/ironing board, high-speed Internet access.

**Courtyard by Marriott Atlanta Buckhead** ★ (Value)   This newly renovated property provides a lot of bang for the buck. It's a favorite among business travelers, but anyone will enjoy it. The Courtyard has a terrific location, near everything that Buckhead has to offer, and within 2 blocks of the Atlanta Financial Center, the Lenox Square and Phipps Plaza shopping malls, and a MARTA station.

The rooms are large and bright, and the suites—perfect for families in town for a few days—come with a full-size pullout couch. Some units are equipped with whirlpool tubs that, surprisingly, are located in the bedroom rather than the bathroom. Ask for one of the end rooms, which are a little larger than the others. Eight units are equipped for travelers with disabilities.

Architects' drawings are on display throughout the hotel, with a large concentration in the aptly named Atlanta's Architect Grill and Bar.

3332 Peachtree Rd. NE (btw. Lenox and Piedmont rds.), Atlanta, GA 30326. ℂ **404/869-0818.** Fax 404/869-0939. www.marriott.com. 181 units. $179–$206 double; $249 suite. Children 17 and under stay free in parent's room. Higher rates during special events. AE, DC, DISC, MC, V. Valet parking $21; self-parking $18. MARTA: Buckhead. **Amenities:** Restaurant; bar; small heated indoor pool; exercise room and access to nearby health club; shuttle service (1-mile radius); room service; laundry service; coin-op washers and dryers. *In room:* A/C, TV, minibar, coffeemaker, hair dryer, iron/ironing board, high-speed Internet access, Wi-Fi, microwave.

**Embassy Suites Atlanta Buckhead** ★★   This all-suite hotel stacks up well against the more expensive hotels in the same area. A favorite with business travelers, the suite arrangement is also ideal for families, and the location can't be beat, with Lenox Square, Phipps Plaza, and many fine restaurants within walking distance. The Buckhead MARTA station is less than a block away.

Each elegantly appointed, 800-square-foot, two-room suite has a bed, pullout queen-size sofa, average-size bathroom with marble vanity, and separate sink in the bedroom. Although the entire hotel is accessible to travelers with disabilities—most of the participants

# The Vine That Ate the South

If you're visiting Georgia in the summer and traveling its interstate highways or country lanes, it's impossible to ignore the wild-looking vine growing along the roadside. That's kudzu, a frighteningly robust plant that upholsters billboards and fences, swallows up whole trees, and creeps eerily toward asphalt lanes, threatening everything in its path. It would surely blanket the pasturing cows if they were to stand still for a couple of days.

A native of the Far East, kudzu was introduced to the United States in the late 1800s and became treasured as a porch vine whose prolific tendrils would shoot straight up at the rate of a foot a day, quickly covering a roof or trellis, providing welcome shade from the midday sun. It was touted as an excellent forage crop (a crop used for grazing and for hay), and because it would grow almost anywhere, it was promoted as a means to control erosion.

By the turn of the 20th century, some horticulturists were having their doubts about kudzu, pointing out (to no avail) that the seemingly virtuous vine had the really bad habit of growing *everywhere* at an alarming rate. However, their warnings went unheeded, and the federal government continued to urge farmers to plant kudzu on worn-out farmland to keep it from washing away. It wasn't until the 1960s that the Soil Conservation Service stopped recommending its use. By then, the dense tangles had a lock on the landscape, not to mention barns and telephone poles.

Nobody's found a practical way to eradicate the stuff yet. Burning it won't work. Chemicals are impotent, unless each root and crown is hunted down relentlessly and sprayed and sprayed for years. And there are no natural predators, unless you count goats or other grazing animals—and there just aren't enough goats to go around. For now, the only thing to do is continue to hack away at the formidable vine—and remember to close our windows at night.

in the wheelchair division of the Peachtree Road Race stay here—10 of the suites are completely equipped for those with disabilities, and two have roll-in showers.

Two popular bonuses: the complimentary cooked-to-order breakfast, served in the 16-story atrium lobby (check out the waterfall!), and complimentary afternoon cocktails.

3285 Peachtree Rd. NW (1 block north of Piedmont Rd.), Atlanta, GA 30326. © **800/362-2779** or 404/261-7733. Fax 404/261-6857. www.embassysuites1.hilton.com. 317 units. $209 suite. Children 17 and under stay free in parent's room. Rates include full breakfast. Rates may be higher during special events, lower during holidays and summer. AE, DC, DISC, MC, V. Valet parking $19; self-parking $16. MARTA: Buckhead. **Amenities:** Restaurant; large outdoor pool/small indoor pool; exercise room; Jacuzzi; sauna; concierge; business center; shuttle service (1-mile radius); laundry service; dry cleaning; coin-op washers and dryers. *In room:* A/C, TV, dataport, fridge, coffeemaker, hair dryer, iron/ironing board, Wi-Fi, microwave.

## Homewood Suites by Hilton Atlanta Buckhead ★★ (Value) This well-run suite hotel has undergone a total renovation recently and is an excellent value, perfect for an extended business stay or a long weekend. Although you won't be within walking

distance of most of the Buckhead attractions or the MARTA station, there is a courtesy van that will take you anywhere within a 3-mile radius. The spacious and homey apartment-style suites have pullout sofas and large kitchen areas with full-size appliances, dishwashers, and toasters. Some of the two-bedroom suites can easily sleep eight people—a great option for large families. Four suites are accessible to travelers with disabilities. The hotel is set back from a busy street, so all units are quiet; ask for one overlooking the pool and patio.

In addition to a complimentary hot breakfast buffet, there is an evening social from Monday through Thursday with free beer, wine, and light snacks or meals.

3566 Piedmont Rd. (btw. Peachtree and Roswell rds.), Atlanta, GA 30305. ℂ **800/225-5466** or 404/365-0001. Fax 404/365-9888. www.homewoodsuites1.hilton.com. 92 suites. $179 1-bedroom suite; $209 2-bedroom suite. Children 17 and under stay free in parent's room. Rates include continental breakfast. Special packages available. AE, DC, DISC, MC, V. Free parking. MARTA: Buckhead; bus 59 stops in front of hotel. Pets accepted with $100 nonrefundable deposit. **Amenities:** Small heated outdoor pool; exercise room; concierge; shuttle service (3-mile radius); business center; secretarial services; laundry service; coin-op washers and dryers. *In room:* A/C, TV, dataport, kitchen, fridge, coffeemaker, iron/ironing board, safe, high-speed Internet access, microwave.

### Residence Inn by Marriott Atlanta Buckhead ★★ (Kids)

Recently renovated, this home-away-from-home was designed to meet the needs of travelers making extended visits, but it's great even if you're spending a single night. Staying here is like having your own apartment, with a private entrance and a large, fully equipped kitchen. Spacious accommodations include comfortable living-room areas; about half the suites have working fireplaces (during the winter, logs are available through the front desk). The most luxurious units are the duplex penthouses with vaulted ceilings, full dining-room/office areas, two standard-size bathrooms, and living-room fireplaces. Two rooms have been modified for travelers with disabilities. The hotel offers a free hot breakfast buffet daily and cocktail-hour parties Monday through Thursday. The location is good, near several excellent restaurants and not far from shopping and nightlife. There's a free shuttle service within a 3-mile radius.

2960 Piedmont Rd. NE (just south of Pharr Rd.), Atlanta, GA 30305. ℂ **800/331-3131** or 404/239-0677. Fax 404/262-9638. www.marriott.com. 136 suites. $169 studio suite; $219 penthouse suite. Discount for extended stay. AE, DC, DISC, MC, V. Free parking. MARTA: Bus 5 from Lindbergh station stops at Pharr and Piedmont rds., about half a block away. Pets accepted with $100 nonrefundable deposit. **Amenities:** Outdoor pool; fitness center; Jacuzzi; shuttle service (3-mile radius); dry cleaning; coin-op washers and dryers; grocery shopping. *In room:* A/C, TV, kitchen (w/fridge, stove, microwave), coffeemaker, hair dryer, iron/ironing board, high-speed Internet access.

### TownePlace Suites by Marriott Atlanta Buckhead ★

This good-value choice caters to both business and leisure travelers, with its extended-stay, all-suite layout. Attractively furnished, large suites were renovated in 2006. They include full kitchens with all the appliances you need for cooking and eating. Bathrooms are standard size. Guests can do their own laundry at no charge. Five rooms are accessible to travelers with disabilities. There isn't a restaurant on the property, but rates include a deluxe continental breakfast. Shuttle van service is within a 3-mile radius of the hotel.

800 Sidney Marcus Blvd. (btw. Lenox and Piedmont rds.), Atlanta, GA 30324. ℂ **404/949-4000.** Fax 404/949-4810. www.marriott.com. 142 units. $154–$179. Children 17 and under stay free in parent's room. Rates include continental breakfast. Higher rates during special events. AE, DC, DISC, MC, V. Free parking. MARTA: Lindbergh; bus 39 stops in front of hotel. Pets accepted with $75 nonrefundable deposit. **Amenities:** Large outdoor pool; small fitness center; shuttle service (3-mile radius); business center; washers and dryers. *In room:* A/C, TV, kitchen (w/microwave, dishwasher, stove), hair dryer, iron, Wi-Fi; high-speed Internet access.

**MODERATE**

**Beverly Hills Inn ★★**   British owner/host Mit Amin offers warm hospitality in this charming B&B, housed in a former women's apartment building from the 1920s. Located on a tree-lined residential street, this is a good spot for an extended stay, especially for families who prefer a B&B atmosphere. On the first floor is a parlor/library where a decanter of port is available all day. Another library is downstairs in the garden room, which has a sky-lit conservatory area filled with plants.

Spacious bedrooms are cheerful and attractive, decorated in a mix of antiques and collectibles. All are equipped with kitchenettes, and there's a private balcony through the French doors. A supermarket is within easy walking distance, should you want to cook in your room, though you may be tempted by the several good restaurants close by. Daily newspapers and local phone calls are complimentary; you'll also find a half-bottle of burgundy in your room upon arrival.

65 Sheridan Dr. NE (just off Peachtree Rd.), Atlanta, GA 30305. (✆) **800/331-8520** or 404/233-8520. Fax 404/233-8659. www.beverlyhillsinn.com. 18 units. $129 single/double/king; $149 balcony suite; $169 2-bedroom suite; $169 whirlpool suite. Extra person $10. Children 11 and under stay free in parent's room. Rates include deluxe continental breakfast. Discounts available for stays of a week or more. AE, DC, DISC, MC, V. Free parking. MARTA: Bus 23 stops at the corner of Peachtree St. and Sheridan Dr. Pets accepted with $125 nonrefundable deposit. **Amenities:** Access to nearby health club; fax/computer; free washers and dryers. *In room:* A/C, TV, kitchenette.

**Country Inns & Suites**   This hotel caters to business and leisure travelers who need a suite and are more interested in spending their money on Buckhead attractions than lodging. Each unit has a bed, a pullout sofa, and a kitchen with full-size appliances. Studios have one TV; suites have two. Outdoor grills are available. A nice touch is the guest supply closet from which visitors can get replacement toiletries and towels whenever they want. Five rooms are accessible to travelers with disabilities. Free coffee and cookies are available 24 hours a day. There's complimentary van service between the hotel and the MARTA Lindbergh station.

800 Sidney Marcus Blvd. (btw. Lenox and Piedmont rds.), Atlanta, GA 30324. (✆) **888/201-1746** or 404/949-4000. Fax 404/949-4010. www.countryinns.com/hotels/gabuckhd. 80 units. $109–$139 double; $189–$209 suite. Rates include continental breakfast. Lower rates for extended stays. AE, DC, DISC, MC, V. Free parking. MARTA: Lindbergh; bus 39 stops in front of hotel. **Amenities:** Outdoor pool; fitness center; shuttle service; concierge. *In room:* A/C, TV, fridge, coffeemaker, hair dryer, iron/ironing board, safe, high-speed Internet access, microwave.

**Fairfield Inn & Suites Buckhead**   A stone's throw from several excellent restaurants and close to everything else in upscale Buckhead, this is an economical choice for business and leisure visitors who are more interested in location than luxury. There's nothing fancy about the Fairfield Inn except for the surrounding neighborhood. The large rooms are well maintained and pleasant, with high ceilings. If you're in town for an extended stay, try to book one of the suites, which have fridges, microwaves, 32-inch TVs, DVD players, and CD players, along with king-size beds and sofabeds. Bathrooms are fairly standard, with the vanity and sink located in the bedroom. *Tip:* Rooms near the elevators and ice machines can be a little noisy, so ask for one away from those locations for a better night's sleep.

3092 Piedmont Rd. NE (btw. Peachtree and E. Paces Ferry rds.), Atlanta, GA 30326. (✆) **404/846-0900.** Fax 404/467-9878. www.marriott.com. 103 units. $139 double; $149 suite. Children 17 and under stay free in parent's room. Rates include deluxe continental breakfast. AE, DC, DISC, MC, V. Free parking. MARTA: Bus 5 from Lindbergh station. **Amenities:** Small indoor pool; Jacuzzi; fitness center; laundry service; dry cleaning; coin-op washers and dryers. *In room:* A/C, TV, coffeemaker, hair dryer, iron/ironing board, high-speed Internet access, microwave.

**Holiday Inn Express Hotel & Suites** ★ (Kids) (Value)   This is a good choice if you're looking for a great Buckhead location at less than the usual Buckhead price. It's within walking distance of several fine restaurants (Pricci is across the street; the Atlanta Fish Market is a few blocks away) and close to Buckhead nightlife. There's also good shopping in the area, as well as a park nearby for the kids. Accommodations include spacious one- and two-bedroom suites with a separate living room, queen-size beds, and a vanity/ dressing area with sink outside the average-size bathroom. Six suites are equipped for travelers with disabilities. The complimentary breakfast buffet is served in a bright room next to the lobby. Evening guest receptions are held Tuesday through Thursday. Complimentary shuttle service is within a 3-mile radius and to Lindbergh MARTA station.

505 Pharr Rd. (about a block off Piedmont Rd.), Atlanta, GA 30305. ℂ **800/972-2404** or 404/262-7880. Fax 404/262-3734. www.ichotelsgroup.com. 87 units. $119–$123 double; $129–$153 suite. Rates include full breakfast. Weekend rates and summer packages available. AE, DISC, MC, V. Free parking. MARTA: Bus 5 from Lindbergh station stops at Pharr and Piedmont rds., about a block away. Pets accepted. **Amenities:** Heated outdoor pool; exercise room; Jacuzzi; business center; shuttle service (3-mile radius); coin-op washers and dryers. *In room:* A/C, TV/VCR, full kitchen w/appliances, hair dryer, high-speed Internet access.

**Hyatt Place Buckhead** ★ (Value)   This rather plain-Jane all-suite hotel is the best bargain buy in the heart of Buckhead. Accommodations here are more like a studio or efficiency than a typical suite, with the "bedroom" separated from the rest of the unit by a low wall. A pullout couch offers some extra sleeping space. The bathrooms are standard size. A complimentary shuttle runs within a 3-mile radius of the hotel.

3242 Peachtree Rd. NE (at Piedmont Rd.), Atlanta, GA 30305. ℂ **877/774-6467** or 404/869-6161. Fax 404/869-6093. www.amerisuites.com. 172 suites. $124–$189 suite. Extra person $10. Children 17 and under stay free in parent's room. Rates include breakfast buffet. AE, DC, DISC, MC, V. Free parking. MARTA: Buckhead. **Amenities:** Small heated outdoor pool; exercise room; access to nearby health club; shuttle service (3-mile radius); business center; dry cleaning; coin-op washers and dryers. *In room:* A/C, TV/VCR, dataport in most suites, minibar, fridge, coffeemaker, hair dryer, iron/ironing board, microwave.

# 4 VIRGINIA HIGHLAND & INMAN PARK

Virginia Highland is a marvelous choice for visitors, as it's within easy walking distance of shops, galleries, and restaurants. The only problem is that there are few accommodations available because this is a mostly residential area. Nearby Inman Park, though not as convenient to attractions, is equally charming. You'll find the following property on the "Midtown Accommodations" map (p. 81).

## MODERATE

**King-Keith House Bed & Breakfast**   The lovely 1890 King-Keith home, built by hardware magnate George King, is in Inman Park, a neighborhood of Victorian homes that is on the National Register of Historic Places. Built in the Queen Anne style, the B&B boasts 12-foot ceilings and carved fireplaces, plus a huge wraparound porch. Beds range from double to king-size, and each room has a private bathroom. The large downstairs suite has a private entrance and sitting room with an extra twin bed. The one-room cottage, which is very spacious, has a king-size bed, sitting area, two-person Jacuzzi, and fireplace.

Coffee is delivered to your room every morning, and the complete breakfast might include French toast, homemade pancakes, or eggs cooked to order. The property is not far from the funky Little Five Points commercial district, the Martin Luther King, Jr., National Historic Site, the Jimmy Carter Presidential Library and Museum, and several restaurants.

889 Edgewood Ave. NE (at Waverly Way), Atlanta, GA 30307. ℂ **800/728-3879** or 404/688-7330. Fax 404/584-8408. www.kingkeith.com. 6 units, including a separate cottage. $110–$170 double; $190 suite; $210 cottage. No charge for up to 2 infants or toddlers. Rates include full breakfast. AE, DISC, MC, V. Free parking. MARTA: 2 blocks from Inman Park station. *In room:* A/C, TV, Wi-Fi.

# 5 DECATUR/LAKE CLAIRE

Originally a streetcar suburb of Atlanta, the quaint and quiet Lake Claire neighborhood is becoming a popular residential area. Don't waste your time looking for the namesake lake—it doesn't exist.

## MODERATE

**Laurel Hill Bed & Breakfast** This B&B is actually two individual houses, and named for the laurel that grows wild on the property. The venture is the result of a lot of hard work by innkeeper Dave Hinman, who lived in one of the homes for about 15 years. When the house next door—a mirror image of his own—became available, he purchased it and renovated both English Tudors to create this bed-and-breakfast. Winding paths lead up through the property to secluded and tranquil seating areas—perfect places for reflecting quietly and enjoying a relaxing moment.

Individually prepared full American breakfasts are served each morning on an open schedule, beginning with the first request and ending with a relaxed last call at 11am. Baked goods, spring water, coffee, and tea are available throughout the day. The dining environment is laid-back and enjoyable, and Dave seems to have a knack for knowing when you'd like to chat and when you just want to enjoy some time alone. (p. 81 for "Midtown Accommodations" map).

1992 McClendon Ave., Atlanta, GA 30307. ℂ **404/377-3217.** Fax 404/262-7618. www.laurelhillbandb. com. 5 units. $109–$119 double Mon–Thurs; $119–$159 double Fri–Sun. Rates include hot breakfast. AE, DISC, MC, V. Free parking. MARTA: Eastlake Rail station is half a mile away. *In room:* A/C, TV, hair dryer.

## INEXPENSIVE

**Garden House Bed & Breakfast** Decatur is one of the fastest growing areas in Atlanta, but it's still severely lacking in places to stay. This bed-and-breakfast, while offering only one suite (there's another bedroom available in a pinch), is a delightful, homey lodging owned by Decatur natives Rhoda and Doug Joyner, who have enjoyed more than 66 years in this city. The couple began their venture in 1996, when Atlanta was preparing to host the Centennial Olympic Games and accommodations were at a premium.

Guests are invited to relax on the spacious screened porch overlooking gardens and a pond with a waterfall. Refreshments, a stocked library, a smoke-free environment, and fresh flowers all add to the experience. The hosts will cook basically whatever their guests prefer, from a full Southern breakfast, with eggs, grits, sausage, and biscuits, to a more gourmet selection of blintzes, quiche, and home-baked walnut wheat bread. They're also able to accommodate special health requirements, such as low-fat or low-sodium diets.

135 Garden Lane, Decatur, GA 30030. ℂ **404/377-3057.** www.gardenhousebedandbreakfastdecatur. com. 1 unit. $90 double; $86 double for 2 or more nights. Rates include full breakfast. MC, V. Free parking. MARTA: Decatur. *In room:* A/C, TV.

# 6 STONE MOUNTAIN PARK

Stone Mountain Park, just 16 miles east of downtown Atlanta, is a recreation area with 3,200 acres of lakes and wooded parkland. It is a major tourist destination, visited by more than 4 million people annually. *Note:* There's an $8 parking fee upon entering the park.

## EXPENSIVE

**Marriott Evergreen Conference Resort** (Kids)  Geared primarily to business groups, Evergreen is also a good choice for vacationing families who want to take advantage of the activities in Stone Mountain Park. A turreted stucco lakefront "castle," Evergreen is nestled in a fragrant pine forest. The large, luxuriously appointed rooms have balconies; lakeview rooms are available. The suites boast a lovely, spacious bedroom; however, those who wind up on the uncomfortable pullout couch in the living room may be in for a restless night. Bathrooms are standard size.

4021 Lakeview Dr., Stone Mountain Park, Stone Mountain, GA 30086. (✆ **770/879-9900.** Fax 770/465-3264. www.evergreenresort.com. 336 units. $139–$299 double; $349 suite. No charge for extra person, but maximum of 5 people allowed in any room or suite. Children 17 and under stay free in parent's room. Packages available. AE, DC, DISC, MC, V. Free parking. **Amenities:** Restaurant; 3 pools (indoor/outdoor/kiddie); 2 18-hole golf courses; 16 tennis courts; fitness center; Jacuzzi; concierge; airport shuttle; business services; room service. *In room:* A/C, TV, dataport, fridge, coffeemaker, hair dryer, iron/ironing board.

**Stone Mountain Inn** (Kids) (Value)  This charming inn, across the street from the tennis venue built for the 1996 Olympics, is managed by Marriott and housed in a two-story, white-colonnade brick building that wraps around a central courtyard. Rooms are lovely, featuring Chippendale-reproduction furnishings; most have large vanity/dressing areas and spacious parlors. Honeymoon suites have king-size, four-poster beds. Almost all of the units have courtyard-facing balconies or patios with rocking chairs. Five rooms are accessible to travelers with disabilities. Tickets for all park attractions are sold at the inn.

1058 Robert E. Lee Dr., Stone Mountain Park, Stone Mountain, GA 30086. (✆ **770/469-3311.** Fax 770/876-5009. www.marriott.com. 92 units. $89–$259 double (rates vary seasonally). Children 11 and under stay free in parent's room. Honeymoon, tennis, golf, and other packages available. AE, DC, MC, V. Free parking. **Amenities:** Restaurant; outdoor pool; business services; shuttle service; coin-op washers and dryers. *In room:* A/C, TV.

## A CAMPGROUND

**Stone Mountain Family Campground**  Nestled in the woods, this large campground with sections for pop-ups, RVs, and tents is a great place to stay. The area has many sites overlooking the lake, especially in the tent section. All sites have barbecue grills, and picnic tables are scattered throughout the area. Public facilities include a dining pavilion, playgrounds, laundries, and showers. The park's beach is close by, and the swimming pool is new. Pets are permitted if kept on a leash. This is a popular place, so be sure to call ahead. You may reserve a spot up to 90 days before you stay; all reservations must be made at least 1 week in advance.

Stone Mountain Park, P.O. Box 778, Stone Mountain, GA 30086. (✆ **800/385-9807** or 770/498-5710. Fax 770/413-5082. www.stonemountainpark.com. $25–$60 per night, depending on type of site and time of year. Rates cover 2 adults and 4 children; additional guests $2 per night. Children 11 and under stay free. AE, DISC, MC, V. Pets accepted. **Amenities:** Outdoor pool; coin-op washers and dryers; barbecue grills; showers.

# 7 DRUID HILLS/EMORY UNIVERSITY

Though it's not a happening section of town in terms of restaurants or attractions, this area, east of Midtown and Buckhead, offers good value for your hotel dollar. And if you have a car, the lodgings listed below are only about a 10-minute drive from the center of things.

## MODERATE

### Courtyard by Marriott Atlanta Executive Park/Emory
This limited-service, moderately priced lodging is slightly outside the usual tourist areas, but it's close to town and convenient to I-85—making it popular with business travelers. Don't expect a spartan, no-frills atmosphere; accommodations feature large desks and sizable dressing-room areas. Suites have full-size pullout sofas, extra phones, and TVs. Eight rooms are accessible to guests with disabilities. There's also airport shuttle service.

1236 Executive Park Dr. (off N. Druid Hills Rd.), Atlanta, GA 30329. © **404/728-0708.** Fax 404/636-4019. www.marriott.com. 145 units. $129 double; $169 suite. AE, DC, DISC, MC, V. Free parking. MARTA: Bus 8 from Brookhaven station. **Amenities:** Restaurant; bar; outdoor pool; exercise room; Jacuzzi; airport shuttle; room service; dry cleaning; coin-op washers and dryers. *In room:* A/C, TV, dataport, coffeemaker, hair dryer, high-speed Internet access.

### Emory Inn
Inspired by the architectural design of Frank Lloyd Wright, this delightful hotel, owned by Emory University, is popular with visitors to Emory and the nearby Centers for Disease Control and Prevention. Rooms, furnished with Early American–style knotty-pine pieces, are attractively decorated. Nine units are accessible to travelers with disabilities. Guests enjoy free use of a vast fitness complex on the university campus, with a heated indoor pool, 12 tennis courts lit for night play, basketball courts, indoor track, racquetball, and a full complement of Nautilus equipment. There's also complimentary shuttle service to the campus and hospital, and an airport shuttle on request.

1641 Clifton Rd. NE (btw. Briarcliff and N. Decatur rds.), Atlanta, GA 30329. © **800/933-6679** or 404/712-6700. Fax 404/712-6701. www.emoryconferencecenter.com. 107 units. From $149 double. AE, DC, DISC, MC, V. Free parking. MARTA: Bus 6 Emory stops in front of the hotel. **Amenities:** Restaurant; outdoor pool; access to campus fitness complex w/heated indoor pool; Jacuzzi; airport shuttle; campus/hospital shuttle; room service; coin-op washers and dryers. *In room:* A/C, TV, coffeemaker, hair dryer, iron.

# 8 DULUTH

Located in Gwinnett County, one of the fastest growing counties in the country, Duluth manages to retain its small-town charm just minutes from the hustle and bustle of the big city. You'll find lots of shopping here, including the Mall of Georgia and Gwinnett Place Mall. Duluth's Buford Highway is also home to an incredible variety of ethnic restaurants, which draw diners from Atlanta looking for everything from Korean to Vietnamese to Caribbean cuisine.

## MODERATE

### Courtyard by Marriott Atlanta Gwinnett Mall
Rooms here are nicely appointed with cherry furnishings, including a dining table and workspace. Both rooms and bathrooms are of average size. Some units have a patio overlooking the pool area. The

Courtyard Cafe, an on-site restaurant, serves an affordable breakfast buffet each morning. For snacks or beverages, the Market is always open. For added convenience, the comfortable new business center provides a computer and laptop stations, along with a printer and high-speed Internet access. The property is in close proximity to the Mall of Georgia on I-85.

3550 Venture Pkwy., Duluth, GA 30096. © **770/476-4666.** Fax 770/623-0198. www.marriott.com. 146 units. $139 double; $154 suite. AE, MC, V. Free parking. **Amenities:** Restaurant; outdoor pool; fitness center; Jacuzzi; coin-op washers and dryers. *In room:* A/C, TV, fridge, coffeemaker, hair dryer, iron/ironing board, high-speed Internet access, microwave.

## INEXPENSIVE

**Candlewood Suites**   Perfect for families or business travelers on the go, Candlewood Suites boasts spacious rooms. An oversize workspace doubles as the kitchen table, dividing the full-size kitchen from the living room. Kick back in a comfy recliner and watch a DVD—which you can borrow free of charge from the front desk—while you munch on popcorn purchased from the on-site convenience store (which is open 24 hr. a day and operates on the honor system). Even the bathrooms are big here. If the weather is nice, you can cook dinner outside, on the grill under the gazebo, for a change of pace.

3665 Shackleford Rd., Duluth, GA 30096. © **678/380-0414.** Fax 678/380-0413. www.ichotelsgroup.com. 122 units. $77–$103 suite. AE, MC, V. Free parking. Pets accepted with $75 nonrefundable fee for stays of 14 days or less. **Amenities:** Fitness center; coin-op washers and dryers. *In room:* A/C, TV, kitchen, coffeemaker, hair dryer, iron/ironing board, high-speed Internet access.

# 9  AIRPORT

There are more than three dozen hotels near the airport, most of them well-known chains. If you're flying out very early or in very late, a room in this area can be quite convenient. Although most airport-hotel guests are business travelers, it's not out of the question for leisure travelers to choose accommodations here. Weekend rates are often very low, and many of the hotels offer free shuttles to the Airport MARTA station, making it easy to reach other parts of the city. Buckhead, for instance, is about 35 minutes away by MARTA rail. The hotels listed below are three of the finest, but there are numerous other chains in the area.

## EXPENSIVE

**Hilton Atlanta Airport ★**   Mercifully, this airport hotel is not under the normal flight pattern. That, and its triple-paned windows, makes it quieter than many hotels, especially the less expensive ones. (For the *most* quiet location, ask for a room with a city view.) The rooms are a good size, with tasteful contemporary decor and one king-size or two double beds. The bathrooms have generous vanities, though the sound of the toilet flush will make you think you're already on the plane. For an excellent value, ask for one of the Executive Corner rooms, which are only $20 more than the standard units. They're twice as big, though, and are spacious enough to accommodate a sofa and two easy chairs in the sitting area. The bathrooms have separate showers and garden tubs. Suites are quite large and luxurious. Twenty-five of the standard rooms have been modified for guests with disabilities. There's a complimentary airport shuttle.

1031 Virginia Ave. (at I-85, exit 73A), Atlanta, GA 30354. © **800/HILTONS [445-8667]** or 404/767-9000. Fax 404/768-0185. www.hilton.com. 503 units. $199–$219 double. Rates may be lower during summer, higher during special events. Weekend packages available. AE, DC, DISC, MC, V. Valet parking $14; self-parking $10. **Amenities:** 2 restaurants; sports bar; outdoor pool; small indoor heated pool; lit tennis court; state-of-the-art fitness center; Jacuzzi; concierge; airport shuttle; business center; salon; room service; laundry service. *In room:* A/C, TV, dataport, minibar, coffeemaker, hair dryer, iron/ironing board.

**Renaissance Concourse Hotel ★**   If you're an airplane buff or you just travel with one, this is the ticket. Built on the site of an old airport terminal in 1992, the Renaissance is literally on the edge of the runway. Each of the renovated guest rooms opens onto the beautiful 11-story interior atrium. Half the rooms also open onto the runway, so you can step out on your balcony and watch the planes take off and land; on the other side, rooms have views of the downtown skyline. It sounds noisy, but the soundproofing is more than adequate, and back in your room, you'll hardly know you're at the airport. The rooms themselves are luxuriously decorated, light, open, and quite large, with spacious bathrooms. Twenty rooms have been specially modified for travelers with disabilities; 19 have roll-in showers. Guests use the complimentary airport shuttle.

1 Hartsfield Center Pkwy., Atlanta, GA 30354. © **404/209-9999.** Fax 404/305-2343. www.marriott.com. 387 units. $159–$215 double. Higher rates during special events. Weekend packages available. AE, DC, DISC, MC, V. Valet parking $10; self-parking $6. **Amenities:** Restaurant; medium outdoor pool; large indoor heated pool; fitness center w/steam rooms and sauna; Jacuzzi; concierge; airport shuttle; business center w/audiovisual support and secretarial services; room service; laundry service. *In room:* A/C, TV, dataport, minibar, coffeemaker, hair dryer, iron/ironing board.

**Sheraton Gateway Hotel Atlanta Airport**   If you're looking for convenience when flying in or out of Atlanta, this is a great location from which to base yourself. Half a mile from the airport—and just 10 minutes from downtown—Sheraton Gateway boasts beautiful marble bathrooms and very comfortable Sheraton Sweet Sleeper beds. The double rooms and bathrooms are of average size. Grab a meal at the 1900 Grill or the 1900 Bar, both serving tasty American fare. Amenities here are similar to those at nearby properties, including AmeriSuites, Hampton Inn, and Holiday Inn Express. There's a complimentary airport shuttle.

1900 Sullivan Rd., Atlanta, GA 30337. © **770/997-1100.** Fax 770/991-5906. www.sheraton.com. 395 units. $159–$269 double; $294–$375 club floor. AE, MC, V. Free parking. **Amenities:** Restaurant; bar; indoor/outdoor pools; Jacuzzi; fitness center; airport shuttle; business center; room service; laundry service. *In room:* A/C, TV, coffeemaker, hair dryer, iron/ironing board, video games, high-speed Internet access.

## 10 SOUTH OF TOWN

### EXPENSIVE

**Serenbe Southern Country Inn ★** (Finds) (Kids)   This retreat is on 284 acres of farmland, 32 miles southwest of Atlanta, amid rolling meadows, horse pastures, verdant woodlands, and fields of sage. Children play in a treehouse, pet the baby animals, or feed the chickens. Activities include croquet, occasional hayrides, marshmallow roasts around a bonfire, fishing from a well-stocked lake, hiking along trails dotted with streams and waterfalls, and moonlit canoe rides.

The 94-year-old main house includes the dining room, where you'll enjoy a hearty breakfast—perhaps cheese grits, baked ham, fresh eggs, fried green tomatoes, and biscuits. The rooms—all with private bathrooms, one with a Jacuzzi tub—are charming and unpretentious, with unique features such as knotty-pine floors strewn with rag rugs, antique furnishings, a bed piled high with decorative pillows, and lace-curtained windows. One room has been modified for guests with disabilities. The lake house has four bedrooms with private entrances and private bathrooms. There's also a communal kitchen with an unstocked fridge, along with a barbecue grill. Rates include a full farm breakfast, afternoon tea, and bedtime sweets.

10950 Hutcheson Ferry Rd., Palmetto, GA 30268. ℂ **770/463-2610.** Fax 770/463-4472. www.serenbe. com. 18 units. $160–$385. Rates include full breakfast. No credit cards. Free parking. Call ahead for directions. **Amenities:** Pool w/Jacuzzi; exercise room; bicycles; fax/dataport; massage; babysitting; washers and dryers. *In room:* A/C, coffeemaker, hair dryer, iron/ironing board.

# Where to Dine

Atlanta's contributions to gastronomy were once mostly limited to Coca-Cola and Varsity hot dogs. Not so today. In the last decade, the dining scene has exploded, and Atlanta has emerged as a sophisticated restaurant town, where establishments have veered away from uninventive American fare and inauthentic down-home Southern cooking (happily, there are still lots of places to feast on authentic down-home Southern cooking).

Innovative chefs, who once left Atlanta for the great food capitals, have brought their expertise and ideas back to the New South. As a result, there's now a little bit of everything available—from all around the world. You can munch on pierogi in East Atlanta, nibble fragrant Thai basil rolls in Virginia Highland, dig into *osso buco* in Buckhead, and so on. There's French cuisine as authentic as any you'll find on the Left Bank, and Italian pasta that tastes like it came from Naples.

The Colonnade and Mary Mac's Tea Room, two bastions of tradition, still turn out some of the best Southern food you'll

ever put in your mouth, but the current trend in many kitchens is to take heirloom Southern recipes and give them a contemporary twist. So pork chops might be stuffed with eggplant and andouille sausage, collard greens sautéed and seasoned with balsamic vinegar, and comfy, familiar grits spiked with Stilton cheese.

The audience for all these culinary concoctions is huge. Atlantans love to eat out, spending half their annual food budget on dining away from home. The debut of a new restaurant is more eagerly awaited than the opening of a new play, and Atlantans avidly peruse the local newspapers to find out about the hottest names in the food game.

Restaurants listed below are divided first by area, then by price, using the following guide: **Very Expensive:** more than $30 per dinner main course; **Expensive:** $20 to $30 per dinner main course; **Moderate:** $10 to $20 per dinner main course; **Inexpensive:** less than $10 per dinner main course.

Valet parking is listed where applicable.

## 1 RESTAURANTS BY CUISINE

### Asian
Bluepointe ★★★ (Buckhead, $$$$, p. 114)
Doc Chey's Noodle House (Virginia Highland & Inman Park, $, p. 131)
Spice Market ★ (Midtown, $$$$, p. 106)

### Bakery/Cafe
Corner Café/Buckhead Bread Company ★ (Buckhead, $, p. 125)

### Barbecue
Fat Matt's Rib Shack (Midtown, $, p. 112)

### Brazilian
Fogo de Chão ★ (Buckhead, $$$$, p. 118)

### Chinese
Little Szechuan (Doraville, $$, p. 136)

Key to Abbreviations: $$$$ = Very Expensive   $$$ = Expensive   $$ = Moderate   $ = Inexpensive

## Contemporary Southern
Horseradish Grill ★ (Buckhead, $$$, p. 121)
South City Kitchen ★ (Midtown, $$$$, p. 105)

## Continental
Pano's & Paul's ★★ (Buckhead, $$$$, p. 119)
Swan Coach House (Buckhead, $$, p. 125)

## Country French
Floataway Café ★★ (Decatur, $$$, p. 133)

## Eclectic
Aria ★★ (Buckhead, $$$$, p. 114)
Brick Store Pub (Decatur, $, p. 135)
R. Thomas Deluxe Grill ★★ (Midtown, $$, p. 111)

## European
Ecco ★★★ (Midtown, $$, p. 109)
Eno ★★ (Midtown, $$$, p. 106)

## European Provincial
Babette's Café ★★ (Virginia Highland & Inman Park, $$, p. 127)

## French
Anis Café & Bistro ★ (Buckhead, $$$, p. 120)
Au Pied de Cochon ★★ (Buckhead, $$$, p. 120)
The Dining Room ★★★ (Buckhead, $$$$, p. 117)
French American Brasserie ★★ (Downtown, $$$, p. 103)
Joël ★★★ (Buckhead, $$$$, p. 118)

## Fusion
Joël ★★★ (Buckhead, $$$$, p. 118)

## Greek
Athens Pizza House (Decatur, $, p. 135)
Avra Greek Tavern (Midtown, $$, p. 109)
Kyma ★★ (Buckhead, $$$, p. 122)

## Ice Cream
Jake's Ice Cream & Sorbets (Decatur, $, p. 135)

## Italian
Floataway Café ★★ (Decatur, $$$, p. 133)
NEO (Buckhead, $$$$, p. 118)
Pasta da Pulcinella ★ (Midtown, $$, p. 111)
Pasta Vino (Buckhead, $$, p. 124)
Pricci ★ (Buckhead, $$, p. 124)
Sotto Sotto ★★ (Virginia Highland & Inman Park, $$, p. 128)
Veni Vidi Vici ★★ (Midtown, $$, p. 112)
Vita ★ (Midtown, $$$, p. 106)

## Mediterranean
Anis Café & Bistro ★ (Buckhead, $$$, p. 120)
The Dining Room ★★★ (Buckhead, $$$$, p. 117)
Eno ★★ (Midtown, $$$, p. 106)

## Mexican
Raging Burrito (Decatur, $, p. 136)
Willy's Mexicana Grill ★ (Downtown, $, p. 104)

## New American
Bacchanalia ★★★ (Midtown, $$$$, p. 105)
Bluepointe ★★★ (Buckhead, $$$$, p. 114)
Buckhead Diner (Buckhead, $$, p. 123)
Canoe ★★ (Vinings, $$$, p. 132)
City Grill ★★★ (Downtown, $$$, p. 103)
Flying Biscuit Cafe ★ (Virginia Highland & Inman Park, $, p. 132)
One Midtown Kitchen ★ (Midtown, $$, p. 110)
Toulouse ★ (Buckhead, $$, p. 125)
Two Urban Licks ★★ (Virginia Highland & Inman Park, $$$, p. 127)
Warren City Club ★ (Virginia Highland, $$, p. 131)
Watershed ★ (Decatur, $$$, p. 134)

Woodfire Grill ★★ (Midtown, $$$, p. 108)

**Pizza**

Athens Pizza House (Decatur, $, p. 135)
Fellini's Pizza (Buckhead, $, p. 126)
Pasta Vino (Buckhead, $$, p. 124)

**Seafood**

Atlanta Fish Market ★★ (Buckhead, $$$, p. 120)
Chops/Lobster Bar ★★ (Buckhead, $$$$, p. 116)
New York Prime ★★ (Buckhead, $$$$, p. 119)
The Palm ★★ (Buckhead, $$$$, p. 119)
Prime ★★ (Buckhead, $$$, p. 123)

**Southern/Regional**

Colonnade ★ (Midtown, $, p. 112)
Home (Buckhead, $$$, p. 121)
Lobby at Twelve ★★ (Midtown, $$, p. 109)
Mary Mac's Tea Room ★ (Midtown, $$, p. 110)
Wisteria (Virginia Highland, $$$, p. 127)

**Southwestern**

Nava ★★ (Buckhead, $$$, p. 122)
Taqueria del Sol ★ (Midtown, $, p. 113)

**Spanish**

La Fonda Latina (Buckhead, $, p. 126)

**Steak**

Bone's ★★★ (Buckhead, $$$$, p. 116)
Chops/Lobster Bar ★★ (Buckhead, $$$$, p. 116)
New York Prime ★★ (Buckhead, $$$$, p. 119)

The Palm ★★ (Buckhead, $$$$, p. 119)
Prime ★★ (Buckhead, $$$, p. 123)

**Sushi/Japanese**

Atlanta Fish Market ★★ (Buckhead, $$$, p. 120)
Magic Fingers Sushi ★★ (Midtown, $$, p. 110)
Prime ★★ (Buckhead, $$$, p. 123)

**Tapas**

Pura Vida (Virginia Highland & Inman Park, $$, p. 128)

**Thai**

Surin of Thailand ★ (Virginia Highland & Inman Park, $$, p. 131)
Tamarind Seed Thai Bistro ★★ (Midtown, $$, p. 111)
Thai Chili ★ (Decatur, $$, p. 133)

**Traditional American**

Blue Ridge Grill ★ (Buckhead, $$$$, p. 114)
Bone's ★★★ (Buckhead, $$$$, p. 116)
Buckhead Diner (Buckhead, $$, p. 123)
George's Restaurant and Bar (Virginia Highland & Inman Park, $, p. 132)
Houston's ★ (Buckhead, $$, p. 123)
Murphy's ★★★ (Virginia Highland & Inman Park, $$, p. 128)
OK Café (Buckhead, $$, p. 124)
Pano's & Paul's ★★ (Buckhead, $$$$, p. 119)
Swan Coach House (Buckhead, $$, p. 125)
The Varsity (Downtown, $, p. 103)
The Vortex (Midtown, $, p. 113)
Woody's Famous Philadelphia Cheesesteaks (Midtown, $, p. 113)

---

## 2 DOWNTOWN

---

Your restaurant choices in downtown Atlanta range from the ultra-elegant City Grill to the world's largest drive-in.

## EXPENSIVE

**City Grill ★★★** NEW AMERICAN    One of Atlanta's most opulent restaurants, City Grill is *the* place for downtown power lunches and couples celebrating a special occasion. The two-level restaurant is located in the lavishly refurbished Hurt Building, and you enter through a marble-walled rotunda with a rosette-and-gold-leaf-adorned dome. The setting is quite grand, but the atmosphere is more relaxed than you might expect, and the dress code accommodates everything from jeans to tuxedos.

Chef Michael Broome specializes in regional American fare straight up with a twist, and primarily uses organic ingredients grown locally. Dishes range from a hickory-grilled, fig-stuffed lamb to a Cornish game hen with pecan-herb dressing. Offering the best wine list in town, City Grill's extensive cellar is stocked with more than 400 wines (most of them French and Californian) in all price ranges, with about 20 selections available by the glass. Pre-theater dining is available.

50 Hurt Plaza (at Edgewood Ave.). (ⓒ) **404/524-2489.** www.citygrillatlanta.com. Reservations recommended. Lunch items $10–$19; dinner items $18–$42. AE, DC, DISC, MC, V. Mon–Fri 11:30am–2pm; Mon–Sat 5–10pm. MARTA: Peachtree Center or Five Points.

**French American Brasserie ★★** FRENCH AMERICAN    New in 2008, FAB—as it's better known—has added some much-needed fine dining to the downtown area. Previously Brasserie Le Coze, FAB serves classic French cuisine and American chops. Take the grand spiral staircase to the canopied rooftop terrace for a great view of the city's skyline, while you enjoy a cocktail and unwind.

Executive chef Stephen Sharp learned to cook in his grandmother's kitchen, but has worked elsewhere in the city, including Four Seasons Park 75 and the Oceanaire Seafood Room. Sharp likes to prepare simple food with complex layers, remaining true to a brasserie concept. Of note is the Le Plateau for two or four people, brimming with oysters, clams, mussels, king crab, shrimp, and lobster with sauces. Colorado lamb loin chops are also a sure bet. The menu is vast, so take your time ordering.

30 Ivan Allen Jr. Blvd. (ⓒ) **404/266-1440.** www.fabatlanta.com. Reservations recommended. Lunch items $14–$30; dinner items $15–$45. AE, DC, DISC, MC, V. Mon–Thurs 11:30am–10pm; Fri–Sat 11:30am–11pm. MARTA: Civic Center.

## INEXPENSIVE

**The Varsity (Kids)** TRADITIONAL AMERICAN    Atlanta grew up around the Varsity, the world's largest drive-in restaurant, opened in 1928 by Frank Gordy (today all six locations are run by his daughter Nancy Simms). This fast-food mecca's greasy feasts are an essential element of the Atlanta experience, and the Varsity draws more celebrities than any other restaurant in town. A 150-foot stainless-steel counter is the hub of the operation, behind which red-shirted cooks and counter people rush out thousands of orders. It's a constant chorus of "What'll ya have? What'll ya have?" with customer responses translated into such esoteric orders as "walk a dog sideways, bag of rags" (a hot dog with onions on the side and potato chips). It takes 200 employees to process the ton of onions, 2,500 pounds of potatoes, 2 miles of hot dogs, 300 gallons of chili, and 5,000 fried pies consumed here by throngs of hungry customers each day.

Order up a slaw dog or a couple of chili burgers (they're only 2 oz. each), with fries, onion rings, and a frosted orange (a creamy frozen orange drink). Barbecued pork, homemade chicken salad, and deviled-egg sandwiches are other options. And since none of this is health food (though it's all fresh and made from scratch), don't resist the fried apple

## (Kids) Family-Friendly Restaurants

**Doc Chey's Noodle House** (p. 131)   This casual neighborhood favorite has two special children's entrees, but there are also several other rice and noodle dishes that will appeal to the younger set.

**Fellini's Pizza** (p. 126)   The New York–style pizza served here is a treat that will please everyone, and it's available by the slice. Salads are also superb, and you can sit outside if you choose.

**Houston's** (p. 123)   There are always lots of families in Houston's, where there's prime rib for the grown-ups, burgers for the kids, and reasonable prices that won't bust the budget. It's casual, but still a good place to take the family for a special occasion.

**OK Café** (p. 124)   OK Café's classic comfort food and jukebox are sure to please kids of all ages.

**Pasta Vino** (p. 124)   Do kids like this place? One 3-year-old from the neighborhood insisted on having his birthday party here so he could have his favorite food—a slice of white-cheese pizza with pesto. There's plenty for parents, too, including fresh veal, seafood, and excellent lasagna.

**Thai Chili** (p. 133)   While there isn't a children's menu here, the restaurant is very kid-friendly and makes families feel right at home, with dishes cooked to order and without any spice at all, if your kids can't take the heat.

**The Varsity** (p. 103)   The greasy feasts at the world's largest drive-in restaurant are big kid-pleasers.

or peach pie a la mode for dessert. The Varsity's interior is spartan, with seating in large, windowed rooms with Formica tables. Big TVs are always on.

61 North Ave. (at Spring St.). ☏ **404/881-1706.** Reservations not accepted. All items under $7. MC, V. Sun–Thurs 10am–11:30pm; Fri–Sat 10am–12:30am. Closed Thanksgiving and Christmas. MARTA: North Ave.

**Willy's Mexicana Grill** ★   MEXICAN   Voted Atlanta's best burritos by *Atlanta* magazine, Willy's isn't exactly a place you'd take someone you really want to impress. However, if it's a close friend who doesn't judge you by the joints you hang out in, this is the place to go. You'll stand in line to direct the construction of your burrito, first selecting the type of tortilla to hold it all together. Protein options include green-mole chicken, grilled cilantro-garlic steak, chipotle-barbecue pork, grilled chicken, and even marinated tofu. Next, you can pile on the goodies, including rice, black beans, roasted peppers, and all your typical burrito toppings, including the freshest salsa I've ever tasted. Aside from burritos, Willy's serves nachos, quesadillas, and tacos—it has the basic menu down. It also serves a few domestic and imported beers. Once you've got the goods, choose a booth along the brightly decorated wall or go outside where it's a bit less hectic.

There are more than a dozen locations in Atlanta, including ones at 2074 N. Decatur Rd. (☏ **404/321-6060**) and 4377 Roswell Rd. NE (☏ **404/252-2235**).

235 Peachtree St. NE. ☏ **404/524-0821.** Reservations not accepted. Burritos $5–$8. No credit cards. Daily 11am–10pm. Located on the square in Decatur (by the courthouse).

Midtown is becoming a hot spot, with new businesses, apartments, and restaurants springing up constantly. This is the theater district, and several restaurants in this part of town are good pre-theater choices.

## VERY EXPENSIVE

**Bacchanalia** ★★★ NEW AMERICAN   When Bacchanalia abandoned the cozy warmth of its pleasantly informal Buckhead cottage for a former meatpacking plant on the outskirts of an industrial area, some fans were nervous that it wouldn't survive in its new locale. But the edgier, airier, more sophisticated space hits just the right note—plus the food is better than ever.

Owner/chefs Anne Quatrano and Cliff Harrison, who consistently win reams of accolades, place an emphasis on using locally produced natural and organic ingredients whenever possible, from farmstead cheeses to heirloom tomatoes to Georgia blackberries, much of which is grown on their own Summerland Farm. Everything is absolutely the freshest, and perfectly prepared. The blue-crab-fritter appetizer with avocado, citrus, and Thai-pepper essence is a signature dish—a plump, sweet, all-lump crab cake that is not to be missed. A longtime dessert favorite is the warm Valrhona chocolate cake, oozing a puddle of rich chocolate from its gooey middle, and served with vanilla-bean ice cream. The American wine list is overflowing with excellent choices, and there's a full bar now, too. Service is smooth and professional, but it's also warm, inviting, and remarkably free of attitude. The team was awarded the James Beard Foundation's "Best Chef in the Southeast" in 2003.

This is one of the best restaurants in town, and reservations are difficult to come by, especially on weekends. When planning a trip to Atlanta, a call to book a table here should be at the top of your list (reservations are taken up to a month in advance). On the same premises, you'll find **Quinones,** a lavish prix-fixe multi-course restaurant that stresses the use of Southern ingredients to create a menu that changes regularly. Dinner is served Friday and Saturday from 6pm. Be sure to save time to browse Star Provisions, the upscale market also on-site. Stocked with excellent meats, seafood, cheeses, wine, pastries, tableware, cookbooks, and other cooking accessories, it's worth a separate trip.

1198 Howell Mill Rd. (just north of 14th St.). ℂ **404/365-0410.** www.starprovisions.com. Reservations essential. Four-course prix-fixe menu $75, higher with wine pairing. AE, DC, MC, V. Mon–Sat from 6pm. Closed Christmas Eve to New Year's Eve and 2 weeks in summer. MARTA: Midtown.

**South City Kitchen** ★ CONTEMPORARY SOUTHERN   South City Kitchen is set in a converted two-story house fronted by a brick patio lined with pear trees. It's a bright space with light filtering through large windows; a bustling exhibition kitchen serves as a visual focus. There's a lot of meeting and greeting here, and the place can be a little loud, but the crowds of well-dressed professionals—sometimes four and five deep at the small bar—seem to thrive on the buzz. If the weather's nice, try the patio, which is more sedate and provides a great people-watching spot.

The seasonally changing menu reflects widely varied Southern influences. This is a good destination if you're not in the mood for a full meal or want to do a little post-theater noshing; there are several options for light fare, such as the she-crab soup (a perennial favorite), and side dishes can be ordered a la carte. If you've never tried grits, this is a good time to take the plunge—the cheese-laced grits are exceptional. Entrees

---

range from jerk-pork tenderloin to shrimp and scallops with garlic gravy over grits. A basket of freshly baked buttermilk biscuits and corn muffins accompanies all main courses. This is also a good stop for Saturday and Sunday brunch (11am–3:30pm)—you'll find everything from vanilla-buttermilk pancakes to a fried green tomato BLT. The wine list includes small signature acquisitions, plus about 20 wines available by the glass.

South City Kitchen has a second location in Smyrna, at 1675 Cumberland Pkwy. (© 770/435-0700).

1144 Crescent Ave. (btw. 11th and 14th sts.). © 404/873-7358. www.southcitykitchen.com. Reservations recommended. Lunch items $7–$17; brunch items $9–$18; dinner main courses $31–$50. AE, DC, MC, V. Daily 11am–3:30pm; Mon–Thurs 5–11pm; Fri–Sat 5pm–midnight; Sun 5–10pm. MARTA: Arts Center.

## EXPENSIVE

**Eno ★★** EUROPEAN/MEDITERRANEAN  Located in Midtown, near several theaters and within walking distance of the Fox, Eno is the perfect place to stop for a pre- or post-theater dinner. It's actually two restaurants in one: a posh dining room, ideal for leisurely dinners, and a wine bar, where you can feast on small plates and appetizers. There are two different menus for the two parts of Eno, and different wine lists, too. In the bar, the 100-odd selections are available by the taste, glass, or bottle; in the dining room, nearly twice that number is available. While dinner is a first-rate food and wine experience, the wine bar, with its more casual attitude, is a lot more fun (though you can easily snack and sip your way into a pretty hefty bill). Goodies range from a delectable braised rabbit and goat-cheese tortellini with fennel pollen and citrus (on the small-plates menu) to whole roasted fish of the day with roasted fennel and potatoes and singed black olives. Regardless of which area you choose to dine in, be sure to save room for the delicate fig and apple tart.

800 Peachtree St. (at Fifth St.). © 404/685-3191. www.enorestaurant.com. Reservations recommended for the dining room. Small plates and appetizers $9–$16; main courses $17–$33. AE, DC, DISC, MC. Tues–Fri 11:30am–11pm (until midnight Fri); Sat 5pm–midnight; Sun 5:30–10pm. MARTA: North Ave.

**Spice Market ★** ASIAN  From restaurants of the same name in New York and Istanbul, Spice Market has made it to Atlanta and chef de cuisine Ian Winslade (formerly of Posh and Bluepointe) is changing our taste buds forever. Inspired by the hustle and bustle of Southeast Asia street life, Spice Market combines exotic curries and spices in bold dishes such as pork vindaloo, red curried duck, and cod with Malaysian chili sauce and Thai basil.

Lunchtime for the busy executive is a snap with Spice Market's $16 Bento Box with limited choices or the 20-minute express "business lunch" for $13 with choices from a Vietnamese chicken salad with grilled eggplant spread, a grilled salmon salad, or *shrimp pad Thai* (Thai-style stir-fried noodles with shrimp). In the evening, you can order a five-course dinner, featuring 10 flavors, for just $48 per person.

188 14th St. NE (in W. Atlanta Midtown). © 404/549-5450. www.spicemarketatlanta.com. Reservations recommended. Lunch items $12–$26; dinner entrees $16–$38. AE, DC, DISC, MC, V. Daily 11:30am–2:30pm; Mon–Sat 5–11pm; Sun 5–10pm. MARTA: Arts Center.

**Vita ★** ITALIAN  Opened in spring 2008 by 30-year restaurant veteran Tony LaRocco, who has owned restaurants in New York City, Hilton Head, and Destin in addition to Atlanta, Vita (which means "life" in Italian) is his latest venture. Family-style Italian-American fare is served up in New York style to the delight of those who have

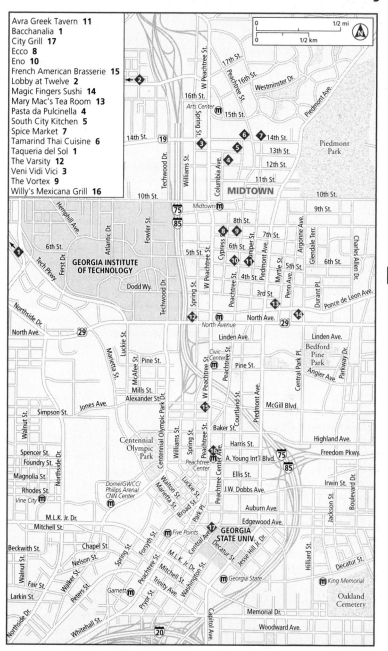

Avra Greek Tavern **11**
Bacchanalia **1**
City Grill **17**
Ecco **8**
Eno **10**
French American Brasserie **15**
Lobby at Twelve **2**
Magic Fingers Sushi **14**
Mary Mac's Tea Room **13**
Pasta da Pulcinella **4**
South City Kitchen **5**
Spice Market **7**
Tamarind Thai Cuisine **6**
Taqueria del Sol **1**
The Varsity **12**
Veni Vidi Vici **3**
The Vortex **9**
Willy's Mexicana Grill **16**

WHERE TO DINE

6

MIDTOWN

## (Fun Facts) True Grits

In the South, a good ol' country breakfast isn't complete unless it includes grits. It's a staple here, kind of like potatoes or rice or pasta are in the rest of the world, and we think everybody else is downright foolish for preferring hash browns or home fries to a heaven-sent bowl of buttered grits. Celestine Sibley, the late *Atlanta Journal-Constitution* columnist, called grits "nature's finest gift to mankind." And Celestine always told it like it was.

Grits are simply crushed kernels of dried corn. A trendier cousin, polenta, is the same thing, just more finely ground and cleaned of all traces of flour. If you've had grits and thought they were bland and tasteless, you probably just didn't have them prepared right. They can be yellow or white (usually white), but the best are stone ground and are cooked for a long time (never instant), boiled with water and salt into a thick porridge and slathered with a big slab of real butter. If you want to expose yourself to ridicule—and ruin your grits—top them with sugar and milk, which is something akin to pouring gravy over a hot fudge sundae.

The beauty of grits is that they soak up flavors like a sponge, allowing them to travel easily from breakfast to dinner. Chicken broth or a little piece of country ham can transform a whole pot, and although many purists gnash their teeth at the thought, some folks cook their grits in milk or cream.

The best addition by far is a little cheese, which turns grits into the ultimate Southern comfort food. Sharp cheddar has been traditional for years, especially in a cheese-grits casserole, but goat cheese added to grits transforms them into a tangy, creamy wonder—a sinful and sophisticated enough dish to serve at a fancy dinner party.

discovered the place. The restaurant's old-world style is comfortable and cheese and olives are imported directly from Italy.

All full salads and pastas serve two to three people, and when you consider a full order of penne with escarole *e fagiole* (white beans and garlic) is just $18, it's quite a bargain. Along with a healthy number of chicken and veal dishes, Vita serves steaks and chops and the fresh mussel appetizer is a reason to return over and over. Of course, cannoli ranks high on the dessert menu, so don't fill up too much. Late hours here make it a popular stop for post-theater or clubbing crowds.

2110 Peachtree Rd., Ste. B. (C) **404/367-8483.** www.vitaatl.com. Reservations for groups of 6 or more. Lunch items $10–$12; dinner entrees (family-style) $13–$54. AE, DC, DISC, MC, V. Mon–Fri 5pm–2am; Sat 11am–2am; Sun 11am–midnight. MARTA: Lindbergh.

**Woodfire Grill** ★★ NORTHERN CALIFORNIAN  Many of us wept tears of joy when chef/owner Michael Tuohy announced that he was opening this restaurant. The interior is warmly decorated, with a stunning copper bar inside the entrance. Entering the dining room, you'll find the wood-fired grill and rotisserie in plain view, providing a dinner theater of sorts for diners whose tables are in the vicinity. Just two complaints: It's noisy, and the hard wood seats leave a little to be desired (pillows are available).

Tuohy dubs Woodfire's cuisine "Northern Californian," and uses the freshest produce, much of it organically grown, and the highest quality meats, seafood, and artisan cheeses. The menu changes daily, so no matter how often you dine here, you'll always find something different. Especially popular is "Rosie the free-range chicken," served on a platter to share. Check out the marble cheese-and-bread carving table and the restaurant's weekly cheese club sandwich. An after-dinner cheese service is available with three or five choices. Woodfire boasts an impressive wine list, with most selections available by the glass. The desserts are quite elaborate, though you might not have room for them.

1782 Cheshire Bridge Rd. ☎ **404/347-9055.** www.woodfiregrill.com. Reservations recommended. Tastes and small plates $8–$14; pizzas $14; entrees $25–$27; platters to share $28–$32; three-course chef's tasting $38; five-course $65. AE, DC, DISC, MC, V. Mon–Sat 5:30–10pm (until 11pm Fri–Sat); Sun 5:30–9:30pm. Complimentary valet parking. MARTA: Lindbergh.

## MODERATE

### Avra Greek Tavern ★ (Value) GREEK

Offering an authentic Greek menu in a charming renovated old Victorian (formerly home to Salt), Avra Greek Tavern is one of few Greek dining opportunities in the entire city. Match that with the fact that it's one of the most reasonably priced restaurants in the area and you've got a win-win dining situation. Portions are a healthy size for the money and the all-Greek wine list adds to the authenticity of the experience. Enjoy enough wine and you might just be out of your chair trying some traditional Greek dance moves. Start with a Greek salad, unlike anything served by those other restaurants just trying to offer some ethnic flair. The moussaka—layers of potato, eggplant, and zucchini, with seasoned ground beef, and baked with béchamel—is true Greek comfort food. Or try the kabobs in chicken, beef, or lamb (the latter is particularly tasty.)

Patrons arrive in jeans or dressed to the hilt; either way, it's okay.

794 Juniper St. ☎ **404/892-8890.** www.avragreektavern.com. Reservations recommended. Lunch entrees $10–$22; dinner entrees $15–$29. AE, MC. V. Fri–Sun 11:30am–4pm; daily 5–10pm (until 11pm Fri–Sat). MARTA: Midtown.

### Ecco ★★ EUROPEAN

Don't look now, but Atlanta's reputation in the culinary world went way, way up in 2008, when Ecco was named "Best Restaurant in the U.S." by the International Restaurant and Hotel Awards. It was second in line for the award of "Best Restaurant in the World," no small feat for a restaurant that just opened in 2006. Featuring a seasonal European menu that teases first with a delicious array of meat and cheese boards, followed by house-made pastas and wood-fired pizzas, Ecco is fast becoming a favorite, especially among locals.

Executive chef Micah Willix, most recently at Seasons 52 in Ft. Lauderdale, has a fairly straightforward approach to cooking, but wows patrons with such dishes as the roasted blue cod with sweet onion, saffron, and rouille, and the *conchiglie* (seashell pasta) with eggplant, San Marzano tomatoes, and garlic. The menu lists a host of small plates and appetizers.

40 7th St. NE. ☎ **404/347-9555.** www.ecco-atlanta.com. Reservations recommended. Entrees $12–$28. AE, DC, DISC, MC, V. Daily 5:30–10pm (until 11pm Fri–Sat); bar and patio 4pm. MARTA: Midtown.

### Lobby at Twelve ★★ SOUTHERN/REGIONAL

Lobby at Twelve features contemporary American cuisine at its finest. Even breakfast is a treat here for guests of the boutique hotel Twelve, which houses the restaurant, or those lucky enough to duck in for a bite on their way to work. Don't miss the ricotta, fried egg, and arugula wrap prepared in the wood oven. Come dinnertime, executive chef Nick Oltarsh wows diners with dishes such as succulently tender braised beef cheeks or his garlic marinated hangar steak. But save room for pastry chef Jonathan St. Hilaire's desserts, especially the sticky toffee pudding with poached pear and *dulce de leche* ice cream.

361 17th St. ℂ **404/961-7370.** www.lobbyattwelve.com. Reservations recommended Fri–Sun. Breakfast items $5–$12; lunch items $12–$24; dinner entrees $12–$28. AE, DC, DISC, MC, V. Mon–Fri 6:30–10:30am and 11:30am–2:30pm, Sat–Sun 7:30am–2:30pm; daily 5:30–10pm (Fri–Sat until 11pm). MARTA: Arts Station, then free shuttle to Atlantic Station.

**Magic Fingers Sushi** ★★ SUSHI/JAPANESE  Though you'll hear this place referred to as M. F. Sushi, I wanted to give you the heads-up as to what the M. F. stands for—"magic fingers," just so you aren't shocked. Atlanta finally has a real, live, honest-to-goodness sushi bar. Chef Chris Kinjo has worked his magic fingers all around the country, and his brother Alex takes care of greeting the guests as they enter this sushi fantasy world. Whether you choose to sit at a table or the sushi bar (where you can keep a close eye on the action), you'll be privy to a menu filled with the freshest fish. It's all there—from tuna to yellowtail, mackerel to eel. Don't wait until you're starving to show up here, as you might wait awhile if it's crowded, especially on the weekends (a typical Atlanta dining problem).

265 Ponce de Leon Ave. ℂ **404/815-8844.** www.mfsushibar.com. Reservations recommended. Sashimi $8–$15 for 3 pieces; nigiri sushi $4–$10; rolls $4–$18 for 6 pieces. AE, DC, MC, V. Mon–Fri 11:30am–2:30pm; Mon–Sat 5:30–10:30pm (until 11:30pm Fri–Sat). Valet parking. MARTA: North Ave.

**Mary Mac's Tea Room** ★ SOUTHERN/REGIONAL  Mary Mac's is a colorful Atlanta institution, a bastion of classic Southern cuisine that has been patronized since 1945 by everyone from truck drivers to bank presidents to Jimmy Carter, who sometimes came by for lunch when he was governor. You'll find a glass of pencils on your table; check off the menu items you desire (they change daily) and hand your selections to your server.

Among the famous lunch and dinner entrees are fried chicken dredged in buttermilk and flour, country-fried steak, and chicken pan pie topped with thick giblet gravy. Steaks, chops, and burgers all come with a choice of side dishes, including expertly prepared fresh veggies. You might also select corn bread with *pot likker,* a tasty ham broth made with turnip greens that first-timers can sample for free. The list of sides is endless, including black-eyed peas, fried green tomatoes, whipped potatoes, fried okra, macaroni and cheese, sweet-potato soufflé, and more. Fresh-from-the-oven corn and yeast rolls are served with lunch; at night, there are hot cinnamon rolls, too. Desserts include peach cobbler and banana pudding—a favorite with locals. There's a full bar, but the drink of choice is sweet tea (sweetened iced tea). Mary Mac's can seat groups of up to 150.

224 Ponce de Leon Ave. NE (at Myrtle St.). ℂ **404/876-1800.** www.marymacs.com. Reservations accepted for groups of 10 or more. Lunch $8–$17; dinner $9–$18. AE, MC, V. Daily 11am–9pm. MARTA: North Ave.

**One Midtown Kitchen** ★ NEW AMERICAN  You'll feel like you're in the heart of New York when you dine at this sophisticated restaurant, the creation of renowned restaurateur Bob Amick. It manages to be both delicious and not too pricey (someone finally figured it out!). Chef Tom Harvey, a Georgia native, heads the kitchen here. The wine list is eclectic and affordable, and the atmosphere is high energy—maybe the high spirits are left over from the restaurant's previous life as a swinging club. Located on the edge of Piedmont Park, One takes the cake when it comes to creativity in powder rooms

(you'll see what I mean). This place is a local favorite, especially with a younger crowd
working their way up the ladder to six figures.

559 Dutch Valley Rd. NE. ℰ **404/892-4111.** www.onemidtownkitchen.com. Reservations recommended. Starters $7–$11; entrees $12–$27. AE, MC, V. Daily 5:30–11pm (until midnight Fri and 10pm Sun). Free valet parking. MARTA: Midtown.

**Pasta Da Pulcinella** ★ Ⓥalue ITALIAN    Pasta Da Pulcinella was known for years as a humble hole in the wall serving up great pasta at rock-bottom prices. Some things have changed since the restaurant moved into new digs. Now tucked away in a charming but crowded cottage, the interior is fancier, though still casual, with table service and a full bar. Prices are fancier, too, but still sensible. What has stayed the same is a commitment to excellent pastas, made from scratch and beautifully presented with a surprising and innovative combination of flavors in each concoction.

The most popular dish is *tortelli di mele*—plump round pasta filled with sweet Italian sausage, browned Granny Smith apples, and Parmesan, then topped with browned butter and sage. You'll see nightly specials each day, but your best bet is to stick with the pastas or risottos. There is a small selection of Italian wines that changes often. Pulcinella is near a number of theaters and makes an easy pre-theater stop.

1123 Peachtree Walk (near 12th St.). ℰ **404/876-1114.** Reservations accepted weekends only for groups of 5 or more. Main courses $12–$20. AE, DC, MC, V. Mon–Fri 11:30am–2:30pm and 5:30–10pm (until 11pm Fri–Sat); Sun 5:30–9pm. MARTA: North Ave.

**R. Thomas Deluxe Grill** ★★ ECLECTIC    Conveniently located in Midtown, R. Thomas is open 24 hours a day, 7 days a week, so there's no excuse to go hungry. Its eclectic menu is about as healthy a choice as you can make in today's world of eat-on-the-go fast food. Now in its 20th year in Atlanta, this Peachtree Street icon will please the meat-eater and the vegetarian alike with delicious fare such as collard greens with millet-corn casserole, mashed potatoes, and shiitake-mushroom gravy. Menu items include gourmet sandwiches, Southwestern fare, pasta dishes, and noodle bowls. Breakfast can be enjoyed at any time—day or night. The store sells books and other items for healthy living.

1812 Peachtree St. NW. ℰ **404/872-2942.** www.rthomasdeluxegrill.com. Entrees $12–$17. AE, MC, V. Daily 24 hr. MARTA: Midtown.

**Tamarind Seed Thai Bistro** ★★ Ⓕinds THAI    If you like Thai, you'll love Tamarind. And if you've never tried Thai food, this is the place to start. Tamarind is a serious, upscale restaurant, and the quality of the food is higher than you'll find in most other Thai restaurants in the city. Once inside, you'll find white tablecloths, fresh flowers, sophisticated decor, and impeccable service. It's a good choice for a romantic evening, business lunch, or pre-theater dinner.

The menu includes all the usual Thai standbys—*pad Thai* (Thai-style stir-fried noodles), chicken-coconut milk soup, fresh basil rolls, curries, and so on—and even the most ordinary dishes are carefully prepared and artfully presented. You won't be disappointed with the more inventive dishes, either, such as *neua yang nam tok,* or "waterfall beef," consisting of tender strips of steak marinated in tamarind and chile peppers and cooked with shallots, sesame seeds, and mint leaves. Keep in mind that Thai cuisine is designed to stimulate five taste senses: sweet, sour, neutral, salty, and hot. And they do mean hot: Tamarind doesn't skimp on the chiles, and many of the dishes are downright fiery. Be sure to pay attention to the "hotness guide" on the menu.

1197 Peachtree St. NE. ✆ **404/873-4888.** www.tamarindseed.com. Reservations recommended. Entrees $11–$29. AE, MC, V. Mon–Fri 11:30am–2:30pm; Mon–Thurs 5–10pm; Fri-Sat 5–11pm; Sun 11am–9pm. MARTA: Arts Center.

**Veni Vidi Vici** ★★ ITALIAN   This elegant theater-district restaurant manages to create an intimate feel in a 5,000-square-foot space. Cutting-edge design (handsome cherrywood wine cabinets, stenciled oak flooring, and sophisticated track lighting that replaces the glow of candles with a pinpoint splash of light on each table) complements the bustling exhibition kitchen.

The specialties here are *piatti piccoli* (small plates, such as skewers of shrimp or prosciutto and pear, traditionally served with cocktails), fresh handmade pastas, and meat or seafood from the wood-fired rotisserie and grill. It's easy to make a meal of the *piatti piccoli* or other appetizers, but the pastas are so lovely that it's a shame to pass them up. Especially good is the house specialty—linguine with plump Little Neck clams in a white or spicy red sauce. Other excellent traditional dishes include the risotto, *osso buco,* and veal scaloppine. The well-chosen wine list is almost 100% Italian.

41 14th St. (btw. W. Peachtree and Spring sts.). ✆ **404/875-8424.** www.buckheadrestaurants.com. Reservations recommended. Piatti piccoli 6.50; lunch items $9.95–$16; dinner pastas $10–$18; dinner main courses $16–$25. AE, DC, DISC, MC, V. Mon–Fri 11:30am–11pm (until 11:30pm Fri); Sat 5–11pm; Sun 5–10pm. MARTA: Arts Center.

## INEXPENSIVE

**Colonnade** ★ SOUTHERN/REGIONAL   This Atlanta institution, established in 1927, serves authentic Southern specialties without any newfangled twists (thank goodness). The Colonnade is unpretentious and comfortable, with most of the seating at butcher-block tables in a large room. A cozy bar with a working fireplace is a nice place to sit if you have to wait for a table—and you probably will.

The fried chicken is some of the best in town—four huge pieces done the way Mama used to make it. The homemade yeast rolls and new whole-wheat rolls will melt in your mouth. In addition to the menu listings, there are economical blue-plate specials and fancier offerings ranging from corned beef and cabbage to frogs' legs. The portions are huge, so it's doubtful you'll have room for dessert. But if you decide to squeeze it in, the butterscotch meringue and banana pudding will satisfy any sweet tooth.

1879 Cheshire Bridge Rd. NE (btw. Wellborne Dr. and Manchester St.). ✆ **404/874-5642.** Reservations not accepted. Entrees $6–$24. No credit cards; personal checks accepted; ATM on-site. Mon–Fri 5–9pm (until 10pm Fri); Sat noon–10pm; Sun 11:30am–9pm. MARTA: Midtown.

**Fat Matt's Rib Shack** BARBECUE   This blues and barbecue shack is a favorite among locals who like their ribs as smoky as their music. Don't expect much in the way of decor. This is truly a shack, where patrons order at the counter, then sit elbow-to-elbow at plastic tables while chowing down on pork ribs, barbecued chicken, and pulled-pork sandwiches. There are sides of coleslaw, baked beans, and Brunswick stew—a Southern concoction that's a cross between a thick gravy and a thicker meat stew. Snack on an "appetizer" of peanuts in the shell, washed down with ice-cold beer, while waiting for your order.

Live music—authentic blues by a variety of local and regional groups—starts every night around 8pm. People pack into the small space, and it's usually standing room only, especially on weekends, so come early if you want to see the show.

1811 Piedmont Rd. (a few blocks south of Cheshire Bridge Rd.). ✆ **404/607-1622.** www.fatmattsrib
shack.com. Reservations not accepted. Ribs and chicken $3.75–$19; chopped pork sandwiches $3.95.
MC, V. Mon–Fri 11:30am–11:30pm (until 12:30am Fri); Sun 1–11:30pm. MARTA: Lindbergh.

**Taqueria del Sol ★** SOUTHWESTERN   This is what fast food ought to be—quick
and good, not to mention affordable. Taqueria del Sol resembles an extremely well-
dressed taco stand, with inventive tacos, enchiladas, side dishes, soups, and chiles. You
put together your own "plate," ordering as much or as little as you'd like. Use your
imagination, picking a couple of tacos (the fish taco is a standout), an enchilada, and
maybe a side of the addictive jalapeño coleslaw. There is usually one special at lunch and
one or two at dinner, which might include a Southwestern interpretation of a Southern
dish, such as boneless fried chicken with ancho mashed potatoes, Low Country gravy,
serrano-chile sauce, and turnip greens. There are 25 or so different kinds of beer to wash
it all down, plus a full bar. Don't expect table service, and do expect to wait during prime
time, but the inconveniences are small, especially if you can snag a table on the covered
patio.

There is a second Taqueria del Sol in Decatur, located at 359 W. Ponce de Leon Ave.
(✆ **404/377-7668**).

1200-B Howell Mill Rd. NW. ✆ **404/352-5811.** www.taqueriadelsol.com. Reservations not accepted.
Tacos $2; sides and soups $2; enchiladas $3; lunch specials around $8; dinner specials under $11. AE, MC,
V. Mon–Fri 11am–2pm, Sat noon–3pm; Tues–Sat 5:30–9pm (until 10pm Fri–Sat). From I-75, take the 14th
St. exit and head west to Howell Mill Rd. Turn right on Howell Mill Rd. The restaurant is a few blocks up
on the left, just before Huff Rd. MARTA: North Ave.

**The Vortex** TRADITIONAL AMERICAN   The laughing-skull logo should give you
a clue that this is a wild little bar and grill with a big attitude. If you're easily offended,
don't go. Or at least don't read the "stuff you really need to know" on the back of the
menu, which, among other things, decrees the restaurant an Idiot-Free Zone and suggests
you don't get a knot in your shorts if you aren't served within 5 minutes. All kinds of
weird flea-market stuff covers the walls, and kids 17 and under are not allowed here.

Attitude aside, this is the place to come for a big, fat, juicy chargrilled burger, one of
the best in town. If you don't want a beef burger, you can substitute a turkey burger,
chicken breast, veggie burger, or bison burger for a nominal charge. Non-carnivores will
find plenty to choose from, including soups, generous sandwiches, and fresh salads. You
can also get breakfast all day, including a build-your-own omelet menu, featuring many
unusual toppings. There's a full bar, out-of-the-ordinary soft drinks, and more kinds of
beer than you can imagine (imports and domestic), not to mention 72 varieties of single-
malt scotch. This is a great people-watching stop and the late hours make it a great place
to eat after a night on the town.

There's another Vortex at 438 Moreland Ave., in Little Five Points (✆ **404/688-
1828**).

878 Peachtree St. NE. ✆ **404/875-1667.** www.thevortexbarandgrill.com. Reservations not accepted.
Weekend brunch menu (served Sat–Sun 11am–3pm) $7–$9; sandwiches $4.50–$7.25; burgers $7–$13.
AE, MC, V. Mon–Wed 11am–2am; Thurs–Sat 11am–3am; Sun 11am–midnight. MARTA: Midtown.

**Woody's Famous Philadelphia Cheesesteaks** (Kids) TRADITIONAL AMERI-
CAN   Gourmet it ain't, but if you and the kids are all tuckered out from a romp in
nearby Piedmont Park, walk on over to this casual little spot for lunch. It's barely bigger
than a glorified hot-dog stand, but serves up excellent Philly cheese steaks, Italian subs,
Polish sausages, and hot dogs. The ordering line (there's no table service) often snakes all

the way out the door, so arrive at off-peak hours or be prepared to wait. There are five small booths inside, but the best place to sit on a nice day is the covered deck—perfect for enjoying an orange freeze or one of Woody's extra-thick, old-fashioned milkshakes.

981 Monroe Dr. NE (at 10th St.). ✆ **404/876-1939.** Reservations not accepted. Hot dogs and sandwiches $3.25–$5.95. No credit cards. Tues–Sat 11am–5pm. MARTA: North Ave.

# 4 BUCKHEAD

Buckhead is home to most of Atlanta's posh restaurants. Keep in mind that this is *the* area to dine, so plan in advance and make reservations as soon as you know where you want to go.

## VERY EXPENSIVE

**Aria ★★** ECLECTIC   Since opening in 2000, Aria has remained a hit among the dozens of top-quality dining choices in the busy Buckhead area. The eclectic gourmet makings of chef/owner Gerry Klaskala are consistently delightful. He seems to have hit the nail on the head with his version of "slow food"—braised, roasted, stewed, and patiently simmered savory meats paired with scrumptious, innovative sides. Here, cooking is considered an art form—and anything less than spectacular is not allowed. Seasonal ingredients are the norm, as are fresh seafood selections. If it's offered, don't miss the chilled Vidalia-onion vichyssoise. Among my favorite entrees is the oak-grilled Springer Mountain chicken with ricotta-stuffed tortellini and spinach. The extensive wine selection wins raves, and delights from pastry chef Kathryn King complete the meal.

490 E. Paces Ferry Rd. ✆ **404/233-7673.** www.aria-atl.com. Reservations recommended. Dinner entrees $31–$50. AE, DISC, MC, V. Mon–Sat 6–10pm. MARTA: Lenox.

**Bluepointe ★★★** ASIAN/NEW AMERICAN   At the corner of Peachtree and Lenox roads, in the heart of upscale Buckhead, is one of the many big stars in the constellation of fine-dining establishments that make up the locally owned and operated Buckhead Life Restaurant Group. Part of the restaurant's success comes from the setting itself: a dramatic, multilevel space with a flashy lounge and sushi bar, soaring ceilings, and a plush contemporary decor with Asian touches. There's a lot of energy and noise in the lounge/sushi bar in the "point" of the building, but it's possible to have a decent conversation in the restaurant portion of the establishment.

The specialty here is seafood, with Asian flavors that give the dishes a contemporary edge. Menus change frequently, depending on what's fresh and available, but might include such delicious options as peanut-crusted grouper in Indian curry, or perhaps scallops with sushi-rice cakes and passion-fruit butter. There are also prime steaks and a delectable lobster. A house specialty is salt-crusted prime rib for two, which looks as if it could serve four people. Everything is beautifully presented, and the service is impeccable.

3455 Peachtree Rd. NE (at Lenox Rd.). ✆ **404/237-9070.** www.buckheadrestaurants.com. Reservations highly recommended. Lunch entrees $10–$35; dinner main courses $26–$56. AE, DC, MC, V. Mon–Fri 11:30am–2:30pm; Mon–Sat 5:30–11pm (until midnight Fri–Sat); Sun 5:30–10pm. Complimentary valet parking. MARTA: Lenox or Buckhead.

**Blue Ridge Grill ★** TRADITIONAL AMERICAN   The Blue Ridge Grill's Adirondacks-style interior has the woodsy warmth of a national park lodge: stone pillars, weathered logs, and a soaring pine ceiling with massive heart pine beams salvaged from an old

Anis Café & Bistro **12**
Aria **14**
Atlanta Fish Market **11**
Au Pied de Cochon **20**
Bluepointe **26**
Bone's **19**
Buckhead Diner **16**
Chops/Lobster Bar **9**
Colonnade **28**
Corner Café/
  Buckhead Bread
  Company **15**
The Dining Room **25**
Fat Matt's
  Rib Shack **30**
Fellini's Pizza **5**
Fogo de Chão **18**
Home **8**
Houston's **27**
Kyma **17**
La Fonda Latina **6**
Nava **10**
NEO **22**
New York Prime **24**
The Palm **21**
Pasta Vino **4**
Pricci **13**
Prime **23**
R. Thomas
  Deluxe Grill **1**
Swan Coach House **7**
Toulouse **3**
Vita **2**
Woodfire Grill **29**

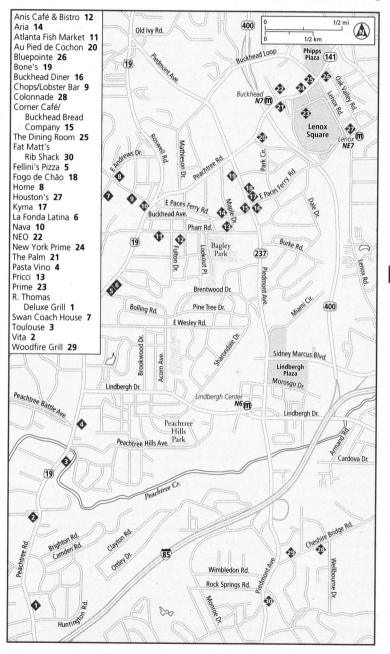

cotton mill. But this spot is as upscale as it is rustic, with antiques, original artwork, and cozy leather booths.

Blue Ridge Grill used to specialize in contemporary Southern cuisine, but the menu is vastly different now, with mostly traditional American fare such as steaks, chops, and seafood. The only remotely Southern items are collard greens and Georgia trout. As in many other restaurants these days, the emphasis is on two-fisted portions: a 22-ounce rib-eye, a 14-ounce veal chop, and huge sides of spinach, mashed potatoes, asparagus, and so on. *Note:* As you drive here along West Paces Ferry Road, remember to look for Northside *Parkway,* not Northside *Drive,* which you'll pass first.

1261 W. Paces Ferry Rd. (at Northside Pkwy., in the Paces Ferry Plaza Shopping Center). © **404/233-5030.** www.blueridgegrill.com. Reservations recommended. Lunch and brunch items $11–$20; dinner main courses $22–$42. AE, DC, DISC, MC, V. Sun–Fri 11:30am–2:30pm; Sun–Thurs 5:30–10pm (until 11pm Fri–Sat). MARTA: Lenox.

**Bone's ★★★** STEAK/TRADITIONAL AMERICAN Atlanta's best and most famous steakhouse, Bone's is a top power-lunch venue for the expense-account crowd, who are provided with notepads and phones at the midday meal. As many deals as steaks are cut here, and the place is rich with celebrity lore. When Bob Hope dined here, everyone respected his privacy until he rose to leave; then the entire dining room gave him a standing ovation. During his presidency, the elder George Bush came in for dinner one night, booking six surrounding tables for his Secret Service men (they ate, too). The setting is traditional masculine-clubby.

The star of the menu is prime-aged, corn-fed Iowa beef, hand-cut on the premises and always prepared exactly as ordered. Thick, juicy lamb chops are excellent alternatives to the beef. Noted for its seafood as well as for its steaks and chops, Bone's flies Maine lobsters in daily and serves fresh Gulf Coast crab and shrimp. Lighter entrees are available at lunch, along with salads, sandwiches, and soups. The wine gallery houses over 500 selections, international in scope, and it highlights French and California vintages. The ultra-rich desserts include "Mountain-high Pie"—layers of chocolate chip, rum raisin, and vanilla ice cream.

3130 Piedmont Rd. NE (half a block below Peachtree Rd.). © **404/237-2663.** www.bonesrestaurant.com. Reservations essential. Lunch items $10–$75; dinner main courses $50–$75. AE, DC, DISC, MC, V. Mon–Fri 11:30am–2:30pm; daily 5:30–10pm (until 11pm Sat). Closed most major holidays. MARTA: Lindbergh.

**Chops/Lobster Bar ★★** SEAFOOD/STEAK Steaks are the specialty at Chops, while lobster (not surprisingly) is the main attraction at the Lobster Bar. However, seafood and lobster are available at Chops, while steaks are also served at the Lobster Bar.

The steakhouse boasts extremely elegant, clubby surroundings—definitely macho, but less so than its arch rival, Bone's (see above). Tri-level seating is in comfortable upholstered armchairs and roomy banquettes. Entrees require a hefty wallet and a hearty appetite for the likes of a 24- or 48-ounce porterhouse steak, a 20-ounce New York strip, triple-cut loin lamb chops, salt- and garlic-crusted prime rib, and so on. You won't need dessert, which is just as well since they're nothing special. A large selection of wines is available; at lunch, filling sandwiches are an option. This is power dining at its best and seats are much in demand, so reserve in advance.

The elegant Art Deco Lobster Bar is reminiscent of the Oyster Bar in New York's Grand Central Terminal. The menu lists steaks and seafood items from Chops, plus additional seafood choices. Lobster is prepared just about every way imaginable—there's lobster cocktail, baked lobster oreganato, lobster bisque, fried lobster tail, steamed

## Picnic Fare & Picnic Spots

There are plenty of opportunities to picnic in Atlanta, and loads of outdoor spots to spread your picnic blanket. Good bets include Centennial Olympic Park downtown, Piedmont Park in Midtown, Stone Mountain Park, and Grant Park. Here are some places that can help you round up a great picnic lunch:

**Alon's Bakery,** 1394 N. Highland Ave. NE (✆ **404/872-6000**), has loads of delectable baked goods (some of the best pastries in town) and a variety of made-to-order sandwiches at reasonable prices. Try the garlic-roasted lamb or the Tuscany (goat cheese, arugula, roasted eggplant). There's also a selection of interesting, easily portable side dishes and salads.

The **BREADGARDEN,** 549 Amsterdam Ave. (✆ **404/875-1166**), is tucked away on a little dead-end street, but it's worth seeking out, especially if you want to picnic in nearby Piedmont Park. This shop started out as a retail bread store, but it now serves up sandwiches on its incomparable freshly baked breads. You can design your own sandwich, but it's hard to come up with anything better than the Mediterranean vegetarian—goat cheese, roasted red peppers, tomatoes, Kalamata olives, eggplant, and olive spread on whole-grain bread.

Adjacent to the Corner Café, the upscale **Buckhead Bread Company,** 3070 Piedmont Rd. (✆ **404/240-1978**), prepares unusual sandwiches to go, as well as authentic French pastries that taste as good as they look.

lobster, and even lobster fingers. You get the picture. The star of the menu is the crab lobster entree, one or two Maine 1-pounders prepared six different ways. For the purist, there's good old live Maine lobster (3–9 lb.), steamed and cracked. And for those who don't like lobster (what are you doing here anyway?), there's a wide variety of impeccably prepared fish, shrimp, and crab. Stone-crab claws are popular during winter months.

70 W. Paces Ferry Rd. (at Peachtree Rd.). ✆ **404/262-2675.** www.buckheadrestaurants.com. Reservations highly recommended. Dinner main courses $28–$100; market prices for lobster. AE, DC, DISC, MC, V. Mon–Fri 11:30am–2:30pm (Chops only); Mon–Thurs 5:30–11pm; Fri–Sat 5:30pm–midnight; Sun 5:30–10pm. MARTA: Lindbergh.

**The Dining Room** ★★★ FRENCH/MEDITERRANEAN    For years, the elegantly comfortable Dining Room at the Ritz-Carlton Buckhead was the domain of nationally celebrated chef Bruno Menard. When Menard left, hotel management launched an international search for a new chef. Enter Arnaud Berthelier, who admits he learned to cook so he could travel. He's found his groove in Atlanta and in the Dining Room, where patrons come expecting a fantastic experience and never leave disappointed. From service to cuisine, it doesn't get much better than this. Berthelier successfully pushes the envelope with the French, Spanish, and North African influences evident in his menu. An impeccable cheese service is available, as well as a host of desserts, including a cart filled with chocolate treats. Among the specialties is a Cuban chocolate tart—very rich but very worth it. Share the experience with a dining partner. Jackets are required for men.

At the Ritz-Carlton Buckhead, 3434 Peachtree Rd. NE (at Lenox Rd.). ☎ **404/237-2700.** www.ritzcarlton. com. Reservations essential, and as far in advance as possible. Dinners $69 (Tues–Thurs three-course) and $125 (Fri–Sat six-course tasting; additional $85 wine pairing). AE, DC, DISC, MC, V. Tues–Thurs 6–9pm; Fri–Sat 6–9:30pm. MARTA: Lenox or Buckhead.

**Fogo de Chão** ★ BRAZILIAN    Atlanta is lucky to be one of a few American cities with an authentic southern Brazilian–style *churrascaria* (grilled-meat restaurant). No vegetarian would be caught dead in this place, as the highlights here are meat, meat, and more meat. From top sirloin, filet mignon, and pork ribs to lamb, rumpsteak, and pork loin, Fogo de Chão seasons each meat selection to perfection before slow-roasting it over a flame to bring out the natural flavors. As you make your way to the 30-item salad bar—one of the best in the city, I might add—and enjoy your side dishes of black beans, fried yucca, garlic mashed potatoes, and cheese bread, the traditional "Gaucho" cooks and waiters will present the savory cuts of meat on skewers and slice them tableside. It's a one-price-fits-all menu. Fogo has become one of the city's most popular restaurants, so reserve in advance if possible.

3101 Piedmont Rd. ☎ **404/266-9988.** www.fogodechao.com. Reservations highly recommended. Lunch $30 per person; dinner $50 per person. AE, DC, MC, V. Mon–Fri 11:30am–2pm and 5–10pm (until 10:30pm Fri); Sat 4:30–10:30pm; Sun 4:30–9:30pm. MARTA: Lindbergh.

**Joël** ★★★ FRENCH/FUSION    Joël Antunes is flying solo these days. Antunes, formerly of the Dining Room at Ritz-Carlton Buckhead fame, is a Frenchman who trained in Nice under Paul Bocuse and went on to win accolades in Lyon, London, and Thailand. His experience as chef of a restaurant in the Oriental Hotel in Bangkok shaped his style, and his cuisine successfully blends Eastern and Western flavors.

Though he's moved on to the Plaza Hotel's Oak Room in New York City, leaving his kitchen under the leadership of longtime friend and chef de cuisine Cyrille Holota, his namesake restaurant includes a 65-seat tapas bar/lounge, two 16-seat private rooms, and a gourmet takeout patisserie with pastries, sandwiches, and light meals. Designed by the Johnson Studio—creators of Canoe, Bluepointe, and Aria—Joël features a clean, sleek design with high windows and classic materials. The space is minimalist and contemporary, and color is used sparingly and dramatically. The 16-seat wine room has a glassed-in wall that holds 5,000 bottles of wine. As if that weren't enough, Antunes boasts that he has the biggest piece of cooking equipment in the country: a 62-foot stainless steel stove, the longest in a stand-alone kitchen in the U.S. Each of his 12 chefs focuses on the preparation of three or four dishes from start to finish, and each has his or her own cooking area along the massive stove. Wow.

The options are limited enough to keep your head from spinning, yet so varied that you don't feel cheated. Whatever you choose, you must save room for dessert or the after-dinner cheese service. Philippe Buttin, formerly of London's famed Mirabelle restaurant, has compiled an impressive 300-selection international wine list with bottles from Chile, Spain, France, Italy, Australia, New Zealand, South Africa, and the United States. An equally impressive reserve list is also available.

3290 Northside Pkwy. (Piazza at Paces). ☎ **404/233-3500.** www.joelrestaurant.com. Reservations recommended. Appetizers $10–$14; entrees $24–$48. AE, DC, MC, V. Tues–Fri 11:30am–2pm; Tues–Sat 5:30–10pm. MARTA: Midtown or Lindbergh.

**NEO** ★ ITALIAN    New in 2008, NEO is the first restaurant to open in the opulent Mansion on Peachtree. Serving a contemporary Italian menu for breakfast, lunch, and dinner, NEO has some standout dishes, including the can't-miss foie gras appetizer at dinner, as well as a melt-in-your-mouth *beef brasato* (beef braised in Barolo wine). Nightly specials are always a good bet, but the risottos and pasta—including a squid ink pasta—are also popular. The restaurant has a great selection of wines, by the glass or by the bottle.

At the Mansion on Peachtree, 3376 Peachtree Rd. © **404/995-7500.** www.rwmansiononpeachtree.com. Reservations recommended. Breakfast items $5–$15; lunch items $14–$24; dinner main courses $27–$44. AE, DC, MC, V. Daily 6:30am–10pm (until 11pm Fri–Sat). MARTA: Lenox or Buckhead.

**New York Prime ★★** SEAFOOD/STEAK   Located next to the Ritz-Carlton Buckhead, this is one of Atlanta's newest—and fast becoming one of the city's favorite—steak-and-seafood see-and-be-seen eateries. Using only USDA prime cuts that melt in your mouth, New York Prime doesn't skimp on the seafood either, offering live lobsters from 3 to a whopping 13 pounds. Triple-cut lamb chops and double-rib veal chops are other popular menu items. Service here is always impeccable, and the dark-wood furnishings and wrought-iron chandeliers give the place a dressed-up, masculine look. All the desserts are homemade and memorable. Finish off your evening with live entertainment—and perhaps a choice cigar—in the Martini Bar.

3424 Peachtree Rd. © **404/846-0644.** www.newyorkprime.com. Reservations recommended. Appetizers $9.50–$18; dinner main courses $21–$45, except for the $84 40-oz. porterhouse for 2. Seafood at market prices. AE, DC, DISC, MC, V. Mon–Sat 5–11pm; Sun 5–10pm. MARTA: Lenox or Buckhead.

**The Palm ★★** SEAFOOD/STEAK   New York's legendary purveyor of juicy prime steaks and succulent outsize lobsters—established in 1926 and still run by its founding family—also has a branch in Atlanta, and it's a beauty. Glossy oak floors, soft lighting, a lofty pressed-tin ceiling, potted palms, and tables spaced for power-lunch privacy create the classic Palm setting—a setting that would not be complete without the restaurant's signature "Wall of Fame," plastered with celebrity caricatures from Frank Sinatra to famous locals Jane Fonda and Ted Turner.

The expense-account crowd is mostly from affluent Buckhead: folks looking for the kind of food served at Chops or Bone's (two premier steakhouses), but in a brasher, more boisterous setting. Preparations are simple here (nothing drizzled or infused); the emphasis is on the freshest seafood and the highest-quality cuts of meat, all served up in satisfying hungry-man portions. The strip steak is huge and divine, done exactly to order. But the most popular entree is the lobster, a hefty critter weighing from 3 to 7 pounds. Other excellent choices are fluffy jumbo-lump crab cakes and linguine with garlicky white-clam sauce. The Palm also serves breakfast, much to the delight of Westin Buckhead hotel guests. Service here is always exceptional.

At the Westin Buckhead Atlanta, 3391 Peachtree Rd. (btw. Lenox and Piedmont rds., just south of Lenox Square). © **404/814-1955.** www.thepalm.com. Reservations recommended. Lunch items $13–$22; dinner main courses $21–$86. Lobster market priced by the lb. AE, DC, MC, V. Daily 11:30am–11pm. MARTA: Lenox or Buckhead.

**Pano's & Paul's ★★** CONTINENTAL/TRADITIONAL AMERICAN   This place has been on the scene since 1979; well-heeled Atlantans consider it a kind of posh private club. And posh it is, especially since a recent renovation turned it into a stylish Art Deco–style space that evokes 1940s sophistication.

The food is excellent, and the service as smooth as silk. Dinner might begin with slow-roasted wild king salmon, accompanied by white asparagus and Swiss chard, and continue with crisply battered lobster tail with Chinese honey mustard (a signature dish). In season, the soft-shell crabs, lightly battered and sautéed crisp, are a succulent treat. If you don't see what you want on the menu, just ask; the staff will make every effort to prepare something that will tempt you. Desserts are as lush as the surroundings, and the wine list is excellent. A $45 four-course prix-fixe menu ($65 with wine pairing) is available Monday through Friday and features creations by chef Gary Donlick.

1232 W. Paces Ferry Rd. (at Northside Pkwy., in the West Paces Ferry Shopping Center). 📞 **404/261-3662.** www.buckheadrestaurants.com. Reservations essential. Main courses $22–$42. AE, DC, DISC, MC, V. Mon–Fri 6–11pm; Sat 5:30–11pm. MARTA: Lenox.

## EXPENSIVE

**Anis Café & Bistro** ★ Ⓥalue FRENCH/MEDITERRANEAN   In the midst of pricey Buckhead, this unpretentious cafe serves up great food at the right price. Set in a converted cottage on a side street, it's the perfect spot for a light lunch or dinner with a French accent. The specialties are Provençal versions of healthy Mediterranean cuisine, and the atmosphere is reminiscent of that region, especially if you're lucky enough to snag a table on the tree-shaded brick patio. The key word here is *informal*. The service is sometimes maddeningly casual, and occasionally there are glitches in the kitchen, but if you relax and pretend you've been invited to a friend's house in the south of France, you won't be disappointed.

Starters include pastis-scented escargots with crispy polenta, garlic and crushed tomatoes. The mussels, which are plump and plentiful, make a full meal when paired with the goat-cheese salad. The saffron linguine and monkfish, with leeks, tomatoes, and white wine butter, is a great entree choice. There are several specialty coffee drinks, including espresso over ice cream. The wine list is quite respectable, and there's a full bar as well.

2974 Grandview Ave. (1 block south of Pharr Rd.). 📞 **404/233-9889.** www.anisbistro.com. Reservations recommended. Lunch $6–$16; dinner entrees $19–$29. AE, DC, MC, V. Mon–Sat 11:30am–2:30pm; daily 6–10pm (until 10:30pm Fri–Sat). MARTA: Lenox.

**Atlanta Fish Market** ★★ SEAFOOD/SUSHI   It's hard to miss this place, and you really don't want to. It's a great mix of whimsy outside (there's a 65-ft. copper fish standing on its tail out front) and serious seafood inside—some of the best you'll find anywhere. Like the Buckhead Diner (see below), the Atlanta Fish Market is simultaneously glitzy and informal. You'll want to dress up, but not too much. Housed in a brick building inspired by a 1920s Savannah train station, it has a dramatic interior with a soaring ceiling, plush leather booths, and distressed pine tables; there's also an enclosed porch that feels very beachy.

The menu is vast, and the seafood as fresh as it's possible to get. To some folks, seafood in the South means fried, and the fried dishes are okay, but the other preparations are exceptional. There are several daily specials and a list of at least a dozen fresh-catch items that can be ordered charbroiled or Hong Kong–style, spiked with soy sauce, ginger, and scallions. You'll also find steaks and chops, as well as a vast number of appetizers, many almost large enough for a meal.

265 Pharr Rd. (btw. Peachtree Rd. and N. Fulton Dr.). 📞 **404/262-3165.** www.buckheadrestaurants.com. Reservations recommended. Sandwiches $9.50–$12; lunch and dinner entrees $19–$35. AE, DC, DISC, MC, V. Mon–Sat 11:30am–11pm (until midnight Fri–Sat); Sun 11:30am–10pm. MARTA: Lenox.

**Au Pied de Cochon** ★★ FRENCH   Located in the InterContinental Buckhead, Au Pied de Cochon is the Atlanta venture of prominent French restaurant group Les Freres Blanc, which operates a Parisian brasserie, also named Au Pied de Cochon. Known for the fresh seafood and the signature roasted "pig trotter"—or pigs' feet, to be frank—the

## Fun Facts — A Buckhead Fish Tale

Traveling down Pharr Road in Buckhead, it's pretty hard not to notice the huge fish sculpture outside the Atlanta Fish Market, one of the city's finest seafood restaurants. The fish, which is perched on its swooped tail and appears to be about to leap over the restaurant, caused quite a commotion when it was first proposed. Although the restaurant was quite enthusiastic about its construction, many folks in the surrounding neighborhoods were not exactly hooked on the idea. Despite protests, the project was approved, and the enormous creature, which resembles a cross between a salmon and a trout, was unveiled in late 1995. Here are some fish facts about a sculpture that, like it or not, is on its way to becoming an Atlanta landmark:

- The fish is about 65 feet high and weighs 50 tons.
- Measured from head to tail, it's 100 feet long, about the size of a large whale.
- It sports more than 600 copper scales, 3½ feet each, which will age to a patina over the years.
- Made of solid copper and steel, it is supported by a welded-iron infrastructure that is connected to a 35-foot-deep steel-and-concrete casing.
- Cost was in excess of $360,000.

restaurant is open 24 hours a day, so there is no excuse for not coming here at some point. This spot provides diners with private booths curtained with red velvet as well as traditional seating options. Nearby, the XO bar specializes in old cognacs. Live jazz music is played Tuesday through Saturday from 6 to 11pm. If you're not up for the action, plan to come early, as the noise from the bar can get pretty intense.

At the InterContinental Buckhead, 3315 Peachtree Rd. NE. © **404/946-9070.** www.aupieddecochon atlanta.com. Reservations recommended. Main courses $17–$32. AE, DC, DISC, MC, V. Daily 24 hr. MARTA: Buckhead.

**Home** ★ SOUTHERN   Focused on farm to table, Home Restaurant and Bar features Southern-inspired, modern fare by chef Jeff Wright. The restaurant serves a limited brunch menu on Sundays, but lunch and dinner dishes run the gamut from pimento cheese or pulled brisket sandwiches to fried chicken confit and shrimp and grits. For the true Southern meal experience, try one of their desserts, including the red velvet cake with cream cheese ice cream (delish!), cornbread cake with coffee ice cream and fresh berries, or—drum roll, please—a Moon Pie Coca-Cola float. You don't get any more Southern than that, folks.

111 W. Paces Ferry Rd. © **404/869-0777.** www.h2sr.com. Reservations suggested. Lunch entrees $7–$16; dinner entrees $22–$35. AE, MC, V. Sun–Fri 11:30am–2:30pm; daily 5–10pm (until 10:30pm Tues–Wed, 11pm Fri–Sat). MARTA: Lenox.

**Horseradish Grill** ★ CONTEMPORARY SOUTHERN   This restaurant had a previous incarnation as the Red Barn Inn, and it still retains some of the rustic atmosphere: wood barn walls, a raftered pine ceiling, and a massive stone fireplace. Big windows overlook the organic garden on one side and Chastain Park on the other; patio seating is under ancient oaks. The view is lovely, whether you're inside or out, but go for the patio if you have a choice. It's also Atlanta's oldest continuously operating restaurant.

Chef Daniel Alterman emphasizes innovative Southern recipes, simply prepared. Ingredients are seasonal and regional: no salmon or lobster, no tomatoes in winter, no turnip greens in summer. The excellent specialties include spicy North Carolina barbecue on corncakes, Georgia mountain trout, hickory-grilled double-cut pork chop, and so on. The wine list is predominantly American, but there are international selections, too. Oatmeal spice cake is the not-to-be-missed dessert. At lunch, there are sandwiches, small plates, and salads. The brunch menu is especially good—try the sweet-potato biscuit with sautéed spinach, grilled andouille sausage, poached eggs, and hollandaise.

4320 Powers Ferry Rd. (at Chastain Park). © **404/255-7277.** www.horseradishgrill.com. Reservations recommended. Lunch items $6–$15; dinner main courses $18–$34. AE, DC, DISC, MC, V. Mon–Fri 11:30am–2:30pm; Mon–Thurs 5:30–10pm; Fri–Sat 5–10pm; Sun 11am–2:30pm and 5–9pm. MARTA: Lenox.

**Kyma ★★** GREEK   Fine Greek dining has finally arrived in Atlanta. One of the newest additions to the Buckhead Life Restaurant Group, Kyma is a contemporary Greek seafood tavern unlike any other. The restaurant is absolutely stunning, with 16-foot solid marble columns weighing 55,000 pounds each, a ceiling lit by twinkling stars, a broken-plate wall mosaic, and a fountain cascading over a marble display of iced fresh whole fish. The predominantly Greek staff adds authenticity to the experience.

Chef Pano I. Karatassos led the menu development for Kyma, showcasing his love of French fundamentals and his clean technique, featuring spices, acidity, and finesse. Kyma will delight you with its cuisine full of true Greek flavors, including *mezedakia* (assorted Greek appetizers), whole fresh fish flown in daily from Mediterranean waters, and favorite spreads. The mezedes are typically shared and enjoyed with ice-cold ouzo, a Greek liqueur flavored with anise. Try a combination tasting of appetizers, from traditional Greek red-caviar mousse to roasted red-pepper purée with feta cheese, to get the full range of flavors and textures. Sides serve two people, so you can choose your main dish and accompaniments separately. You might not be able to pronounce anything on the menu, but the waitstaff is used to the grunt-and-point method.

3085 Piedmont Rd. © **404/262-0702.** www.buckheadrestaurants.com. Reservations required. Entrees $19–$42. AE, DC, MC, V. Mon–Sat 5–11pm. MARTA: Lindbergh.

**Nava ★★** SOUTHWESTERN   Nava's tri-level earth-toned interior is gorgeous—the work of architect Bill Johnson, who is known for creating fabulous settings. There's a bundled spruce ceiling beamed with tree trunks, a *kiva*-style fireplace, a copper-hooded exhibition kitchen, and a rustic and elegant decor rich with Southwestern and Native American art.

Don't come here expecting a beans-and-burritos Tex-Mex meal. This is truly inventive Southwestern cuisine; you'll find enchiladas and tostadas and the like, but they're stuffed with such treats as rock shrimp and jalapeño honey mustard, or ancho-chile steak and portobello mushrooms. You can even make a meal from the long list of starters—an easy way to sample the creative menu. The appetizer of mussels dry-roasted in a hot iron skillet and served in spicy chipotle broth is a favorite among regulars. Save room for the roasted-banana enchilada, served with warm caramel sauce—a great combination. Nava's extensive wine list was composed to complement the contemporary Southwestern dishes.

There's also a large selection of tequilas, beers, and margaritas; the prickly-pear margarita **123** is a big seller.

3060 Peachtree Rd. (at W. Paces Ferry Rd.). ℂ **404/240-1984.** www.buckheadrestaurants.com. Reservations recommended. Lunch items $10–$17; appetizers $7.50–$13; dinner main courses $18–$34. AE, DC, DISC, MC, V. Mon–Fri 11:30am–2:30pm and 5:30–11pm; Sat 5–11pm; Sun 5:30–10pm. MARTA: Lenox.

**Prime ★★** SEAFOOD/STEAK/SUSHI    Don't be put off by the fact that this restaurant is located in a shopping mall. For one thing, it's in Lenox Square, *the* shopping mall of the Southeast. And what better finish to a shopping spree than a martini and a steak, or sushi? If you're going to indulge, you might as well go all the way. And this is an extremely indulgent place—a suave, hip atmosphere with food to match. It's a steakhouse, but it's bright and contemporary rather than dark and clubby.

Do start with a martini. The French say hard liquor spoils the meal, but hey, this isn't France—and several specialty martinis are available. The sushi is the freshest you can get, the steaks are sublime and huge, and the seafood is stylish. At lunch, you'll find lighter entrees, sandwiches, and a divine lobster salad with citrus vinaigrette (no mayo). Sundays feature dollar sushi and hot sake from 4 to 9pm.

3393 Peachtree Rd. NE (upstairs at the main entrance to Lenox Square shopping mall). ℂ **404/812-0555.** www.h2sr.com. Reservations recommended. Lunch items $6.95–$15; dinner main courses $17–$29. AE, DC, DISC, MC, V. Mon–Sat 11:30am–10pm (until 11pm Fri–Sat); Sun 4–10pm. MARTA: Buckhead or Lenox.

## MODERATE

**Buckhead Diner ★★** NEW AMERICAN/TRADITIONAL AMERICAN    As sleek as a Thunderbird convertible, the exterior of this nouvelle diner glitters with neon tubing and chrome, and the posh interior conjures up images of the *Orient Express*. It's almost always crowded, so be prepared to wait at peak times (it's usually worth it—the place is full of hustle and bustle and lots of fun). Open since 1987, the diner has a full bar, including excellent Bloody Mary's.

Main courses are a mix of Mom and modern, some quite heavy on the calories (but who's counting?). Longtime favorites include the veal and wild-mushroom meatloaf with celery mashed potatoes, as well as the ahi tuna burger. The sweet and spicy calamari appetizer is a favorite. If you order nothing else, be sure to get the homemade potato chips slathered with melted Maytag blue cheese—big enough for the table to share, and I bet you won't be too embarrassed to lick the plate. Dessert must-haves include a to-die-for chocolate-chip crème brûlée. All the breads are baked fresh daily at the Buckhead Bread Company (see below).

3073 Piedmont Rd. (at E. Paces Ferry Rd.). ℂ **404/262-3336.** www.buckheadrestaurants.com. Reservations not necessary. Snacks, sandwiches, and salads $6–$16; lunch items $7.95–$24; dinner main courses $18–$28. AE, DC, DISC, MC, V. Mon–Sat 11am–midnight; Sun (including brunch) 10am–10pm. MARTA: Lenox.

**Houston's ★** Kids TRADITIONAL AMERICAN    Part of an Atlanta-based group with restaurants throughout the country, Houston's serves up lavish portions of fresh, top-quality fare in an exciting yet informal spot. It's always packed with people, and service is as snappy as the food. There's usually a wait, but you won't mind spending time on the front patio, a terrific people-watching spot, or in the bar. (If you're in a rush during lunch, eat at the bar.)

Thick, hickory-grilled burgers are a specialty, as are the tender, meaty ribs, served with a choice of side dishes: skillet beans, fries, coleslaw, or couscous. A lighter main course is the salad of sliced grilled chicken, tossed with chopped greens and julienned tortilla strips in a honey-lime vinaigrette, garnished with a light peanut sauce. For dessert, you can indulge in a huge, chewy brownie topped with vanilla ice cream and Kahlúa.

There are several locations around town, including one in Buckhead in the Brookwood Square Shopping Center, 2166 Peachtree Rd., at Colonial Homes Drive (© **404/351-2442**).

3321 Lenox Rd. (at E. Paces Ferry Rd.). © **404/237-7534.** www.hillstone.com. Reservations not accepted. Burgers and salads $9–$17; main courses $13–$30. AE, MC, V. Daily 11am–10pm. MARTA: Lenox.

## OK Café (Kids) TRADITIONAL AMERICAN

The specialties here are down-home classics served in a simple setting of leather booths and old-style Formica tables. A jukebox is stocked with oldies, and waiters wear white diner uniforms. There's a witty sculpture of a money tree in the dining room—perhaps to pay homage to the moneyed crowd, which comes here for updated comfort food.

The place is full of memories of Mom: Blue-plate specials such as meatloaf, pot roast, and roast turkey with corn-bread dressing are all served with corn muffins and two side dishes (the best is six-cheese macaroni). Sandwiches, burgers, salads, and thick, old-fashioned shakes are other options. They also have a dessert list to die for, including coconut cake, hot pecan pie, and banana bread pudding. It's a good spot to bring the whole family, especially if you have kids who turn up their noses at anything more complex than mashed potatoes. OK Café is also known for its country-style breakfasts and brunches. Takeout is available.

1284 W. Paces Ferry Rd. NW (at Northside Pkwy., in the West Paces Ferry Shopping Center). © **404/233-2888.** www.okcafe.com. Reservations not accepted. Burgers, salads, and sandwiches $7–$12; lunch and dinner $12–$14. AE, DC, DISC, MC, V. Daily 7am–11pm (until midnight Fri–Sat). MARTA: Lenox.

## Pasta Vino (Kids) (Value) ITALIAN/PIZZA

This may not be the very best Italian restaurant in town, but the combination of high quality and low prices makes it a favorite neighborhood stop—and a great choice when you want good food but don't want to dress up and go "out." Billy Petrucci runs this little trattoria; his father, Nico, runs chic, upscale Abruzzi in the same shopping center.

The yeasty, chewy pizzas, most of which are available by the slice, are as good as they come. Seafood and veal, served with a side of pasta marinara, are done especially well. And the mussels appetizer is large enough for an entree. The best traditional Italian dish on the menu is the lasagna, made with the most tender noodles, a little ground beef, delicate béchamel and tomato sauces, and lots of mozzarella. It's worth twice the price. The eggplant lasagna is even better. The house salad is made with boring iceberg lettuce, so choose the huge Caesar instead and split it. The wine is limited to the house varieties—one white, one red—but they're not bad. This place is extremely kid-friendly and usually filled with families from the local, well-heeled neighborhood. The patio is a great spot in summer.

2391 Peachtree Rd. NE (in the Peachtree Battle Promenade at Peachtree Battle Ave.). © **404/231-4946.** www.pvbuckhead.com. Reservations not accepted. Pizzas $14–$21; pastas $10–$19; main courses $13–$21. MC, V. Mon–Fri 11:30am–2pm; daily 5–9pm (until 10pm Fri–Sat). MARTA: Lenox or Buckhead.

## Pricci ★ ITALIAN

Pricci is strikingly glamorous, with part of its drama stemming from an open kitchen where a team of white-toqued chefs engage in a culinary frenzy around an oak-fired pizza oven. The decor is also theatrical—Art Deco chrome and brass dividers, rich decorative woods, cozy banquettes, and a snazzy bar. The downside is the noise; it's hard to escape all the dining clatter.

Pricci's fare is hearty regional Italian cuisine: thin-crusted oak-fired pizzas, pastas such **125**

as beef short-rib ravioli, *osso buco* with borlotti beans and gremolata, and so on. The specialty of the house, which serves two, is an excellent whole roasted fish with grilled asparagus. A good value on the lunch menu is the three-pasta tasting. The award-winning wine list highlights every wine-producing region of Italy and features a good selection of grappa (an Italian brandy).

500 Pharr Rd. (at Maple Dr.). ℰ **404/237-2941.** www.buckheadrestaurants.com. Reservations recommended. Lunch $8.95–$15; pizzas, pastas, and risottos $8.50–$15; dinner entrees $13–$25. AE, DC, DISC, MC, V. Mon–Fri 11:30am–2:30pm; daily 5–11pm (until 10pm Sun). MARTA: Lenox.

**Swan Coach House** (Finds) CONTINENTAL/TRADITIONAL AMERICAN If you visit the Atlanta History Center in Buckhead (p. 140), this delightful restaurant is a great lunch option. It's a genteel spot with a "ladies' lunch" ambience, and the menu mirrors the setting, featuring fare such as salmon croquettes with cucumber relish and Dijon dill sauce. There's even a 1950s-style congealed salad on the list. The best choice, which has been on the menu for 30 years, is the Swan's Favorite: chicken salad in pastry timbales served with cheese straws and creamy frozen fruit salad. For dessert, order the French silk swan—a meringue base filled with chocolate mousse and covered with whipped cream and slivered almonds. There's a full bar.

*Note:* You don't have to visit the Atlanta History Center to dine here; the restaurant has a separate entrance. A gift shop and art gallery adjoin the dining room.

At the Atlanta History Center, 3130 Slaton Dr. NW. ℰ **404/261-0636.** www.swancoachhouse.com. Reservations accepted for groups of 10 or more. Main courses $12–$15. AE, MC, V. Mon–Sat 11am–2:30pm. Closed New Year's Day, Memorial Day, July 4th, Labor Day, Thanksgiving, and Christmas. MARTA: Lindbergh.

**Toulouse** ★ (Finds) NEW AMERICAN The name is French, but the cuisine is New American, with influences from the south of France. Toulouse is tucked away behind a strip of shops along Peachtree Road; it's a bit hard to spot, but you'll be glad you sought it out. The neighborhood crowd, attired in anything from blue jeans to black tie, likes to keep this place a secret, revealing it only to friends and special visitors. It's casual and charming, a spacious loft with a large wooden bar and an open kitchen in full view.

The menu changes seasonally, perhaps more often depending on the whims of the chef, but you're likely to find some of the house specialties always available. A good bet is the plump roast chicken done to perfection in a wood-fired oven, accompanied by arugula bread salad. Another favorite is the braised lamb shank with a Kalamata olive/sweet-pepper sauce and roasted vegetables. The excellent wine list has lots of good values and recently landed Toulouse a top ranking from *Wine Spectator.* There's no corkage fee on Sundays.

2293 Peachtree Rd. NE (south of Peachtree Battle Ave.). ℰ **404/351-9533.** www.toulouserestaurant. com. Reservations recommended. Main courses $16–$25. AE, DC, MC, V. Daily 5:30–10pm (until 11pm Fri–Sat). MARTA: Lenox or Buckhead.

## INEXPENSIVE

**Corner Café/Buckhead Bread Company** ★ BAKERY/CAFE This spot is a combination of an upscale cafe and a gourmet bakery. The cafe portion is more casual and relaxed than the Buckhead Diner, its glitzy cousin across the street, but the food is still upscale. The menu is large and varied, with wonderful soups and hearty sandwiches on bread baked in the neighboring bakery. There are also interesting main-dish salads,

WHERE TO DINE

BUCKHEAD

including the longtime favorite, a chicken-, egg-, and tuna-salad trio. Weekday breakfasts include fresh-baked pastries, crepes, Belgian waffles, and traditional fare such as poached eggs with cheddar-cheese grits. Weekend brunch is a busy time here, with a fancier menu that features delicious dishes such as two pan-poached eggs with portobello mushrooms and crispy prosciutto topped with a port-wine glaze.

About half the space is given over to a vast bakery, the Buckhead Bread Company, which displays many varieties of fresh-baked bread each day—everything from focaccia flavored with fresh rosemary and basil to honeyed eight-grain loaves studded with roasted sunflower seeds. The gorgeous pastries have a French pedigree that will transport you to the Left Bank. You can get your sweets to go, or enjoy them on the small patio with a cup of specialty coffee.

3070 Piedmont Rd. (at E. Paces Ferry Rd.). (C) **404/240-1978.** www.buckheadrestaurants.com. Reservations not accepted. Sandwiches and main-dish salads $8.25–$12; brunch items $7.95–$14. AE, DC, DISC, MC, V. Mon–Fri 6:30am–3:30pm; Sat–Sun 8am–3:30pm. MARTA: Lenox.

**Fellini's Pizza** (Kids) PIZZA  You won't get chèvre or cilantro on your pizza here, but you will get traditional toppings such as anchovies, Italian sausage, meatballs, pepperoni, fresh mushrooms, and onions. These cheesy New York–style pies have thin, doughy crusts that exude the heavenly aroma of fresh-baked bread. Besides the pizzas, some of which are available by the slice, there are immense, well-stuffed calzones. The beer is always ice-cold.

Fellini's is a classic pizza joint, and a damn good one at that. It's a wacky place, very atypical for Buckhead. Most of the seating is at tables on a large outdoor patio centered on a tiered fountain, with statues of angels and gargoyles. Because it fronts Peachtree Road, it's a great spot to sit and watch the city go by. If you're wilting from the heat, you can always retreat to the funky, spare interior.

There are several additional locations; the most convenient for visitors are in Buckhead, at 1991 Howell Mill Rd. ((C) **404/352-0799**), and in Midtown, at 909 Ponce de Leon Ave. ((C) **404/873-3088**).

2809 Peachtree Rd. (at Rumson Rd.). (C) **404/266-0082.** www.fellinisatlanta.com. Reservations not necessary. Slice $2.05–$3.95; medium pie $12 and up; calzones $5.50 and up. No credit cards. Mon–Sat 11am–2am; Sun noon–midnight. MARTA: Lenox or Buckhead.

**La Fonda Latina** SPANISH  Funky and festive, La Fonda is a brightly painted little hole in the wall consisting of a small interior dining area with an open kitchen, a covered outdoor patio, and an open-air rooftop patio with seating in wooden booths amid lots of plants. Outdoor areas are heated in winter and cooled by large fans in summer.

The food is both fresh and refreshingly authentic. You might simply order up a bottle of *vino blanco* and a delicious *ensalada mixta* (tuna, black olives, lettuce, onions, and peppers in a classic vinaigrette that you can soak up with Cuban bread). There are several different kinds of quesadillas, three types of paella (traditional, seafood, and vegetarian), Latin sandwiches served on crusty Cuban bread, and a nicely grilled chicken served with rice and beans. Try the creamy, homemade flan for dessert.

La Fonda has three other locations, including 923 Ponce de Leon Ave. ((C) **404/607-0665**).

2813 Peachtree Rd. NE (btw. Rumson Rd. and Sheridan Dr.). (C) **404/816-8311.** www.fellinisatlanta.com. Reservations recommended. Main courses $6.25–$12.50. MC, V. Mon–Thurs 11:30am–11pm; Fri–Sat 11am–midnight; Sun noon–11pm. MARTA: Lenox or Buckhead.

A meal in this charming district can be an occasion to see a non-touristy part of Atlanta. Come a little early so you can browse the area's great little shops and galleries. For dining establishments, see the map on p. 129.

## EXPENSIVE

**Two Urban Licks** ★★ NEW AMERICAN   One of Atlanta's hottest dining spots, Two Urban Licks is among a handful of area restaurants turned gold by creators Bob Amick and Todd Rushing of Concentrics Restaurants. (Others include One Midtown Kitchen, Piebar, and Murphy's.) Two's executive chef, Scott Serpas, has created a menu of fiery American cooking in a high-energy, urban environment. Specializing in wood-fired meat selections such as suckling pig, fish, and barbecue, the restaurant cooks dishes "in the round" on a 14-foot rotisserie in a wide-open kitchen, smack-dab in the middle of the bustling eatery. Try the seafood gumbo—Big Easy style. Just as exciting as the menu here is the innovative domestic wine program, consisting of 42 stainless-steel barrels of wine displayed in a 26-foot glass-and-steel temperature-controlled tower just inside the front door. Enjoy live blues at 8pm Wednesday through Saturday; on Sundays at 6pm, there's the Low Country boil.

820 Ralph McGill Blvd. ✆ **404/522-4622.** www.twourbanlicks.com. Reservations recommended. Main courses $19–$28. AE, MC, V. Mon–Thurs 5:30pm–midnight; Fri–Sat 5:30pm–1am; Sun 5:30–10pm. MARTA: Five Points and bus 16.

**Wisteria** ★ SOUTHERN   In this former grocery store, chef Jason Hill has given Southern cuisine his own twist, starting with the black-eyed pea hummus with sweet potato chips and his green tomato fries with bleu cheese dip. This casual, upscale setting is perfect for special events and the wine list is brief but interesting. Belly up for supper when you can enjoy such down-home delights as jumbo shrimp and grits or Southern fried catfish over a warmed green tomato, okra, and spicy crawfish ragout with remoulade.

471 N. Highland Ave. ✆ **404/525-3363.** www.wisteria-atlanta.com. Reservations recommended. Main courses $16–$30. AE, DC, DISC, MC, V. Daily 5:30–10pm (until 11pm Fri–Sat). MARTA: North Ave.

## MODERATE

**Babette's Café** ★★ EUROPEAN PROVINCIAL   Owner/chef Marla Adams has put together a menu that's decidedly anti–haute cuisine, full of excellent interpretations of comfy, everyday provincial dishes. The crowd is made up of loyal locals, and the French farmhouse ambience matches the fare.

The restaurant has some of the best mussels in town. Start off with the mussel appetizer, and don't let the offbeat combination of ingredients scare you off. Bivalves are Adams's specialty, and this unusual dish—steamed mussels with white wine, strawberries, and serrano peppers—is excellent. A longtime favorite entree—grilled lamb loin chops with red-wine reduction and shoestring potatoes—is kept on the menu by popular demand.

Most of the selections from the reasonably priced wine list are available by the glass, part of Adams's strategy to encourage customers to sample different wines. There are special prix-fixe dinners held each season, the most famous of which is at New Year's. It's a re-creation of the food and wine from the book *Babette's Feast,* for which the restaurant is named. Babette's is a great place to stop after a visit to the Carter Center, which is just around the corner.

573 N. Highland Ave. (just north of Freedom Pkwy.). ✆ **404/523-9121.** www.babettescafe.com. Reservations recommended, and required for wine dinners held once a season. Brunch items $7–$26; dinner main courses $15–$26. AE, DC, DISC, MC, V. Tues–Sat 5:30–10pm; Sun 10:30am–2pm and 5–9pm. MARTA: North Ave.

**Murphy's ★★★** TRADITIONAL AMERICAN   Murphy's, a wine-and-cheese shop that evolved into a restaurant and bakery, comprises a cozy warren of rooms. It's one of the most popular places in Atlanta for weekend brunch. The interior is charming and inn-like, with French doors flung open and ceiling fans spinning in nice weather. Up front is the bakery/wine shop, with glass display cases overflowing with pastries, crusty fresh-baked breads, and luscious desserts. At dinner, you'll find a variety of entrees, including sautéed rainbow trout with sweet-potato hash. For lunch, the hefty sandwiches are always winners, especially the crab-cake version with smoky chile mayo; there's a selection of pastas and salads as well. Brunch includes egg dishes, breads, waffles, pancakes, salads, and sandwiches.

Murphy's is a popular destination for locals in the surrounding neighborhood, which is full of young professionals who like casual dining. It's a good stop if you're exploring the Virginia Highland area; if there's a wait, you can kill some time in the nearby shops. Murphy's is also perfect for dessert and coffee, which is otherwise hard to find around here.

997 Virginia Ave. NE (at N. Highland Ave.). ✆ **404/872-0904.** www.murphysvh.com. Call-ahead seating for dinner only. Lunch, brunch, and breakfast items $5–$13; dinner main courses $11–$24. AE, DC, DISC, MC, V. Mon–Thurs 11am–10pm; Fri 11am–midnight; Sat 8am–11pm; Sun 8am–10pm. MARTA: North Ave.

**Pura Vida** TAPAS   With cuisine inspired by that of the Latin Caribbean and South America, plus some Spanish influences thrown in for good measure, Pura Vida is the best tapas eatery in the city. Among the tasty $6-to-$10-a-plate tapas designed to share are the *empanada de picadillao de pollo.* Translated, that would be turnovers stuffed with chicken, olives, capers, raisins, and diced eggs served with chile–sugarcane vinegar. Another popular plate is the Ponce de Leon—18-month cured Serrano ham, Spanish chorizo, and olives. Pura Vida also offers an extensive wines-by-the-glass menu, as well as specialty drinks such as "Sex in Santiago," its version of a cosmopolitan cocktail. Folks come here not only to eat, but also to enjoy the activities of the Pura Vida Social Club: On Fiesta Friday, patrons can join in dancing the salsa, mambo, and merengue or just sit back and enjoy the sights. Some nights, the city's dramatic tango community performs the Argentine tango while guests enjoy Argentine wines. Monday nights feature mojitos and dominos. (I hear the game is making a comeback.) The atmosphere is fun, but if you're not up for noisy crowds, plan to dine early.

656 N. Highland Ave. ✆ **404/870-9797.** www.puravidatapas.com. Reservations recommended. Tapas $6–$10. AE, DC, DISC, MC, V. Mon–Thurs 5:30–10pm; Fri–Sat 5:30–11:30pm; Sun noon–3:30pm. MARTA: North Ave.

**Sotto Sotto ★★** ITALIAN   Sotto Sotto means "hush hush" in Italian. How ironic: The food is divine here, but the noise is incredible. It seems that half of Atlanta has determined this is the place of the moment and now tries to wedge into the tiny restaurant on the same night, at the same time. It's an energetic crowd, and they all appear quite content to shout at one another over their seafood risotto. If you don't mind noise, then by all means go. But if you're looking for a quiet, romantic spot, forget it.

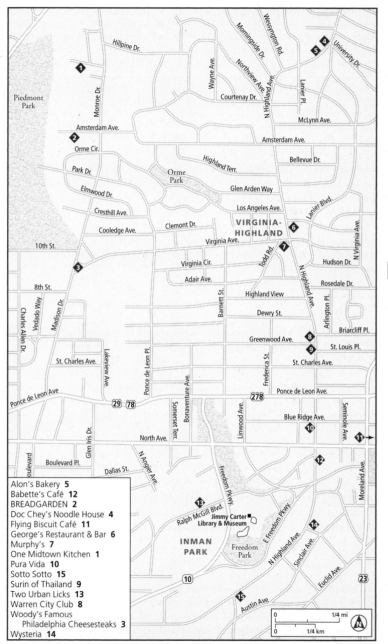

**WHERE TO DINE**

**6**

**VIRGINIA HIGHLAND & INMAN PARK**

Piedmont Park

Hillpine Dr.

Wayne Ave.

Morningside Dr.

Wessyngton Rd.

Northview Ave.

N Highland Ave.

Lanier Pl.

University Dr.

Courtenay Dr.

McLynn Ave.

Monroe Dr.

Amsterdam Ave.

Amsterdam Ave.

Orme Cir.

Bellevue Dr.

Park Dr.

Highland Terr.

Orme Park

Glen Arden Way

Lanier Blvd.

Elmwood Dr.

Los Angeles Ave.

Cresthill Ave.

Clemont Dr.

VIRGINIA-HIGHLAND

N Virginia Ave.

Cooledge Ave.

Virginia Ave.

10th St.

Virginia Cir.

Todd Rd.

Hudson Dr.

8th St.

Adair Ave.

Rosedale Dr.

Charles Allen Dr.

Vedado Way

Madison Dr.

Barnett St.

Highland View

N Highland Ave.

Arlington Pl.

Briarcliff Pl.

Dewry St.

St. Charles Ave.

Lakeview Ave.

Ponce de Leon Pl.

Greenwood Ave.

Frederica St.

St. Louis Pl.

St. Charles Ave.

Ponce de Leon Ave.

Glen Iris Dr.

Somerset Terr.

Bonaventure Ave.

Linwood Ave.

Blue Ridge Ave.

Seminole Ave.

North Ave.

Boulevard Pl.

Dallas St.

N Angier Ave.

Freedom Pkwy.

Moreland Ave.

Ralph McGill Blvd.

Jimmy Carter Library & Museum

E Freedom Pkwy.

N Highland Ave.

Sinclair Ave.

INMAN PARK

Freedom Park

Euclid Ave.

Austin Ave.

0     1/4 mi
0     1/4 km

Alon's Bakery **5**
Babette's Café **12**
BREADGARDEN **2**
Doc Chey's Noodle House **4**
Flying Biscuit Café **11**
George's Restaurant & Bar **6**
Murphy's **7**
One Midtown Kitchen **1**
Pura Vida **10**
Sotto Sotto **15**
Surin of Thailand **9**
Two Urban Licks **13**
Warren City Club **8**
Woody's Famous
    Philadelphia Cheesesteaks **3**
Wysteria **14**

## Outdoor Dining

Food always seems to taste better outdoors, and Atlanta's temperate climate makes alfresco dining possible 6 to 8 months out of the year. It's true that there are always some stifling midsummer days, but things usually cool off enough in the evening to make outdoor dining quite pleasant. Many of these places heat their patios during the winter, closing them only on the most frigid days. Here are a few prime spots:

**Anis Café & Bistro** (p. 120): This tree-shaded spot outside a converted Buckhead bungalow is reminiscent of a terrace in the south of France. You can easily imagine you're in Provence here.

**Canoe** (p. 132): Lovely gardens surround a covered terrace on the banks of the Chattahoochee River, creating a perfect setting. Wear your best Ralph Lauren outfit.

**Fellini's Pizza** (p. 126): Have a beer or a slice of pizza, and watch the world sail down Peachtree Road.

**French American Brasserie** (p. 103) Known to its friends as FAB, this downtown spot offers a great view of the city's skyline from its canopied rooftop seating area and bar.

**George's Restaurant and Bar** (p. 132): There are only a few tables outside this plain neighborhood tavern, but it's in the heart of trendy Virginia Highland, prime people-watching territory.

**Horseradish Grill** (p. 121): If you're looking for a place to propose, this is it. A candlelit patio is set under ancient oaks and overlooks lovely Chastain Park.

**Nava** (p. 122): Located at the busy intersection of Peachtree and West Paces Ferry roads, but comfortably set back from the street, the lovely brick terrace here is a great perch from which to watch all the Buckhead activity while sipping margaritas and nibbling appetizers.

**South City Kitchen** (p. 105): There's limited seating outside this converted Midtown house, but it's a perfect spot to watch the comings and goings of all the beautiful young people who dine here.

**The Warren City Club** (p. 131) The Warren in popular Virginia Highland has a delightful third-level garden terrace where guests can enjoy cocktails or a full meal.

That's the bad news. There's lots of good news: the wood-roasted fish, Sotto Sotto's specialty (the chef fillets it tableside); the meltingly tender homemade pastas and creamy risottos; the inventive appetizers; the attentive service; and the small but tempting selection of desserts. The unbelievably rich chocolate soup (yes, soup) of dark Belgian chocolate with hazelnut whipped cream and sugar croutons will make you swoon. The bartender makes a top-notch martini, and the all-Italian wine list is extensive, with several excellent selections by the glass. You may have to wait to be seated even if you have a reservation, but it's worth it.

**Surin of Thailand** ★ THAI   This charming Thai restaurant opened in 1991 to big crowds, and it continues to enjoy hearty acclaim. The place is full of neighborhood regulars and suburbanites looking for consistent Asian cooking in an upbeat, contemporary setting—bare oak floors, candlelit tables covered in royal-blue cloths, and cheerful yellow walls. On weekends, arrive early or late to avoid a wait, and try for a table in the window or along the wall. There's more seating in the small back rooms, but the noisy and crowded main dining area is much more fun.

The same menu is offered throughout the day, with specials at both meals. The fresh basil rolls are some of the best around. Another appetizer favorite is chef Surin Techarukpong's exquisite deep-fried edible "baskets" filled with shrimp, chicken, and corn, served with a piquant vinegar-chile-peanut sauce. Entrees range from seafood dishes to traditional noodles and curry. If it's on the specials menu, opt for *neur nam tok*—strips of grilled beef tenderloin seasoned with lime, hot serrano chile peppers, fresh basil, fish sauce, and green onion; it's eaten rolled in cabbage leaves. For a cool finale, try the creamy homemade coconut ice cream or one of the mango, green tea, or ginger versions.

810 N. Highland Ave. (at Greenwood Ave.). ℭ **404/892-7789.** www.surinofthailand.com. Reservations not accepted. Lunch items $7–$8.50; dinner main courses $10–$20. AE, DC, DISC, MC, V. Mon–Fri 11:30am– 2:30pm; Sat–Sun noon–2:30pm; daily 5:30–10:30pm (until 11:30pm Fri–Sat). MARTA: North Ave.

**Warren City Club** ★ NEW AMERICAN   Don't let the name scare you away—you can be a member of this club, but don't have to be in order to enjoy the great food in a comfortable setting, including an outdoor deck. The Warren offers a full bar and comfortable seating areas around five wood-burning fireplaces. Dishes include Captain Crunch–crusted salmon, pepperoni and portabella lasagna, and of course, the Warren burger.

The party goes on until 2am, with DJ music and dancing. The $4 mimosa brunches are a can't-miss, with menu items ranging from $8 to $13. Wine Wednesdays and stand-up comedy on Sunday nights (doors open at 7pm, show starts at 9pm) are popular events. You'll find an extensive list of fine wines and special spirits.

818 N. Highland Ave. (at Greenwood Ave.). ℭ **404/475-1991.** www.thewarrencityclub.com. Appetizers $8–$13; entrees $13–$22. AE, MC, V. Wed–Sat 6pm–2am; Sun brunch 11am–3pm. MARTA: North Ave.

## INEXPENSIVE

**Doc Chey's Noodle House** (Kids) ASIAN   This may not be the most authentic noodle house in the city, but it's a neighborhood standby that won't let you down if you're looking for a good, inexpensive meal. It's kid-friendly, too, and offers two children's meals (Chinese chicken soup or chicken, carrots, and broccoli over rice) that should please finicky little eaters. The rest of us have a lot to choose from: fragrant basil rolls, Chinese scallion pancakes, soup bowls, noodle bowls, rice bowls, and salads, each with a Thai, Chinese, Japanese, or Vietnamese accent. You can ask for most dishes to be prepared vegetarian-style. The decor is nothing fancy, but the patio is large and pleasant, the Asian beer is cold, and at these prices, there's not much to complain about.

There's another Doc Chey's in Emory Village near Emory University, 1556 N. Decatur Rd. (ℭ **404/378-8188**), open for lunch Monday through Saturday and dinner nightly.

1424 N. Highland Ave. (at University Dr.). ℭ **404/888-0777.** www.doccheys.com. Reservations not accepted. Main dishes $5–$10. AE, DISC, MC, V. Daily 11:30am–10pm. MARTA: North Ave.

**Flying Biscuit Cafe** ★ (Finds) NEW AMERICAN   This totally unpretentious neighborhood hangout has the best biscuits in town, but that's not all that makes folks willing to wait up to an hour and a half for a table. A cozied-up storefront near the funky Little Five Points area, this place has a round-the-clock breakfast menu that will get you over the worst day-after-the-night-before, plus an assortment of dishes that are best described as comfort food for the granola crowd. Breakfast and lunch are served all day. You can get a cup of coffee while you wait outside for your table, but to avoid the serious crowds, come on a weekday or in the early afternoon. If you have any sullen teenagers in your party, they'll think you're really cool for bringing them here.

Orange-scented French toast with raspberry sauce and honey crème anglaise is hard to beat, especially when accompanied by homemade turkey-and-sage sausage. But the aptly named Love Cakes, a mix of black beans and cornmeal, sautéed and topped with tomatillo salsa, sour cream, feta, and raw onion spears, will steal your heart away. Though there's a vegetarian slant to the menu, there's also plenty to please carnivores, from the grilled turkey meatloaf and soy breakfast sausage to the ever-changing warm chicken salad atop organic field greens. Look for nightly chicken, seafood, and pasta specials, too.

There's a second location in Midtown, at 1001 Piedmont Ave. (© **404/874-8887**).

1655 McLendon Ave. (at Clifton Rd.). © **404/687-8888.** www.flyingbiscuit.com. Reservations not accepted. Breakfast $5.95–$8.95; main courses $6.95–$14. AE, MC, V. Daily 7am–10pm (until 10:30pm Fri–Sat). MARTA: Midtown.

**George's Restaurant and Bar** (Value) TRADITIONAL AMERICAN   Smack in the middle of trendy Virginia Highland, surrounded by chic boutiques and cafes, is a comfy old neighborhood tavern—nearly a juke joint—that's managed so far to buck the gentrification sweep. This place, which has been operated by the Najour family for over 40 years, is not trendy, so don't expect wild-mushroom risotto or seared tuna. Instead, gear up for solid bar fare—burgers, sandwiches, fries, and the like. The refreshingly unpretentious attitude attracts neighborhood regulars and a couple of book-discussion groups, which meet here regularly.

Good bets are the substantial homemade black-bean soup and the crispy onion rings—even better than the Varsity's. When you order a burger, be sure to specify how you want it done. The charbroiled chicken salad, chunks of tender breast atop mixed greens, is nicely prepared. On a sunny day, grab a table on the sidewalk out front; it's a great place for watching the world (and some unusual folks) go by.

1041 N. Highland Ave. NE (near Virginia Ave.). © **404/892-3648.** Reservations not accepted. Main courses $3.95–$8.50. AE, MC, V. Mon 11:30am–10:30pm; Tues–Thurs 11:30am–11pm; Fri–Sat 11:30am–midnight; Sun 12:30–9:30pm. MARTA: North Ave.

# 6 VININGS

## EXPENSIVE

**Canoe** ★★ NEW AMERICAN   Canoe's cuisine is exceptional, and the setting is divine—a picturesque spot on the Chattahoochee River, surrounded by heavenly gardens. The interior is ultra-upscale boathouse, with polished wood, classy fabrics, and fun, sophisticated metalwork (wrought-iron kudzu vines trail through the dining room). The canoe motif is everywhere; there's even a canoe-shaped phone booth.

The menu is American with Asian accents. The appetizer of duck-stuffed crispy Georgia quail with grilled endive, dried cherries, and roasted peanuts is a great start to dinner. If it's available, try the slow-roasted rabbit with Swiss chard, apple wood bacon ravioli, and candied garlic jus. Any of the fish are good, but for a regional dish with a twist, try the seared Georgia mountain trout with smoked salmon ravioli, asparagus, and caramelized fennel. The excellent wine list is encyclopedic, and even includes a few organic options. If the weather is good, ask for a table on the large, canopied patio.

4199 Paces Ferry Rd. NW (at the Chattahoochee River), in Vinings. ℂ **770/432-2663.** www.canoeatl.com. Reservations essential on weekends. Lunch items $9.50–$18; brunch items $7–$16; dinner main courses $20–$33. AE, DC, DISC, MC, V. Mon–Fri 11:30am–2:30pm; Mon–Thurs 5:30–10pm; Fri–Sat 5:30–11pm; Sun 10:30am–2:30pm and 5:30–9:30pm.

## 7  DECATUR

### EXPENSIVE

**Floataway Café** ★★ COUNTRY FRENCH/ITALIAN  Tucked away on a secluded industrial street in a renovated warehouse near Emory University, the Floataway Café is not easy to find, but people have been flocking here since the restaurant opened in 1998. This is the second venture by Anne Quatrano and Clifford Harrison of the renowned Bacchanalia in Midtown; the restaurant and menu here are less formal, but the food is of the same high quality. The only drawback to this place is that it can be as loud as a working warehouse. Ask for a table away from the bar, which can be quite boisterous.

The menu changes daily, with an emphasis on fresh and local organic produce and unusual ingredients. You'll find succulent wood-grilled or roasted meats and seafood, homemade pastas, even a couple of pizzas—all inventively prepared. One favorite is a house specialty: grilled steak with pommes frites and red-wine shallot butter. You can make a meal of the starters: Ricotta-stuffed sautéed squash blossoms and prosciutto with Georgia figs are two that shouldn't be passed up if they're available. The wine list has an international slant and complements the food.

1123 Zonolite Rd., Ste. 15 (west of the intersection of Johnson and Briarcliff rds.), Decatur. ℂ **404/892-1414.** www.starprovisions.com. Reservations essential. Main courses $18–$32. AE, DC, MC, V. Tues–Sat from 6pm.

### MODERATE

**Thai Chili** ★ THAI  Owner Robert Khankiew, who was a chef at several other local Thai restaurants, has been packing people in since he and his family opened the doors of this friendly restaurant. The dishes are authentic, the flavors bold, and the dining room casual yet polished (tablecloths, soft lighting).

Start off with traditional basil rolls with plum sauce, or try the *namsod*—minced pork with chile, ginger, onion, and lime juice, which you roll up in a cabbage leaf. The spicy basil lamb (charbroiled chops with mushroom and onions) is succulent and exceptional, and the curries are quite good. When in doubt, stick with the daily specials or the chef's special section of the menu; all are good bets. There is no children's menu, but the restaurant is very kid-friendly. On weekends, you're likely to wait if you arrive without a reservation.

2169 Briarcliff Rd. NE (at LaVista Rd. in the BriarVista Shopping Center), Decatur. ℂ **404/315-6750.** www. thaichilicuisine.com. Reservations recommended for dinner. Lunch items $8–$14; dinner main courses $9–$23. AE, DISC, MC, V. Sun–Thurs 11am–10pm; Fri–Sat 11am–11pm.

## Cheesecake Fit for a President

Sweet potatoes are a staple in many Southern homes, and they find their way into recipes that never cease to surprise me. From sweet-potato casserole and sweet-potato pie to the popular sweet-potato biscuits served during brunch at the Horseradish Grill (p. 121), this tasty tuber is very versatile. One Atlanta treat in particular does true justice to this spectacular spud: the sweet-potato cheesecake from **Sweet Auburn Bread Company.** The creation of Atlanta chef Sonya Jones, this sweet treat is known far and wide. In fact, former president Bill Clinton stopped by the market to try it for himself. Let's just say he didn't let any go to waste.

Trained at the Culinary Institute of America in Hyde Park, N.Y., Jones grew up in the restaurant business watching every move her mother made around the kitchen. She fell in love with baking. After graduating from the CIA, she went on to share her culinary talents as a baking and pastry-chef instructor at a local technical college. Soon she had opened her own bakery and was turning out pound cakes, buttermilk and lemon chess pies, even cakes made from towers of Krispy Kreme doughnuts. But it was in 1998 that her name would become synonymous with the famed sweet-potato cheesecake. "I wanted to come up with something really Southern and yet gourmet," she said of the smooth sweet pie resting atop a pound-cake crust. The cheesecake has been featured in numerous magazines and newspapers and even on the Food Network. Now her goods are available in 22 Starbucks coffee shops around Atlanta, two of which are owned by Magic Johnson.

Formerly housed in the Sweet Auburn Curb Market, her bakery is now right at home at 234 Auburn Ave. NE, in the same neighborhood where she grew up and learned to love baking as a young girl. Retail hours are Monday through Friday from 7:30am to 5pm and Saturday from 8am to 3pm. Special orders may be placed by calling © **404/221-1157** or visiting the website at www.sweetauburnbread.com.

**Watershed** ★ NEW AMERICAN    When executive chef Scott Peacock left the highly successful Horseradish Grill a few years ago, who would have thought that he'd land in a sandwich shop housed in a former gas station in Decatur? Okay, it's better than it sounds. Owned in part by Emily Saliers, one of the Indigo Girls, and bearing the name of one of the folk duo's songs, Watershed works on several levels—hip restaurant, wine bar, and retail store featuring wine, cookbooks, kitchen-related items, and other gifty little things. All of these attractions are found in a bright, airy, retro-style space whose industrial feel is softened by its pastel decor.

There are three or four entrees on the lunch menu, but sandwiches are the thing here—highly inventive and served on a variety of buttered, toasted breads. Two standouts include the version with Bosc pear, Maytag blue cheese, applewood-smoked bacon, toasted walnuts, and arugula; and the white-truffle chicken salad with sultanas and pine nuts. Oh, yes, and you can't ignore the tangy but comforting pimento-cheese sandwich made with extra-sharp cheddar. At dinner, more entrees are added to the seasonal list of sandwiches, sides, and soups. You might find a whole roasted trout with garlic and lemon, or perhaps tender braised pork over creamy polenta. Tuesday is fried-chicken night, so arrive early to avoid a long wait. The wine list is extensive and well chosen, and the desserts, from the chocolate/pecan-praline parfait to the organic Georgia pecan tart, are scrumptious.

406 W. Ponce de Leon Ave. (just west of the square), Decatur. ✆ **404/378-4900.** www.watershed restaurant.com. Reservations recommended. Lunch entrees $8–$14; dinner entrees $12–$27. AE, MC, V. Mon–Sat 11am–10pm; Sun brunch 10am–3pm.

## INEXPENSIVE

**Athens Pizza House** Ⓥⓐⓛⓤⓔ GREEK/PIZZA   Who says pizza has to have an Italian pedigree? The Papadopoulos family migrated here more than 20 years ago from Connecticut, and they've been serving up Greek specialties and their interpretation of pizza ever since. Their restaurant draws a large number of families and Emory University students from the surrounding area. The interior is ultra-casual, with Naugahyde booths and Formica-topped tables, and you'll be welcome in shorts or jeans.

There's quite a variety of Greek dishes, from gyros to pastitsio to rotisserie-cooked lamb. Portions are generous, prices are reasonable, and everything is authentic. It's home-style rather than fancy—exactly what you would get if the Papadopouloses invited you over for dinner. The signature creation is the pizza, and if you've never had it Greek-style, it's worth a try. It has a thick, yeasty crust and comes in several varieties; the best is the vegetarian special, with fresh tomatoes, onions, sweet green peppers, Kalamata olives, and a generous portion of feta cheese. A good ending is the honey-soaked baklava.

*Note:* There are several Athens Pizza restaurants and Athens Pizza Express takeout stores around town. Check the phone book for other locations.

1341 Clairmont Rd. (at N. Decatur Rd.), Decatur. ✆ **404/636-1100.** www.athenspizzaatlanta.com. Reservations not accepted. Pizzas $6.45–$20; main courses $8.50–$12. AE, DC, DISC, MC, V. Sun–Fri 10am–11pm; Sat 11am–11pm.

**Brick Store Pub** ECLECTIC   On the square in Decatur, this pub has old-world charm without being dark and gloomy, and features the most eclectic beer menu in Atlanta. Each of the 17 drafts—from Germany, England, and even the Czech Republic—is served in its own special glass. The 79 bottled beers might make it difficult for you to decide, and Brick Store also offers 26 single-malt scotches, nine Irish whiskeys, and eight small-batch bourbons. Many patrons come here for the drinks as much as for the diverse food. Starters include such treats as baked brie or roasted-red-pepper hummus with warm pita points. Pierogi primavera (potato-and-cheese-stuffed pasta served in a Parmesan sauce) is another popular item, as are the potato wedge fries with lots of salt and vinegar. Sit around the horseshoe bar for a real pub experience, or opt for one of several tables outdoors.

There are several great shops in the area for some before- or after-dinner shopping; you'll also find a coffee shop and an ice-cream shop.

125 E. Court St. (on the square), Decatur. ✆ **404/687-0990.** www.brickstorepub.com. Reservations not accepted. Salads, sandwiches, and burgers $3.50–$7; dinner entrees $7–$9. AE, MC, V. Mon 11am–1am; Tues–Sat 11am–2am; Sun noon–10pm.

**Jake's Ice Cream & Sorbets** ICE CREAM   Ice cream just doesn't get any better than this. Jake's has a true following in Atlanta and devoted fans will stand in line, outside, in the freezing cold and rain if that's what it takes to get the goods. Among the most popular flavors are Chocolate Slap Yo' Mama, the seasonal Honey Fig, Toasted Coconut Joy-scream, the delicious Wabi Sabi Tiramisu, and the signature Brown Shugah Vanilla.

515 N. McDonough St. (under Eddie's Attic in the Little Shop of Stories), Decatur. ✆ **404/377-9300.** www.jakesicecream.com. Reservations not accepted. AE, DC, MC, V. Tues–Sat 11am–10pm; Sun noon–10pm. MARTA: Five Points.

**Raging Burrito** MEXICAN   A Decatur favorite, the Raging Burrito is the place to go when you need a salsa, guacamole, and margarita fix, not to mention the out-of-this-world burritos. From the barbecued-chicken burrito with caramelized onions and cilantro to the Sydney Salad burrito with fresh guacamole (voted best in town year after year) and a salad filling, Raging is sure to satisfy even the biggest hunger pangs. Choose from flour, wheat, spinach, or sun-dried tomato tortillas to build your dream burrito. Chase down the chow with any of 50 tequilas offered, and you might be hanging around at an outside table for a while. Nachos, quesadillas, and vegetarian chili are also popular menu items. Brunch is offered on Sundays. This is also home to Azul Tequila Lounge.

141 Sycamore St. (on the square), Decatur. ✆ **404/377-3311.** www.ragingburrito.com. Reservations not accepted. Burritos $4.50–$8. AE, DC, DISC, MC, V. Daily 11am–10pm (until 11pm Fri–Sat).

# 8 DORAVILLE

## MODERATE

**Little Szechuan** CHINESE   Little Szechuan is a perennial favorite among the ethnic restaurants that now line Buford Highway in northeast Atlanta. It's nothing fancy, but the price is right. Most of the patrons are Chinese or regulars (or both), who make a point of seeking out good ethnic food. Two Chinese-restaurant clichés are pointedly absent here: egg rolls and fortune cookies. When you're seated, you'll be given a small bowl of spicy sprouts to munch on while you peruse the extensive menu. And when your check arrives at the end of the meal, it will be accompanied by a piece of fresh, seasonal fruit—perhaps a slice of watermelon.

The standout entree is also the most expensive: fresh steamed red snapper with black-bean sauce. It's best when you request it spiced up a little. (Even though the name of the restaurant would suggest otherwise, not everything on the menu is spicy Szechuan-style Chinese.) The wine selection is extremely limited (and the red wine has been known to arrive slightly chilled), so it's best to forget it and have an ice-cold Tsing-Tao beer instead.

5091-C Buford Hwy. (just north of Shallowford Rd. in Northwoods Plaza), Doraville. ✆ **770/451-0192.** Lunch combination plates $4.65–$8.75; dinner entrees $7.25–$20. MC, V. Mon and Wed–Fri 11:30am–3pm; Wed–Mon 5–9:30pm.

# What to See & Do in Atlanta

People used to say Atlanta was a great place to live, but you wouldn't want to visit. Not anymore. In fact, because of traffic and other major pains in this city, some say just the opposite—give me a weekend in Atlanta and let me live elsewhere. To each his own.

A lot has happened since Atlanta's humble beginnings as a railroad depot, and the city is rich in historic attractions—Civil War sites, landmarks of the civil rights movement, and monuments to the businesses that have energized the city's development (such as World of Coca-Cola). And all those elements that make Atlanta a great place to live make the city a terrific place to visit, too. You can take a stroll through a world-class botanical garden, visit the world's largest indoor aquarium, picnic in a scenic park, raft down a river, visit a major art museum, splash through the Olympic-rings fountain, take in an enchanting puppet show, and much more.

Consider the CityPass and see six of Atlanta's top attractions for $69 (it's a bargain, take my word for it), while avoiding most ticket lines at the same time. For info call ⓒ 770/256-0490 or visit www.city pass.com.

MARTA stops near attractions are listed where applicable. If you need information on bus routes, call ⓒ 404/848-4711.

## 1 THE TOP ATTRACTIONS

**The APEX (African-American Panoramic Experience) Museum**  This museum chronicles the history of Sweet Auburn, once Atlanta's foremost black residential and business district, and serves as a national African-American museum and cultural center. The museum's Trolley Car Theater, a replica of a turn-of-the-20th-century tram that ran on Auburn Avenue, shows a 12-minute multimedia presentation, *Sweet Auburn: Street of Pride,* acquainting visitors with the area's history. Sweet Auburn also comes to life in tableaux such as a replica of an Auburn Avenue barbershop and a re-creation of the 1920s-era Yates & Milton's Drugstore (Atlanta's first black pharmacy), featuring some original furnishings. There are interactive displays for children, too. The APEX recently added a tribute to the late Maynard Holbrook Jackson, Jr., Atlanta's first black mayor. Inquire about special events and workshops taking place during your visit to Atlanta.

Across the street, at 100 Auburn Ave., is **Herndon Plaza,** where you can see a permanent exhibit on the Herndon family (former slave Alonzo F. Herndon founded the Atlanta Life Insurance Company) and changing shows featuring the works of African-American artists.

135 Auburn Ave. (at Courtland St.). ⓒ **404/523-2739.** www.apexmuseum.org. Admission $4 adults, $3 seniors and students, free for children 4 and under. Tues–Sat 10am–5pm; also Sun 1–5pm in Feb and June–Aug. Closed Thanksgiving, Christmas, and New Year's Day. MARTA: Bus 3 from the Five Points station.

**Atlanta Botanical Garden**    This delightful botanical garden, occupying 30 acres in Piedmont Park, includes the Fuqua Orchid Center, a children's garden, an education center, and the Dorothy Chapman Fuqua Conservatory. In the $4.8-million, 25,000-square-foot Fuqua Orchid Center, a collection of rare high-elevation orchids, which flourish on cool, wet mountains in South America, are being grown in the warm Southeast. Typically, one would have to go to San Francisco or Seattle to see such plants. There is beauty here year-round, but peak orchid-bloom season lasts through March.

Equally exciting is the 16,000-square-foot, glass-walled Dorothy Chapman Fuqua Conservatory, housing rare and endangered tropical and desert plants—and a fascinating exhibit of poison dart frogs (more about them later). With acres of irreplaceable rainforest being bulldozed every minute, the plant species in the conservatory seem all the more special. Approached via an arbored promenade and fronted by a lily pond, the entrance to the conservatory has a revolving globe showing the many regions of the world where plant life is endangered.

The focal point of the conservatory is the misty Tropical Rotunda, housing fern collections, cycads (the most primitive seed-bearing plants known), epiphytes (plants that don't require soil to grow), gorgeous orchids, carnivorous plants, a wide variety of begonias, and towering tropical palms. It's a lush and humid jungle, with brightly hued tropical birds warbling overhead, a splashing waterfall, and winding pathways lined with fragrant hibiscus, ginger, and flowering jasmine vines. Of special interest is a double coconut palm from the Seychelles, growing from the largest and heaviest seed in the plant kingdom. Its first 12-foot leaves have already begun to grow, but it will be 100 years before the tree reaches its full height.

In the midst of all this is an intriguing exhibit of Central and South American poison dart frogs—small, active ground dwellers in unbelievably bright colors (yellow, orange, lime green, cobalt blue) and vivid patterns. About 12 species are exhibited in three large terrariums filled with tropical rainforest plants and designed to simulate the climates in the frogs' native lands. This exhibit is a big hit with visiting children.

Another main section of the garden highlights plants that thrive in North Georgia's extended growing season. Displays in this area include a rock garden, a dwarf conifer garden, an English knot herb garden, a tranquil moon-gated Japanese garden, a rose garden, and annual and perennial displays. The delightful children's garden, with its wonderful climbing structures and whimsical sculptured fountains, has become a hot spot for young families.

Another section of the garden consists of two wooded areas. The 5-acre Upper Woodland features a paved path, a fern glade, camellia and hosta gardens, gurgling streams, beautiful statuary, and a habitat designed to show visitors how to attract wildlife to their own backyards. Still more rustic is Storza Woods, 15 acres of natural woodlands and one of the few remaining hardwood forests in the city. Even though its path is unpaved, it makes for an easy and interesting walk.

The arid Desert House displays Madagascan succulents, such as a unique family of spiny plants called *Didiereaceae.* Here, too, are "living stones" (desert succulents that nature designed to look like pebbles to protect them from predators), tree aloes, caudiciforms (with swollen stems and roots for storing water), and conifers from Africa. The building also houses an orangery of tropical mango, papaya, star-fruit, litchi, coffee, and citrus trees. An "Olympic" olive tree presented by Greece in honor of the 1996 Centennial Olympic Games in Atlanta resides here as well.

There are flower shows throughout the year, along with lectures and other activities. Call to find out what's scheduled during your visit. The Café serves sandwiches, salads, and snacks, and it also has a children's menu. It's open Tuesday through Sunday, with outdoor seating available. A marvelous gift shop is on the premises; your purchases help support the garden.

1345 Piedmont Ave. NW (adjacent to Piedmont Park at Piedmont Ave. and the Prado). © **404/876-5859.** www.atlantabotanicalgarden.org. Admission $12 adults, $9 students and seniors, free for children 3 and under. A taped audio tour is available in 5 languages for a small fee. Tues–Sun 9am–5pm, until 7pm during daylight saving time. The Conservatory, Orchid Center, and gift shop open at 10am. The gardens are closed every Mon except Mon holidays. All areas accessible to visitors with disabilities. Free parking. MARTA: North Decatur bus 36 from the Arts Center station Tues–Sat; Monroe/Lindbergh bus 27 on Sun.

### Atlanta Cyclorama & Civil War Museum ★★

Though it sounds like something out of Disney World, the Atlanta Cyclorama was created in the 1880s, and the concept— a huge, 360-degree cylindrical painting viewed from a rotating platform—dates back a century earlier. Cycloramas were the rage of 18th- and 19th-century Europe, Russia, Japan, and, later, the United States, depicting subject matter ranging from the splendors of Pompeii to Napoleonic battles. Enhanced by multimedia effects and faux terrain extending 30 feet from the painting into the foreground, they were the forerunners of newsreels, travelogues, and TV war coverage.

The one you'll see here—a 42-foot-high cylindrical oil painting, 358 feet in circumference (on about 16,000 sq. ft. of canvas)—depicts the events of the Battle of Atlanta, on July 22, 1864, in meticulous detail. It took 11 Eastern European artists, working in the United States in the studio of William Wehner, 22 months to complete the project.

For 21st-century tourists, the concept and story of the Cyclorama are as interesting as the action depicted, and the restoration is incredibly impressive. Though painted on fine Belgian linen in the painstaking style of the 19th-century art academies, the work suffered in moves from city to city, and later (when motion-picture epics made cycloramas passé) from neglect. Well-intentioned but incompetent attempts at restoration caused further damage. In the 1970s, a severe storm waterlogged the painting, causing seemingly irreversible damage. But Mayor Maynard Jackson recognized the historical and artistic importance of the Cyclorama; under his auspices, $11 million was raised for its restoration. It took $2^1/_2$ years for renowned conservator Gustav Berger and his crew to repair the damaged work, a process that included mending more than 700 rips in the canvas. The fascinating story of the Cyclorama's development and restoration is related in a video near the auditorium entrance.

The Cyclorama's central theme is General John B. Hood's desperate attempt to halt General William Tecumseh Sherman's inexorable advance into the city. Comprehensively narrated, and complete with music and sound effects (including galloping horses and cannon fire), it vividly depicts the troop movements and battles on the day that the Confederates lost 8,000 men and the Yankees lost 3,722. A figure highlighted far beyond his historical importance is General John A. Logan of the Federal Army of Tennessee (who commissioned the painting at a cost of $42,000 as a campaign move in his bid for the Union vice presidency). He's shown gloriously galloping into the fray, bravely exposing himself and his men to enemy fire. (The work was originally called *Logan's Great Battle.*) A 14-minute film about the Battle of Atlanta precedes the Cyclorama viewing. The total program lasts about 35 minutes.

The building housing the Cyclorama also contains a museum of related artifacts, the most important being the steam locomotive *Texas* from the 1862 "Great Locomotive

Chase." Other exhibits include displays of Civil War arms and artillery, Civil War–themed paintings, portraits of Confederate and Union leaders, "life in camp" artifacts and photographs, and uniforms. You'll need about an hour and a half to see the museum in full if you visit both floors.

*Note:* No video cameras are allowed inside the Cyclorama auditorium.

800 Cherokee Ave. (in Grant Park). ✆ **404/658-7625.** www.atlantacyclorama.org. Admission $8 adults, $7 seniors, $6 children 6–12, free for children 5 and under. Tues–Sun 9am–4:30pm. Shows begin every half-hour starting at 9:30am. Closed Thanksgiving, Christmas, New Year's Day, and Martin Luther King, Jr., Day. By car, take I-20 E. from downtown to exit 59A. Free parking. MARTA: From Five Points Station take bus 97 to Grant Park.

**Atlanta History Center ★★★**   The Atlanta History Center chronicles the past of Georgia and the Southeast, as well as the history of Atlanta, with a vast collection of photographs, maps, books, newspaper accounts, furnishings, Civil War artifacts, and decorative arts. It occupies 32 woodland acres, with self-guided walking trails and five gardens. Plan to spend the better part of a day here. And call ahead, or inquire on the premises, about lectures, films, festivals, and other events that take place on a regular basis; activities range from sheep-shearing demonstrations to decorative-arts forums. When you call, also check on house-tour times for the day of your visit (these tours are described below). *Note:* House-tour tickets are limited and can be purchased only on the day of your visit. Arrive early to avoid disappointment.

Begin your visit at the **Atlanta History Museum,** where you can buy tickets and get information about historic house tours and other activities. The museum is the single best place to go for a cultural record of the city and the South. The major permanent exhibit, "Metropolitan Frontiers: Atlanta, 1835–2000," traces Atlanta's history from the Native Americans and rural pioneer settlements to the present day. Displays, enhanced by hands-on discovery areas and informative videos, feature hundreds of photographs, documents, and artifacts. Included is an entire 1890s shotgun house, a fire engine that was used in Atlanta's great fire of 1917 (when 50 city blocks were ravaged by flames), a rare 1920 Hanson Six touring car, and a model of Atlanta's most complex interstate intersection, known locally as "Spaghetti Junction."

A $10-million, 20,000-square-foot addition houses an exhibition about the 1996 Centennial Olympic Games in Atlanta. This highly interactive, three-level addition opened in 2006 to coincide with the 10th anniversary of the Atlanta games.

Also on the center's grounds is the beautifully restored **Swan House,** the 1928 estate of Edward Hamilton Inman, scion of an old Atlanta family. The house and gardens were designed by renowned architect Philip Trammell Shutze and are considered his finest residential work. The formal gardens include terraced lawns and waterfalls, retaining walls with recessed ivy arches, and fountain statuary. Swan House is fronted by a classical colonnaded porte-cochere leading to a circular entrance hall with Ionic columns and a dramatic floating stairway. In the entrance hall, you'll notice that the fanlight over the door features a swan, announcing the theme of the house. There is supposed to be at least one swan emblem or decoration in each room—see if you can find them. The house is interesting not only architecturally, but also for its eclectic contents and furnishings, which comprise a veritable museum of decorative arts. It's a fascinating glimpse into the lifestyle enjoyed by upper-crust Atlantans in the early–20th century.

**Tullie Smith Farm** gives a sense of the life of Georgia's mid-19th-century farmers. A two-story "plantation-plain" house built in the early 1840s, it was brought to Atlanta along with period outbuildings in 1972. This was no Tara-like colonnaded mansion—

just an everyday farmhouse whose occupants lived in rustic simplicity. Costumed docents give tours throughout the day, and there are frequent demonstrations of 19th-century farm activities. In a bedroom with a rope bed and a crib (always occupied by the youngest baby), a docent will demonstrate how to use a spinning wheel. The basket of pomander balls in this room was typical—the 19th century's answer to today's air fresheners. You'll find weaving demonstrations in the back room. During cooler months, demonstrations of hearth cookery take place in the whitewashed kitchen, where herbs hang from the rafters. Additional outbuildings include a barn, corncrib, root cellar, blacksmith shop, and smokehouse. The gardens and grounds are authentic to the period.

Leave some time to stroll the gardens, most notably the forested mile-long **Swan Woods Trail.** It includes plants native to Georgia, plus the Garden for Peace, home to a sculpture by noted Soviet artist Georgi Dzhaparidze and Atlanta artist Hans Godo Frabel. If you're visiting during lunchtime, the **Swan Coach House** (p. 125) is a delightful restaurant on the premises.

130 W. Paces Ferry Rd. (at Slaton Dr.). © **404/814-4000.** www.atlantahistorycenter.com. Admission $15 adults, $12 seniors and students 13 or older, $10 children 4–12, free for children 3 and under. General admission is all-inclusive. Mon–Sat 10am–5:30pm; Sun and some holidays noon–5:30pm. Ticket sales end at 4:30pm. Closed Thanksgiving, Christmas Eve, Christmas, and New Year's Day. MARTA: Take MARTA rail to Lenox station; from there take bus 23 to Peachtree St. and W. Paces Ferry Rd., then walk 3 blocks west on the latter.

**Birth Home of Martin Luther King, Jr.** ★★  Martin Luther King, Jr., was born in this two-story Queen Anne–style house on January 15, 1929, the oldest son of a Baptist minister and an elementary-school music teacher. His childhood was a normal one. He preferred baseball to piano lessons, liked to play board games, and got a kick out of tearing the heads off his older sister's dolls (nonviolence came later). To quote his sister, Christine King Farris, "My brother was no saint ordained at birth; instead he was an average and ordinary man, called by . . . God . . . to perform extraordinary deeds."

King lived here through the age of 12, and then moved with his family to a house a few blocks away. A visit provides many insights into the formative influences on one of the greatest leaders of our time. The Rev. A. D. Williams, King's maternal grandfather and pastor of Ebenezer Baptist Church, bought the house in 1909. Reverend Williams was active not only in the church, but also in the community and in early manifestations of the civil rights movement. He was a charter member of Atlanta's NAACP and led a series of black registration and voting drives as far back as 1917. He was instrumental in getting black officers onto the Atlanta police force. Martin Luther King, Sr., moved in on Thanksgiving Day, 1926, when he married Williams's daughter Alberta. When Reverend Williams died in 1931, King became head of the household and took over Williams's pulpit at Ebenezer Church.

The King family retained ownership of the house at 501 Auburn Ave. even after they moved away. King's younger brother, Alfred Daniel, lived here with his family from 1954 to 1963. In 1971, King's mother deeded the home to the King Center. It has since been restored to its appearance during the years of King's boyhood. The furnishings are all originals or period reproductions, and some personal items belonging to the family are on display. Christine was actively involved in the restoration, providing a wealth of detail about the former appearance of the house, as well as anecdotal material about life in the King family.

Tours of the house, conducted by national park rangers, begin in the downstairs parlor, where you'll see family photographs showing Martin Luther as a child. The parlor was used for choir practice, for the dreaded piano lessons, and as a rec room where the family gathered around the radio to listen to shows like "The Shadow." In the dining room, world events were regularly discussed over meals, and every Sunday, before dinner, each child was required to recite a newly learned Bible verse from memory. You'll also see the coal cellar (stoking coal was one of King's childhood chores); the children's play area; the upstairs bedroom of King's parents, in which Christine, Martin Luther, and Alfred Daniel were born; Reverend Williams's den, where the family gathered for nightly Bible study; the bedroom King shared with his brother ("always in disarray," says Christine); and Christine's bedroom.

*Note:* In summer, especially, tickets often run out early; for your best chance at touring the home, arrive at 9am.

501 Auburn Ave. (C) **404/331-6922.** www.nps.gov/malu. Free admission. Tickets are available at the National Park Service Visitor Center, 450 Auburn Ave. Accessible only by tour. Tours depart from Fire Station No. 6 (at Boulevard and Auburn Ave.) about every 30 min. in summer, every hour the rest of the year. June 15–Aug 15 daily 10am–6pm; Aug 16–June 14 daily 10am–5pm. Closed Thanksgiving, Christmas, and New Year's Day. From I-75/85 S., exit at Freedom Pkwy./Carter Center (exit 248-C). Turn right at first stoplight onto Boulevard. Follow signs to Martin Luther King, Jr., National Historic Site. MARTA: King Memorial station is about 8 blocks away, or take bus 3 east from the Five Points station.

**Centennial Olympic Park** ★★★ (Kids) Centennial Olympic Park, one of the most enduring legacies of the 1996 Olympic Games, is a living monument to the city's memories—both good and bad—of that seminal event. Conceived as a town square, it represents the heart of the Olympic effort, the site where everyone flocked to celebrate the games. And when the games resumed after the bombing in the park that claimed one life, it was where people gathered to try to revive the Olympic spirit. Ongoing upgrades keep the park in tip-top shape for the more than three million visitors who come here each year.

A 21-acre swath of green space and bricks, the park was carved out of a blighted downtown area. It was closed after the games and redesigned for permanent use before reopening in 1998. Once again the universal gathering place it was intended to be, it's an oasis of rolling lawns crisscrossed by brick pathways and punctuated by artwork, rock gardens, pools, and fountains. There are usually a few free events each month—festivals, artists' markets, concerts, and other performances, some private, some open to the public. The park is home to a number of concert series, a huge Fourth of July celebration, and the Holiday in Lights, including an ice skating rink. Call for a complete listing of happenings or visit their website.

If you're visiting the park on your own, and not coming for a specific event, your first stop should be the Visitor Center on Andrew Young International Boulevard, in the southwest corner of the park, across from the CNN Center. This is where you'll find information about the park. If you bought a $35 commemorative brick in 1996, someone will help you locate it among over 500,000 engraved bricks that were used to pave the plaza and walkways. Even if you didn't buy a brick, it's fun to wander around and read the names and messages (some pretty intriguing) engraved on them.

The best part of the park is the Fountain of Rings and its 251 water jets in the shape of the five interlocking Olympic rings. It's the focus of a vast paved plaza bordered by 23 flags honoring the host countries of the summer games from 1996 and earlier. If you're here in summer, you and the kids can frolic in the Fountain of Rings (wear shoes, please, and bring a bathing suit), a good way to cool off in the sizzling Southern heat. Don't be

> ### (Fun Facts) **Pricey Parkland**
>
> If you really, really, really had a good time at Centennial Olympic Park, you can have it all to yourself for a small fee. Though it's a public park, it's also a money-maker managed by the Georgia World Congress Center Authority, and parts of the park are sometimes rented for various business functions, parties, and other celebrations. There have even been a few weddings. You can rent the entire park for, um, $15,000. If you're short on cash, you can always buy the park for $1 million in Monopoly money as it's a featured Atlanta location in the Monopoly Here and Now board game. Call ✆ **404/222-7275** for facility rental details.

shy—just about everybody in Atlanta has done this at one time or another. If getting drenched is not your thing, you can still enjoy one of the "concerts" put on by the Fountain—choreographed water and light displays, during which the water jets, which normally shoot 12 feet into the air, can reach 35 feet during special effects.

Located along the east border are the Quilt Plazas, five plazas of contrasting bricks that tell the story of the Centennial Olympic Games. The best "quilt" is also the most moving. Titled the *Quilt of Remembrance,* it pays respect to the bombing victims and contains colored marble from five continents. Be sure to read the inscriptions on its borders.

265 Park Avenue W. NW (at Baker St). ✆ **404/222-PARK (7275).** www.centennialpark.com. Free admission. Daily 7am–11pm. MARTA: Omni/Dome/GWCC or Peachtree Center.

**CNN Studio Tour ★★★**　This tour of the world's largest newsgathering organization is lots of fun and a uniquely Atlanta experience. The CNN Center is headquarters for CNN, CNN International, and Headline News. During 50-minute guided walking tours, visitors get a behind-the-scenes look at the high-tech world of 24-hour TV network news in action.

You'll find the tour desk in the main lobby near the base of an eight-story escalator. While you're waiting for the tour to begin, you can have a videotape made of yourself reading the day's top stories from behind a CNN anchor desk. The tour starts in an exhibit area where you'll find timelines covering the history of CNN and Turner Broadcasting, interactive kiosks where you can surf the CNN websites or access clips from the top 100 stories that CNN has covered, memorabilia from some of those events, and a journalism ethics display. A theater that re-creates CNN's main control room allows you to experience the behind-the-scenes elements of a news broadcast.

Next, you'll enter a special-effects studio and get a glimpse of the technology that goes into the production of global news. Here you'll discover the magic of a high-tech Blue Chromakey system (it's what's used to broadcast that big map behind the weather folks), see how on-air graphics are made, and learn the secrets of the TelePrompTer.

On another level, visitors get a bird's-eye view of the main CNN newsroom from a glass-walled observation station. From here, you'll see the hustle and bustle of writers composing news scripts. If a live broadcast is in progress—and chances are good that one will be—you can see CNN newscasters at work. Tour guides are knowledgeable and can answer virtually any question.

The longer, more extensive VIP tour allows visitors to actually step out onto the main CNN newsroom floor and explore production areas not normally accessible to the public.

After your visit, stop by the Turner Store, which carries network-logo clothing and gift items, along with MGM movie paraphernalia. For sports fans, there's the Braves Clubhouse store, featuring the Atlanta Braves logo on every item you can imagine. There are several restaurants and numerous fast-food outlets in the atrium of the CNN Center, as well as a few shops. Keep in mind that the tour includes quite of bit of walking and a very steep escalator ride, which carries you to great heights to begin your visit. Those afraid of heights might want to consider skipping the tour.

CNN Center, Marietta St. (at Techwood Dr.). ☎ **404/827-2300** or 877/4CNN-TOUR [4266-8687]. www.cnn. com/studiotour. Admission $12 adults, $11 seniors, $9 children 4–18. A more in-depth, Morning Express tour costs $49 (includes breakfast, souvenirs, and more behind-the-scenes opps). *Note:* Reservations highly recommended. Tours are given daily every 10 min. 9am–5pm. Arrive early for the tour you wish to take, as most tours sell out. Closed Easter, Thanksgiving, and Christmas. MARTA: Omni/Dome/GWCC. Many parking lots around the building.

**Ebenezer Baptist Church**    Founded in 1886, Ebenezer was a spiritual center of the civil rights movement from 1960 to 1968, during which time Martin Luther King, Jr., served as co-pastor. King's grandfather, the Rev. A. D. Williams, dedicated the church to "the advancement of black people and every righteous and social movement." His son-in-law and successor, Martin Luther King, Sr., worked for voting rights and other aspects of black civil and social advancement, following Williams's activist example. Later, Martin Luther King, Jr., would join his ancestors in pursuing justice for African Americans.

The congregation has built a new sanctuary directly across the street, but the older building, where Martin Luther King, Jr., preached, continues to be open to the public. Short but informative tours of the sanctuary, conducted by members of the Ebenezer congregation, are given Monday through Friday from 9am to 4pm, Saturday from 9am to 2pm, and Sunday from 2 to 4pm. One of the best things to do is attend a Sunday-morning worship service in the new sanctuary. The public is welcome—and you'll realize just *how* welcome when the members of the congregation leave their seats at the beginning of the service to shake the hands of as many visitors as possible. It's a living testimonial to all that the church's most famous son stood for. Sunday services are at 7:45 and 10:45am. The sanctuary is usually packed, so it's a good idea to arrive well ahead of time. Groups of six or more should call the church office at ☎ **404/688-7263** to make reservations. An ecumenical service also takes place here every year during King Week (Jan 9–15).

407–413 Auburn Ave. NE. ☎ **404/688-5001** or 404/688-7263. Free admission (donations appreciated). Mon–Sat 9am–5pm; Sun 1–5pm. From I-75/85 S., exit at Freedom Pkwy./Carter Center. Turn right at first stoplight onto Boulevard. Follow signs to Martin Luther King, Jr., National Historic Site. MARTA: King Memorial station is about 8 blocks away, or take bus 3 from the Five Points station.

**Fernbank Museum of Natural History** ★★ Kids    The largest museum of natural sciences in the Southeast, this architecturally stunning facility borders 65 acres of pristine forest. Architect Graham Gund has achieved a marvelous integration of interior/exterior space: The building, which nearly eclipses the attractions inside, centers on a soaring three-story, sky-lit Great Hall—an Italianate brick atrium with spiral staircases, lofty columns, and windows revealing the woodlands beyond. Look closely at the museum floors, where ancient fossil remains from the late Jurassic period are embedded.

When the Great Hall was designed, it was meant to one day be the home of a large-scale permanent dinosaur exhibition, and in 2000, Fernbank became the only place in the world to display a complete mounted skeleton of *Argentinosaurus,* the largest dinosaur ever found. The dramatic permanent exhibit, "Giants of the Mesozoic," features the

90-foot-long plant-eater as it defends its nest of eggs against the 45-foot-long *Giganoto-saurus,* the largest meat-eater ever classified. Hovering above in the 86-foot-tall hall are two flying *Pterosaurs.* Dinosaurs just don't get any bigger than this, and it's a little hair-raising to walk into the hall and see these beasts towering over the tiny humans below.

There are several other permanent exhibits, including "A Walk Through Time in Georgia," which uses the state as a microcosm to tell the story of the earth's development through time and the chronology of life upon it. Visitors travel back 15 billion years to experience the origins of the universe (the Big Bang) and the formation of galaxies and solar systems, and into the future to consider the fate of our planet. Eighteen galleries re-create landform regions from the rolling pine-forested foothills of the Piedmont Plateau to the mossy Okefenokee Swamp, from the Cumberland Plateau (where you can walk through a typical limestone cavern) to the marshy Coast and Barrier islands. Exhibits are enhanced by creative films and videos, informational audiophones, interactive computers, sound effects, and old-fashioned field guides—not to mention more than 1,500 fabricated plants and mounted specimens of birds and animals.

"Sensing Nature" tantalizes your senses with hands-on exhibits that explore how we experience the natural world. The room swims with computers, colored lights, and mirrors, and you can step into a life-size kaleidoscope, play with perspective, gaze into infinity, see physical evidence of sound waves, and mix colors on a computer.

The Children's Discovery Room, open daily June through August and on a limited basis during the school year, includes Fantasy Forest, a colorful play area designed for preschoolers (ages 3–5), where kids can become bees and pollinate flowers, climb a tree house, walk through a swamp, and play at being farmers. The state-shaped Georgia Adventure is a similar discovery room for ages 6 to 10.

While you're here, be sure to catch a stunning IMAX film (buy tickets as soon as you enter the museum; they sometimes sell out). The immense screen—five stories high and 72 feet wide—puts you right in the middle of all the action.

Other museum attractions include a wetlands exhibit, a dramatically colorful living coral reef aquarium, a unique shell display, a gemstone collection, and the McClatchey Collection of jewelry and textiles from the old Silk Road countries. The museum store is stocked with entertaining and educational gifts and books, and there's a restaurant with arched windows overlooking Fernbank Forest and outdoor patio seating. See p. 216 for a description of the adult-geared Martinis & IMAX Friday nights.

767 Clifton Rd. NE (off Ponce de Leon Ave.). ✆ **404/929-6300** for information, 404/929-6400 for tickets. www.fernbank.edu. Admission $15 adults ($23 includes an IMAX theater ticket), $14 seniors and students ($21 includes an IMAX theater ticket), $13 children 3–12 ($19 includes IMAX theater ticket), free for children 2 and under. IMAX theater admission alone $13 adults, $12 seniors and students, $11 children 3–12, free for children 2 and under. Mon–Sat 10am–5pm; Sun noon–5pm. The IMAX theater until 10pm on Fri nights Jan–Nov for Martinis & IMAX. Closed Thanksgiving and Christmas. Free parking. MARTA: Bus 2, ask driver to drop you at Clifton Rd. Walk north and Fernbank is first drive on right.

**Fox Theatre ★★**  Originally conceived as a Shriners' temple in 1916, this lavish, block-long Moorish-Egyptian fantasyland ended up as a movie theater when the Shriners realized that their grandiose plan had far exceeded their budget. In 1927, they sold the temple to movie magnate William Fox, who created a peerless pleasure palace. French architect Oliver J. Vinour designed the building, using motifs of the Middle East, including replicas of art and furnishings from King Tut's tomb.

Atlanta's new theater opened in 1929 as a masterpiece of Eastern splendor, its Moorish facade, onion domes, and minarets in exotic contrast to the surrounding Victorian boardinghouses. A brass-trimmed marble kiosk imported from Italy served as a ticket booth. The 140-foot entrance arcade led to a lushly carpeted lobby with blue-tiled gold-fish pools. The auditorium was an Arabian courtyard under a twinkling starlit sky that, with state-of-the-art technology, could be transformed to a sky at sunrise or sunset. A striped Bedouin canopy sheltered the balcony, and sequin- and rhinestone-studded stage curtains depicted mosques and Moorish horsemen.

As the show began, a gigantic gilded 3,610-pipe Möller organ rose majestically from its vault, its rich chords accompanied by a full orchestra. A medley of popular songs, cartoons, a follow-the-bouncing-ball sing-along, a stage-show extravaganza by a bevy of Rockette-like chorines called the Fanchon and Marco Sunkist Beauties, and a newsreel preceded every main feature. At night, there were dances in the Egyptian Ballroom, designed to replicate Rameses' temple. Even the men's lounge was exotically appointed with hieroglyphic adornments, winged scarab-motif friezes, bas-reliefs of royal figures, and throne chairs.

Unfortunately, the Fox's opening coincided with the Great Depression, and it proved impossible to maintain its opulence. In 1932, the company declared bankruptcy and closed its doors. The theater reopened 3 years later for occasional concerts. By the 1940s, it was a successful concern once more, and in 1947, the Metropolitan Opera began performing here for a week each year—an offering that lasted 2 decades. An oversize panoramic screen was installed in the 1950s, along with a 26-speaker stereo system. But like monumental movie palaces nationwide, the Fox inevitably declined in the age of television. In 1975, its doors were padlocked once again.

An organization of concerned citizens called Atlanta Landmarks raised $1.8 million and saved the Fox from the wrecking ball in 1978, foiling Southern Bell's plans to purchase and demolish it to make way for a regional headquarters building. Ever since, it's been a thriving entity, featuring Broadway shows, headliners, dance companies, and comedy stars. Best of all, the theater has been restored to its former glory, its fabulous furnishings and fixtures all refurbished or replaced with replicas.

You cannot explore the building on your own, so call to find out when you can take a tour, or come to see a performance in the theater.

660 Peachtree St. NE (at Ponce de Leon Ave.). ⓒ **404/881-2100** for performance tickets, 404/688-3353 for tours. www.foxtheatre.org. Tours $10 adults, $5 seniors and students. The Atlanta Preservation Center conducts walking tours of the Fox Theatre and the surrounding area Mon, Wed, Thurs, and Sat; call to verify times before you go, as tours are occasionally canceled due to production rehearsals. MARTA: North Ave.

### Georgia Aquarium ★★★ (Kids)

Since it opened to continual massive crowds in late 2005, the world's largest aquarium has had Atlanta abuzz about its 8 million gallons of fresh and marine water, home to more than 100,000 animals representing 500 species from around the globe. The aquarium continues to add to its collection, including a 9-foot 456-pound manta ray named Nandi, who joined the waters in 2008. A dolphin exhibit is planned to open in 2010.

The aquarium includes five stunning permanent exhibits, including Cold Water Quest, Georgia Explorer, Ocean Voyager, River Scout, and Tropical Diver, each featuring inhabitants of those environments. Visitors are fascinated by the ghostly beluga whales in the Cold Water Quest, along with Australian weedy sea dragons, giant Pacific octopus, and Japanese spider crabs. Georgia Explorer includes an interactive gallery with touch pools of horseshoe crabs, sea stars, stingrays, and shrimp. See a loggerhead sea turtle and right whales, which live just off the Georgia coast. Feel like a scuba diver in a sea of fish

# Water, Water Everywhere

Folks in Atlanta were pretty sure the Georgia Aquarium would be a big hit, but even the most optimistic about this world-class project underestimated the numbers of people who'd be clamoring to see the newest showcase of the Southeast. Nine months after its opening in November 2005, the world's largest indoor aquarium was already welcoming its three-millionth visitor.

Aquarium benefactor Bernie Marcus had it pegged pretty well, though—he predicted the facility would welcome three million people within its first year. The aquarium is a gift to the people of Georgia from Marcus, cofounder of Home Depot, and his wife, Billi, through the Marcus Foundation.

The initial crowds were so huge, sales of annual memberships were actually suspended because management feared that hordes of return visitors would overwhelm their ability to welcome first-time guests. Of the first three million visitors, more than 50,000 were Atlanta-area teachers and students, who were among the earliest supporters of the facility. The aquarium has now served as Atlanta's second-largest tourism boost since the Centennial Olympic Games were held here in 1996.

Since the opening, aquarium visitors and staff have found both reason to celebrate and reason to mourn. From an announcement of $14 million in building improvements less than a year after opening to the early 2007 passing of Gasper, one of two beluga whales housed here, the Georgia Aquarium continues to draw international attention.

as you walk through an acrylic tunnel surrounded by water and creatures in the Ocean Voyager exhibit. Watch out for the gigantic whale sharks that call this tunnel home; they'll swim right over your head. River Scout highlights wildlife of rivers from Georgia to Asia, including a large exhibit of Amazonian fish. See electric fish from Africa and get up close and personal with a toothy piranha. Kids delight at the playful Asian small-clawed otters who spend their days playing and eating. Tropical coral reefs round out the exhibit Tropical Diver, where kids love to look for "Nemo" among the hundreds of sea creatures that pop in and out among the reef. Three jellyfish exhibits are also located here, performing a mesmerizing watery ballet.

A number of behind-the-scenes tours are available, including Journey with Gentle Giants, an opportunity to swim or scuba-dive with whale sharks and tons of other fish in the Ocean Voyager exhibit. Fees are steep: $190 for swimmers and $290 for certified divers, but where else could you have this experience in a metropolitan setting? The swim/dive tour is limited to six people a day and reservations are booked months ahead, so plan early. For another $50 you can purchase a DVD of yourself swimming with the fishes to take home to impress friends and family. Other tours are less expensive and allow guests to visit areas typically off limits to see how these creatures are cared for by staff.

While numbers have leveled out since the opening year, crowds are still big enough that tickets are issued based on your preferred time to enter the aquarium. Tickets to the 4-D theater are a few bucks extra, or for an additional $50, visitors can experience a behind-the-scenes tour. Advance booking online is highly recommended. Café Aquaria serves grilled items, pasta, pizza, salads, sandwiches, and more.

If you plan to see the World of Coca-Cola and the Georgia Aquarium, a Pemberton Pass will save you a few bucks. In addition, the two attractions share a huge covered parking garage with a $10 fee. Pemberton Place includes an expansive lawn, perfect for a picnic, as well as a cafe and public restrooms.

225 Baker St. ☏ **404/581-4000.** www.georgiaaquarium.org. Admission $26 adults, $22 seniors, $20 children 3–12. Sun–Fri 10am–5pm; Sat 9am–6pm. 365 days, but holiday hours vary slightly. Covered parking (attached) $10. MARTA: Peachtree Center or Dome/GWCC/PhilipsArena/CNN.

**High Museum of Art ★★★**    The High's $130-million, three-building expansion truly brought the museum to world-class status. The additions include more gallery space for the museum's permanent collection, enlarged special-exhibit space, a coffee bar, and a new retail shop. Not to be overshadowed, the original facility—designed by architect Richard Meier and part of the Woodruff Arts Center complex—is itself a work of art. A dazzling white-porcelain–tiled building with an equally pristine white interior, the museum houses four floors of galleries connected by semicircular pedestrian ramps girding a spacious, sun-filled four-story atrium.

The permanent collection here includes more than 10,000 pieces, among them a significant group of 19th- and 20th-century American paintings. Hudson River School artists such as Thomas Cole and Frederic Church are featured, as are Thomas Sully, John Singer Sargent, and William Harnett. The Virginia Carroll Crawford Collection of American Decorative Arts comprehensively documents trends in decorative arts from 1825 to 1917. The Samuel H. Kress Foundation collection includes Italian paintings and sculpture from the 14th through the 18th centuries. The Uhry Print Collection contains important works by French Impressionists and post-Impressionists, German expressionists, and 20th-century American artists. Also notable are collections of sub-Saharan African art, a folk-art collection, and works by noted 19th- and 20th-century American and European photographers.

In addition to the permanent collection, which is shown on a rotating basis, the museum hosts a number of major traveling exhibitions each year, complemented by films, lectures, workshops, gallery talks, concerts, and other events, including Friday Jazz, the third Friday of each month. Ask at the desk about special events during your visit. Free guided gallery tours of the High's permanent collection are offered Tuesday through Sunday at 1pm; free guided family tours are given every Saturday and Sunday at 2pm. Special headsets for audio guides are available for special exhibits.

The museum's wonderful gift shop boasts an impressive stock of books, prints, and interesting art-related objects. Since the opening of the contemporary Table 1280, the on-site restaurant, many now visit the High specifically for the food. It serves American-inspired fare as well as a delightful mix of small plates of seasonal ingredients, and the meal can be as memorable as the museum visit. The restaurant is open Tuesday through Saturday from 11am to 2pm for lunch, Sunday from 11am to 2pm for brunch, and Tuesday through Sunday from 5 to 10pm for dinner and tapas. The lounge remains open until midnight Tuesday through Saturday. Don't miss this experience.

1280 Peachtree St. NE (at 16th St.). ☏ **404/733-HIGH [4444].** www.high.org. Admission $18 adults, $15 seniors and students with ID, $11 children 6–17, free for children 5 and under. Fees subject to change for special exhibitions. Tues–Wed and Fri–Sat 10am–5pm; Thurs 10am–8pm; Sun noon–5pm. Closed July 4th, Thanksgiving, Christmas, and New Year's Day. MARTA: Arts Center (a covered walkway links the station to the museum). Parking is available in the garage across from the museum.

**Jimmy Carter Library & Museum**    Set on 30 acres of gardens, lakes, and waterfalls, this impressive presidential library houses some 27 million pages of documents, memoranda, and correspondence from Jimmy Carter's White House years. There are also 1.5 million photographs and hundreds of hours of audio- and videotapes. The library's hilltop site is a historic one; it was from this spot that Sherman watched the Battle of Atlanta.

In the extensive museum, you'll find an exact replica of the Oval Office during Carter's presidency—an exhibit enhanced by a recording of Carter speaking about his experiences in that office. A large display of "gifts of state" runs the gamut from a Dresden figurine of George and Martha Washington (a gift from Ireland) to a carpet from the Shah of Iran. You'll also see the table setting used when the Carters entertained Chinese Vice Premier Deng Xiaoping and his wife in the State Dining Room; a video of artists such as the late pianist Vladimir Horowitz performing in the East Room; campaign memorabilia; and a large display devoted to the activities of Rosalynn Carter. Other exhibits focus on Carter's support of human rights (there's a letter from Soviet dissident Andrei Sakharov and Carter's reply); his boyhood days (you'll see his sixth-grade report card and a photo of the Plains High basketball team); and his pre-presidential life as a peanut farmer, governor, and state senator.

There are informative videos throughout, including an interactive "town meeting" video through which visitors can ask Carter questions on subjects ranging from world affairs to his personal life. Another intriguing participatory video lets you respond to a terrorist crisis and learn the probable consequences of your choice.

Consider having lunch here. There's an excellent cafeteria, run by one of the city's top catering companies, with patio seating overlooking a Japanese garden and pond. If you're still in a political mood, stop at nearby **Manuel's Tavern,** a local pub at 602 N. Highland Ave. that's popular with journalists and politicians. President Carter himself stops in occasionally.

441 Freedom Pkwy. (exit 248-C off I-75/85). ℭ **404/865-7100.** www.jimmycarterlibrary.org. Admission $8 adults, $6 seniors 55 and over, free for children 16 and under. Mon–Sat 9am–4:45pm; Sun noon–4:45pm. Library Mon–Fri 8:30am–4:30pm. Closed New Year's Day, Thanksgiving, and Christmas. Free parking.

**The King Center ★**    Martin Luther King, Jr.'s commitment to nonviolent social change lives on at this memorial, museum, and educational center. A nongovernmental member of the United Nations, the center works with government agencies and the private sector to reduce violence within individual communities and among nations.

The tour of the center, which is self-guided, begins in Freedom Hall, where memorabilia of King and the civil rights movement are displayed. Here, you can see King's Bible and clerical robe, a handwritten sermon, a photographic essay about his life and work, and, on a grim note, the suit he was wearing when a deranged woman stabbed him in New York City. Also on display is the key to his room at the Lorraine Motel in Memphis, Tenn., where he was assassinated. In an alcove off the main exhibit area is a video about King's life and works. Additional exhibits include a room honoring Rosa Parks (whose refusal to give up her seat on a city bus led to the Montgomery bus boycott), and another honoring Mahatma Gandhi, whose emphasis on nonviolence was a major influence on King.

The center's library and archives house the world's largest collection of books and other materials documenting the civil rights movement, including Dr. King's personal papers and a rare 87-volume edition of *The Collected Works of Mahatma Gandhi,* a gift

# Searching for Margaret Mitchell

More than 6 decades after Margaret Mitchell published *Gone with the Wind*, the novel continues to attract new fans and fascinate people around the world. And thousands of them come to Atlanta each year looking for some trace of Tara or the woman who wrote about it.

Well, Tara doesn't exist, no matter how much the book and movie brought it to life for us. The white-columned mansion we equate with Tara was more the product of Hollywood's fancy than of Mitchell's imagination. She begged filmmakers to represent the house as she envisioned it, as a plain structure without columns, which is far closer to the reality of a working plantation than the image that's been perpetuated.

Until the Margaret Mitchell House & Museum opened in 1997, evidence of Mitchell herself was nearly as elusive as the fictional Tara. An extremely private person, she left a will stipulating that her papers and manuscripts be burned upon her death. Only a portion of the manuscript of *Gone with the Wind* was spared—enough to prove that Mitchell was its author. Several places where Mitchell lived fell victim to development or were destroyed in 1917, when a great fire swept the city.

Still, it's possible to walk the streets of Atlanta and find traces of the famous author, either by viewing exhibits honoring her or by retracing some of her steps:

- **1401 Peachtree St.** The house is gone, but a plaque commemorates the site of the home where Mitchell spent her adolescence. She ordered that the house be torn down after her death, possibly because she wasn't happy there. Her mother's dream house, it was a white, two-story Colonial Revival with Doric columns. MARTA: Arts Center.

- **Margaret Mitchell House & Museum,** 990 Peachtree St., at 10th Street (✆ 404/249-7015). In 1925, newlywed Mitchell and her husband, John Marsh, moved into apt. 1 on the bottom floor of this building, living here until 1932. It was in "the dump," as she called it, that Mitchell wrote much of her novel. See p. 152 for details. MARTA: Midtown.

- **Georgian Terrace,** 659 Peachtree St. It was here in 1921 that debutante Mitchell shocked polite society by performing an Apache dance—all the rage in Paris—with her partner at a charity ball. As a result, she was blackballed from the Junior League. Years later, when the Junior League held a costume ball the night before the world premiere of *Gone with the Wind*, Mitchell declined their invitation to be the guest of honor. It was also here that Mitchell handed over her manuscript to Harold Latham, an editor for Macmillan. MARTA: North Avenue.

- **Margaret Mitchell Square,** intersection of Peachtree and Forsyth streets and Carnegie Way. It's possible to walk right by this spot and not even know that you've just passed one of the few public memorials to Atlanta's most famous author, which is probably just the way Mitchell would have preferred it. (Friends and acquaintances say she would have disliked the idea of a monument to her life.) The understated square contains a fountain, an inscription, and a sculpture symbolizing the columns of Tara. A block away is the famous intersection known as Five Points, which Mitchell referred to in her book. MARTA: Peachtree Center.

- Across the street from the square is the **Atlanta-Fulton Public Library** (© **404/730-1700**), which has a permanent Margaret Mitchell exhibit on its third floor. Among the interesting memorabilia, you'll find numerous photographs, a facsimile copy of one of the pages of the original manuscript, and Mitchell's library card. The library also possesses Mitchell's personal literary collection, including the books she used to research *Gone with the Wind,* her typewriter, and her Pulitzer Prize. If you sign the guest book at the exhibit, look back through the previous pages. You'll be astounded at the number of people from overseas who have visited the display. The current library is the site of an earlier building, the Carnegie Library, where Mitchell did much of her research. Her father was one of the founders of the library, and in the years after his death, Mitchell made many contributions in his name. The Carnegie Library was razed in 1977 to make way for the present building. Open Monday from 9am to 6pm, Tuesday through Thursday from 9am to 8pm, Friday and Saturday from 9am to 6pm, and Sunday from 2 to 6pm. MARTA: Peachtree Center.
- Across Peachtree Street is the rose-granite **Georgia-Pacific Building,** built on the site of the Loew's Grand Theatre, where *Gone with the Wind* had its premiere on December 15, 1939. The theater burned in 1979, but there's an inscription to the right of the main entrance to the current building. See if you can find the misspelling. MARTA: Peachtree Center.
- **Accident scene,** Peachtree and 13th streets. On August 11, 1949, Mitchell and her husband were crossing the street to attend a play. Mitchell accidentally darted into the path of a taxi rounding the curve, was struck, and died 5 days later. MARTA: Peachtree Center.
- **Gravesite,** 240 Oakland Ave. SE. Mitchell was laid to rest in Oakland Cemetery on August 17, 1949. Only 300 guests were allowed to attend, but fans invaded the cemetery after the service, many taking funeral flowers as souvenirs. The cemetery (© **404/688-2107**), which is an interesting place in and of itself, is open daily from dawn to dusk. Admission is free, and a map of famous graves is available for a small fee at the cemetery office Monday through Saturday from 9am to 5pm, Sunday from 1 to 5pm. MARTA: King Memorial.
- **Atlanta History Center,** 730 W. Paces Ferry Rd. (© **404/814-4000**). For a look at what plantation life was really like, visit the Tullie Smith Farm on the grounds of the history center. The house itself, built in 1845 and moved here in 1972, is a plain, columnless two-story building, typical of an antebellum working plantation in North Georgia. See p. 140 for more details on the Atlanta History Center. MARTA: Arts Center.

For more information on Margaret Mitchell, read *Looking for Tara,* a small but informative guidebook to Mitchell's Atlanta. It's written by Don O'Briant and is available in local bookstores.

from the government of India. The library is open by appointment only for scholarly research.

In addition to serving as a museum and hub of social-justice activity, the center is Martin Luther King, Jr.'s final resting place, a living memorial to this inspiring leader that is visited by tens of thousands each year. Dr. King's white-marble crypt rests outside in the Freedom Plaza, surrounded by a beautiful five-tiered Reflecting Pool, a symbol of the life-giving nature of water. The tomb is inscribed with his words: "Free at Last. Free at Last. Thank God Almighty I'm Free at Last." An eternal flame burns in a small circular pavilion directly in front of the crypt, and the late Coretta Scott King is laid to rest here as well. The Freedom Walkway, a vaulted colonnade paralleling the pool, will eventually be painted with murals depicting the civil rights struggle. Located at the end of Freedom Walkway is the Chapel of All Faiths, symbolizing the ecumenical nature of Dr. King's work and the universality of the basic tenets of the world's great religions.

A store on the premises sells King memorabilia and a wide selection of books and audiovisual resources. Ranger talks focusing on the community and the civil rights movement take place frequently on Freedom Plaza.

449 Auburn Ave. (btw. Boulevard and Jackson St.). © **404/526-8900.** www.thekingcenter.org. Free admission. Mon–Fri 8:30am–5:30pm. Closed Thanksgiving, Christmas, and New Year's Day. From I-75/85 S., exit at Freedom Pkwy./Carter Center. Turn right at first stoplight onto Boulevard. Follow signs to Martin Luther King, Jr., National Historic Site. MARTA: King Memorial station is about 8 blocks away, or take bus 3 east from the Five Points Station.

**Margaret Mitchell House & Museum (Birthplace of Gone with the Wind)** ★  Seven decades after it was first published, *Gone with the Wind* continues to fascinate people around the world. But until this attraction opened in 1997, after a 10-year effort to preserve the house from demolition, disappointed pilgrims found precious little evidence here of the famous book or its author. Now the house and museum are a must-see for visiting *GWTW* fans.

It's rather surprising that it took so long for restoration efforts to get underway on the dilapidated Tudor Revival apartment house where Margaret Mitchell wrote most of her epic novel and lived with her husband, John Marsh, from 1925 to 1932. The structure was built as a single-family dwelling in 1899, then moved to the back of the lot in 1913 and converted into a 10-unit apartment building 6 years later. It remained an apartment building until 1979, when it was abandoned and eventually boarded up. When the newlyweds moved in, they called it "the dump." It was not an affectionate nickname; according to a friend of Mitchell's, she disliked living here (finances left few alternatives) and would probably be offended by the notion of its restoration. But the house has attracted its share of visitors—from all 50 states and more than 70 countries.

The house and museum tell the complex story of the famous novelist. Guided tours, which last 1 to 1½ hours, begin in the visitor center. Before beginning the tour, guests enter the theater to see a 17-minute film titled *It May Not Be Tara,* featuring an overview of Mitchell's life, and interviews with some of her friends and family members. Also in the theater is an exhibit of photos taken of Mitchell in her teens and 20s. The tour of the house includes a visit to the Mitchell-Marsh apartment, which is furnished much as it was when the couple lived here. Mitchell wrote much of her novel in the front room, seated at a typewriter and desk below the beveled-glass windows in the small corner alcove. Like most writers, she preferred to keep her literary efforts private and would throw a towel over her typewriter when friends dropped in—which was often.

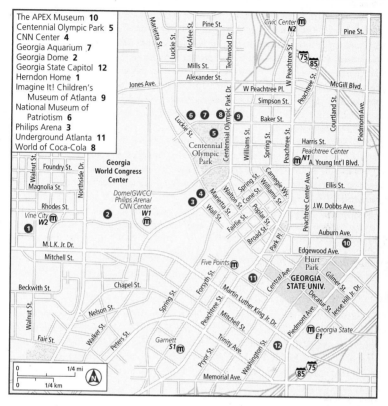

The APEX Museum **10**
Centennial Olympic Park **5**
CNN Center **4**
Georgia Aquarium **7**
Georgia Dome **2**
Georgia State Capitol **12**
Herndon Home **1**
Imagine It! Children's
    Museum of Atlanta **9**
National Museum of
    Patriotism **6**
Philips Arena **3**
Underground Atlanta **11**
World of Coca-Cola **8**

**WHAT TO SEE & DO IN ATLANTA**

**7**

**THE TOP ATTRACTIONS**

The museum contains movie memorabilia and chronicles the making of the movie, its premiere in Atlanta, and the impact that the book and movie had on society. The tour concludes in the museum shop, which features a variety of *GWTW* collectibles. If you finish your tour around mealtime and you're ready for a real change of pace, walk a few blocks south on Peachtree Street to the Vortex (p. 113), a rowdy burger joint and bar that serves some of the best hamburgers in town.

990 Peachtree St. (at 10th St.). ✆ **404/249-7015.** www.gwtw.org. Admission $12 adults, $9 seniors and students, $5 children 4–12, free for children 3 and under. Mon–Sat 9:30am–5pm; Sun noon–5pm. Closed Thanksgiving, Christmas Eve, Christmas, and New Year's Day. Free parking. MARTA: Midtown.

**Martin Luther King, Jr., National Historic Site** Under the auspices of the National Park Service (NPS), this area of about 2 blocks around Auburn Avenue was established to preserve the birthplace and boyhood surroundings of the nation's foremost civil rights leader. Designated a national historic site, these blocks include King's boyhood home and the Ebenezer Baptist Church, where King's father and grandfather were ministers and King served as a co-pastor. Free tours of King's birth home start at Fire Station No. 6, which was recently restored by the NPS; tickets are available on a first-come, first-served basis at the National Park Service Visitor Center, 450 Auburn Ave., across from the King Center. For more information on King's birth home, see p. 141.

Other Auburn Avenue attractions, not under NPS auspices, include the King Center, where King is buried (see above), and the APEX Museum (p. 137). Several additional surrounding blocks have been designated as a preservation district; this area is known as Sweet Auburn. John Wesley Dobbs, maternal grandfather of former Atlanta mayor May-nard Jackson, is the person who first called it such, after Oliver Goldsmith's *The Deserted Village,* the first line of which reads, "Sweet Auburn! loveliest village of the plains." Mayor Jackson says his grandfather called the area "sweet" because the keys to black liberation existed here in the form of "the three Bs—bucks, ballots, and books." (See chapter 8 for tips on exploring the area.)

The NPS Visitor Center provides a complete orientation to area attractions and includes a theater for audiovisual and interpretive programs, interactive exhibits, and a bookstore. It's fronted by a beautifully landscaped plaza with a reflecting pool, King's crypt (which his wife had returned to the site several years ago), and an outdoor amphi-theater for NPS programs.

450 Auburn Ave. ℭ **404/331-6922.** www.nps.gov/malu. Free admission. Labor Day to Memorial Day weekend daily 9am–5pm; rest of year daily 9am–6pm. Closed Thanksgiving, Christmas, and New Year's Day. MARTA: Bus 3 from the Five Points station.

**Michael C. Carlos Museum of Emory University** (Finds) Emory University began its antiquities collection in 1875, and this intriguing museum dates to 1919, when it was founded to display the art and artifacts collected by Emory faculty in Egypt, Cyprus, Greece, Sicily, the Sea of Galilee, and the sites of ancient Babylon and Palestine. Today, the museum also maintains collections of ancient art and archaeology from Rome, Central and South America, the Near East, and Mesoamerica; works of the native cul-tures of North America; art of Asia and Oceania; and some 1,000 objects from sub-Saharan Africa. Additionally, a sizable collection of works on paper encompasses illuminated manuscript pages, drawings, and prints from the Middle Ages and the Renaissance to the 20th century.

The museum is housed partly in a 1916 Beaux Arts building that is on the National Register of Historic Places; architect Michael Graves redesigned the interior in 1985. The remainder of the collections occupy a 35,000-square-foot exhibition space (also designed by Graves). The first-floor galleries feature exhibits from the extensive permanent collec-tion—objects that were part of the daily life of people from five continents as early as the 7th millennium B.C. They include Bronze and Iron Age clay pots, jugs, loom weights, and oil lamps from Palestine; Egyptian mummies, pottery, cosmetic containers, and headrests; Greek and Cypriot pottery, flasks, and statuary; and Mesopotamian pottery, coins, tools, sculpture, and cuneiform tablets inscribed with ancient writing. Also on this level: the Thibadeau Pre-Columbian collection, comprising more than 1,300 objects spanning 2,000 years of creativity—gold jewelry, pottery, and statues, including many ceramic, volcanic stone, greenstone, and gold sculptures from ancient Costa Rica.

The upper floor is used for changing exhibits ranging in subject matter from Pueblo Indian pottery to Impressionist art. Throughout the museum, 210 plaster casts of ancient architectural elements—reliefs, friezes, column capitals, and decorative elements from temples and monuments—adorn hallway and lobby walls.

Allow at least an hour to see the collections. There are many interesting workshops, lectures, films, and gallery tours here; call to find out what's on during your stay. A nice

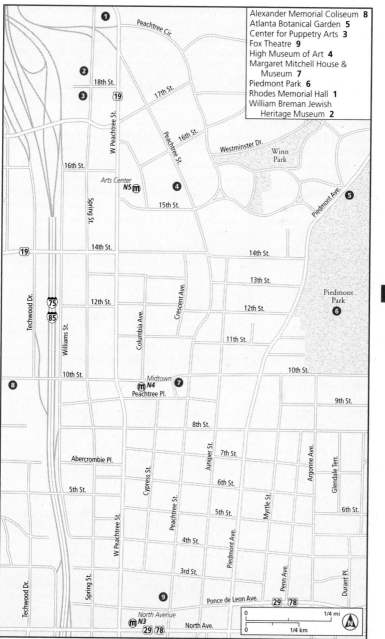

Alexander Memorial Coliseum **8**
Atlanta Botanical Garden **5**
Center for Puppetry Arts **3**
Fox Theatre **9**
High Museum of Art **4**
Margaret Mitchell House &
  Museum **7**
Piedmont Park **6**
Rhodes Memorial Hall **1**
William Breman Jewish
  Heritage Museum **2**

WHAT TO SEE & DO IN ATLANTA

**7**

THE TOP ATTRACTIONS

museum shop tempts with a variety of educational books and gifts, as well as jewelry inspired by the collections. Caffè Antico, on the third floor, serves a seasonal menu of salads, sandwiches, and entrees and is open Monday through Saturday, 11am to 4pm and Sunday noon to 4pm.

571 S. Kilgo St. (near the intersection of Oxford and N. Decatur rds. on the Main Quadrangle of the Emory campus). ✆ **404/727-4282.** www.carlos.emory.edu. Admission $7. Tues–Sat 10am–5pm; Sun noon–5pm. Closed major holidays. Parking can be difficult on the Emory campus. Paid visitor parking is available in the Fishburne Parking Deck and at the B. Jones Center lot. After 6pm, free parking is available in any space on campus not marked by an orange PARK or handicap sign. MARTA: Bus 6 Emory from Candler Park station or Lindbergh station, or bus 36 N. Decatur from Avondale station or Arts Center station.

**Oakland Cemetery ★ Finds**     Listed on the National Register of Historic Places, this outstanding 88-acre Victorian cemetery was founded in 1850. It survived the Civil War and remained the only cemetery in Atlanta for 34 years. Among the more than 48,000 people buried here are Confederate and Union soldiers (including five Southern generals), prominent families, paupers, governors and mayors, golfing great Bobby Jones, and *Gone with the Wind* author Margaret Mitchell. There's a Jewish section (consecrated by a temple), a black section (dating from segregation days), and a potters' field (a section for unknown or poor people). Two monuments honor the Confederate war dead. Standing at the marker that commemorates the "Great Locomotive Chase," you can see the trees from which the Yankee raiders were hanged; the Confederate train conductor Captain William Fuller is buried nearby. The cemetery is not only famous for historical reasons, but also because it is a virtual outdoor museum of Gothic and Classical Revival mausoleums, bronze urns, stained glass, and Victorian statuary.

Almost every grave has a story. Real-estate tycoon Jasper Newton Smith had a life-size statue of himself erected on his grave so he could watch the city's goings-on into eternity. (The sculptor originally gave Smith a tie, but Smith, who never wore one, refused to pay for the piece until the tie was chiseled off.) Dr. James Nissen, Oakland's first burial, feared being buried alive; his will directed that his jugular vein be severed prior to interment. And John Morgan Dye was a baby who died during the siege of Atlanta; his mother walked through the raging battle to the cemetery carrying the small corpse. The smallest grave, however, is that of "Tweet," a pet mockingbird buried in its family's lot.

Though you can visit whenever the cemetery is open, try to come when you can take a guided tour. It's a fascinating way to learn about the history of the graveyard and about graveyard symbolism (a lopped-tree-trunk marker indicates a life cut short or goals unachieved, rocks on a grave denote a life built on a solid foundation, a shell means resurrection, and so on). Every October, there's a celebration to commemorate the cemetery's founding, with turn-of-the-20th-century music, food, and storytelling.

A 5-year, $15-million restoration aimed at reviving the cemetery as a park got underway in early 2003, and Atlanta residents certainly seem to be taking to the idea—dozens of people jog and walk on the rolling terrain every day, and picnickers are a common sight. However, a tornado swept through in the spring of 2008, damaging several sections, which are well on their way to repair now, many being improved from their pre-storm condition. Leashed pets are welcome.

248 Oakland Ave. SE (main entrance at Oakland Ave. and Martin Luther King, Jr., Dr.). ✆ **404/688-2107.** www.oaklandcemetery.com. Free admission. Daily dawn to dusk; visitor center Mon–Sat 9am–5pm; Sun 1–5pm. Purchase an informative, self-guided walking-tour map brochure at the visitor center for $1. Guided walking tours available Mar–Nov for $10 adults, $5 seniors and students. Free parking inside the cemetery. MARTA: King Memorial.

**Stone Mountain Park ★ (Kids)**   A monolithic gray-granite outcropping (the world's largest) carved with a massive monument to the Confederacy, Stone Mountain is a distinctive landmark on Atlanta's horizon and the focal point of its major recreation area, which includes 3,200 acres of lakes and beautiful wooded parkland. Having celebrated its 50th anniversary in 2008, Stone Mountain is Georgia's number-one tourist attraction, and one of the 10 most-visited paid attractions in the United States.

Stone Mountain itself was formed about 300 million years ago, when intense heat and pressure caused molten material just below the earth's surface to push upward. That material cooled slowly (it took 100 million years) and formed compact, uniform crystals. Initially, a 2-mile-thick overlay of the earth's surface covered the hardened granite, but over the next 200 million years, that layer eroded, exposing the mountain we see today. The dome-shaped rock rises 1,683 feet above sea level and covers 583 acres. Half of Georgia and part of North Carolina rest on the mountain's base.

Make your first stop the **Discovering Stone Mountain Museum** to get some perspective on the mountain's history. Exhibits take you through an intriguing chronological journey from the area's past into its present.

Although the best view of the mountain is from below, the vistas from the top are spectacular. Visitors who are part mountain goat can take the **walking trail** up and down its moss-covered slopes, especially lovely in spring when they're blanketed in wildflowers. The trail is 1.3 miles each way. Or you can ride the **Skyride cable car** to the top, where you'll find an incredible view of Atlanta and the Appalachian Mountains. The best approach is to take the cable car up, and then walk back down. A new view can be had from the **Sky Hike** attraction, a quarter-mile family adventure course four stories high.

For a different perspective, check out the park from onboard a World War II amphibious vehicle: The park's **Ride the Ducks Tour** is a 40-minute adventure that moves from land into the waters of Stone Mountain Lake. Tours run from 11am daily; tickets are $9 for ages 3 and up, or $6 when added to the One-Day All-Attractions Pass. Duck Tours are included on the One-Day Pass on "Limited Attraction Days" (Mon–Thurs in the fall) at no additional charge.

---

**(Fun Facts)   The Face of a Mountain**

Over half a century in the making, Stone Mountain's neoclassical carving—90 feet high and 190 feet wide—is the world's largest bas-relief sculpture. Originally conceived by Gutzon Borglum, it depicts Confederate leaders Jefferson Davis, Robert E. Lee, and Stonewall Jackson galloping on horseback throughout eternity. Borglum started work on the mountain sculpture in 1923, but abandoned it after 10 years due to insurmountable technical problems and rifts with its sponsors. (He went on to South Dakota, where he gained fame carving Mount Rushmore.) No sign of his work remains at Stone Mountain, but it was his vision that inspired the project. Augustus Lukeman took over in 1925, but 3 years later, the work still far from complete, the family that owned the mountain lost patience and reclaimed the property. It wasn't until 1963, after the state purchased the mountain and surrounding property for a park, that work resumed under Walter Kirtland Hancock and Roy Faulkner. It was completed in 1970.

A highlight at Stone Mountain is the **Lasershow Spectacular,** an astonishing display of laser lights and fireworks with animation and music. The brilliant laser beams are projected on the mountain's north face, a natural 1-million-square-foot screen. Shows are presented on Saturdays at 8:30pm from March through October, except from Memorial Day weekend through Labor Day, when they take place every night at 9:30pm. They're free with park admission. Bring a picnic supper and arrive early to get a good spot on the lawn at the base of the mountain.

Other major park attractions include the **Stone Mountain Scenic Railroad,** an open-air train that chugs around the 5-mile base of Stone Mountain. The ride takes 40 minutes and includes a live "train robbery" skit. Trains depart from Railroad Depot, an old-fashioned train station, where there's a restaurant with all the fixings for a fried-chicken picnic, just in case you forgot to bring your own.

The **Antique Car and Treasure Museum** is a jumble of old radios, jukeboxes, working nickelodeons, pianos, Lionel trains, carousel horses, and clocks, along with classic cars. The *Scarlett O'Hara,* a paddlewheel riverboat, cruises the 363-acre Stone Mountain Lake.

Visitors can now travel back in time at **Crossroads** ★, where you can explore an 1870s rural Southern town, complete with a cast of authentically costumed characters who sing, play instruments, tell stories, and demonstrate crafts such as glass-blowing, candle-making and blacksmithing. In addition to the town's quirky and talented characters, other special treats include a gristmill and bakery, a general store with candy and ice-cream production facilities, and a boardinghouse restaurant that serves up tasty Southern cuisine, from chicken and dumplings to fried catfish. If you plan to eat, you might want to stop by and add your name to the list before you explore the town, as there is often a wait.

Another part of the Crossroads attraction is the **Great Barn,** a hit with children and adults. Join in the fun as you help "harvest" fruits and vegetables throughout this multi-level foam factory to rack up points for your team. The **Treehouse Challenge** is a one-of-a-kind outdoor adventure that pits boys against girls to control balls on a large track that links the two tree houses (sort of a life-size pinball game). The town's centerpiece is the **Tall Tales of the South** theater, where visitors use special glasses to view a 3-D film with 4-D (yes, four) special effects. The frog's tongue, which stretches into the movie audience from its perch on a swamp log, is just one of the surprises of the experience. Small children might not enjoy the film, as some of the effects are a bit unnerving.

The 19-building **Antebellum Plantation** offers self-guided tours assisted by hosts in period dress at each structure. Highlights include an authentic 1830s country store; the 1845 Kingston House (which represents a typical overseer's house); the clapboard slave cabins; the 1790s Thornton House, elegant home of a large landowner; the smokehouse and well; the doctor's office; a barn, a coach house, and crop-storage cribs; a privy; a cook house; and the 1850 neoclassical Tara-like Dickey House. The grounds also contain formal gardens and a kitchen garden. It takes at least an hour to tour the entire complex. Often (especially in summer), there are Civil War reenactments, craft and cooking demonstrations, storytellers, and balladeers on the premises. Children will enjoy getting up close and personal with the critters at Grandpa's Farm at the Plantation, featuring domesticated farm animals such as pigs and goats.

Additional activities: golf (on top-rated courses designed by Robert Trent Jones and John LaFoy), miniature golf, 15 tennis courts, a sizable stretch of sandy lakefront beach

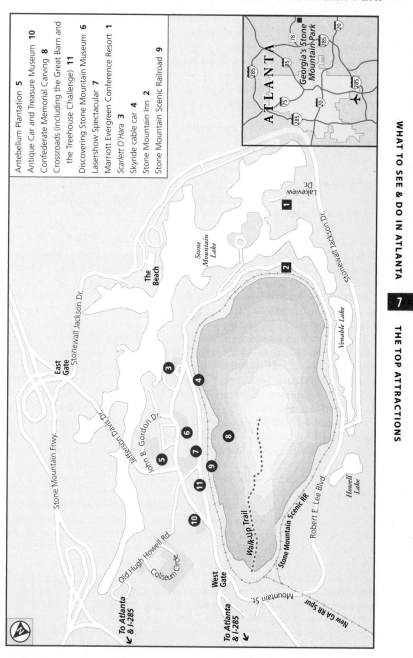

Antebellum Plantation **5**
Antique Car and Treasure Museum **10**
Confederate Memorial Carving **8**
Crossroads (including the Great Barn and
   the Treehouse Challenge) **11**
Discovering Stone Mountain Museum **6**
Lasershow Spectacular **7**
Marriott Evergreen Conference Resort **1**
*Scarlett O'Hara* **3**
Skyride cable car **4**
Stone Mountain Inn **2**
Stone Mountain Scenic Railroad **9**

ATLANTA

Georgia's Stone Mountain Park

Lakeview Dr.

Stonewall Jackson Dr.

Stone Mountain Lake

The Beach

East Gate

Stonewall Jackson Dr.

Stone Mountain Frwy.

Jefferson Davis Dr.

John B. Gordon Dr.

Venable Lake

Howell Lake

Robert E. Lee Blvd.

Stone Mountain Scenic RR

Walk-Up Trail

Old Hugh Howell Rd.

Coliseum Circle

West Gate

Mountain St.

New GA RR Spur

To Atlanta & I-285

To Atlanta & I-285

with four water slides, carillon concerts, rowboats and paddleboats, bicycle rental, fishing, hiking, picnicking, and more.

Stone Mountain is one of the most beautiful parks in the nation and hosts a number of major events throughout the year, so visit its website for dates and details. Consider spending a few days of your trip here; it's a great place for a romantic getaway or a family vacation. See p. 95 for details about on-site accommodations. If you can only spare a day, it's an easy drive (about 30 min.) from downtown.

U.S. Hwy. 78E, Stone Mountain (16 miles east of downtown Atlanta). © **800/317-2006** outside metropolitan Atlanta, or 770/498-5690. www.stonemountainpark.com. A ticket for all major attractions is $25 adults, $22 seniors/military, $20 children 3–11. Year-round, gates 6am–midnight. Major attractions fall and winter 10am–5pm; spring and summer 10am–8pm. Parking $8 a day (one-time-only charge if you stay on the grounds) or $35 for 12-month pass. Attractions only are closed Christmas Eve and Christmas; park remains open. MARTA: Take MARTA to the Avondale station, where you can transfer to a bus to Stone Mountain Village. The park is 4 blocks from the village.

**World of Coca-Cola** ★★ (Kids) An exposition showcasing the world's most popular soft drink, World of Coca-Cola sounds like a huge Coke commercial—and it is. But it's also one of the biggest attractions in the city and a must-see for anybody who's ever had a taste of the Real Thing (and who hasn't?). Now in a new 75,000-square-foot facility that opened downtown near Centennial Park, the CNN Center, and the Georgia Aquarium in 2007, the museum is bigger and better than ever, housing a massive collection of Coca-Cola memorabilia, along with numerous interactive displays, high-tech exhibits, an art gallery, and video presentations.

The self-guided tour begins with a pre-show in the memorabilia-laden Coca-Cola Loft, which includes the oldest artifact, a 1905 "Drink Coca-Cola" Christmas bell decoration, advertising the fizzy beverage for 5¢. From here, visitors gain entrance to the Happiness Factory Theater, where a short film gives them a glimpse into the magic behind every bottle of Coke. Milestones of Refreshment, a series of 10 galleries, traces the history of Coca-Cola from its 1886 debut at Jacob's Pharmacy in downtown Atlanta to its current worldwide fame. Gathering in the Hub, visitors have an opportunity to meet the Coca-Cola polar bear and have their photo taken with him. Adults and kids alike are mesmerized by the Bottle Works exhibit, a working bottling line that allows visitors to stand in the midst of the process. Watch for the small glass bottles to be filled and then be sure to pick up one as your free souvenir before leaving.

The second level holds much, much more—this experience is a total immersion in Coca-Cola. The upper level includes everyone's favorite exhibit—Taste It!—where visitors can have free samples of more than 60 soft drink products from around the world. (**Warning:** You'll soon figure out that America's idea of refreshing isn't the same as that of other countries—some drinks are disgusting.) You'll want to let the kids run wild on the lawn outside once they've loaded up on sugar and caffeine here, but what the heck, drinks are on the house, right? The Pop Culture Gallery showcases Coca-Cola as an icon of popular culture and includes artistic expressions of those inspired by the soft drink, including paintings, furniture, home decor and advertisements.

The Secret Formula 4-D Theater airs a film featuring an eccentric scientist on a quest to uncover the mysterious secret formula for Coke. And a Perfect Pauses Theater showcases some of the best Coca-Cola television advertising throughout the years, as well as three short films on the product. The tour ends in the massive gift shop (you can't leave without going through here first—smart marketing, huh?), which sells a mind-boggling array of Coca-Cola logo items, everything from T-shirts to Coke polar bears.

Allow about 90 minutes to drink it all in. Weekdays are the prime time to visit if you want to avoid long lines. If you plan to see the World of Coca-Cola and the Georgia Aquarium, a Pemberton Pass will save you a few bucks. In addition, the two attractions share a huge covered parking garage with a $10 fee. Pemberton Place includes an expansive lawn, perfect for a picnic, as well as a cafe and public restrooms.

121 Baker St. NW. ✆ **404/676-5151.** www.woccatlanta.com. Admission $15 adults, $13 seniors 55 and over, $9 children 3–12, free for children 2 and under with adult admission. Sun–Thurs 10am–5:30pm; Fri–Sat 9am–6:30pm. Closed Easter, Thanksgiving, and Christmas; abbreviated hours on Christmas Eve and New Year's Eve. Parking garage on Central Ave. off Martin Luther King, Jr., Dr. MARTA: Peachtree Center or Dome/GWCC/Philips Arena/CNN Center.

# 2 MORE ATTRACTIONS IN ATLANTA AND BEYOND

**Callanwolde Fine Arts Center** A magnificent Gothic-Tudor–style mansion built for Coca-Cola heir Charles Howard Candler in 1920, Callanwolde today serves as a fine-arts center for city residents. Ongoing classes are given in pottery, painting, photography, drawing, and more, and there are numerous workshops for both adults and children. The estate occupies 12 acres in the Druid Hills section of Atlanta, an area planned by Frederick Law Olmsted, designer of New York's Central Park. You may be surprised that most of the rooms are bare; only Callanwolde's exquisite walnut paneling, beautifully carved ceilings and moldings, grand staircase, magnificent marble and stone fireplaces, and leaded-glass windows evoke its luxurious past.

Visitors are welcome to peruse shows of local artists in the Petite Hall gallery upstairs; enjoy the lawns and formal gardens, which are maintained by the county; and take in the concerts, storytelling evenings, 1- and 2-day workshops, and dance performances. Check the website to see what's going on when you're in town, as attending an event here is the best way to experience the estate. Especially memorable is Christmas at Callanwolde, when the entire house is decorated for the season, crafts shops are set up in different rooms, and special events and performances are scheduled for children and adults.

980 Briarcliff Rd. NE (north of Ponce de Leon Ave.). ✆ **404/872-5338.** www.callanwolde.org. Free admission, except for special events. Mon–Fri 10am–8pm; Sat 10am–3pm. Self-guided tours available at all times, except during special events. MARTA: Bus 6 (Emory route) from Edgewood/Candler Park or Lindbergh stations.

**Château Elan Winery & Resort** Surrounded by verdant countryside just 40 minutes north of Atlanta, the four-diamond/four-star Château Elan is a hilltop winery that replicates a 16th-century-style French estate. Though its first wines were produced in 1985, the winery has already garnered more than 200 awards.

Guided tours are given Monday through Friday between 11am and 6pm, Saturday and Sunday between noon and 4pm. Self-guided tours are free, or $5 with wine tasting for those 21 and over, except on Saturdays when tours are $10 and include a souvenir glass. On view are the crushing and pressing machines, oak barrels used to age and flavor the wines, the cask room, and the bottling area. The tours conclude with a wine tasting. Grapes ripen in July and August, so if you're here during harvesting in August and September, you'll actually see the winemaking procedure. More than 300 tons of grapes are harvested and processed each year. Saturday cooking demonstrations in the winery's Culinary Studio are popular events, but limited to 20 people at $20 per pop.

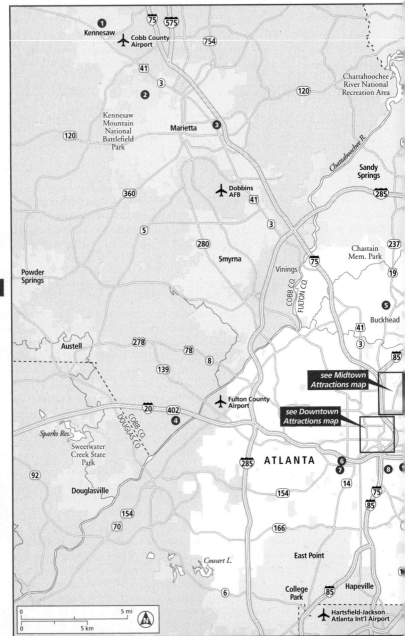

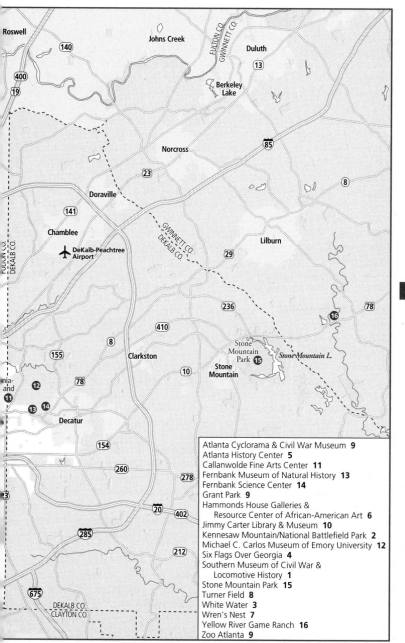

Atlanta Cyclorama & Civil War Museum **9**
Atlanta History Center **5**
Callanwolde Fine Arts Center **11**
Fernbank Museum of Natural History **13**
Fernbank Science Center **14**
Grant Park **9**
Hammonds House Galleries &
   Resource Center of African-American Art **6**
Jimmy Carter Library & Museum **10**
Kennesaw Mountain/National Battlefield Park **2**
Michael C. Carlos Museum of Emory University **12**
Six Flags Over Georgia **4**
Southern Museum of Civil War &
   Locomotive History **1**
Stone Mountain Park **15**
Turner Field **8**
White Water **3**
Wren's Nest **7**
Yellow River Game Ranch **16**
Zoo Atlanta **9**

The interior of the château, a stage-set version of a Paris street, has a quarry-stone floor, wrought-iron fences, and street lamps. The building houses a gallery with monthly exhibits by regional and national artists, displays of antique European winemaking equipment, and a wine market.

There are also some on-premises restaurants, so plan to eat lunch or dinner here. **Café Elan,** open daily from 11am to 10pm, serves sandwiches, salads, and light entrees. It's a charming setting, with seating under a green awning. **Paddy's Irish Pub,** open Friday through Sunday at noon, the rest of the week at 2pm (closing hours vary), serves traditional Irish fare and spirits. Seating just 28 guests, the fancier **Le Clos,** with pale-pink walls, lace-curtained French doors, and tables covered with crisp white linen, is open for dinner Thursday through Sunday evenings, with seatings from 6 to 9pm. A five-course prix-fixe meal features haute-cuisine entrees; appropriate Château Elan wines are served with each course. Reservations are imperative; men are required to wear a coat and tie.

You might also consider an overnight stay at the 277-room **Inn at Château Elan,** a luxurious resort where facilities include three golf courses (two 18-hole and one par-3, 9-hole) and seven tennis courts (offering pro shops and instruction), an equestrian center, a full-service European-style health spa and salon, an outdoor Olympic-size pool, an indoor heated pool, a fitness center, and a rock-climbing tower. Room rates begin at $180 double; call for details and to inquire about golf, tennis, spa, and other packages. If the lovely grounds beckon, you can order a gourmet picnic basket from the kitchen at the hotel.

100 Rue Charlemagne Dr., Braselton (30 miles north of Atlanta at exit 126 off I-85). © **800/233-WINE [9463]** or 678/425-0900. www.chateauelan.com. Daily 10am–9pm.

**Georgia State Capitol** It wasn't until after the Civil War (1868) that Atlanta became, once and for all, the state capital; its present capitol building, completed July 4, 1889, was hailed as a testament to the city's recovery. Modeled after the nation's Capitol, another neoclassical edifice atop a "crowning hill," its 75-foot dome, covered in gold leaf and topped by a Statue of Freedom, is a major Atlanta landmark. The building is fronted by a massive four-story portico with a pediment supported by six Corinthian columns set on large stone piers. In the rotunda, with its soaring 237-foot ceiling, are busts of famous Georgians, including signers of the Declaration of Independence and the Constitution. The governor's office is off the main hall. The capitol building's public spaces are currently being restored to their 1889 grandeur.

Grand staircases in both wings rise to the third floor, where you'll enter the House of Representatives and, across the hall, the Senate chambers. The legislature meets for 40 days, beginning the second Monday in January (it can also be called into special sessions); all of its sessions are open to the public. The fourth floor houses legislative galleries and the Georgia Capitol Museum, with exhibits on cotton, peach, and peanut growing; cases of mounted birds, fish, deer, insects, and other species native to Georgia; rocks and minerals; American Indian artifacts; and more. Note, too, the museum displays on the first floor.

Tours begin on the main floor; this level also serves as an information center for city and state attractions. The tours take 45 minutes; allow at least another 30 minutes to browse around on your own afterward. Highlights of the grounds are detailed in a brochure available at the tour desk. ***Note:*** For security reasons, your bag will be searched when you enter.

If you're visiting in December or January, take note of two special treats: A beautifully decorated 40-foot tree adorns the rotunda at Christmas, and on January 15, Dr. Martin Luther King, Jr.'s birthday, there's a memorial program featuring speeches by local dignitaries, including the governor.

206 Washington St. (at Martin Luther King Blvd.). ✆ **404/656-2844.** www.sos.state.ga.us. Free admission. Mon–Fri 8am–5pm. Tours given year-round at 10, 11am, 1, 2, and 3pm, with additional times Sept–April of 10:30am and 1:30pm. Self-guided tours are possible any time the capitol is open. Closed major holidays, including state holidays. Parking lot behind the capitol building on Capitol Ave. is closed to the public during legislative sessions; other lots are on Martin Luther King, Jr., Dr. at Central Ave. and on Courtland St. between Martin Luther King, Jr., Dr. and Central Ave. MARTA: Georgia State.

### Hammonds House Galleries & Resource Center of African-American Art

Occupying the 1857 Eastlake Victorian–style former home of Dr. Otis T. Hammonds, a black anesthesiologist and art patron, Hammonds House is a national center for the exhibition, preservation, research, and documentation of African-American art and artists. The permanent collection includes Hammonds's extensive compilation of works by African-American and Haitian artists, as well as his African masks and carvings. These works are complemented by later acquisitions, including pieces by Romare Bearden, William H. Johnson, Robert S. Duncanson, and Elizabeth Catlett. The permanent collection is shown on a rotating basis and is supplemented by exhibitions featuring the work of renowned black artists from all over the world. The Resource Center, housing documents on African-American art and artists, is open to the public by appointment.

The house is located in the thriving West End neighborhood, which was declared a historic district in 1991. While you're in the area, take a look at the other lovingly restored Victorian bungalows and houses. A short walk away is the Atlanta University Center, the largest historically African-American education complex in the world, home to prestigious Morehouse College. Dr. Martin Luther King, Jr., is Morehouse's most famous alumnus; a chapel was built on the campus to honor his memory.

503 Peeples St. (at Lucile St., 2 blocks north of Ralph David Abernathy Blvd.). ✆ **404/612-0500.** www.hammondshouse.org. Admission $4 adults; $2 seniors, children, and students. Tues–Fri 10:30am–4:30pm. MARTA: Bus 71 from the West End station or bus 67 from West Lake station.

### Herndon Home

Alonzo Herndon was born in 1858, during the last decade of slavery. After emancipation, he worked as a field hand and sharecropper, supplementing his meager income by selling peanuts, homemade molasses, and axle grease. He arrived in Atlanta in the early 1880s, taking on work as a barber and eventually owning several barbershops of his own. Herndon used the earnings from these shops to acquire Atlanta real estate, and by 1900, fewer than 40 years out of slavery and with only a year of formal education, he was the richest black man in Atlanta. In 1905, Herndon purchased a church burial association, which, with other small companies, became the nucleus of the Atlanta Life Insurance Company, today the nation's second-largest black-owned insurance company.

In 1910, Herndon built this elegant 15-room house in the Beaux Arts–neoclassical style, complete with a stately colonnaded entrance. Herndon and his wife, Adrienne McNeil, a drama teacher at Atlanta University, were the primary architects of the house, and construction was accomplished almost completely by African-American artisans. Because their son Norris occupied the home until 1977, much of the original furniture remains, and there are family photographs throughout. Adrienne died about a week after the house was completed.

The house tour begins in a receiving room with a 10-minute introductory video called *The Herndon Legacy.* The tour then takes you through the reception hall; the music room, with rococo gilt-trimmed walls and Louis XV–style furnishings; the living room, with a frieze on its walls depicting the accomplishments of Herndon's life; the dining room, furnished in late Renaissance style with family china and Venetian glass displayed in a mahogany cabinet; the butler's pantry; and the sunny breakfast room. Upstairs, you'll see the bedroom used by Herndon's second wife, Jessie, with its Jacobean suite and Louis XV–style furnishings; Herndon's Empire-furnished bedroom, where a book from a Republican National Convention is displayed on a table, letting you know his political bent; the collection room (Norris collected ancient Greek and Roman vases and funerary objects); Norris's bedroom; a sitting room; and a guest bedroom.

587 University Place (btw. Vine and Walnut sts.). *C* 404/581-9813. www.herndonhome.org. Admission $5 adults, $3 students and children. Tues and Thurs 10am–4pm, with tours on the hour. Tours available by appt. on Sat. Closed New Year's Day, July 4th, Thanksgiving, Christmas Eve, and Christmas. MARTA: Vine City.

**Kennesaw Mountain/National Battlefield Park**   This 2,884-acre park, run by the National Park Service, was established in 1917 on the site of a crucial Civil War battle in the Atlanta campaign of 1864. Some two million visitors come annually to explore the Confederate entrenchments and earthworks, some of them equipped with actual Civil War artillery.

The action began in June 1864. A month earlier, General Ulysses S. Grant had ordered Sherman to attack the Confederate army in Georgia, telling him to "break it up, and go into the interior of the enemy's country as far as you can, inflicting all the damage you can upon their war resources." In response to this order, Sherman's army, 100,000 strong, pushed back Confederate forces composed of General Joseph E. Johnston's 65,000 men. By June 19, Union troops had driven Johnston's men back to a well-prepared defensive position on Kennesaw Mountain. Southern engineers had built a line of entrenchments in its rocky slopes, allowing the Confederates to cover every approach with rifle or cannon. An Ohio officer later commented that if the mountain had been constructed for the sole purpose of repelling an invading army, "it could not have been better made or placed."

On June 27, following a few weeks of skirmishing, Sherman, underestimating the strength and still-feisty morale of the rebels, attempted to break through Confederate lines and annihilate the troops in a grand no-holds-barred assault from two directions. Confederate General Samuel French described the onset of the attack: "As if by magic, there sprang from the earth a host of men, and in one long, waving line of blue the infantry advanced and the battle of Kennesaw Mountain began." Weeks of torrential rain had turned these battlegrounds into muddy mire, adding significantly to the misery on both sides.

Sherman's men were repelled by massive bursts of firepower and huge rocks that the Confederates rolled down the mountain at them. Union casualties far outnumbered Confederate losses in this first attack. Meanwhile, 8,000 Union infantrymen in five brigades attacked from another angle; in this battle, the Union lost 3,000 men, the Confederates 500, resulting in a tremendous Confederate victory on these grounds.

Allow at least 2 hours for exploring. Start your tour at the **visitor center,** where you can pick up a map, watch a 20-minute film about the battle, and view exhibits of Civil War artifacts, medicine, and memorabilia. On weekdays, you can drive or hike up the mountain to see the actual Confederate entrenchments and earthworks. On weekends, it may be too crowded to drive, but you can take a shuttle bus for a nominal fee or you can hike (the steep trail is about 2 miles round-trip, so wear comfortable shoes). You'll find interpretive signs at key spots and, on weekends and holidays from Memorial Day through Labor Day, interpretive programs give further information about the battle. You'll also want to drive to **Cheatham Hill,** site of some of the fiercest fighting. There are 16 miles of hiking trails for those who want a more extensive tour (trail maps are available at the visitor center), and picnicking is permitted in designated areas, some of which boast barbecue grills. The scenery is gorgeous, so even if Civil War battles are not your thing (that is, if you're reluctantly accompanying an enthusiastic spouse or friend), you'll find some beautiful hiking or driving.

Old Hwy. 41 and Stilesboro Rd., Kennesaw. © 770/427-4686. www.nps.gov/kemo. Free admission. Park daily 7:30am–8pm; visitor center daily 8:30am–5pm. Closed six major holidays. Take I-75 N. to Barrett Pkwy. and then follow the signs.

**National Museum of Patriotism**   This facility opened on July 4, 2004, but moved in November 2008 into a new home at the Hilton Garden Inn of downtown Atlanta. The museum was the dream of Nick Snider, retired vice president of United Parcel Service, who wanted to inspire and educate people on the subject of patriotism. A collector of World War II patriotic sweetheart jewelry and collectibles, Snider now shares these exhibits with museum visitors, who will also see inspiring videos that highlight the spirit of America; interactive, educational displays honoring the U.S. armed forces; and exhibits on the American flag, the Medal of Honor, women patriots, and the diversity of patriotism. In addition, the museum houses Georgia's only exhibit on the September 11, 2001, terrorist attacks. Traveling exhibits have included "The Patriotic Work of Norman Rockwell," "Patriotism in Cinema," and "Patriotic Posters."

275-B Baker St. (in the Hilton Garden Inn). © 877/276-1692 or 404/875-0691. www.museumof patriotism.org. Admission $15 adults, $12 seniors, $10 for students, free for children 4 and under. Daily 9am–6pm. MARTA: Dome/GWCC/Philips Arena/CNN.

**Rhodes Memorial Hall**   Rhodes Hall is one of a few remaining pre–World War I Peachtree Street mansions—a significant reminder that Peachtree was once a fashionable residential street. The house was designed shortly after the turn of the 20th century by Willis Franklin Denny (at the time Atlanta's leading residential architect) as a home for affluent Atlanta businessman Amos Giles Rhodes and his family.

Its medieval-baronial-cum-High-Victorian-Romanesque style was inspired by Rhineland castles. The Stone Mountain granite exterior is replete with arched Romanesque windows, battlements and buttresses, parapets, towers, and turrets. A large Syrian-arched veranda wraps the east and north facades. The interior is grandiose, with maple- and mahogany-bordered oak parquet floors, mosaics surrounding the fireplaces, and a gracefully winding, hand-carved Honduran mahogany staircase with nine stained-glass stairwell panels depicting "The Rise and Fall of the Confederacy." The house and stables originally occupied 150 acres of land and included servants' quarters, a carriage house, and other outbuildings. When it was built, this site was in suburbia, an afternoon's drive from downtown.

Upon Rhodes's death in 1929, his residence was deeded to the state of Georgia in keeping with his desire to preserve his home. The house was entered on the National Register of Historic Places in 1974. Today, it is the headquarters for the Georgia Trust for Historic Preservation and is in an ongoing process of restoration. To date, the original

> ## ⓕFun Facts Did You Know?
>
> - Atlanta has 100 streets that include the word "Peachtree."
> - Georgia's major agricultural crop is peanuts, not peaches.
> - Atlanta's earliest streetlights burned whale oil.
> - The world's largest bas-relief sculpture (Stone Mountain—90×190 ft.) and the world's largest painting (the Cyclorama, using 20,000 sq. ft. of canvas) are in Atlanta.
> - In 1916, Georgia Tech's Yellow Jackets set a world record football score: 222 to 0 against Cumberland College.
> - Because it has received over $250 million from Coca-Cola, Emory University is known as "Coca-Cola U."
> - *Fortune* magazine consistently rates Atlanta one of the nation's best places to do business.
> - Not a single scene from the movie *Gone with the Wind* was filmed in Georgia, though a few bushels of Georgia red clay were transported to the Hollywood set to add verisimilitude.
> - Hartsfield-Jackson is the country's busiest airport and is consistently ranked among the best airports in the world. Eighty percent of the U.S. population is within a 2-hour flight of Atlanta.

dining-room suite and some other furnishings are in place, and all the mahogany woodwork and decorated ceilings on the first floor have been restored. The original landscaping—with white and red cedars, dogwoods, banana trees, and a circular flower bed—has been re-created in the front yard.

You can see the house only by guided tour. On weekdays, the 45-minute Historical Tours explain Rhodes Hall's background while guiding visitors through the first floor of the house. The special Behind-the-Scenes Tours, on Sunday at noon, are comprehensive 3-hour experiences that explore the entire house.

1516 Peachtree St. NW (at Peachtree Circle). ⓒ **404/885-7800.** www.rhodeshall.org. Historical tours of first floor only, $5 adults, $4 seniors, students and children 6–12, free for children 5 and under. Behind-the-Scenes Tours $8 (no discounts apply). Tours on the hour every hour. Tues–Fri 11am–4pm; Sat 10am–2pm; Sun noon–3pm. Closed major holidays. Free parking in designated lot behind building on Spring St. MARTA: Arts Center.

**Southern Museum of Civil War and Locomotive History**   Previously the Kennesaw Civil War Museum, this museum is now operated in association with the Smithsonian Institute, which means that Civil War and transportation objects from the Smithsonian will be incorporated into the exhibits here.

It was here that the wild adventure known as the "Great Locomotive Chase" began. The Civil War had been underway for a year on April 12, 1862, when Union spy James J. Andrews and a group of 21 Northern soldiers disguised as civilians boarded a locomotive called the *General* in Marietta, buying tickets for diverse destinations to avert suspicion. When the train made a breakfast stop at the Lacy Hotel in Big Shanty, they seized the locomotive and several boxcars and fled northward to Chattanooga. The goal of these daring raiders was to destroy tracks, telegraph wires, and bridges behind them, thus cutting off the Confederate supply route between Virginia and Mississippi.

Conductor William A. Fuller, his breakfast interrupted by the sound of the *General* chugging out of the station, gave chase on foot, then grabbed a platform car and poled along the tracks. With him were a railroad superintendent and the *General*'s engineer. At the Etowah River, Fuller and crew commandeered a small locomotive called the *Yonah* and made better progress. Meanwhile, the raiders tore up track behind them, and when the pursuers got close, the raiders slowed them down by throwing ties and firewood onto the tracks. Andrews, a very smooth talker, managed to convince station attendants en route that he was on an emergency mission running ammunition to Confederate General Beauregard in Mississippi.

Fuller's chances of catching the *General* improved when he seized the southbound *Texas* and began running it backward toward the raiders, picking up reinforcements along the way and eventually managing to get a telegraph message through to General Danville Leadbetter, commander at Chattanooga. The chase went on, with Andrews sending uncoupled boxcars careening back toward Fuller as obstructions. Fuller, who was running in reverse, merely attached the rolling boxcars to his engine and kept on. At the covered Oostanaula Bridge, the raiders detached a boxcar and set it on fire in hopes of finally creating an impassable obstacle—a burning bridge behind them. But the *Texas* was able to push the flaming car off the bridge. It soon burned out, and Fuller tossed it off the track and continued.

By this time the *General* was running low on fuel and water, the *Texas* was hot on its heels, and the raiders realized that all was lost. Andrews gave his final command: "Jump off and scatter! Every man for himself!" All were captured and imprisoned within a few days. Some escaped, others were exchanged for Confederate prisoners of war, and the rest were hanged in Atlanta, most of them at a site near Oakland Cemetery. Though the mission failed, the raiders, some of them posthumously, received the newly created Medal of Honor for their valor.

The museum, occupying a building that was once the Frey cotton gin, houses the *General* (still in running condition, but don't get any ideas); a walk-through caboose; exhibits of Civil War artifacts, memorabilia, and photographs (including those relating to the chase and its participants); and exhibits on railroads. You can view a 20-minute narrated video about the chase, but if you really want the full story, rent the Disney movie *The Great Locomotive Chase,* starring Fess Parker as the dashing Andrews. (You can also buy a copy in the museum gift shop.)

The museum is 3 miles from Kennesaw Mountain/National Battlefield Park (p. 166), so consider visiting both of these Civil War–related sights on the same day.

2829 Cherokee St., Kennesaw. ☎ 770/427-2117. www.southernmuseum.org. Admission $7.50 adults, $6.50 seniors 60 and over, $5.50 children 4–12, free for children 3 and under. Guided tours given every half-hour. Mon–Sat 9:30am–5pm; Sun noon–5pm. Closed major holidays. Free parking. Take exit 273 off I-75 N. and follow the signs.

## Underground Atlanta (Overrated)

In 1969, a group of Atlanta businesspeople decided to create an underground entertainment complex of restaurants, shops, and bars in the historic hub of the city, centered on the Zero Milepost that marked the terminus of the Western & Atlantic Railroad in the 1800s. The area had flourished until the early 1900s, until it became so congested that permanent concrete viaducts were constructed over it, elevating the street system and routing traffic over a maze of railroad tracks.

Merchants moved their operations up to the new level, using the lower level for storage space. For most of the 20th century, it remained a deserted catacomb.

The 1969 entertainment development idea was great, but unfortunately the complex declined and closed after a little more than a decade. In 1989—after a public-private infusion of $142 million—a larger, livelier Underground reopened to much fanfare, becoming once again an entertainment mecca and urban marketplace. Local civic leaders pinned their hopes for downtown revival on the complex, and for some time it looked as if the concept would work. But, beset by lease disputes, financial problems, and changes of management, Underground has failed to sustain its early promise, and its most recent management company struggles to overcome the complex's seedy reputation.

Occupying 12 acres in the center of downtown, Underground Atlanta sports oscillating searchlights emanating from a 138-foot light tower, an outdoor staging area used for performances and concerts, and the cascading waters of Peachtree Fountain Plaza. Underground comprises about 75 retail operations and restaurants, many of them national chains. Markers throughout the complex indicate historic sites. Their origins are fascinating, so be sure to pick up an information sheet at the visitor booth and take your own self-guided tour. Humbug Square—where street vendors and con artists flourished in the early 1900s—has a colorful market with turn-of-the-20th-century pushcarts and wagons displaying offbeat wares. The complex is still worth a look if you're in the downtown area, but keep in mind that it's mostly a tourist attraction at this point. It's still struggling to find its place in the urban mix, perhaps because locals prefer the shopping and entertainment areas in Buckhead and Virginia Highland.

The **Atlanta Convention & Visitors Bureau** (© **404/222-6688**) operates its most comprehensive center in Underground Atlanta, at 65 Upper Alabama St. Open Monday through Saturday from 10am to 6pm, Sunday from noon to 6pm, it includes displays and interactive exhibits depicting the city's rich history. There's also **AtlanTIX!,** a ticket booth where visitors can purchase day-of-show, half-price tickets to theater, dance, and other live performances throughout the metro area.

50 Upper Alabama St. (bounded by Wall St., Central Ave., Martin Luther King, Jr., Dr., and Peachtree St.). © **404/523-2311** or 877/859-4891. www.underground-atlanta.com. Free admission. Mon–Sat 10am–9pm; Sun 11am–7pm. Some restaurants and clubs until midnight (or later) nightly. Paid parking in the garages off Martin Luther King, Jr., Dr. MARTA: Five Points station has a short pedestrian tunnel that connects directly with Underground Atlanta.

**William Breman Jewish Heritage Museum**   This museum, the largest of its kind in the Southeast, offers a unique glimpse into Atlanta's history, exploring Jewish heritage with a special emphasis on the Atlanta Jewish experience. Two main galleries juxtapose the destruction of the Holocaust with the reemergence of Jewish communities in Atlanta and throughout the world. The stories are told through photographs, documents, and memorabilia uncovered in the attics and basements of local families and individuals. Especially moving are the stories and possessions generously shared by Holocaust survivors living in Atlanta.

In addition to the two main galleries, there's a Discovery Center with hands-on activities related to the exhibitions, a community archive, a genealogy center, a library, and a gift shop.

1440 Spring St. NW (in the Selig Center at 18th St.). © **678/222-3700.** www.thebremen.org. Admission $10 adults, $6 seniors, $4 students, $2 children 3–6, free for children 2 and under. Mon–Thurs 10am–5pm; Fri 10am–3pm; Sun 1–5pm. Archives by appt. only. Closed Sat, major Jewish holidays, and some secular holidays. Limited free parking. MARTA: Arts Center.

Though the following attractions are great choices if you're traveling with kids, don't pass them up even if you're not. Especially worthwhile are the Center for Puppetry Arts, Imagine It! Children's Museum of Atlanta, Wren's Nest, and Zoo Atlanta (visit in conjunction with Atlanta Cyclorama and Oakland Cemetery). In addition, be sure to take the kids to the Fernbank Museum of Natural History (p. 144), the Birth Home of Martin Luther King, Jr. (p. 141), and the King Center (p. 149), all described earlier in this chapter.

### Center for Puppetry Arts ★ (Kids)

Dedicated to expanding public awareness of puppetry as a fine art and to presenting all of its international and historical forms, the center opened in 1978, with Kermit the Frog cutting the official ribbon (he had a little help from the late Jim Henson). Staff and loyal visitors are all aglow with the latest acquisition: more than 500 of the late Henson's Muppets, as well as props, videos, and memorabilia from such classics as "The Muppet Show" and "Sesame Street." The collection will be housed in a Jim Henson Wing when the center opens its new location in 2012. Until then, a number of Henson puppets are on display at the current location.

It encompasses a 300-seat theater, a smaller theater, gallery space, and a permanent museum. The puppet shows are marvelous—sophisticated, riveting, full-stage productions with elaborate scenery. Some are family-oriented; others, with nighttime showings, are geared to adults. Call ahead to find out what's on (reservations are essential). You can also call a week or so in advance to enroll yourself or your kids in a puppet-making workshop.

The center's permanent exhibit, "Puppets, The Power of Wonder," is stunning, featuring one of the largest and finest puppet collections in North America. It includes such treasures as ritualistic African figures, Punch and Judy, Henson's Pigs in Space, turn-of-the-20th-century Thai shadow puppets, Indonesian *wayang golek* puppets used to tell classic stories (a centuries-old tradition), Chinese hand puppets, rod-operated marionettes from all over Europe, original Muppets, pre-Columbian clay puppets that were used in religious ceremonies (ca. A.D. 1200), and Turkish shadow figures made of dried animal skins. Visitors get the opportunity to use joysticks to manipulate more than 350 of these puppets. A video hosted by Jim Henson provides an overview of puppetry and takes visitors around the world to meet masters of the art. Another gallery features visiting exhibits from other countries. Reservations are required for guided 1-hour tours of the permanent exhibit.

The gift shop is like no other, with oodles of marionettes, one-of-a-kind handmade puppets, masks, videos, and other related items.

1404 Spring St. NW (at 18th St.). © **404/873-3391.** www.puppet.org. Museum admission $8 adults, $7 seniors and students, $6 children, or free if you see a show or take a workshop. Show tickets $16. Workshops $6–$15. Tues–Sat 9am–5pm; Sun 11am–5pm. Closed New Year's Day, Memorial Day, July 4th, Labor Day, Thanksgiving, and Christmas. Limited free parking. MARTA: Arts Center.

### Fernbank Science Center (Kids)

Owned and funded by the DeKalb County School System, this museum/planetarium/observatory, located adjacent to the 65-acre Fernbank Forest, is an educational partner of the Fernbank Museum of Natural History (p. 144). Plan to visit the entire complex on the same day. There's a 1.5-mile forest trail here, with trees, shrubs, ferns, wildflowers, mosses, and other plants marked for identification. An extensive rose garden is next-door to the museum.

The indoor facility houses exhibits such as a video display on geological phenomena (volcanoes, earthquakes, mountain formation, and so on); a gem collection; an exhibit tracing the development of life in Georgia from 500 million to 1 million years ago; a complete weather station; fossilized trees; the original *Apollo 6* space capsule and space suit (on loan from the Smithsonian); computer games; a replica of the Okefenokee Swamp, complete with sound effects; and models of dinosaurs that roamed Atlanta in prehistoric times. At the Observatory, which contains the largest telescope in the world dedicated to public education, an astronomer gives talks and helps visitors to spot celestial objects. Planetarium shows are held daily.

156 Heaton Park Dr. NE (at Artwood Rd. off Ponce de Leon Ave.). ✆ **678/874-7102.** www.fernbank.edu. Free admission to exhibit hall, Mon–Wed noon–5pm; Thurs–Fri noon–10pm; Sat 10am–5pm. Planetarium shows $4 adults, $3 students and seniors. Planetarium shows vary (see website for latest info). Observatory Thurs–Fri 9 (or whenever it gets dark) to 10:30pm, weather permitting. Forest trails Mon–Fri 2–5pm; Sat 10am–5pm. From downtown, go east on North Ave. to Piedmont Ave. and turn left. Turn right on Ponce de Leon Ave., drive 4$\frac{1}{2}$ miles, and turn left at the light onto Atwood Rd. Turn right on Heaton Park Dr. Fernbank is on the left across from Fernbank Elementary School.

**Imagine It! Children's Museum of Atlanta** (Kids)  Opened in 2003, Imagine It! is a 30,000-square-foot children's museum conveniently located across the street from Centennial Olympic Park, in an area undergoing some exciting urban renaissance. Based on Howard Gardiner's theory of multiple intelligences, Imagine It! features colorful hands-on exhibits and activities that allow children the opportunity to look, listen, touch, and explore in order to discover firsthand how things work. Fun is the priority in this high-energy environment (the learning just sneaks up). There are four major learning zones: Fundamentally Food, Let Your Creativity Flow, Tools for Solutions, and Leaping into Learning, the specialty zone for toddlers. The Morph Gallery has changing exhibits, such as Bob the Builder, the Amazing Castle, and Curious George's Let's Get Curious.

The museum is recommended for children 2 to 8, but all are welcome. However, all grown-ups must be accompanied by a kid, and all kids must be accompanied by a grown-up. Snacks and drinks are available in the Eats and Treats area, and Chick-fil-A offers a limited menu during lunch hours. Due to high visitor volume, Imagine It! encourages visitors to purchase advance tickets online to ensure entrance to the museum upon arrival. Make a day of it and visit Centennial Park, the new World of Coca-Cola, or the Georgia Aquarium across the street either before or after your museum visit.

275 Centennial Olympic Park Dr. NW. ✆ **404/659-KIDS [5437].** www.imagineit-cma.org. Admission $11 (plus tax) for adults and children 2 and above, free for children 1 and under. Advance ticket reservations encouraged. Mon–Fri 10am–4pm; Sat–Sun 10am–5pm. Closed Thanksgiving and Christmas. Parking available throughout the area. MARTA: Peachtree Center.

**Six Flags Over Georgia** (Kids)  One of the state's major family attractions, Six Flags provides a great day's entertainment. Arrive early (at least 30 min. before opening), note where you've parked in the vast lot, and take 10 minutes or so to plan out your show and ride schedule.

The park's various areas have themes centered around different regions, from Southern (Cotton States, Confederate, Georgia, Lickskillet, and Promenade) to European (France, Britain, Spain) to American (U.S.A.) to Gotham City (featuring Batman The Ride). Costumed Looney Tune characters (Sylvester, Daffy Duck, and others) roam the park greeting kids (check out the gazebo in the Promenade section to meet that wascally wabbit Bugs Bunny). Summertime is busy in the park's water-themed venue, Skull Island, a

Caribbean pirate adventure, with six slides and a spewing volcano among other watery playground treats.

Thrill rides include several additional watery options, such as Splashwater Falls (a plummet down a soaring 50-ft. waterfall), a log flume, and Thunder River (a simulated white-water rafting adventure). White-knuckle coasters include the Georgia Scorcher (one of the Southeast's tallest and fastest stand-up roller coasters), Ninja (the "black belt" of roller coasters, turning riders upside down five times and offering thrilling loops, dives, and corkscrew turns), the Georgia Cyclone (a classic wooden coaster with 11 dramatic drops, patterned after Coney Island's famous thrill ride), the Great American Scream Machine (another classic wooden coaster), and Mind Bender (a triple-looper). Other highlights are Batman The Ride (a twisting roller coaster with ski-lift-like seats), Great Gasp (a 20-story parachute jump), Riverview Carousel (a merry-go-round from the early 1900s), and Free Fall (ever wonder what it would be like to fall off a 10-story building?). A less dizzying adventure is Monster Mansion, a Disneyesque boat ride through an antebellum mansion haunted by more than 100 animated monsters. And there's much, much more.

Shows vary from year to year, but they usually include a major musical revue, a country-music show, a golden-oldies show, thrill cinema adventures on a 180-degree screen, and an animated character show. In addition, headliners such as SheDaisy and John Michael Montgomery play the 8,072-seat (with lawn seating for 4,000) Southern Star Amphitheatre.

There are restaurants and snack bars throughout the park, though you might consider bringing a picnic.

275 Riverside Pkwy. SW (at the Six Flags exit off I-20 W.), Austell. © **770/948-9290.** www.sixflags.com/georgia. Admission $40 (plus tax) adults, $30 (plus tax) seniors 55 and over and children 48 in. and under, free for kids 2 and under. A nominal fee is charged for amphitheater concerts. Weekends only Mar to mid-May and Sept–Oct; daily Memorial Day to Labor Day. Gates 10am; closing hours vary. Parking $15.

**White Water** (Kids) A Six Flags park encompassing 40 acres of wet, splashy fun, White Water is the largest water park in the South, with over 30 slides. Its star attraction is the $1-million Tree House Island, a four-story fantasy treehouse with more than 100 different activities—curvy slides, net bridges, water cannons, chutes, and more. A 1,000-gallon bucket of water empties over the whole attraction every few minutes. Other park highlights include Cliffhanger, a 990-foot free fall (one of the tallest such attractions in the world); the 735-foot Run-A-Way River, an enclosed tunnel raft ride; the "Atlanta Ocean," a 750,000-gallon wave pool; and a host of different slide and splash experiences. There's much more, including a special section for children 48 inches and under called Little Squirt's Island, with 25 tot-size water attractions. Adjacent Captain Kid's Cove has dozens of additional activities for kids 12 and under. Restaurants and snack bars are on the premises, as are rental lockers ($13–$19) and shower facilities. Swimsuits are essential and no outside food, beverages, or coolers are allowed.

Next to White Water is **American Adventures** (© **770/428-5217**; www.americanadventuresfunpark.com), a year-round indoor/outdoor family amusement park with children's rides in the Fun Forest (bumper cars, a small roller coaster, a tilt-a-whirl, and others); a classic carousel; a go-cart track; a penny arcade with more than 130 games; Professor Plinker's Laboratory (a large children's play area with ball crawls and nets to climb); 18-hole miniature golf; and the Foam Factory, a huge, multilevel interactive play area with scads of foam-ball activities. It's all geared to children 12 and under. A family-style restaurant is on the grounds. Admission to American Adventures is $20 for a full-day pass or $16 for three hours. Or pay just for those attractions you want to use.

Some attractions are free for adults accompanying children, and most attractions offer discounted pricing for adults. American Adventures is connected to the water park, so you can go back and forth if you want, though you'll pay entrance fees to both. Hours vary with the season, so call first.

250 N. Cobb Pkwy. NE (exit 265 off I-75), Marietta. ☎ **770/424-9283.** www.sixflags.com/georgia. Admission $37 adults, $27 children under 48 in. tall. Parking $10. Weekends only starting in mid-May 10am–6pm; daily Memorial Day to late summer and Labor Day weekend 10am to late evening (closing hours vary). Closed early Sept to Apr.

**Wren's Nest** (Kids)   Named for a family of wrens that once nested in the mailbox, Wren's Nest is the former home of Joel Chandler Harris, who chronicled the wily deeds of fictional African characters Br'er Rabbit and Br'er Fox. It's been open to the public since 1913, when Harris's widow sold it to the Uncle Remus Memorial Association.

Harris's literary career began at the age of 13, when he apprenticed on the *Countryman,* a quarterly plantation newspaper. During the 4 years that he spent learning at the *Countryman,* young Harris spent many an evening hanging about the slave quarters, drinking in African folk tales and fables spun by George Terrell, a plantation patriarch who became the prototype for Uncle Remus. When the *Countryman* went out of business, Harris went on to other newspapers, working his way up to editorial writer at the *Atlanta Constitution* by his early 30s. There, filling in for a sick colleague, he remembered the plantation stories of his youth and evoked Uncle Remus to fill his column. Enthralled readers clamored for more, and the rest is history.

The house itself is an 1870s farmhouse with a Queen Anne–style Victorian facade added in 1884. Harris lived here from 1881 until his death in 1908, doing most of his writing in a rocking chair on the wraparound front porch. On the 30-minute tour, you'll see a good deal of memorabilia: the stuffed great horned owl over the study door (a gift from Theodore Roosevelt, whose White House Harris visited); the original wren's-nest mailbox on the study mantel; and all of Harris's books, along with signed first editions from major authors of his day (an unverified Mark Twain among others) displayed in a bookcase. Guided tours are held every half-hour on Tuesday, Thursday, and Saturday.

The house itself is certainly more than worthy of a visit here, but a favorite attraction is the **storytelling** every Saturday at 1pm, when the resident storyteller shares stories culled from African and African-American folklore; it's a real treat.

1050 Ralph David Abernathy Blvd. (2 blocks from Ashby St.). ☎ **404/753-7735.** Admission $8 adults, $7 seniors and students, $5 children 3–12, free for children 2 and under. Tues–Sat 10am–2:30pm. Closed major holidays. Take I-20 W. to Lowery Blvd., turn left on Ashby St., then right on Ralph David Abernathy Blvd.; Wren's Nest is 2 long blocks down on the left. MARTA: Bus 71 from West End station.

## Impressions

*I seem to see before me the smiling faces of thousands of children—some young and fresh—and some wearing the friendly marks of age, but all children at heart, and not an unfriendly face among them. And while I am trying hard to speak the right word, I seem to hear a voice lifted above the rest saying, "You have made some of us happy." And so I feel my heart fluttering and my lips trembling and I have to bow silently and turn away and hurry into the obscurity that fits me best.*

—Joel Chandler Harris, former owner of Wren's Nest, who died on July 3, 1908. He wrote these words, which later appeared on his gravestone.

**Yellow River Game Ranch** (Kids) Bordering the Yellow River, this 24-acre animal preserve allows for close encounters of the four-legged kind—a chance to view, pet, feed, and generally mingle with some 600 animals (always including quite a few babies) who live in open enclosures or right out in the open, along a 1-mile oak- and hickory-shaded forest trail. The ranch is home to one of the largest buffalo herds east of the Mississippi. Owner Art Rilling knows every animal on the ranch by name and can give you chapter and verse on each one's personality, preferences, and, in some cases, romantic history. The animals know they're among friends here and are highly socialized, so you'll have a unique chance to study them up close. Keep in mind that all these animals smell like, well, animals. If a barnyard atmosphere bothers you, don't visit.

Inhabitants include donkeys named Rhett and Scarlett, Georgia black bears that stand up and beg for marshmallows, goats, dozens of rabbits in Bunny Burrows (kids can pet the bunnies), an assortment of interesting-looking chickens, a herd of buffalo, sheep, burros, goats, ponies, and a groundhog named General Beauregard Lee (we are in Georgia, after all) who lives in a white colonnaded Southern mansion complete with miniature satellite dish.

Consider packing a picnic lunch. There are tables throughout the property, and one especially nice picnic area overlooks the river.

4525 Hwy. 78, Lilburn. (C) **770/972-6643.** www.yellowrivergameranch.com. Admission $8 adults, $7 children 2–11, free for children 1 and under. Daily 9:30am–6pm; ticket sales end at 5pm. Closed major holidays. Take I-85 N. to I-285 E. Exit at State Hwy. 78 and follow it east for 10 miles.

**Zoo Atlanta** ★★ (Kids) This delightful 40-acre zoo dates from 1889, when George W. Hall (aka "Popcorn George") brought his traveling circus to town. Employee claims for back wages forced Hall to relinquish his menagerie, and the animal entourage was purchased by a prominent Atlanta businessman who donated the collection to the city as the basis for a zoological garden in Grant Park. It grew considerably over the years and was a popular local attraction, but had fallen into disrepair by the mid-1980s. Director Terry Maple was brought in to rescue the zoo and oversee a multimillion-dollar renovation.

The turnaround has been dramatic. Today, Zoo Atlanta is one of the finest zoos in the country, with animals housed in large open enclosures that simulate their natural habitats. The zoo participates in breeding programs, many of them focusing on endangered species, and is home to endangered animals that include black rhinos, Sumatran orangutans, 19 western lowland gorillas, two African elephants, two Komodo monitors, and big-mouthed African dwarf crocodiles. The Australian-themed Outback Station in the Orkin Children's Zoo introduced two new species—red kangaroos and kookaburras. The Living Treehouse, a revitalized home for drill baboons, Mona monkeys, and red ruffed lemurs, also houses an open-air aviary for 15 species of African birds. Turner Broadcasting made a $5 million donation in 2004, the single largest gift in Zoo Atlanta history. The money allowed the zoo to enhance the public offerings and educational programs in its Conservation Action Resource Center.

Currently, the exhibit creating the biggest stir is the Asian Forest, home to Lun Lun and Yang Yang, two giant pandas and their first offspring, Mei Lan, born in 2006 after a couple years of pressure on the two to procreate. The happy couple welcomed their second baby in 2008, much to the delight of the public and fans who kept up with the cub's progress via webcam on the zoo's website. The cub, named Xi Lan ("Atlanta's Joy" in Chinese), through a public vote—by tradition remained unnamed until he was 100 days old—was the only giant panda born in the U.S. in 2008. The two Chinese natives and their adorable offspring are a huge hit with adults and children alike. Although the pandas' rowdiest period is in the afternoon, they put on quite a show most of the day: munching bamboo, tussling with each other, playing on their log swing, or climbing on the swinging ladder. When Lun Lun has had enough of Yang Yang's roughhousing, she heads for the water. In the summer, the two can be especially entertaining; if it's really sweltering, zoo officials give each of them a huge block of ice to help them cool off. Yang Yang likes to hug his until it melts.

Your first stop at the zoo will probably be Flamingo Plaza. Farther on, Mzima Springs and Masai Mara house elephants, rhinos, lions, zebras, giraffes, gazelles, and other African animals and birds. The landscape in this section resembles the plains of East Africa, with honey locust trees and yuccas, and the lion enclosure replicates an East African *kopje* (rocky outcropping). Frequent animal demonstrations, African storytelling, and educational programs take place under the Elder's Tree in Masai Mara. Here you'll find the young waterbuck, daughter of Kokopelli (who was aptly named for the ancient fertility god).

The lushly landscaped Ford African Rain Forest—one of the most popular sections—centers on four vast gorilla habitats separated by moats. Studies on gorilla behavior take place here, and there are usually quite a few adorable babies (they're hard to spot sometimes, so be sure to ask if there are any to be seen). The zoo's longtime mascot, Willie B. (named after former Atlanta mayor William B. Hartsfield), died in 2000, but his daughters Kudzoo and Olympia live in the forest and usually put on a pretty good show. The best time to visit is around 2pm, when the gorillas are fed. Also in this section is a walk-through aviary of West African birds, an exhibit of small African primates, and the Gorillas of Cameroon Museum. Landscaping includes burned-out areas of forest and deadfall trees—gorillas do not live in manicured gardens. In addition, the rainforest is home to the zoo's African lions, including three cubs new to the property in 2008: Christos, Mikalos, and Athanaisi.

In the Ketambe section, several families of high-climbing orangutans show off their skills among the trees and bamboo clusters of an Indonesian tropical rainforest. If you're lucky enough to be here at feeding time—around 2:30pm—you might see them swinging on ropes from tree to tree. In the Sumatran Tiger Forest, rare Sumatran tigers prowl a lush forest, sometimes dipping into a stream or waterfall. Nearby is a superb Reptile House—the zoo is home to one of the finest reptile collections in the country—and a special exhibit area, often used to house visiting animals.

A zoo train travels through the Children's Zoo area. Here, you'll find a playground and petting zoo where kids can get friendly with llamas, sheep, pot-bellied pigs, goats, and more. There are aviaries here, too. Kids (and adults) will love the entertaining and informative free animal shows at the zoo; these shows are held in the Wildlife Theater during summer, and African elephant demonstrations are given daily year-round. The zoo's "Wild Like Me" indoor play experience highlights similarities between people and animals.

## Fond Farewell

When Willie B., the beloved Zoo Atlanta gorilla, died a number of years ago, so many people came to his memorial service to pay their last respects that many had to be turned away. In all, close to 8,000 mourners managed to attend.

## Coo at the Zoo

It's no secret who the main attraction is at Zoo Atlanta these days. Adorable little Xi Lan ("Atlanta's Joy" in Chinese)—who remained nameless until she reached 100 days old—is bringing in well-wishers by the droves. But if you can't get to Atlanta in person, you can keep up with nearly every bodily function of this little fuzz ball on the zoo's website. She can even be viewed Monday through Friday from 10am until 5pm via the online "Panda Cam."

All this fuss isn't much ado about nothing: It's a long-awaited celebration and culmination of breeding giant pandas in captivity, and this is Zoo Atlanta's second success story. After a number of years of breath holding and matchmaking, the zoo had its first tiny giant panda delivered in 2006. (Maybe all the happy couple needed was a little *privacy?* After all, who can perform under that kind of pressure!)

The firstborn—Mei Lan—which translates to "Atlanta Beauty," was named through an online poll hosted by the local daily newspaper, the *Atlanta Journal-Constitution,* garnering 20% of the more than 57,000 votes submitted. Mei Lan was one of ten names from which voters had to choose; these names were selected by many facets of the panda conservation community, including zoo staff, zoo volunteers, a special Zoo Atlanta sponsor, local media, and the people of China. She has proven to be a good big sister to Xi Lan. While visitors are hard-pressed to disagree on the amount of "cuteness" the new addition emits, scientists continue to debate whether giant pandas belong to the bear family, the raccoon family, or a separate family of their own. Until any new developments are quantified, giant pandas remain categorized in the bear family, which seems to make those gift-shop stuffed bears even more irresistible.

There are snack bars (including a McDonald's) throughout the zoo. You can also picnic in tree-shaded areas in Grant Park just outside the zoo. The Zoo Atlanta Trading Company sells zoo memorabilia and gifts.

800 Cherokee Ave. (in Grant Park). © **404/624-5600.** www.zooatlanta.org. Admission $19 adults, $15 seniors, $14 children 3–11, free for children 2 and under. Strollers can be rented. Daily 9:30am–5:30pm; ticket booths close at 4:30pm. Closed Thanksgiving and Christmas. Free but limited parking. Take I-75 S. to I-20 E. Get off at the Boulevard exit (59A) and follow signs to Grant Park. MARTA: Bus 97 from the Five Points station or bus 397 from the King Memorial station.

## 4 SPECIAL-INTEREST TOURS

The **Atlanta Preservation Center,** a private nonprofit organization headquartered at 327 St. Paul Ave. (© **404/688-3353**), offers a variety of 1- to 2-hour guided walking tours of the city. Cost of each tour is $10 for adults and $5 for seniors, students, and children. Tours of the Fox Theatre are given year-round; the remaining options are noted below. Call or visit www.preserveatlanta.com for days, hours, and departure points.

# Run the Peachtree

The Peachtree Road Race is more than just the world's largest 10K road race. It's a social event in Atlanta, as thousands of spectators line Peachtree Street, Atlanta's main drag, to cheer the runners.

If you're lucky enough to be in town on July 4th, you can do the same. Pack a breakfast and station yourself just about anywhere along Peachtree from Lenox Square to 14th Street. Or go straight to the finish in Piedmont Park and take part in the chaos of the finale. Be sure to arrive early. The wheelchair division of the race begins at 7am, and the official footrace begins at 7:30am. Peachtree is closed to traffic that morning, and you'll have difficulty crossing the street—even on foot—after 7am.

The race is quite a sight to behold, as 55,000 runners surge down Peachtree, a far cry from the 110 runners who gathered to run the first race in 1970. (The only spectators then were a few surprised pedestrians walking their dogs.) The race is so popular now that it takes 500 volunteers to coordinate the start and 50 minutes for the final group to pass the starting line. By then, the winner has already covered the 6.2-mile distance and rested for at least a quarter of an hour.

Don't even think about entering the race at the last minute. Many more applicants than can be accommodated vie for the available spots, and the event always closes out in a few days. You can, however, run the course on other days of the year. There are sidewalks all the way down Peachtree, so it's a fairly safe course. Here's the route you should follow:

Start at the corner of Peachtree and Lenox roads, right across from Lenox Square. Proceed down Peachtree through Buckhead. Along the way, you'll pass by some of Atlanta's most elegant neighborhoods. Just after West Wesley Road, you'll have a magnificent view of the downtown skyline. Don't let the easy, downward trend of the first few miles fool you. This is a tough run, and just about halfway through the course, there's a fairly steep incline—appropriately dubbed Heartbreak or Heart Attack Hill. (Fortunately, the top of the hill is right in front of Piedmont Hospital.) In Midtown, proceed on Peachtree to 10th Street, turn left, and continue to the end of the course, which is at the Charles Allen Drive entrance to Piedmont Park. To return to Lenox Square, backtrack to the Midtown station on 10th Street a block off Peachtree, and take MARTA to the Buckhead or Lenox station.

For more information, call the Atlanta Track Club at ℰ **404/231-9064.**

On the **Fox Theatre Tour,** you'll explore this restored 1920s Moorish movie palace in depth. The theater's auditorium resembles the courtyard of a Cairo mosque, and the architecture and interior were influenced by the discoveries at King Tut's tomb (p. 145 for a full description of the theater). This tour is subject to change due to special events or matinee performances.

Grant Park, the centerpiece of a revitalized neighborhood, became a favorite spot thanks to its beautiful lake, numerous springs, and amusement area. It's now home to the Atlanta Cyclorama and Zoo Atlanta. The **Grant Park Tour** (Sun in Mar–Nov) uses the park as the setting for a walk through Atlanta's history, from antebellum times (you'll see the Grant Mansion and Confederate fortifications) through the Victorian era to the present day.

The **Historic Downtown Tour** (Fri–Sat in Mar–Nov) is an architectural survey of Atlanta's downtown, from Victorian buildings to modern high-rises. You'll learn about the architects, the businesspeople, and the prominent families who created the city's early commercial center. The tour includes peeks at historic interiors.

The **Inman Park Tour** (2pm Sun in Mar–Nov, Twilight Tours Apr–Oct) visits Atlanta's first trolley suburb, where you'll see preserved and restored Victorian mansions (exterior views only). Highlights include the homes of Coca-Cola magnates Asa Candler and Ernest Woodruff.

The **Sweet Auburn/Martin Luther King, Jr., Historic District Tour,** offered only as a special prearranged group tour, focuses on the area that 20th-century African-American entrepreneurs developed into a prosperous commercial hub. You'll also visit the church where Martin Luther King, Jr., preached, and discover landmarks of the civil rights movement.

**Frederick Law Olmsted's Druid Hills Tour** (Mar–Nov, Twilight Tours Apr–Oct) explores the neighborhood that was the setting for the play and film *Driving Miss Daisy.* The gracious parklike area was laid out by noted landscape designer Frederick Law Olmsted and contains many architecturally important homes.

**Margaret Mitchell's Ansley Park Tour** (Twilight Tours Apr–Oct) explores one of Atlanta's first garden suburbs (today a charming Midtown neighborhood), partly designed by Frederick Law Olmsted. Its broad lawns, majestic trees, parks, and beautiful houses make for a lovely tour. It's easy to get lost in Ansley Park, so if you want to explore the area, this walking tour is a good idea.

The **Historic Midtown Tour** (Mar–Oct) explores the many faces of the booming Midtown area, from its bungalows and skyscrapers to its restaurants and churches.

## 5 PARKS & OUTDOOR PURSUITS

## PARKS
### Grant Park
Named for Confederate Capt. Lemuel P. Grant, who helped build Atlanta's defense line, Grant Park (bordered by Sydney St., Atlanta Ave., Boulevard, and Cherokee Ave.) still contains vestiges of his fortifications. Near the intersection of Boulevard and Atlanta Avenue, you can see the remaining earthwork slopes of Fort Walker, a commanding artillery bastion with its original gun emplacements. Its cannons and caissons can be seen in the museum area of the Atlanta Cyclorama (p. 139), one of Grant Park's two major attractions. The other is Zoo Atlanta (p. 175). The park is open daily from 6am to 11pm; it's best to visit during daylight hours.

### Piedmont Park ★
Piedmont Park, the city's most popular and centrally located recreation area (with its main entrance on Piedmont Ave. at 14th St.), was once a farm and a Civil War encampment. Its first public usage was by the elite Gentlemen's Driving Club, which bought the

property as a site for horseback riding and racing. It soon became a venue for state fairs, including the spectacular Cotton States and International Exposition of 1895. In 1904, the property's 180-plus acres of woodsy meadow and farm were transformed into a city park with a varied terrain of rolling hillsides, verdant lawns, and lush forest around Lake Clara Meer.

Today, Piedmont Park is the setting for many popular regional events such as concerts and music festivals. It contains softball fields, soccer fields, public tennis courts, a public swimming pool, and paths for jogging, skating, and cycling. The park hosts a Green Market from 9am to 1pm every Saturday from May through mid-December, selling locally grown produce, artisan cheeses, fresh-cut flowers, and other merchandise. The park gets a lot of use, and in some spots can be downright scruffy-looking, but the Piedmont Park Conservancy and the city of Atlanta continue to upgrade the landscaping. A visitor center, where you can find information on the park and the surrounding area, is located at the Piedmont Avenue and 12th Street entrance. The park is a great place for children, with plenty of open, car-free spaces. Don't let the kids miss PlayScape at the 12th Street entrance; created by well-known sculptor Isamu Noguchi, it's a climbable series of brightly colored geometric shapes complete with ladders and slides. The people-watching in the park is superb, and the Midtown skyline beyond is magnificent. The Atlanta Botanical Garden (p. 138) is next-door.

Parking can be impossible, especially during special events, and authorities are quick to tow cars parked illegally. It's easiest to take MARTA to the Arts Center station and walk the few blocks down 14th Street. During special events, it's usually possible to take a shuttle to and from the station.

A great way to see the park and soak up some of its history is on a **walking tour** sponsored by the Piedmont Park Conservancy. These free tours depart from the visitor center at 11am on the first and third Saturdays in May through early December. During the 1¹/₂-hour tour, guides will point out many historic areas, including remnants of the 1895 Piedmont Exposition, the Walker Farm, and the 1895 Cotton States and International Exposition. Call ℭ **404/876-4024** for information.

## Stone Mountain Park
See p. 157 for a full description of Stone Mountain Park, one of the best places in the region for all kinds of outdoor activities: picnicking, boating (rowboating, canoeing, and sailing), biking (rentals are available), fishing, hiking, golfing, playing tennis, and swimming. The entrance fee (which includes parking) is $8 per car per day; an annual pass is $35.

## OUTDOOR PURSUITS
### Biking
See "In-Line Skating & Biking," below.

### Fishing
There's good trout fishing on the Chattahoochee River, in the North Georgia Mountains, about 1¹/₂ hours from downtown. Many lakes in the area are good for bass and striper; these include **Lake Lanier,** a 38,000-acre reservoir about 45 minutes away. Fishing licenses, which can be bought at most sporting-goods stores, Wal-Marts, Kmarts and online at www.gadnr.org, are $3.50 for 1 day and $9 for 3 or more days (for Georgia residents; non-residents slightly higher). A trout-fishing stamp is $5, or $13 for non-Georgia residents.

The **Fish Hawk,** 3095 Peachtree Rd. (© **404/237-3473;** www.thefishhawk.com), has been selling quality tackle for over 25 years. Specializing in fly-fishing, the store carries all kinds of fishing gear and outdoor clothing and can also supply the requisite license. The staff is extremely knowledgeable and can tell you where to find the fish you seek and anything you need to know about applicable state regulations. They also offer a fishing guide service. Hours are Monday through Friday from 9:30am to 6pm, Saturday from 9am to 5pm.

For additional information, serious anglers can contact the **Georgia Department of Natural Resources,** License and Boat Registration Unit (© **800/366-2661;** www.gadnr.org).

## Golf

The **Stone Mountain Golf Club** (© **770/879-9900;** www.stonemountaingolf.com) is a beautiful nationally ranked public facility, boasting some areas that are adjacent to the park's lake. Robert Trent Jones, Sr., designed 18 of the 36 holes. A pro shop is on the premises, and lessons are available. For weekends and holidays, reserve the Tuesday prior to the day you want to play; at other times, reserve a week in advance. A restaurant/clubhouse has a large deck overlooking the lake. Greens fees, including cart and taxes, are $49 Monday through Thursday, $55 on Friday, and $64 on Saturday, Sunday, and holidays; prices may be lower in the off season. There is a parking fee of $8 per car to enter the park. The course is open daily from 7am to dark.

## In-Line Skating & Biking

Piedmont Park is the place to skate, and the nearby **Skate Escape,** 1086 Piedmont Ave. NE, at 12th Street (© **404/892-1292;** www.skateescape.com), is the place to rent equipment. This establishment has all kinds of bicycles and skates for rent or sale, plus helmets, bike locks, and accessories. You can also buy skateboards here. Conventional and in-line skates can be rented for $6 per hour, $15 per day; three-speed or children's bikes are $6 per hour, $25 per day. If you have an out-of-state driver's license, a major credit card is required as ID; alternately, you can leave a deposit of $150 for skates, $250 for bikes. Skate Escape is open Monday through Friday from 11am to 6:30pm, Saturday and Sunday from 11am to 6pm, and the folks here will give you good advice about routes through the park. MARTA: Midtown.

Also see the information on the PATH Foundation under "Nature Walks & Scenic Strolls," below.

## Nature Walks & Scenic Strolls

Atlanta offers many wonderful places for quiet nature walks and easy day hikes. Below are just a few of the options.

The **Atlanta History Center,** 130 W. Paces Ferry Rd. (© **404/814-4000**), described fully on p. 140, stands on 32 woodland acres and has self-guided walking trails and five gardens. You'll discover many plants native to the region along the forested mile-long Swan Woods Trail.

The **Chattahoochee River National Recreation Area** is a series of parklands that punctuate the 48 miles along the Chattahoochee River—from Buford Dam at Lake Lanier, north of the city, to Paces Mill at Vinings, just outside Atlanta's northwestern limits. Along the way, trails range from flat, easy walks to more strenuous ridge and valley hikes. Lace up your sneakers to enjoy some of the unspoiled parts of the scenic Chattahoochee River. Admission is free, but there is a $3 parking fee. For maps and more information, contact the National Park Service (© **678/538-1200;** www.nps.gov/chat).

**Stone Mountain Park,** 16 miles east of downtown on U.S. 78, is also covered in more detail in this chapter (p. 157). It has thousands of acres of beautiful wooded parkland and lakes. There's a walking trail that goes up and down the moss-covered slopes of the mountain; you'll be delighted by the wildflowers that bloom here each spring. Twenty acres of wildlife trails crisscross the park, passing through natural animal habitats and a petting zoo. Hard-core hikers will enjoy the challenging hiking trails.

Sixteen miles of extensive hiking trails meander through the beautiful scenery at **Kennesaw Mountain/National Battlefield Park,** Old Hwy. 41 and Stilesboro Road, Kennesaw (© 770/427-4686). Trail maps are available at the visitor center. See p. 166 for more information.

**Piedmont Park,** centrally located with its main entrance on Piedmont Avenue at 14th Street, provides a glorious setting for strolls, jogs, and bike rides. The wonderful **Atlanta Botanical Garden** is next-door. See p. 179 for a full description of the park, and p. 138 for coverage of the botanical garden.

**Château Elan,** 30 miles north of Atlanta at exit 126 off I-85 in Braselton (© 678/425-0900), has nature trails along St. Emilion Creek (forested with tulip, poplar, oak, hickory, and beech trees) and by Romanée–Conti Pond. There are picnic areas on the lovely grounds, and custom picnic boxes can be purchased at Café Elan. See p. 161 for a complete description of the château's offerings.

The **Fernbank Science Center,** 156 Heaton Park Dr. NE (© 678/874-7102), has 1.5 miles of paved trails with trees, wildflowers, and plants labeled for identification. This unspoiled natural environment is home to many animals and birds; in addition, a small pond teems with aquatic life. See p. 171 for a complete description of the science center.

The nonprofit **PATH Foundation** (© 404/355-6438; www.pathfoundation.org) is dedicated to creating and maintaining a network of walking and biking trails in metropolitan Atlanta. So far, the organization has completed more than 100 miles of greenway trails. The most accessible is around **Chastain Park** in the northern part of the city; it's an easy, paved 2.6-mile trail looping around the rolling hills of the park and golf course. The **Atlanta–Stone Mountain Trail,** which goes from the Carter Center to Stone Mountain Park, is another popular trek. Maps are available at most biking and sporting-goods stores. Call the above phone number for more information and advice about where to begin your journey.

## River Rafting/Canoeing/Kayaking

The **Nantahala Outdoor Center** (© 888/905-7238; www.noc.com) leads white-water rafting adventures on the scenic Chattooga River in North Georgia (it's the one you saw in the movie *Deliverance*) and the Ocoee River in Tennessee (which was an Olympic venue). Put-in points for both rivers are about a 2-hour drive from Atlanta. Trips vary in length (from a few hours to a few days) and difficulty.

The Chattooga has Class II and III rapids in Section III, and Class III, IV, and V in Section IV. The roller coaster Ocoee has Class III and IV rapids only. Kids must be at least 10 years old for easy trips, 12 or older for more difficult rapids. The company also offers canoeing and kayaking trips, plus excursions of varying difficulty on other rivers. All of the expeditions are immensely popular, so make reservations as far in advance as possible.

Prices vary depending on the length and difficulty of the trip, and weekends are more expensive than weekdays, summer trips more expensive than spring and fall. Half-day trips begin at about $35, full-day trips at about $85; both rates include equipment, a guide, and transportation from the outpost to the river. Rafting season is April 1 to October 31, with occasional trips in March and November.

The **Chattahoochee River National Recreation Area** (see "Nature Walks & Scenic Strolls," earlier) has several spots where canoers, kayakers, and rafters have access to the cold, slow-moving Chattahoochee River. Call the National Park Service (✆ **678/538-1200**) for more information. Watercraft can be rented year-round from the **Chattahoochee Outdoor Center** (✆ **770/395-6851**) at the Johnson Ferry and Powers Island units in the recreation area.

## Swimming

Almost every Atlanta hotel has a swimming pool. In addition, there is a sandy lakefront beach (complete with water slides) in Stone Mountain Park (p. 157).

If you're *really* serious about getting wet, there's also **White Water,** exit 265 off I-75 on North Cobb Parkway in Marietta (✆ **770/424-9283**), a water theme park described in detail on p. 173.

## Tennis

The City of Atlanta Parks and Recreation Department operates 12 outdoor hard courts at **Piedmont Park** (✆ **404/853-3461**), all of them lit for night play. No reservations are taken; it's first-come, first-served. There's free parking at the courts, and showers and lockers are available on the premises. Hours are Monday through Thursday from 10am to 9pm, Saturday 9am to 6pm, and Sunday from 10am to 6pm. Fees are $3 per person per hour during the day, $5 per person per hour when courts are lit.

The city also has 13 outdoor clay courts and 10 outdoor hard courts (16 are lit) at the **Bitsy Grant Tennis Center,** 2125 Northside Dr., between I-75 N. and Peachtree Battle Avenue (✆ **404/609-7193**). Courts are available on a first-come, first-served basis; no reservations are taken. There are showers and lockers available. The courts are open Monday 10am to 8pm, Tuesday and Wednesday 10am to 9pm, Thursday 9am to 9pm, Saturday 9am to 4pm, and Sunday 9am to 6pm. Hours from Labor Day to April are abbreviated; call ahead for details. Court fees are around $6 per person per hour on a soft court and $3 per person per hour on a hard court, depending on the hour of play. There's a lot of team tennis played here, so call ahead to check court availability. For information about other city courts, call the **Office of Recreation** (✆ **404/817-6766**).

# 6 SPECTATOR SPORTS

Atlanta has five professional major league teams: the Braves, the Hawks, the Falcons, the Thrashers, and the Dream. Good tickets can be extremely hard to come by during a winning season, so plan in advance. Tickets can be obtained from the individual teams or through **Ticketmaster** (✆ **800/326-4000** or 404/249-6400; www.ticketmaster.com). Note that a service charge will be added to each ticket purchased through Ticketmaster.

## AUTO RACING

From beginning to end, **Atlanta Motor Speedway** has race fans covered. Hosting two NASCAR Sprint Cup races a year—one in early March and one on Labor Day weekend—as well as NASCAR Nationwide Series and NASCAR Camping World Truck Series events, this track in Hampton, 30 miles south of Atlanta, is where folks come to see the big boys run. The smart fans are those who come in a day early and camp or RV—they get to avoid the traffic. The others aren't so lucky. Unreserved campsites are $60 during race week. Reserved camping for self-contained RVs is $100 to $150;

hookups are available. If you don't want to wait for a free parking space for your car, $75 reserved vehicle parking is in the Champions Reserve Lot. Race tickets are usually available right up until the start of the race, and some are quite reasonably priced. Tours of the speedway are available through the gift shop. Call ℂ **770/946-4211** or visit www. atlantamotorspeedway.com for more information.

Situated on 700 scenic wooded acres about 45 minutes north of downtown Atlanta, **Road Atlanta** is one of the Southeast's premier road-racing motor-sports facilities. Its 2.5-mile Grand Prix racecourse has a challenging combination of turns, elevation changes, and high-speed straightaways. A year-round season includes sports-car, motorcycle, truck, and vintage/historic racing, among other events. Call ℂ **800/849-RACE [7223]** or 770/967-6143, or go to www.roadatlanta.com, for information and a schedule of events. Tickets usually run $20 to $75, with higher prices for the Petit Le Mans, a 1,000-mile race. Infield parking is $5. Road Atlanta is located in Braselton on Georgia Hwy. 53 between I-85 and I-985 (take I-85 N. to exit 129, make a left, and follow the signs).

## BASEBALL

Although they've won the World Series only once in recent memory, in 1995, the **Atlanta Braves** consistently post a terrific record. In 1997, the team moved to Turner Field, a stadium that was modified to function as a world-class ballpark after hosting the Centennial Olympic Games (see "Stadiums," below, for details). The regular season runs from the first week of April until the first week of October; post-season play is over by the end of October.

Advance-purchase seats run from $6 (in the Upper Pavilion) to $56 (on the Dugout Level), and ticket availability is proportional to the team's success. Call customer service (ℂ **404/522-7630**) for more information, or visit the website at www.atlantabraves. com. You can charge tickets online or by phone through **Ticketmaster** (ℂ **800/326-4000** or 404/249-6400; www.ticketmaster.com), or buy directly from the stadium box office, which is located at the northwest corner of the ballpark. It's open Monday through Friday from 8:30am to 6pm, Saturday from 9am to 5pm, and Sunday from 1 to 5pm. Even if you can't get tickets in advance, it's sometimes possible to get $1 Skyline tickets (bleacher seats) and $5 standing-room-only tickets. Skyline tickets are available only on game day and go on sale 3 hours before game time. Fans are limited to one ticket per customer, and immediate entry to the ballpark is required. Standing-room-only tickets are sold only on game day and are available 1 hour before the first pitch, but only when all other tickets for the game have been sold. Check the designated ticket window in the main ticket area.

---

ⓕ **Fun Facts** **Foul Play**

Kudzu, a fast-growing vine that smothers anything and everything in its path, once stopped an Atlanta Braves baseball game. On August 29, 2000, in the ninth inning of a game between the Braves and the Cincinnati Reds, the lights abruptly went out at Turner Field. It seems that a kudzu vine had snaked around a critical terminal area, causing the 12-minute blackout. It was the first-ever kudzu delay in Major League Baseball. The Braves lost 4 to 2.

# BASKETBALL

The **Atlanta Hawks** are the local men's NBA franchise, and their season runs from November to April. The Hawks play in Philips Arena, which was built downtown on the site of the old Omni Coliseum, adjacent to CNN Center, and opened in September 1999 (see "Stadiums," below, for details). Tickets range from $10 for a nosebleed seat to $90 for something up close and personal. Call **Ticketmaster** (© **800/326-4000** or 404/249-6400; www.ticketmaster.com) or © **404/827-3865** for information.

New to Atlanta and to the WNBA since 2008, the fledgling **Atlanta Dream** is the local women's professional basketball franchise, with a season that runs from May to September. The Dream plays in Philips Arena, adjacent to CNN Center (see "Stadiums," below, for details). Tickets range from $9 to $45 for regular seating areas and $53 to $212 courtside. Call © **404/604-2626** for information.

On the college front, the **Georgia Tech Yellow Jackets** play in the highly competitive Atlantic Coast Conference (ACC). Their season runs from mid-November to early March, and home games are played in Alexander Memorial Coliseum, on the campus at 10th and Fowler streets (see "Stadiums," below, for details). Tickets range from $13 to $31, but they are often difficult to come by. Available tickets go on sale at the Coliseum on the day of the game. Call © **888/832-4849** or 404/894-5447 for information.

# FOOTBALL

The **Atlanta Falcons** are the city's NFL franchise, playing eight games (plus exhibition games) each season in the Georgia Dome (see "Stadiums," below, for details). Watching a game in the Dome is an interesting, noisy experience. The regular season begins in September and runs through December, with post-season games played in January. Pre-season games begin in August. Ticket prices are $25 to more than $200, depending on how close to the action you want to sit. For information, call © **404/249-6400** or visit www.atlantafalcons.com.

As for college football, the "Ramblin' Wrecks from **Georgia Tech**" have played their home games at 43,000-seat Bobby Dodd Stadium/Grant Field, on campus at North Avenue and Techwood Drive, since 1913. The season runs from September to November. Call © **888/832-4849** or 404/894-5447 for information. Tickets are $25 and $40 and are usually available, except for home games against the University of Georgia, which are always sold out. Games are played on Thursday nights and Saturday afternoons. Parking is limited; taking MARTA to the North Avenue station is the best option. Go early and stop at the Varsity for a hamburger or a hot dog; it's on North Avenue between the MARTA station and the stadium.

# HOCKEY

The **Atlanta Thrashers,** an NHL team named after Georgia's state bird, took to the ice in 1999 in Philips Arena, which was built downtown on the site of the old Omni Coliseum (see "Stadiums," below). The season runs from October through April, and tickets run from $10 to $200. Call © **404/584-PUCK [7825]** or visit www.atlantathrashers. com for information. Take MARTA to Omni/Dome/GWCC.

# STADIUMS

**Alexander Memorial Coliseum**  This 10,000-seat stadium—renovated for the Olympics—is home to Georgia Tech's Yellow Jackets college basketball team. Parking is limited around the stadium; it's easiest to take MARTA.

Georgia Institute of Technology, 10th and Fowler sts. © **404/894-5400** for information. MARTA: North Ave.

**Georgia Dome**   Atlanta's $214-million, 71,500-seat domed mega-stadium, home of the Atlanta Falcons, hosted Super Bowl XXVIII in 1994, several Olympic events in 1996, and Super Bowl XXXIV in 2000. In addition, it is the site of the annual Chick-fil-A Bowl (formerly Peach Bowl) each January, and it hosted the NCAA Men's Basketball Final Four in 2002 and 2007. The Dome also holds tennis matches, tractor pulls, college basketball games, track and field events, and Supercross events. Behind-the-scenes tours of the Georgia Dome are available Tuesday through Saturday on the hour from 10am to 3pm for $6 per adult and $4 per senior or student. The stadium's oval shape provides a good view of the action from every seat. Check the papers or call the number below to find out what's on during your stay. Parking is extremely limited and expensive; take MARTA and walk to the Dome instead.

1 Georgia Dome Dr. (at International Blvd. and Northside Dr.). ☎ **404/223-9200** or www.gadome.com for information. MARTA: Omni/Dome/GWCC.

**Philips Arena**   This spectacular $213-million arena, home to the NHL Atlanta Thrashers, NBA Atlanta Hawks, and WNBA Atlanta Dream, was built on the site of the old Omni Coliseum. Tours of the arena are available daily every half-hour: from 9am to 6pm on non-event days, and 9am to 5pm on event days. The 1-hour tours take in the Hawks' and Thrashers' locker rooms, the press box, and the luxury suites. Tickets are $7 for adults, $5 for seniors, $4.50 for children 4 to 12, and free for kids 3 and under. The Philips Experience is an interactive station with five hands-on activities to test your skills in basketball, hockey, and other fun challenges.

The Hawk Walk, which connects the CNN Center with Philips Arena, is worth a look if you're a sports fan. It's an indoor street that sells food, beverages, and Atlanta Hawks, Thrashers, and Dream merchandise. Huge video screens display live action at the arena or shows from one of the Turner networks, while giant billboards flash ticker information from the CNN channels.

100 Techwood Dr. NW (at Marietta St.). ☎ **404/827-2300.** www.philipsarena.com. MARTA: Omni/Dome/GWCC.

**Turner Field** ★★   This spectacular 50,000-seat ballpark started life as an 80,000-seat stadium built to host the Centennial Olympic Games in 1996. After housing the opening and closing ceremonies and numerous track and field events during the Olympics, the north end of the stadium (with approximately 35,000 seats) was demolished and the rest of the structure was modified to accommodate baseball.

Turner Field is built in the style of old-time ballparks, but also includes a number of attractions besides the baseball game itself. The folks who run the stadium like to call it a baseball theme park, and it's not a bad idea to come to the game early and take in the various attractions, especially if you have children along. The **Braves Museum and Hall of Fame** features memorabilia commemorating legendary stars and key moments in

---

**Fun Facts   A Grand Golfer**

Robert Tyre "Bobby" Jones, who won golf's Grand Slam at the age of 28, never became a professional golfer. Jones, who rarely played in tournaments after 1930, went on to practice law in Atlanta. One of the city's public golf courses is named for him.

Braves history (take a gander at the bat Hank Aaron used to hit his 715th home run). The museum is open to ticket holders on game days 3 hours before game time and 1 hour after the completion of the game. **Scouts Alley** is designed to teach fans about the fine art of scouting. Fans can test their hitting and throwing skills, call up scouting reports on former and current Braves, play a trivia game, call a play-by-play inning of a game, learn about Hank Aaron's "hot" spot, and much more. At the **Cartoon Network's Tooner Field,** kids can hang out with Cartoon Network characters or play interactive games in the Digital Dugout. At the **East Pavilion,** fans can have their images inserted into either a baseball card or a photo of a great moment in Braves history. The **Braves Clubhouse Store** is full of Braves-themed merchandise, some of which is available only at the stadium.

Finally, it's possible—and fun—to tour Turner Field. Tours depart every half-hour Monday through Saturday from 9:30am to 4pm and Sunday from 1 to 4pm on non-game days, and Monday through Saturday from 9:30am to noon on game days. Cost is $10 for adults, $5 for children 3 to 12, and free for children 2 and under. Tours include the museum, the dugout, the press box and broadcast booth, the clubhouse, Scouts Alley, and more. On non-game days, there's ample free parking in the north lot. Call ✆ **404-614-2311** for more information.

If all this activity makes you hungry, head to the **West Pavilion**—where you can snack on famous food items from other ballparks—or to the **Braves Chop House,** a casual restaurant that overlooks the Braves' bullpen.

Museum-only tickets are $5 on non-game days, $2 on game days; the museum hours vary according to the game schedule.

755 Hank Aaron Dr. SW. ✆ **404/522-7630.** www.turner.com. Parking $8–$12. Parking for visitors with disabilities in the South lot, east of I-75/85, on a first-come, first-served basis. MARTA: Free parking at MARTA rail stations; ride the train ($1.50) and then take the free shuttle from the Five Points station to the stadium. Shuttle service begins 1 hr. before game time and continues for 1 hr. after the game ends. There's also a shuttle from Underground Atlanta. Or take MARTA to the Georgia State University station and walk several blocks to the stadium. Call MARTA (✆ **404/848-4711**) for more information.

WHAT TO SEE & DO IN ATLANTA

7

SPECTATOR SPORTS

# A Walking Tour of Sweet Auburn

You never really understand a city until you walk around it a bit, and Atlanta's climate allows for walking tours almost year-round.

In addition to the tour below, consider taking one of the guided walking tours beginning on p. 63. Also, note that certain attractions detailed in chapter 7 are walking tours in and of themselves: for example, Stone Mountain Park, Kennesaw Mountain/National Battlefield Park, Oakland Cemetery, and the Atlanta History Center in Buckhead.

Sweet Auburn, the focus of the following walking tour, includes the Martin Luther King, Jr., National Historic Site, which comprises about 2 blocks along Auburn Avenue, plus the surrounding preservation district (about 10 more blocks). A neighborhood that nurtured scores of 20th-century black businesspeople and professionals, it contains the birthplace, church, and gravesite of Martin Luther King, Jr. The area was a vibrant commercial and entertainment district for

black Atlantans from the late 1800s until the 1930s, when it went into a steep decline. In the 1980s, the area where Martin Luther King, Jr., was born and raised was declared a national historic site, and now, under the auspices of the National Park Service, portions of Auburn Avenue are in an ongoing process of restoration. Although parts of the area are still in sad disrepair, new landscaping has beautified some of the street, and several homes on the "Birth Home" block have been restored to their 1920s appearance. For more information about the national historic site, contact the **National Park Service** at ✆ **404/331-6922** or visit the website at www.nps.gov.

This walking tour provides insight into black history, the civil rights movement, and black urban culture in the South. If you're traveling with children, it's a wonderful opportunity to teach them about a great American. The major points of interest are covered in detail in chapter 7.

| WALKING TOUR | SWEET AUBURN |
|---|---|
| Start: | The corner of Howell and Irwin streets. To get here, take I-75/85 S. and exit at Freedom Parkway/Carter Center. Turn right at the first light onto International Boulevard. Follow signs to the Martin Luther King, Jr., National Historic Site. You can park in a lot on the north side of Irwin Street between Boulevard and Jackson Street. By MARTA: King Memorial station is about 8 blocks away, or you can take bus 3 east from the Five Points station. |
| Finish: | Auburn Avenue and Courtland Street. |
| Time: | Allow a half-day to explore this area thoroughly. If you want to include a tour of Martin Luther King, Jr.'s, Birth Home (stop no. 3)—and a visit to this area would not be complete without it—start out early in the day and obtain your tickets at the National Park Service Visitor Center at 450 Auburn Ave. Only a limited number of tickets are available each day. |

## A Spot of History

Dr. Martin Luther King, Jr., won the Nobel Peace Prize in 1964 at the age of 35, the youngest person ever to do so. He was killed 4 years later.

Begin your stroll at:

### ❶ Howell and Irwin streets

Walk south along Howell Street, where renovated historic homes and housing (designed to harmonize with the architecture of the neighborhood) provide testimony to the area's continuing renaissance. Note 102 Howell St., built between 1890 and 1895, which was the home of Alexander Hamilton, Jr., Atlanta's leading turn-of-the-20th-century black contractor. Its architectural details include Corinthian columns and a Palladian window.

Turn right on Auburn Avenue. As you proceed, look for interpretive markers indicating historic homes (mostly Victorian and Queen Anne) and other points of interest en route to 499 Auburn Ave., home of:

### ❷ The King Center

The organization here (© **404/526-8900;** www.thekingcenter.com) continues the work to which King was dedicated—reducing violence within individual communities and among nations. Freedom Plaza, on the premises, is King's final resting place. Stop in to take a self-guided tour of exhibits on King's life and the civil rights movement. Admission is free; the center is open every day from 9am to 5pm. See p. 149 for more details.

Now double back a few blocks east to 501 Auburn Ave., the:

### ❸ Birth Home of Martin Luther King, Jr.

Free half-hour guided tours are given on a continual basis, daily from 9am to 5pm, at King's birthplace. On weekends, especially, arrive early—demand for tickets often exceeds supply. Tickets are obtained at the National Park Service Visitor Center, at 450 Auburn Ave. See p. 141 for more details on the Birth Home.

Walk back toward stop no. 2, noting the turn-of-the-20th-century homes in the area, such as the:

### ❹ Double "Shotgun" Row Houses

Standing at 472–488 Auburn Ave., these two-family dwellings with separate hip roofs were built in 1905 to house workers for the Empire Textile Company. They were called "shotgun" because rooms were lined up in a row, and one could (theoretically) fire a shotgun straight through the whole house.

Continue west on Auburn Avenue. At the corner of Auburn Avenue and Boulevard is:

### ❺ Fire Station No. 6

This is one of Atlanta's eight original firehouses, completed in 1894. The two-story Romanesque Revival building was situated to protect the eastern section of the city. The station houses a museum, open daily from 9am to 5pm, where exhibits include restored fire engines and vintage firefighting paraphernalia. Note the Italianate arched windows on the second story. Admission is free.

Continuing west on Auburn Avenue, a notable stop on your tour is at 407 Auburn Ave., where you'll find the:

### ❻ Ebenezer Baptist Church

This church (© **404/688-7263**), founded in 1886, is where Martin Luther King, Jr., served as co-pastor from 1960 to 1968. Short but informative tours are given Monday through Friday from 9am to 4pm, Saturday from 9am to 2pm, and Sunday from 2 to 4pm. The church has built a new sanctuary across the street, but the original building remains as a historic site under the auspices of the State Department of Parks and Recreation. The church is open Monday through Saturday from 9am to 5pm. See p. 144 for more details.

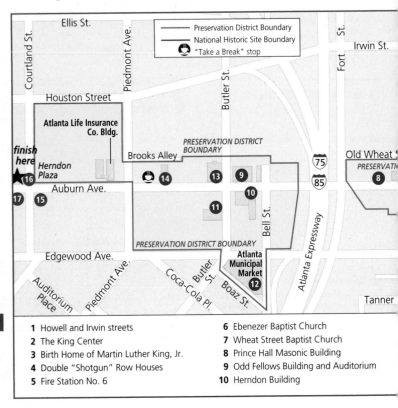

A WALKING TOUR OF SWEET AUBURN

8

SWEET AUBURN

1 Howell and Irwin streets
2 The King Center
3 Birth Home of Martin Luther King, Jr.
4 Double "Shotgun" Row Houses
5 Fire Station No. 6
6 Ebenezer Baptist Church
7 Wheat Street Baptist Church
8 Prince Hall Masonic Building
9 Odd Fellows Building and Auditorium
10 Herndon Building

One block west, at 365 Auburn Ave., is the:

### ❼ Wheat Street Baptist Church

This church has served a congregation since the late 1800s. Auburn Avenue was originally called Wheat Street in honor of Augustus W. Wheat, one of Atlanta's early merchants. The name was changed in 1893.

Farther west, on Auburn Avenue between Hilliard and Fort streets, is the:

### ❽ Prince Hall Masonic Building

This was an influential black lodge led for several decades by John Wesley Dobbs. Today, it houses the national headquarters of the Southern Christian Leadership Conference.

On the other side of the expressway, at 228–250 Auburn Ave., note the:

### ❾ Odd Fellows Building and Auditorium

This was another black fraternal lodge, which originated in Atlanta in 1870. Completed in 1914, the building later became headquarters for an insurance company.

Across the street, at 231–245 Auburn Ave., is the:

### ❿ Herndon Building

This building, erected in 1924, is named for Alonzo Herndon, an ex-slave who went on to found the Atlanta Life Insurance Company. By 1930, the Auburn business

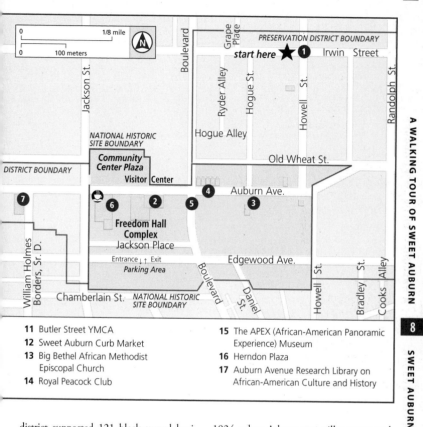

**11** Butler Street YMCA

**12** Sweet Auburn Curb Market

**13** Big Bethel African Methodist Episcopal Church

**14** Royal Peacock Club

**15** The APEX (African-American Panoramic Experience) Museum

**16** Herndon Plaza

**17** Auburn Avenue Research Library on African-American Culture and History

district supported 121 black-owned businesses and 39 black professionals.

**Make a left on Butler Street and you'll see the:**

### ⓫ Butler Street YMCA

Built in the early 1900s, this was a popular meeting place for civil rights leaders. Today, the building is augmented by a modern YMCA across the street.

**Continue south along Butler Street to the:**

### ⓬ Sweet Auburn Curb Market

The market is located just below Edgewood Avenue. Formerly called the Municipal Market, this historic market dates to 1924, when Atlanta was still a segregated city. Whites shopped within, while blacks were only permitted to patronize stalls lining the curb. The market's current name reflects that era. Today, it sells groceries and fresh produce—including many regional and ethnic items, such as ham hocks and chitlins ("We sell every part of the pig here but the oink," says the owner). Fully cooked ethnic meals are available as well, and there is seating so you can dig in right away. Open Monday through Thursday from 8am to 6pm, Friday and Saturday from 8am to 7pm.

> **TAKE A BREAK**
> The **Sweet Auburn Curb Market,** 209 Edgewood Ave. (© **404/659-1665**), is a delightful mix of scents and sights. Seating is scattered throughout in case you just can't wait to get home to eat your purchases. Variety abounds, with fresh fish, meats, veggies, salads, and flowers to take home, plus fully cooked foods from every corner of the earth—everything from specialty cheesecakes to chitlins. Open Monday through Saturday from 8am to 6pm.

Walk back to Auburn Avenue on Butler Street and turn left. To your right, at 220 Auburn Ave., is the:

### ⑬ Big Bethel African Methodist Episcopal Church

This church was originally built in the 1890s, destroyed by fire, and then rebuilt in 1924. In the 1920s, John Wesley Dobbs called the Bethel "a towering edifice to black freedom."

Farther along, at 186 Auburn Ave., is the:

### ⑭ Royal Peacock Club

This music club's walls were painted from floor to ceiling with peacocks. Closed for years, it presented top black entertainers such as Ray Charles, Aretha Franklin, and Dizzy Gillespie in its heyday.

At 135 Auburn Ave., the corner of Auburn Avenue and Courtland Street, is:

### ⑮ The APEX (African-American Panoramic Experience) Museum

This museum features exhibits on the history of Sweet Auburn and the African-American experience, including a children's gallery with interactive displays. You can call © **404/521-2739** to see if there's anything special happening at the museum while you're in town. See p. 137 for further details.

Cross the street to:

### ⑯ Herndon Plaza

Here, you can see exhibits on the high-powered Herndon family, including patriarch Alonzo Herndon, a former slave who started the Atlanta Life Insurance Company.

If you'd like to do further research on the history of Auburn Avenue—or on any aspect of African-American history and culture—continue on to 101 Auburn Ave., the:

### ⑰ Auburn Avenue Research Library on African-American Culture and History

This is the place to go for answers about African-American history. Operated by the Atlanta-Fulton County Library System, the library's collection includes literature, documents, rare records, and more. A Heritage Center on the premises features special exhibits, workshops, seminars, lectures, and other events. Open Monday through Thursday from 10am to 8pm, and Friday through Sunday from noon to 6pm.

# Shopping

Atlanta is the shopping mecca of the Southeast, period. Visitors might *say* they come to Atlanta to steep themselves in Southern history, take in a play or two, or contemplate the masterpieces in a museum. But what they really want to do is trot on over to Buckhead for a little retail therapy.

It's not just that there's a lot of shopping here, but the fact that it's so varied. There are chic boutiques that can hold their own with the best of Los Angeles or New York, flea markets bursting at the seams with antiques and collectibles, giant department stores, and interesting little browsable areas such as Virginia Highland. And even if you don't want to buy anything, it's great fun to wander around the shopping areas, checking out the locals and taking the pulse of the city.

## 1 GREAT SHOPPING AREAS

### ATLANTIC STATION

Open and growing since 2006, **Atlantic Station** (© 404/733-5000; www.atlanticstation.com), is a mixed-use development, much of which includes shops with everything from books and boots to furniture and furs. Covering 138 acres, it's as ambitious a development as any this country has seen, and includes one million square feet of open-air retail and entertainment venues, including a two-story movie theater. You can easily spend a full day browsing the stores, which include American Eagle Outfitters, Ann Taylor and Ann Taylor Loft, City Sports, Dillard's, DSW, Express, Gap, Nine West, Old Navy, West Elm, and Z Gallerie. It's also the location of the city's first IKEA, a shopping experience in itself. This is not only the first branch in the Southeast, but also the first in the world to serve grits and sweet tea in its restaurant. Once you shop 'til you drop, stop in at the Grape, a casual wine bar with outstanding small-plate gourmet fare and a great variety of wines from around the world. Find a new one you really like? Pick up a bottle from their wine shop right next-door. They have several locations around the city, so visit www.yourgrape.com for more information and scheduled wine tastings.

Atlantic Station is located on 17th Street, just west of I-75. To get here, take MARTA to the Arts Center station, then hop a free shuttle to Atlantic Station.

### BUCKHEAD

The stamping ground of well-to-do Atlantans, Buckhead is the ultimate shopping area, with two major malls and lots of little boutiques, antiques shops, and galleries. If you're serious about shopping, this is the place to start. Even though the area has an upscale reputation, don't let that stop you. There's lots of variety, and the competition can mean excellent bargains.

The hot spot for the best of Buckhead is at the corner of Peachtree and Lenox roads, where two major malls—**Phipps Plaza** and **Lenox Square**—face off against each other (see section 2 of this chapter for details). If your time is limited, pick one of these malls and spend the morning or afternoon there. For about $6, you can park in the "up front" lot, right outside the main entrance.

If you have more time and are interested in art, antiques, or decorative accessories, head straight to **Bennett Street,** where you'll find a healthy concentration of stores in a 2-block strip. There are also many options in **Buckhead West Village,** near the intersection of Peachtree and West Paces Ferry roads. Shops also line the rest of Peachtree Road as well as smaller side streets. Serious interior decorators will want to make the trip to **Miami Circle.**

## Bennett Street

Located just off Peachtree Road on the south edge of Buckhead is a quaint little street that's become one of the most interesting shopping destinations in the city. Once a supply path linking Atlanta to the surrounding countryside during the Civil War, Bennett Street evolved into a thriving warehouse district around the turn of the 20th century. Those warehouses have been transformed into a handy concentration of shops and galleries specializing in art, decorative accessories, and antiques.

Exploring the street makes for a pleasant afternoon ramble, but if you don't have time to wander the whole strip, check out the Stalls and the Interiors Market, both of which house many dealers in one location. Most shops are open Monday through Saturday from 10am or 11am to 5pm, and a few are open Sunday from 1 to 5pm. Bennett Street—little more than a dead-end alley—is only a couple of blocks long, but it's built on a hill, so wear comfortable shoes. It's just off Peachtree Road between Collier Road and Peachtree Battle Avenue. To get here from downtown, take bus no. 23 from the Arts Center MARTA station to the 2100 block of Peachtree Road.

Here's some of what you'll find along Bennett Street.

**Bennett Street Gallery**  This gallery features contemporary glass, ceramics, jewelry, and fine art, including paintings in oil, acrylic, casein (a plastic substance), and watercolors. 22 Bennett St. NW. ✆ **404/352-8775.** www.bennettstgallery.com.

**Interiors Market**  This is a large consortium of antiques and art dealers all under one roof. Locals looking for just the right home accessory know to start here or at the Stalls (see below) rather than schlepping around to all the different shops in town. There's an ever-changing variety of objects here, with myriad booths featuring everything from fine antiques to old books. 55 Bennett St. NW. ✆ **404/352-0055.** www.interiorsmarket.com.

**Nottingham Antiques**  Direct importers of European antique pine furniture, this shop also sells custom furniture. 45 Bennett St. NW. ✆ **404/352-1890.** www.nottingham antiques.com.

**The Stalls**  Just like the Interiors Market, this is a large assortment of dealers under one roof, which increases the odds that you'll find that special piece you've been searching for. The quality of the antiques and accessories is excellent, attracting designers from around the country. For lunch, you can stop at the Stalls Café, which serves an excellent grilled sandwich—pimento cheese with bacon and tomato. 116 Bennett St. NW. ✆ **404/352-4430.** www.thestalls.com.

## Miami Circle

Most design centers are open to the trade only, and this street of showrooms and warehouses started out that way. But now, most of the nearly 100 merchants on Miami Circle in Buckhead are open to the public. It's a virtual smorgasbord of furnishings and accessories—from fine European and American antiques to country and primitive pieces. There's antique and reproduction pine, painted furniture, antique statuary, heirloom wicker, fine artwork, majolica, custom and antique rugs, antique books and bookcases, **195** clocks, antique chandeliers, and at least one warehouse of designer fabrics.

This is not a quaint street suitable for a pleasant stroll, but it is a great place to browse for serious merchandise. Most establishments are open Monday through Saturday from 10am to 5pm, and some are open on Sunday as well. If you need something shipped home, it's not a problem. Miami Circle is off Piedmont Road, just a half-mile south of Peachtree Road and about a third of a mile north of the Lindbergh MARTA station.

## West Village of Buckhead

The intersection of Peachtree and West Paces Ferry roads is the heart of the original Buckhead community. On the east side of Peachtree Road is the center of Buckhead nightlife; the retail shops are on the west side of Peachtree Road, where you'll find everything from art and antiques to women's apparel. The West Village, as the area surrounding the intersection is called, is bounded by West Paces Ferry Road, Roswell Road, and East Andrews Drive. If you're navigating the city via public transportation, use the Buckhead MARTA station to access shopping in this area.

There are a couple of places to stop for a snack or lunch as you wander through the neighborhood. You can stop in at **Fadó** at 3035 Peachtree Rd. (✆ **404/841-0066**), an "authentic" Irish pub that serves commendable Gaelic fare; especially good is the *boxty* (filled Irish potato pancake) and the corned beef and cabbage.

Here's some of what you'll discover in the West Village.

**Boxwoods** It's hard to see everything in this delightful shop in one visit. There are intriguing gifts and serious gardening accessories, as well as numerous antiques, lamps, fresh flowers, and greenery. Open Monday through Saturday from 10am to 6pm. 100 E. Andrews Dr. NW. ✆ 404/233-3400. www.boxwoodsonline.com.

**Lagerquist Gallery** The contemporary fine art in this, Atlanta's oldest fine-arts gallery, includes sculpture, paintings, watercolors, and works on paper by regional, national, and international artists. Open Tuesday through Saturday from 10am to 5pm, plus Mondays by appointment only. 3235 Paces Ferry Place NW. ✆ 404/261-8273. www.lagerquist gallery.net.

**Patagonia** There's a lot here for outdoor enthusiasts, no matter what sport you enjoy—canoeing, paddling, skiing, cycling, climbing, surfing, and on and on. You'll find plenty of equipment, as well as boots, outerwear, and organic cotton clothing for men, women, and children. Open Monday through Friday from 10am to 7pm, Saturday from 10am to 6pm, and Sunday from noon to 6pm. 34 E. Andrews Dr. NW. ✆ 404/266-8182.

**Peoples** The women's clothing in this friendly shop—suits, tops, skirts, dresses, jackets, and swimwear—is contemporary, with clean, classic lines. It's a sleek, well-chosen collection you won't find in department stores. Open Tuesday through Saturday from 10am to 5pm. 3236 Roswell Rd. NW. ✆ 404/816-7292.

**Razzle Dazzle** Razzle Dazzle has been on the Buckhead scene since 1975. Sportswear is the main staple here (great pants, sweaters, jackets, and so on), but there are also stunning little dresses, some evening wear, hats, and a wonderful assortment of jewelry, some of it handmade. You'll find lines by Ella Moss, Splendid, Free People, and more. Open Monday through Saturday from 10:30am to 5pm. 49 Irby Ave. NW. ✆ 404/233-6940. www. razzledazzleatlanta.com.

## Cool Coca-Cola Facts

The world's most popular soft drink, Coca-Cola, was invented in Atlanta. Here's just how much the world loves it:

- If all the Coca-Cola ever produced were to erupt from "Old Faithful" at its normal rate of 15,000 gallons per hour, the geyser would flow continually from A.D. 307 to the present.
- If all the Coca-Cola ever produced were in 8-ounce bottles laid end-to-end, they would reach to the moon and back 1,057 times. That's one round-trip per day for 2 years, 10 months, and 23 days.

**Signature Shop & Gallery**  Everything here is one of a kind, handcrafted by contemporary American artists: dinnerware, turned wood bowls, decorative and functional ceramics, pewter vessels, sterling jewelry and utensils, quilts, furniture, and more. Open Tuesday through Saturday from 10am to 5:30pm. 3267 Roswell Rd. NW. *☏* **404/237-4426.** www.thesignatureshop.com.

**White Dove**  White Dove is full of feminine, sexy, upscale clothing for day and evening. Many of the fabrics are delicate and antiquey—silky rayons, linens, chiffons, and gauzy cottons—and the hats are festooned with silk flowers. Open Tuesday through Saturday from 11am to 6pm. 18 E. Andrews Dr. NW. *☏* **404/814-1994.**

## CHAMBLEE'S ANTIQUE ROW

Antique Row (www.antiquerow.com), on New Peachtree Road at Broad Street and North Peachtree Road, is a quaint collection of shops located in historic buildings, some dating as far back as the 1800s. Nearby, there are a few antiques malls, which conveniently house many dealers under one roof. The largest is the **Broad Street Antiques Mall,** 3550 Broad St. (*☏* **770/458-6316**), which has around 100 dealers.

In the assorted shops and malls, you'll find antique American and European furniture, glassware, pottery, Victoriana, Orientalia, wicker, collector toys, quilts, Coke memorabilia, jewelry, architectural antiques, Olympics collectibles, and crafts items. Hours vary with each store. Most are open Monday through Saturday from 10am to 5:30pm, Sunday from 1 to 5:30pm. It's a little tough to get here if you don't have a car, but you can take a MARTA train to the Chamblee station, which is about ³/₄ mile from the shops. On weekdays, take the no. 132 Tilly Mill bus from there; on weekends, walk or take a taxi.

## DECATUR

Decatur is finally getting some respect as a destination for dining, entertainment, events, and even shopping. With dozens of small boutiques and galleries, Decatur can hold its own when it comes to shoppers looking for one-of-a-kind buys, fine art, and great bargains. From clothing and shoes to books and jewelry, the area has a little of everything and plenty of fun places for a quick bite or full afternoon of wine and noshing.

**Boogaloos**  If you're looking for the latest in fashion for women for a special night on the town or a date with a new guy (or even an old one), this cute shop carries all the lines today's young women love. Look for clothing lines such as Seven for All Mankind, BCBG Generation, Citizens of Humanity, Envi and more. The fourth Friday of every month is Fab Friday, with 20% off all full-price merchandise—and wine and hors d'oeuvres! 246 W. Ponce De Leon Ave. ✆ **404/373-3237**. www.boogaloosboutique.com.

**Heliotrope**   This shop is packed with fun stuff, from holiday decor, candles, and practical-joke ammo to greeting cards, jewelry, and tableware. If you need a gift, you can find it here, regardless of whom you are shopping for. 248 W. Ponce de Leon Ave. ✆ **404/371-0100**. www.heliotropehome.com.

**Squash Blossom Boutique**   Opened in 1999 by mother and daughter Ettie Wurtzel and Talia Wurtzel Blanchard, Squash Blossom recently doubled its space—and its inventory. Located on the square in Decatur, this shop features hip women's clothing by Echo, Nick & Mo, Hanky Panky, and Bobi, and accessories, including bags, hats, scarves, and jewelry. 113 E. Court Sq. ✆ **404/373-1864**. www.squashblossomboutique.com.

**Whit's End**   Selling men's casual clothing and accessories as well as gift items, Whit's End carries clothing lines such as Fossil, Columbia, Kuhl, and Woolrich. This place has been voted as the "Best of Decatur Gear for Your Guy" in *Atlanta* magazine, so if your man doesn't dig shopping, swing by and pick up something to surprise him. 431 W. Ponce De Leon Ave. ✆ **404/377-3310**. www.whitsenddecatur.com.

**Wiggle**   Even if you don't have kids of your own, this is a fun place to ooh and aah over cute clothes for tikes. The shop has apparel for babies, boys, and girls from infant size through size eight. Toys, art, and shoes round out the offerings. Wiggles does monogramming, too, whether on a piece you buy from them or something you bring in. They also do free gift wrapping! 305 E. College Ave. ✆ **404/373-2522**. www.wiggleatlanta.com.

## LITTLE FIVE POINTS

An area similar to Virginia Highland (p. 199), though a lot funkier and much rougher around the edges, Little Five Points is a happening and offbeat shopping district. There are still authentic hippies here—and enough young people with wildly colored hair and pierced body parts to give you a '60s flashback. Little Five Points is close to Virginia Highland, so head over that way if you crave additional browsing; you can cover both areas in a few hours. In addition to the shops, there are a number of taverns and cafes in the area. Plan to have lunch at the Flying Biscuit Cafe (p. 132), which is about a mile up McLendon Avenue.

Begin your stroll on Moreland Avenue just north of Euclid Avenue, and then proceed southwest along Euclid Avenue. Most shops are open Monday through Saturday from 11am to 7 or 8pm, and Sunday from noon to 6pm. But note this is a very laid-back shopping district, so hours can change on a whim. Paid parking is available on weekends in the expanded parking lot around Junkman's Daughter on Moreland Avenue. Take MARTA to the Five Points station to access this area.

Below are some of the shopping highlights of Little Five Points.

**Abbadabbas's**   If you're searching for comfortable shoes and want something a tad offbeat, step into this wild little shoe store that's been a fixture for years. You'll find Birkenstocks, Doc Martens, and Converse, to name a few, as well as a great assortment of socks. There are four other locations around town. 421-B Moreland Ave. NE (btw. Euclid and North aves.). ✆ **404/588-9577**.

**A Cappella Books**   You'll discover new, used, and out-of-print books here, many on topics including the counterculture, literature, history, and the arts. There are signed editions, too. 484 Moreland Ave. ✆ **404/681-5128**.

**The Clothing Warehouse**   Vintage Levi's are the main attraction here, but there's also a selection of other casual used clothing for both men and women. 420 Moreland Ave. NE (btw. Euclid and North aves.). © **404/524-5070.**

**Junkman's Daughter**   This funky 10,000-square-foot megastore looks like a transplant from New York's East Village. The merchandise includes inexpensive club clothing for men and women (often bizarre and totally tasteless), including T-shirts and shoes. The staircase leading to the mezzanine is in the shape of a 20-foot-tall red high-heeled shoe. 464 Moreland Ave. NE (btw. Euclid and North aves.). © **404/577-3188.**

**René René**   *Atlanta* magazine named René René the city's best women's clothing shop in the "funky club scene" category. It's true, but some of owner René Sanning's designs are also sophisticated—possibly even wearable for work. Among the offerings is a glamorous, Old Hollywood–style evening line that has attracted such customers as Faye Dunaway and Halle Berry. Don't miss the interesting accessories. 1142 Euclid Ave. (btw. Moreland and Colquitt aves.). © **404/522-RENE [7363].**

**Sevananda**   This natural foods co-op market is a health junkie's dream. Sevananda—ancient Sanskrit for "the joy of service," offers fresh, local and organic produce, natural foods, vitamins and supplements, and the largest selection of bulk herbs and spices in the city. Even if you aren't in the market for fresh wheatgrass, you won't be able to pass up the freshly prepared foods, from baked goods and soups to sandwiches and entrees. Also look for earth-friendly household and pet products. 1142 Euclid Ave. (btw. Moreland and Colquitt aves.). © **404/522-RENE [7363].**

**Stefan's Vintage Clothing**   Most of Stefan's merchandise is vintage clothing for men and women from the early 1900s through the early 1960s, plus accessories like cigarette cases, cuff links, evening bags, hats, and period costume jewelry. There are cashmere overcoats, lingerie items, cocktail and evening gowns, tuxedos, wedding gowns, Hawaiian shirts, bowling shirts, and suits. Prices are low, and the merchandise is usually in flawless condition. It's definitely the best shop in Little Five Points. 1160 Euclid Ave. NE (btw. Moreland and Colquitt aves.). © **404/688-4929.**

---

**(Moments)   I Scream for Ice Cream**

If you happen to be in the Virginia-Highland shopping district in the afternoon or evening, stop in for an authentic Italian gelato at the funky **Paolo's Gelato Italiano,** 1025 Virginia Ave. NE. The place closes for a few hours midday Tuesday through Friday, but opens at noon daily. Also in the area, **Cold Stone Creamery,** 1220 Caroline St., limits its flavors only by your imagination, as you get to choose your ice-cream flavor as well as dozens of delicacies that are mixed in on a cold marble slab (hence the name). If you're not feeling creative, choose from the shop's own combinations, including Chocolate Devotion, Birthday Cake Remix, and Cookie Minster. Open daily from 11am to 11pm. Decatur shoppers can enjoy another favorite—**Jake's Ice Cream** (p. 135), located at 515 N. McDonough St. (under Eddie's Attic). Jake's is open Tuesday through Saturday from 11am to 10 pm and Sunday noon to 10pm.

---

**(Finds)  A Little Bit of Italy in Atlanta**

A local chef's love of all things Italian has resulted in one of the country's hottest gourmet food lines. **Bella Cucina Artful Food** sells handmade pesto—one of which is highly regarded by none other than Oprah Winfrey—and fresh pasta sauces, coarse-grain and honey mustards, and fruit preserves prepared with farm produce and beautifully packaged right here in Hotlanta. Now you can buy the stuff at the company's retail store, Bella Cucina, 1050 N. Highland Ave. (© **404/ 347-6476;** www.bellacucina.com; MARTA: Civic Center).

---

**Wax n Facts**   Looking for that ancient Bob Dylan album that your college girlfriend got custody of when you broke up? It's probably here, along with tons of other old vinyl. 431 Moreland Ave. NE (btw. Euclid and North aves.). © **404/525-2275.**

# VIRGINIA HIGHLAND

This charming area of town, centered on North Highland Avenue between University Drive and Ponce de Leon Avenue, boasts antiques shops, boutiques, and art galleries. There are three major areas for shopping: North Highland just south of University Drive; the intersection of North Highland and Virginia avenues; and just north of Ponce de Leon Avenue around St. Charles Place. It's about a mile and a half from one end of Virginia Highland to the other, but it's a nice walk, and there are cafes where you can stop and take a break. For lunch, try Murphy's (p. 128). If you have limited time to browse, go straight to the intersection of North Highland and Virginia avenues and take in the stores there. This area is accessible by MARTA through the Five Points station.

Here's some of what you'll find in the Virginia-Highland area.

**Mitzi & Romano**   Mitzi Ugolini carries cool and contemporary women's clothing, plus great jewelry and accessories, including fantastic handbags. Most of the selection is affordable. Don't miss the sale section at the back of the store. Open Monday through Thursday from 10am to 9pm, Friday and Saturday from 10am to 10pm, and Sunday from 11am to 7pm. 1038 N. Highland Ave. (btw. Virginia and Los Angeles aves.). © **404/876-7228.**

**Mooncake**   The ever-changing inventory of whimsical wearables for women here might include cloche and straw hats, flowing dresses, unusual silk separates, and hand-crafted jewelry. The retro-style clothing looks vintage, but everything is new. You'll also find body and bath items, hair accessories, diaries, and greeting cards. Open Monday through Saturday from 11am to 7pm and Sunday noon to 5 or 6pm. 1019 Virginia Ave. NE (just off N. Highland Ave.). © **404/892-8043.**

**Natural Body International**   This appealing shop invites you to pamper yourself with all manner of skin treatments, oils, soaps, lotions, and cosmetics, as well as an extensive line of aromatherapy products. All offerings are natural and animal- and environment-friendly. An on-site day spa features a full line of beauty treatments. Open Monday 10am to 6pm, Tuesday through Friday from 10am to 8pm, Saturday from 10am to 7pm, and Sunday from noon to 6pm. There are several other Atlanta locations, including one in Buckhead at 2385 Peachtree Rd., Ste. 3A (© **404/869-7722**); the hours vary. 754 Peachtree St. NE. © **404/876-2131.** www.naturalbody.com.

**10,000 Villages**   Even though 10,000 Villages is not unique to Virginia Highland, every item sold here is unique in itself. A fair trade retailer of handmade jewelry, home decor, and gifts, 10,000 Villages helps support and improve the lives of thousands of artisans in Asia, Africa, Latin America, and the Middle East. Open Monday to Friday from 11am to 6pm, Saturday from 10am to 6pm, and Sunday from noon to 6pm. 1056 St. Charles Ave. NE. (✆ **404/892-5307.**

## THE WEST SIDE

If you want to end your shopping day with dinner at Bacchanalia (p. 105), be sure to call well in advance for reservations. You can, however, grab a quick lunch at Taqueria del Sol (p. 113).

To reach the West Side, take I-75/85 from downtown, exit at 14th Street, take 14th Street west to Howell Mill Road, turn right, and go to the intersection of Howell Mill and Huff roads. Don't miss the additional stores on Foster Street, about a block down Huff Road, but note that the artists' studios at the end of the street are not open to the public. (And please don't feed the goats and chickens grazing in front of the studios.) Take MARTA to the Arts Center station to reach this area.

Below are some of the shopping highlights in this area.

**Bungalow Classic**   Simple, comfortable, elegant furniture is what you'll find here, along with linens, books, lamps, and other home accessories. Open Tuesday through Saturday from 10am to 6pm. 1197 Howell Mill Rd. NW, Ste. 110. (✆ **404/367-8522.** www.bungalowclassic.com.

**The Garden Path**   This is a full-service nursery and landscape company with a selection of gardening paraphernalia and teak furniture. Open Tuesday through Saturday from 10am to 6pm. 1198-B Howell Mill Rd. NW. (✆ **404/355-0788.**

**Provenance Antiques**   This store started out small a few years ago, but recently expanded into a larger space that offers more room for the large and interesting collection of antiques, chandeliers, bed linens, rugs, tableware, and accessories. Open Monday through Saturday from 10am to 6pm. 1157 Foster St. NW. (✆ **404/351-1217.**

**Star Provisions**   Owned by Bacchanalia restaurant, Star Provisions is a cooks' marketplace unlike any other in Atlanta. There's a small offering of locally grown organic produce, a cheese shop, a comprehensive wine shop, a bakery, and a specialty fish and meat market featuring Niman Ranch's fantastic meats. There's also a large selection of unique tableware, cookbooks, and other gourmet-quality provisions such as olives, tea, coffee, olive oil, vinegar, and pasta. This place is nirvana if you're a serious foodie, but even if you're not, it's fun to look around and get a sample or two of cheese. And just try to sneak by the bakery, with its fabulous array of goodies, including Bacchanalia's legendary Valrhona chocolate cakes—divine confections with gooey chocolate middles. Open Tuesday through Saturday from 11am to 8pm. 1198 Howell Mill Rd. NW. (✆ **404/365-0410.** www.starprovisions.com.

## STONE MOUNTAIN VILLAGE

**Stone Mountain Village,** just outside the West Gate of Stone Mountain Park (bounded by Second and Main sts. north and south, Lucille St. and Memorial Dr. east and west; (✆ **770/879-4971;** www.stonemountainvillage.com), is worth a visit. This has been a shopping area since the 1800s, and many of the shops are housed in historic buildings. Antiques, crafts, and collectibles are among the most popular merchandise here, so this is the place to stock up on country furniture, imported toys, dolls, baskets, homemade jams, handmade patchwork quilts and quilting fabrics, handcrafted dulcimers, Civil War memorabilia, and out-of-print books. Hours for most shops are Monday through Saturday from 10am to 6pm; many are also open Sunday from 1 to 5pm. Parking is free at several lots in town.

It's great fun to wander around this quaint village, and there's usually some festive event going on—an arts-and-crafts fair, live entertainment, and so on. During the Christmas season, the streets are candlelit and the village becomes a magical place populated by St. Nick, elves, carolers, and harpists. Be sure to stop by the **Village Visitor Center,** housed in a restored 1915 caboose at the corner of Main and Poole streets, to find out about special sales and events. It's open Monday through Saturday from 10am to 4pm, Sunday from 1 to 4pm.

Stop for a meal at the nearby **Village Corner Bakery, Tavern, and German Restaurant,** 6655 Memorial Dr., at Main Street (ⓒ **770/498-0329**). For breakfast, there are croissants, German apple pancakes, and ham-and-egg platters with homemade biscuits. At lunch, you can chow down on sandwiches, salads, quiche, soups, and home-baked desserts. And the dinner menu features German specialties such as Wiener schnitzel and sauerbraten. Wash it all down with one of the restaurant's German-style beers. The restaurant is open Tuesday through Saturday from 8am to midnight, Sunday from 10am to 8pm.

---

# 2 DEPARTMENT STORES & MALLS

**Discover Mills**   This is Atlanta's newest collection of specialty shops and outlets—200 in all, some offering up to 70% off on designer fashions and brand names. Just 30 minutes northeast of downtown, Discover Mills features a Bass Pro Shops Outdoor World, Burlington Coat Factory, Children's Place Outlet, Eddie Bauer Outlet, Kenneth Cole Outlet, Limited Too, Mikasa Factory Store, Neiman Marcus Last Call, Off Broadway Shoe Warehouse, Off 5th (Saks Fifth Avenue outlet), Osh Kosh B'Gosh Outlet, Samsonite Company Store, and Sun & Ski Sports. Open Monday through Saturday from 10am to 9:30pm, Sunday from 11am to 7pm. 5900 Sugarloaf Pkwy., Lawrenceville. ⓒ **678/847-5000.** www.discovermills.com.

**Lenox Square**   Vast, upscale Lenox Square, which started out as a humble shopping center in 1959, has grown into one of the most popular shopping destinations in the Southeast. Its interesting mix of stores, many of them exclusive to the region, takes it beyond the usual cookie-cutter mall, and the formula attracts locals and visitors alike. You can buy just about anything here, from hiking boots to an engagement ring—and even if you're not in the mood to buy, there's great people-watching.

Anchors include Neiman Marcus, Macy's, and Bloomingdale's department stores. There are 250 shops, restaurants, kiosks, and services in the mall, including six movie theaters and several fine-dining restaurants. One of the best restaurants is Prime (p. 123). Among the best-known stores are Ann Taylor, Anthropologie, BCBG, Betsey Johnson, Brooks Brothers, Burberry, Cartier, Club Monaco, Coach, Hermès, J. Crew, Kate Spade, Kenneth Cole, Louis Vuitton, Nicole Miller, Polo/Ralph Lauren, Sephora, St. John, Stuart Weitzman, Urban Outfitters, and Williams-Sonoma. Pottery Barn, Restoration Hardware, and Crate & Barrel all carry a selection of home furnishings and accessories, including many items that are usually available only by catalog.

Open Monday through Saturday from 10am to 9pm, Sunday from noon to 6pm, with extended hours during the Christmas season. A few stores close early on Saturday night.

There's valet parking ($6) and a free shuttle to Phipps Plaza at the main entrance on Peachtree Road. 3393 Peachtree Rd. NE (at Lenox Rd.). © **404/233-6767.** www.simon. com. MARTA: Lenox.

**Mall at Peachtree Center**  Part of the vast Portman-designed Peachtree Center complex, this downtown mall has around 70 shops, restaurants, and services on three levels. It's not exactly a shopping destination, but its location near major downtown hotels makes it convenient if you're in need of certain goods or services. There are a few apparel shops, including Brooks Brothers, and other stores with gifts, jewelry, books, cards, and candy. Services include florists, hairstylists, FedEx, UPS, a dry cleaner, and an optician. A food court dishes up everything from gyros to chocolate-chip cookies, and full-service restaurants include some decent choices: Benihana and Azio. Most stores are open Monday through Saturday from 10am to 6pm. Peachtree St. at International Blvd. © 404/654-1296. www.peachtreecenter.com/mall. MARTA: Peachtree Center.

**Mall of Georgia**  Atlanta's newest megamall, Mall of Georgia is about a half-hour drive from downtown and worth every mile. Anchoring this vast shopping haven are Dillard's, Nordstrom (and Nordstrom Rack), and Macy's. They're joined by 225 of the biggest names in retail, including Ann Taylor, A/X Armani Exchange, Coach, J. Crew, Old Navy, Pottery Barn, Restoration Hardware, Talbots, and Williams-Sonoma. Dining and entertainment options abound here, with Max Lager's American Grill, outdoor cafes, and a 500-seat amphitheater. Mall hours are Monday through Saturday from 10am to 9pm and Sunday from noon until 6pm. 3333 Buford Dr., Buford, GA 30519. © 678/482-8788. www.simon.com.

**Phipps Plaza**  Just across the street from Lenox Square is Phipps Plaza, Atlanta's most exclusive shopping venue and one of its prettiest as well, with spacious promenades and grand interior courts. Nordstrom, Parisian (a Birmingham, Alabama–based department store with a fantastic women's shoe department), and Saks Fifth Avenue anchor the mall's 100-plus shops and restaurants. The exclusive Ritz-Carlton Buckhead hotel is just a few steps away.

Phipps Plaza's posh emporia (many of them area exclusives) include A/X Armani Exchange, Barneys New York CO-OP, Cole Haan, Elie Tahari, Gianni Versace, Giorgio Armani, Gucci, Intermix, Jeffrey Atlanta, Juicy Couture, Max Mara, Niketown, Origins, Ross-Simons (for jewelry, china, and silver), Talbots, Theory, Tiffany & Co., and Tory Burch. You'll also find chic boutiques selling ladies' and men's apparel, luggage, jewelry, home furnishings, and specialty gifts.

Services include valet parking ($6) and a free shuttle to Lenox Square at the Lenox Road entrance. There are several restaurants, including the Tavern at Phipps, which has a pleasant, clubby atmosphere. Also on the premises: a food court and a 14-screen movie theater. Stores are open Monday through Saturday from 10am to 9pm, Sunday from noon to 5:30pm. 3500 Peachtree Rd. NE (at Lenox Rd.). © **800/810-7700** or 404/262-0992. www.simon.com. MARTA: Lenox.

**Underground Atlanta**  This 12-acre stretch of shops and restaurants is not as vibrant as it was several years ago, but it can still be fun to browse if you're staying downtown. There are dozens of shops, plus vendors in Humbug Square selling merchandise off antique pushcarts. Shopping options include clothing stores for men, women, and children, running the gamut from lingerie to sportswear. There are also cart vendors and novelty stores such as Atlanta Dollar, a bargain mecca.

Of course, there's a food court with a number of dining options. For lunch, you might try Johnny Rockets, an entertaining 1950s-style burger joint that the whole family will enjoy. If you're driving, there's parking in two garages off Martin Luther King, Jr., Drive. Open Monday through Saturday from 10am to 9pm, Sunday from noon to 6pm. Alabama St. (btw. Peachtree St. and Central Ave.). © **404/523-2311.** www.underground-atlanta.com. MARTA: Five Points.

## 3 MORE SHOPPING AROUND TOWN

### ANTIQUES/FLEA MARKETS

Atlanta is home to several permanent flea markets selling everything from custom furniture to antique toys, but the most exciting markets are those that set up shop once a month. The lineup of dealers—from all parts of the country—is ever-changing, so no matter how often you go, you'll always see something new and fresh.

If you're in search of real finds, shop on the first day as soon as the market opens—that's when local dealers swoop in to snatch up the best merchandise. Serious bargaining often takes place in the closing hours of the last day, when many dealers are anxious to avoid lugging their wares home with them. Be sure to keep your admission ticket; it's good for the whole weekend.

**Kudzu Antique Market**    You can spend half a day browsing this 25,000-square-foot antiques market, featuring one of the best collections of folk art in Atlanta as well as more than 100 dealers selling antiques, furniture, vintage clothing, '50s and '60s retro, garden art, lighting, and more. Open daily from 11am to 7pm. 2928 E. Ponce de Leon Ave. © **404/ 373-6498.** www.kudzuantiques.com.

**North Atlanta Antique Show**    Formerly the Pride of Dixie Antiques Market, this is more of a true antiques market than a flea market, featuring 700 dealers who have searched the countryside for fabulous finds. You'll see fine antique furniture as well as interesting primitive painted pieces, heirloom jewelry and silver, antique books, baskets, rugs, linens, roll-top desks, and much more. The market is held inside an air-conditioned building, so weather is not a factor. Open the fourth weekend of each month, Friday and Saturday from 9am to 6pm, Sunday from 11am to 5pm. Admission is $4 for the weekend. Parking is free. At the North Atlanta Trade Center, north of Atlanta. Take I-85 N. to the Indian Trail exit (about 25 min. from downtown), and then follow the signs. © **770/279-9853.**

**Paris on Ponce**    This 50,000-square-foot bohemian warehouse in the heart of Midtown features everything from 18th-century antiques to new designer furniture. This is one of the neatest retail spaces for seeing things you never would have dreamed existed, yesterday or today. Open Thursday through Saturday from 10am to 6pm and Sunday from noon to 6pm. 716 Ponce de Leon Place NE. © **404/249-9965.** www.parisonponce.com.

**Scott Antique Markets**    Scott is an immense and immensely popular market that has been so successful that it's had to open another location across the highway from its original spot. It's now garnered much of the market here, following the closing in late 2006 of the popular Lakewood Antiques Market. There are spaces for 2,400 booths, all indoors, and the antiques and collectibles are some of the finest you'll see anywhere. This market is similar in atmosphere to the North Atlanta Antique Show, but much bigger, with loads of heirloom furniture, jewelry, silver, and so on, as well as a huge assortment of collectibles.

There's a free shuttle between the two Scott markets, so it's easy to visit both locations. The markets are held on the second weekend of every month. Open Friday and Saturday from 9am to 6pm, Sunday from 10am to 4pm. Admission is $3. Free parking is available. At the Atlanta Exposition Center, south of the city. Take I-75 S. to I-285. Go east on I-285 to exit 55 (Jonesboro Rd.) and follow the signs. ℂ **404/366-0833.** www.scott antiquemarket.com.

## BOOKSTORES

In addition to the independent bookstores in Atlanta, the nationwide chains of Barnes & Noble, Borders, and Doubleday are all represented locally. The main **Barnes & Noble,** 2900 Peachtree Rd. (ℂ **404/261-7747;** MARTA: Lenox), can be found in Buckhead, just a few minutes south of Lenox Square. The main **Borders,** 3637 Peachtree Rd. (ℂ **404/237-0707;** MARTA: Lenox), is also in Buckhead, 3 blocks north of Lenox Square.

**Books & Cases**   There are some recent used books here, but the big attraction is the vast collection of antique books, especially the complete leather-bound sets. There are also old Bibles, children's books, scholarly books, antique and reproduction bookcases, and rare prints. Open Monday through Saturday from 10am to 5:30pm. 800 Miami Circle NE, Ste. 100 (just off Piedmont Rd.). ℂ 800/788-9107 or 404/231-9107. MARTA: Buckhead.

**Charis Books & More**   Marketed as an "independent feminist bookstore," Charis is located in the funky Little Five Points district and specializes in diverse and unique children's books, feminist and cultural studies books, and lesbian/gay/bi/trans fiction and nonfiction. Open Monday and Tuesday from 10:30am to 6:30pm; Thursday from 10:30am to 7:30pm; Wednesday, Friday, and Saturday from 10:30am to 8pm; and Sunday from noon to 6pm. 1189 Euclid Ave. ℂ 404/524-0304. www.charisbooksandmore.com.

**Engineer's Bookstore**   The largest technical bookstore in Atlanta, Engineer's has an incredible selection of computer and engineering titles as well as the graduate and undergraduate texts for Georgia Tech. Relocated in 1993 to make way for the Olympic Village dormitories, Engineer's Bookstore has been in business since 1954. Open Monday through Friday from 9am to 5:30pm, Saturday from 10am to 2pm. 748 Marietta St. NW (at Means St., just off Tech Pkwy. and approx. 1 mile from Georgia World Congress Center). ℂ 800/635-5919 or 404/221-1669. www.engrbookstore.com. MARTA: North Avenue.

**Outwrite Bookstore & Coffeehouse**   Selling books, magazines, and CDs, this casual Midtown spot caters to the gay and lesbian community and is a sort of clearinghouse for information on local issues and activities. The coffee and pastries are good, and the atmosphere is comfortable. Open daily from 10am to 11pm. 991 Piedmont Ave. (at 10th St.). ℂ 404/607-0082. www.outwritebooks.com. MARTA: Midtown.

**Tall Tales Book Shop, Inc.**   This general bookstore in the Emory University area has a large selection of mainstream titles with an emphasis on literature. All large publishers, as well as university and small presses, are represented. The staff is knowledgeable and will be happy to process special orders. Open Monday through Thursday from 9:30am to 9:30pm, Friday and Saturday from 9:30am to 10pm, and Sunday from 12:30 to 6:30pm. 2105 LaVista Rd., No. 108. ℂ 404/636-2498. MARTA: Lindbergh.

## FACTORY & DISCOUNT OUTLETS

**North Georgia Premium Outlets**   This 140-store center is a cut above most outlet complexes, with designers and manufacturers such as Anne Klein, BCBG, Bose, Brooks Brothers, Calvin Klein, Coach, Cole Haan, Gap, Kenneth Cole, Nike, Nine West, Saks

It's definitely worth the trip. Open Monday through Saturday from 10am to 9pm, Sunday from noon to 6pm. 800 Hwy. 400 S. (35 min. north of Atlanta), Dawsonville. ℂ **706/216-3609.** www.premiumoutlets.com.

## FARMERS' MARKETS

**Atlanta State Farmers' Market** The State Farmers' Market is a vast 146-acre outdoor facility where stall after stall is piled high with produce. There are also vendors of home-canned pickles, jams, and relishes; plants and flowers; and seasonal items such as pumpkins in October, and holly and Christmas trees in December. It's a colorful spectacle. You can have a good meal at a restaurant on the premises. Open 24 hours daily except Christmas. 16 Forest Pkwy., Forest Park, GA. ℂ **404/675-1782.** www.pickyourown.org. Take I-75 S. to exit 23; the market is on your left.

**DeKalb Farmers' Market** Even if you have no intention of purchasing, this incredible market, started in 1977 by Robert Blazer, merits a visit. A mind-boggling array of international food items is temptingly displayed in a 140,000-square-foot building. Tables are laden with mountains of produce from broccoli to bok choy, not to mention winter melons and water chestnuts, lily root, curry leaves, breadfruit, Jamaican jerk marinade, Korean daikon radish, a multiplicity of mushrooms, chickpea miso, a vast beer and wine section, dried fruits, plants and flowers, seafood, meat, poultry, every imaginable fresh herb and hot pepper, fresh-baked breads and pastries, stalks of sugarcane, many varieties of cheese, frogs' legs, conch meat, quail, and on and on. As you shop, you can nibble whatever is offered at sample tables throughout the facility. There's also a small cafeteria on the premises. The market is about a 20-minute drive from downtown. Open daily from 9am to 9pm except Thanksgiving and Christmas. 3000 E. Ponce de Leon Ave., Decatur. ℂ **404/377-6400.** MARTA: Avondale.

**Harry's Whole Foods** Like the DeKalb Farmers' Market, this megamarket must be seen to be believed. An Atlanta icon since 1987, Harry's features mountains of fresh produce, incredible selections of cheese, seafood, meats, gourmet items, wines, and beers, plus more exotica than you can imagine. While DeKalb attracts a more international clientele (although the selection of goods is not necessarily more international in scope), Harry's is a bit more upscale and polished, and attracts many suburbanites, probably because of its locations. DeKalb has a wider variety of organic foods and produce, while

SHOPPING

**9**

MORE SHOPPING AROUND TOWN

---

Ⓜ**oments** **Fresh Market Fare**

If your idea of fun is watching other people cook for you, stop in at the Morningside Farmers' Market on a Saturday morning. Each week at 9:30am, one of the city's top chefs gives a free cooking demonstration, and the lucky audience gets to sample the results. Afterward, browse the market, a small but beautiful array of organic, locally grown vegetables, fruits, herbs, and flowers. There are also handmade soaps, beeswax candles, primitive furniture, beaded jewelry, and other assorted artisanal items. The market, at 1393 N. Highland Ave., is open on Saturdays in late April through December from 8 to 11:30am. Call ℂ **404/313-5784** for details.

Harry's does better at baked goods, prepared foods, and cheeses. Saturday and Sunday are crowded at all markets, but the bustle seems to add to the fun if you don't have to do any serious shopping.

Open Monday through Saturday from 8am to 9pm, Sunday from 9am to 8pm. There is another Harry's located at 70 Powers Ferry Rd., Marietta (℗ **770/578-4400**). 1180 Upper Hembree Rd., Alpharetta. ℗ **770/664-6300**. From I-85 N., take Hwy. 400 north toward Roswell. Turn right onto Alpharetta Hwy./Hwy. 120 and left onto Upper Hembree Rd.

## FASHIONS

See sections 1 and 2 of this chapter for more store listings.

**The Bilthouse** Set in an old cottage in Buckhead, this is the place to go if you're looking for something casual that's a little out of the ordinary. Most of the clothing is designed for comfort—which is not to say that it doesn't also look great—and much of it is made of natural fabrics. There are linen shifts and separates, cotton sweaters, tights, flowing skirts, lots of one-of-a-kind dresses, and more for women of all ages. There's also unique furniture, jewelry, children's clothing, artwork by local artists, and little goodies for body and bath. Open Monday through Saturday from 9:30am to 6pm. 511 E. Paces Ferry Rd. NE (5 blocks west of Peachtree Rd., on the corner of Maple Ave.). ℗ **404/816-7702**. MARTA: Buckhead.

**K&G Men's Center** K&G is tucked away in an industrial area with a number of other discount stores, but it's definitely worth seeking out. This huge warehouse is crammed with a large selection of top-quality men's clothing, men's shoes, and furnishings. You'll find truly excellent suits, including tuxedos. There are other K&G stores, all in the suburbs, but this is the original. To reach Ellsworth Industrial Drive, take I-75 N., exit at Howell Mill Road, go west to Chattahoochee Avenue, turn right, and then take the next right. Open Monday through Saturday from 9:30am to 9pm, and Sunday from 11am to 7pm. 1750 Ellsworth Industrial Dr. NW (at Chattahoochee Ave.). ℗ **404/352-3471**.

**Luna** A good variety of strictly up-to-the-minute women's clothing and accessories are found here: sportswear, ultra-feminine evening wear, suits, jewelry, handbags, and cool shoes. Open Monday through Saturday from 10am to 7pm, and Sunday from noon to 5pm. 3167 Peachtree Rd. (south of Piedmont Rd.). ℗ **404/233-5344**. MARTA: Lenox.

**A Pea in the Pod** This cleverly named boutique chain features maternity clothes, but we're not talking T-shirts with an arrow pointing to your stomach. These are gorgeous clothes, from really chic sportswear to elegant business garb to evening wear. Open Monday through Saturday from 10am to 9pm, Sunday from noon to 5:30pm. In the Phipps Plaza mall, 3500 Peachtree Rd. (at Lenox Rd.). ℗ **404/816-9747**. MARTA: Lenox.

**Potpourri** If you're in search of upscale traditional women's apparel, Potpourri will fit the bill. There are lots of lovely sportswear separates, as well as dresses, belts, costume jewelry, and other accessories. Open Monday through Friday from 10am to 6pm and Saturday from 10am to 5pm. 3718 Roswell Rd. NW (just north of Piedmont Rd.). ℗ **404/365-0880**. MARTA: Buckhead.

## GIFTS, ART & COLLECTIBLES

Also see the stores listed in the hot shopping neighborhoods in section 1 of this chapter.

**Erika Reade** The emphasis here is on interesting home-related accessories and furnishings—paintings, antique and primitive furniture, mirrors, exquisite bed linens, and tabletop items. You'll find French soaps and candles, hand-blown glass, jewelry, wonder- **207** ful gifts for adults and children, and much more. It's all absolutely up-to-date and extremely tasteful. Open Monday through Thursday from 10am to 6pm, Friday and Saturday from 10am to 5pm. 3732 Roswell Rd. (just north of Piedmont Rd.). ℭ **404/233-3857.** MARTA: Lindbergh.

## HARDWARE/WOODWORKING

**Highland Hardware**   This isn't a hardware store; it's an institution. Woodworkers come from all over the country to browse Highland's huge selection of woodworking supplies and tools, and still more order from its voluminous catalog. But even if you don't know a router from a band saw, it's fun to roam through the large, high-ceilinged store, which has an old-fashioned, neighborly feel. Highland also stocks regular hardware, gardening merchandise, annuals, and perennials. Call in advance if you're interested in attending one of the many woodworking programs or workshops. Open Monday through Friday 9am to 6pm (Thurs until 8pm), Saturday from 8:30am to 6pm, and Sunday from noon to 5pm. 1045 N. Highland Ave. NE (at Los Angeles Ave.). ℭ **404/872-4466.** www.tools-for-woodworking.com. MARTA: Five Points.

## KITCHENWARE

**Cook's Warehouse**   There's everything you need here—except the kitchen sink—for setting up a gourmet kitchen: top-of-the-line cookware, dinnerware, quality knives, small appliances, cookbooks, chef's clothing, oodles of gadgets, a selection of olive oils and vinegars, and much more. There's a full schedule of cooking classes and demonstrations, too, so check the website for details. Open Sunday from 12:30 to 5:30pm, Monday through Thursday from 10am to 7pm, and Friday and Saturday from 10am to 6pm. 549-1 Amsterdam Ave. NE (1 block west of Monroe Dr.). ℭ **404/815-4993.** www.cookswarehouse. com. MARTA: Arts Center.

## SPORTING GOODS

**REI (Recreational Equipment Inc.)**   This Seattle-based company sells everything imaginable for the outdoor enthusiast: clothing, shoes, outerwear, and accessories for biking, hiking, camping, rock climbing, canoeing, kayaking, and so on. The staff is extremely knowledgeable, and the sales are frequent and fabulous.

Open Monday through Saturday from 10am to 9pm, Sunday from 11am to 6pm. There's another REI just north of the city at 1165 Perimeter Center W. NE (ℭ **770/901-9200**). 1800 Northeast Expwy. (on the I-85 access road; take the Clairmont Rd. exit and go south). ℭ **404/633-6508.** www.rei.com. MARTA: Brookhaven.

# Atlanta After Dark

This is a city that sizzles after dark, with numerous music clubs featuring jazz, rock, country, and blues, plus a comprehensive cultural scene that includes symphony, ballet, opera, and theater productions. If that's not enough, major artists headline regularly at Atlanta's many large-scale performance venues.

Nightlife turns up all over Atlanta, but the biggest concentration of clubs and bars is in Buckhead (near the intersection of Peachtree and E. Paces Ferry rds.); in Virginia Highland (at the intersection of Virginia and N. Highland aves., and on N. Highland just north of Ponce de Leon Ave.); in Little Five Points (near the intersection of Moreland and Euclid aves.); and downtown near Peachtree Center.

The **Buckhead** scene is often like a huge, unruly fraternity party, with lots of people and cars cruising the streets. It gets rowdier as the night goes on, and has been marked by violence on several occasions. In 2002, following scores of complaints from area residents, the Atlanta Police Department began closing a couple of roads in the Buckhead area every Friday and Saturday night to discourage some of the cruising; traffic jams and things have been improving ever since. **Virginia Highland** is full of upper-20- and 30-somethings and professionals. **Little Five Points** is an eclectic mix of wildly, weirdly dressed folks and neighborhood regulars. **Downtown** hosts many out-of-town visitors and convention goers.

To find out what's going on during your stay, consult the **Atlanta Journal-Constitution.** Its "Access Atlanta" section, published every Thursday, highlights movies, plays, festivals, gallery openings, and other happenings for the upcoming weekend.

There's also an extensive listing of live music. A calendar of events is published other days of the week, but it's not as complete. The newspaper's website at www.ajc.com allows you to access a week's worth of newspaper features, including the events calendar and "Access Atlanta."

A free newspaper called **Creative Loafing,** available at hundreds of locations around town (hotels, restaurants, shops, MARTA stations, sidewalk stands, and so on), lists numerous events and has special sections for "Gay and Lesbian Activities" and "Singles." Visit its website at www.creativeloafing.com or call ✆ **800/950-5623** to get a copy of the paper before you visit.

It's often possible to purchase tickets directly from the box office where the event is taking place. In addition, tickets to many performances are sold by **Ticketmaster**—call ✆ **404/249-6400** (for large performances) or ✆ **404/817-8700** (for smaller cultural events) to charge by phone. Online, you can reserve tickets at www.ticketmaster.com. Ticketmaster has more than 100 locations throughout Georgia, including all Publix Supermarkets, where customers can purchase tickets in person, though they must be paid for in cash. If you're staying in a large hotel, your concierge service will usually be able to obtain tickets to even the most popular events.

Day-of-show half-price tickets are available at the **AtlanTIX!** ticket booth at the Atlanta Convention & Visitors Bureau in Underground Atlanta (p. 169) and at Lenox Square (p. 201). Customers can see which plays and other live performances have tickets available that day, purchase a voucher for the show, and pick up the ticket at the show's box office before curtain time. Vouchers must be paid for in person; phone sales are not available. Call ☏ **404/588-9890** or visit www.atlanta performs.com for more information.

A quick point before you head out: *Forbes* magazine has listed Atlanta as the number one city for singles, noting the city's "hopping nightlife" as one of the highlights, so get out there and groove.

A word of warning, however: Atlanta's nightclubs are frequently gone with the wind with no prior notice whatsoever, so call ahead to make sure your planned destination is still in business.

---

# 1 THE PERFORMING ARTS

## BALLET

**Atlanta Ballet** The oldest continuously operating ballet company in the United States, the Atlanta Ballet usually presents six productions each fall-through-spring season. Performances range from classics to new works and include *The Nutcracker* every December. Tickets are available through **Ticketmaster** (☏ **404/817-8700**) or on the day of the performance at the Fox Theatre box office or the Cobb Energy Performing Arts Centre box office, depending on show location. Performances held at the Fox Theatre, 660 Peachtree St. NE (at Ponce de Leon Ave.). ☏ **404/873-5811.** Also at the Cobb Energy Performing Arts Center, 2800 Cobb Galleria Pkwy. ☏ **770/916-2800.** www.atlantaballet.com. Tickets $10–$50. MARTA: North Ave. (to Fox Theatre).

## CLASSICAL MUSIC

**Atlanta Symphony Orchestra** The Atlanta Symphony Orchestra performs under music director Robert Spano and principal guest conductor Donald Runnicles. Complementing the orchestra is the 200-voice Atlanta Symphony Orchestra Chorus, enabling performances of large-scale symphonic/choral works. The season runs from September to May in the Woodruff Arts Center, and there are summer concerts at Verizon Wireless Amphitheatre at Encore Park as well as in Chastain Park Amphitheatre. The box office is open Monday through Friday from 10am to 8pm, Saturday and Sunday from noon to 8pm. Most performances begin at 8pm.

The ASO's annual schedule is extensive. The main offering is the **Master Season Series.** Master Season concerts, held on selected Thursday, Friday, and Saturday evenings in the plush 1,762-seat Atlanta Symphony Hall, feature renowned guest artists such as violinist Robert McDuffie, cellist Marin Alsop, pianist Olli Mustonen, soprano Sylvia McNair, and mezzo-soprano Susan Graham. Other events during the season are Sunday-afternoon **Family Concerts** geared toward children, **Casual Classics** on selected Saturday afternoons, holiday concerts during the Christmas season, and a tribute to Martin Luther King, Jr., in mid-January.

The ASO's **Classic Chastain Series** concerts are held in the 7,000-seat Chastain Park Amphitheatre from June to August, featuring headliners such as Tony Bennett and Natalie Cole performing with the ASO. All tickets except lawn seating are reserved. It's customary to bring elaborate picnics and wine to these events. In addition to the Chastain series, the ASO gives free evening concerts in parks throughout the Atlanta area during the summer; these run the gamut from full symphony performances to light classical concerts.

## (Tips) Playing Southern

Want to talk like a Southerner? An easy way to start is with "y'all." But remember that "y'all" is always plural, NEVER singular. For instance, when talking to two or more people it's okay to say "Are y'all coming with me tonight?" But if you pose the same question to just one person who happens to know Southernspeak, he'll probably snicker (politely). And don't even think about saying "you all" instead. Y'all got that?

Opened in May 2008, the Verizon Wireless Amphitheatre at Encore Park in Alpharetta is the summer home of the Atlanta Symphony Orchestra. The venue boasts 7,000 fixed seats under a roof and 5,000 lawn seats.

*Note:* At press time, plans were still underway for the future construction of a $300-million Atlanta Symphony Center in Midtown. Performances held at the Woodruff Arts Center, 1280 Peachtree St. NE (at 15th St.). © **404/733-5000** (box office) for information and tickets. www.atlantasymphony.org. Most tickets $19–$55. Parking available in the Arts Center Garage on Lombardy Way btw. 15th and 16th sts. MARTA: Arts Center.

## OPERA

**Atlanta Opera**    Under the direction of Dennis Hanthorn, the Atlanta Opera has five fully staged productions during the spring and fall at the Fox Theatre. Principal performers are drawn from top opera companies across the United States and Europe. Recent productions included Verdi's *Otello* and Puccini's *Turandot.* Only four performances are given of each opera, and tickets can be difficult to obtain, so charge them in advance if possible. Performances held at the Cobb Energy Performing Arts Centre, 2800 Cobb Galleria Pkwy., Alpharetta. © **800/35-OPERA [67372]** or 404/881-8801 for information. www.atlantaopera. org. Tickets $17–$126. Single tickets available through the Cobb Energy Centre box office (in person only) and Ticketmaster (© **404/817-8700**).

## THEATER

The **Alliance Theatre Company** is the major theater company in Atlanta, but there are many other excellent companies with performances ranging from experimental to classic. Most are located near downtown and Midtown, but there are a number in the suburbs. Some of the notables include **Actor's Express** (© 404/607-7469; www.actors-express. com), **Ansley Park Playhouse** (© 404/875-1193; www.ansleyparkplayhouse.com), **Dad's Garage** (© 404/523-3141; www.dadsgarage.com), **Horizon Theatre Company** (© 404/584-7450; www.horizontheatre.com), **Theatre Decatur** (© 404/373-5311), **Peachtree Playhouse** (© 404/875-1193; www.peachtreeplayhouse.com), **7 Stages Theatre** (© 404/523-7647; www.7stages.org), **Shakespeare Tavern** (© 404/874-5299; www. shakespearetavern.com), **Theatre Gael** (© 404/876-1138), **Theatre in the Square** (© 770/422-8369; www.theatreinthesquare.com), and **Theatrical Outfit** (© 678/528-1500; www.theatricaloutfit.org). Check the *Atlanta Journal-Constitution* on Thursday to see what's on during your visit. There are also performances by the **Georgia Shakespeare Festival** (© 404/264-0020; www.gashakespeare.org) each summer and fall.

**Alliance Theatre Company**   The Alliance Theatre Company, under the direction of
Susan V. Booth, is the largest regional theater in the Southeast. The company produces
about 10 plays a year on three different stages, and the season runs from September
through June, with occasional productions during the summer as well. Many well-known
actors have played these stages, among them Jane Alexander, Richard Dreyfuss, the late
Esther Rolle, and Morgan Freeman. Recent seasons have included Dickens's *A Christmas
Carol* (performed annually); *Medea*, starring Phylicia Rashad; and the world premiere of
Elton John and Tim Rice's musical *Aida*. The **Alliance Children's Theatre** presents plays
geared to youngsters from January to May. Tickets for children's productions are $20 for
adults and $15 for children. The box office is open Monday through Friday from 10am
to 8pm, Saturday and Sunday from noon to 8pm. Most performances begin at 8pm.
Performances held at the Woodruff Arts Center, 1280 Peachtree St. NE (at 15th St.). ✆ 404/733-
5000 (box office) for information and tickets. www.alliancetheatre.org. Tickets $25–$45. "Rush
tickets" often available for $15 on the day of a performance; they must be purchased in person
at the box office after 5pm. Parking available in the Arts Center Garage on Lombardy Way btw.
15th and 16th sts. MARTA: Arts Center.

## MAJOR ENTERTAINMENT VENUES

In addition to the venues listed below, many stadiums host major concerts from time to
time. These include the Alexander Memorial Coliseum and Bobby Dodd Stadium at
Grant Field at Georgia Tech, Road Atlanta, Philips Arena, and the Georgia Dome. See
"Spectator Sports" in chapter 7 (p. 183) for details on some of these stadiums.

**Atlanta Civic Center**   The Civic Center offers a wealth of entertainment options in
its 4,600-seat auditorium, hosting headliners, touring Broadway shows, traveling symphony and opera companies, and fashion shows. 395 Piedmont Ave. NE (btw. Ralph McGill
Blvd. and Pine St.). ✆ 404/523-6275 for general information. www.atlantaciviccenter.com. MARTA:
Civic Center (about 5 blocks away); buses go to the door.

**Chastain Park Amphitheatre** ★★ (Moments)   This delightful 7,000-seat outdoor
facility presents concerts under the stars from May to October, featuring big-name performers. Everyone brings food—a picnic on the grass, at your amphitheater seat, or at a
table for up to six is a tradition. Some people even bring gourmet feasts, flowers, and candelabra for an extra-special experience. If you don't feel like piecing together a picnic, you
can pre-order your meal from **Proof-in-the-Pudding,** an on-site caterer. Meals are wonderful and come with enough food for four or more. For a fee, the company will dress your
table and have everything ready when you arrive; all you'll have to do is open the wine and
light the candles. It can be difficult to get tickets at times, so order as far in advance as possible (months ahead if you can). The Atlanta Symphony Orchestra (p. 209) accompanies
some performers here. 449 Stella Dr. NW (in Chastain Park at Powers Ferry Rd.). ✆ 404/733-5000,
or 404/817-8700 for Ticketmaster. www.classicchastain.com. MARTA: Lenox.

**Cobb Energy Performing Arts Centre**   The first major performing arts facility
built in metro Atlanta in four decades, Cobb Energy Centre hosts Broadway shows, ballet, concerts, educational shows, family performances, operas, and other events. The
venue includes a 2,750-seat theater, a 10,000-square-foot ballroom, and 1,000 on-site
parking spaces. New home to the Atlanta Opera and many performances of Atlanta Ballet, the Cobb Energy Centre is just north of the city in Alpharetta. 2800 Cobb Galleria
Pkwy. ✆ 770/916-2800 for information, or 404/817-8700 for Ticketmaster. Tickets available at the
on-site ticket booth in person only. www.cobbenergycentre.com.

**Fox Theatre** ★★    Built in 1927, when movie theaters were conceived along lavish lines, the Fox is a Moorish-Egyptian extravaganza complete with arabesque arches, onion domes, and minarets. Its exotic interior reflects the Egyptomania of the 1920s—a phenomenon resulting from archaeologist Henry Carter's discovery of the treasure-laden tomb of King Tut. Throne chairs, scarab motifs, and hieroglyphics are seen throughout the theater, and the auditorium evokes a Middle Eastern courtyard under an azure sky. The Fox is home to some performances of the **Atlanta Ballet** (discussed above). In addition, a wide spectrum of headliners play the Fox, along with diverse entertainment ranging from Broadway musicals to rock 'n' roll. See p. 145 for details on the Fox's history and architecture, as well as information on tours. 660 Peachtree St. NE (at Ponce de Leon Ave.). ✆ **404/881-2100** for information, or 404/817-8700 for tickets. www.foxtheatre.org. Many paid parking lots nearby. MARTA: North Ave.

**HiFi Buys Amphitheatre**    The $15-million outdoor HiFi Buys Amphitheatre—formerly Coca-Cola Lakewood—accommodates 19,000 people with 7,000 reserved seats, plus a sloping lawn that holds an additional 12,000. Needless to say, this is a vast facility used for major shows. Eric Clapton, Elton John, Pearl Jam, and Aerosmith have all performed here. There are picnic tables with umbrellas on the grounds, and though you can't bring in food or drink, a wide variety of refreshments are available, including beer, champagne, fruit, cheese, sandwiches, and pizza. 2002 Lakewood Way (at the Lakewood exit off I-75/85, 3½ miles south of downtown). ✆ **404/443-5000.** Take I-75 or I-85 S. to Lakewood Fwy. exit and follow signs. MARTA: Lakewood/Fort McPherson (shuttle buses take patrons to and from the station).

**Rialto Center for the Performing Arts**    Located close to the center of downtown on the campus of Georgia State University, this wonderful 900-seat facility hosts a variety of performances, from theater to dance to all types of music. It opened as a theater in 1916, and then became the Rialto movie house before being converted into a multipurpose venue in the late 1990s. 80 Forsyth St. ✆ **404/413-9849.** www.rialtocenter.org. Paid parking in nearby lots. MARTA: Peachtree Center.

**Variety Playhouse**    Built in the 1930s as a neighborhood movie theater for Little Five Points, the Variety is now an intimate concert hall offering an eclectic array of performances, from folk rock to jazz, that are definitely worth checking out. There are frequent album-release parties here. 1099 Euclid Ave. (near Washita St.). ✆ **404/524-7354** for information. www.variety-playhouse.com. Paid parking lot on Euclid Ave. near Colquitt Ave. MARTA: Inman Park or bus 3 (Auburn Ave.).

# 2  THE CLUB & MUSIC SCENE

Nightclubs come and go, so it's always a good idea to call ahead. Most clubs are open until 2, 3, or even 4am.

## BLUES CLUBS

**Blind Willie's**    This well-known club features live blues from around the country, but local bands are part of the scene as well. The bar usually opens about 7pm, and there's a limited bar menu, but the big attraction is the music, which starts around 10pm. This place gets too packed to move in when there is a big show. 828 N. Highland Ave. (just north of Ponce de Leon Ave.). ✆ **404/873-2583.** www.blindwilliesblues.com. Cover varies. MARTA: Five Points.

**Fat Matt's Rib Shack** This barbecue joint packs 'em in every evening for a taste of **213** smoky ribs, beer, and local blues. The food is as good as the sultry music, which starts every night at 8pm. See p. 112 for more information. 1811 Piedmont Ave. (a few blocks south of Cheshire Bridge Rd.). ℰ 404/607-1622. www.fatmattsribshack.com. MARTA: Lindbergh and a short cab ride.

**Northside Tavern** Home of the locally and internationally acclaimed Mudcat blues band, this hole in the wall was obviously a gas station in a previous life. Though the digs aren't anything to write home about and the location might look a bit shady, the music here is fantastic. Mudcat plays every Wednesday night and one weekend a month—when they aren't performing in Europe. Yes, Europe. Don't worry if you miss the Mudcats, though; this place offers excellent live blues every day of the week. Cold beer, a full bar, and a couple of pool tables round out the offerings. 1058 Howell Mill Rd. NW. ℰ **404/874-8745.** www.northsidetavern.com. Cover varies. MARTA: Arts Center.

## A COMEDY CLUB
**The Punchline** This popular suburban comedy club, about a 40-minute drive from downtown, features pros on the national comedy-club circuit—the comedians you see on Leno and Letterman. Jeff Foxworthy got his start here. Doors open an hour before showtime. Reasonably priced food is served, and there's a full bar. Thursday and early Friday shows are smoke-free. Though you can buy tickets at the club, they often sell out, so it's best to reserve by phone. You must be 21 or older and have a valid ID to get in. It's open Tuesday through Sunday, with showtimes usually beginning around 8pm. 280 Hilderbrand Dr. NE (off Roswell Rd. in the Balconies Shopping Center), Sandy Springs. ℰ **404/252-5233.** www.punchline.com. Cover $15–$20, depending on day of the week. MARTA: Sandy Springs.

## DANCE CLUBS
**HALO Lounge** HALO is one of the most beautiful bars in Atlanta, featuring a back-lit onyx bar. Some of the coolest DJs in town spin here, making HALO a favorite among Atlantans no matter what their sexual preference. Thursday is the most popular night for the gay crowd. Food is served Monday to Saturday from 5 to 11pm. *Note:* Don't miss the entrance—the address is Peachtree Street, but the door is off Sixth Street. 817 W. Peachtree St. NW. ℰ **404/962-7333.** www.halolounge.com. Occasional cover varies. $5 covered parking on Cypress St. MARTA: Midtown.

**Johnny's Hideaway** "Atlanta's Only Nightclub for Big Kids" has been one of Atlanta's top nightspots for the over-40 crowd for 30 years. Ebullient host Johnny Esposito is a well-known Atlanta character, though his age now keeps him from being on hand nightly to greet guests. Locals jokingly refer to the nightspot as "God's waiting room," a dig at the "old folks" who still come here to party (including the couple in their 80s you might spot tearing up the dance floor if you arrive early). The music sweeps through the decades at this Buckhead treasure, from the big-band era to the '80s, attracting a crowd of all ages. The music gets "younger" as the night wears on, and the patrons do, too. This is a place for serious dancing, and though it's unpretentious, there are celebrities (such as George Clooney and Robert Duvall) who drop by when in town. The majority of the bartenders here have been on staff for over 25 years and can make a night of sitting at the bar a lot of fun, if you get there early enough to claim a stool. They'll even keep your purse safe behind the bar so you can dance the night away. Check out the Frank Sinatra Room, filled with more than 100 pieces of memorabilia. A reasonably priced menu lists items ranging from deli sandwiches to prime-rib main courses. Attire is dressy-casual. Open daily. 3771 Roswell Rd. (2 blocks north of Piedmont Rd.). ✆ 404/233-8026. www.johnnyshideaway.com. $5 cover on Sun for live music. MARTA: Buckhead.

**Masquerade**  Popular with the college-age crowd, Masquerade is housed in a century-old, stone-walled, Romanesque former factory. Its interior is divided into three main areas—Heaven, Hell, and Purgatory—all appropriately decorated. Up in Heaven is a concert hall featuring live local and national acts. Hell is a DJ dance party, and Purgatory is the game room, with pool tables and other non-music diversions. Closed on Sunday. 695 North Ave. NE (just east of Boulevard). ✆ 404/577-8178. www.masq.com. Cover $5–$8 in Hell and Purgatory, $5–$20 (depending on the performer) in Heaven. Parking $3–$5. MARTA: North Ave.

**Opera Atlanta**  Formerly Eleven50, this elegant Miami-type club draws a mixed crowd. The atmosphere is very laid-back, and well-known DJs visit on weekends. Opera has three dance areas featuring a different style of music in each, from top 40 to rock to salsa and merengue. Cover is typically $15 and up, depending on the DJ's status and what night of the week you visit. Also a popular venue for private parties and celebrity sightings. 1150-B Peachtree Rd. ✆ 404/874-0428. www.operaatlanta.com. MARTA: Lenox.

**Sutra**  Voted one of the top 100 nightclubs in the country, Sutra is sexy and chic, where all the pretty people meet to drink and dance. In the heart of Midtown, Sutra features the talents of one of the most popular DJs in the city, and it draws big crowds. Guests are asked to "dress to impress," no ball caps, jerseys, or athletic wear allowed. Cover varies depending on event. 1136 Crescent Ave. NE ✆ 404/607-1160. www.sutralounge atl.com. MARTA: Art Center.

## FOLK, ACOUSTIC & BLUEGRASS CLUBS

**Eddie's Attic**  Eddie's Attic is a popular venue for acoustic singer/songwriters. In fact, the Indigo Girls, Billy Pilgrim, and Shawn Mullins all started their careers here. The place is divided into three sections: The main bar is perfect for music lovers, with its small stage, intimate seating arrangement, and excellent acoustics. Rowdier folks will like the poolroom and the covered patio, where there's a full bar and TV monitors playing the live performance from the main stage. The entire family is welcome for the 7pm smoke-free shows on Friday and Saturday. There is a full menu, offering mostly typical bar fare. 515-B N. McDonough St., Decatur (next to the old courthouse on the square). ✆ 404/377-4976. www.eddiesattic.com. Cover $5–$25, depending on the performer and whether you want to secure a good seat or take your chances with general admission. Parking available on the square or at the lot on Church St., directly behind Eddie's. MARTA: Decatur.

**Red Light Cafe**  This classic San Francisco–style coffeehouse, a funky high-ceilinged space decked out with tables and comfy sofas, offers a mix of art, music, conversation, and food and beverages. The big attraction is the music—local bluegrass, folk, rock, and jazz. Locals jam at 7pm and Wednesdays are open mic. You can order salads, fresh pastas, and sandwiches, and there's a good selection of bottled and draft beers, including some locally brewed choices. Closed on Mondays. 553 W. Amsterdam Ave. (west of Monroe Dr.). ✆ 404/874-7828. www.redlightcafe.com. Cover varies. MARTA: Arts Center.

## JAZZ CLUBS

**Dante's Down the Hatch** (Finds)  For over 33 years, Dante Stephensen has manned the decks of this jazz supper club, part of an entertainment complex built around the illusion of a well-rigged 18th-century schooner tied to the wharf of a mythical Mediterranean seating areas, but the most romantic spot is a semi-enclosed private "cabin" on the lower deck, where a trio plays traditional jazz 6 days a week. Earlier in the evening, classical folk guitarists perform on the "wharf," and on weekend nights, a solo pianist plays on the ship prior to the show. Dante's has an expansive wine list, with about 90 bottles at $36 and less. If you wish to have dinner during the show, the specialty is fondue, available by reservation only. Amazingly, the menu is available in 55 languages. 3380 Peachtree Rd. NE (across the street from the Lenox Square mall). © 404/266-1600. www.dantesdownthehatch. com. Cover $7–$9 for seating on the jazz ship; free on the wharf. MARTA: Buckhead.

**Sambuca**    Part restaurant, part jazz club, Sambuca is the third in a new chain of jazz cafes (the first two were in Texas). The big attraction here is the large, chic bar, where a jazz combo plays on the bandstand each night and a crowd fills the dance floor. Upscale couples and singles are often four-deep at the bar, and everyone is sharply dressed. Shows start at 7:30pm and the cover depends on who is performing. Some nights there is no cover, just a two-drink minimum. If your main interest is the music, come early for a table near the bandstand. There's almost always a wait to get in, especially as the evening wears on. 3102 Piedmont Road NE (btw. Peachtree and E. Paces Ferry rds.). © 404/237-5299. www.sambucarestaurant.com. No cover; 2-drink minimum. MARTA: Lindbergh.

---

# 3 THE BAR SCENE

In addition to the neighborhood establishments listed below, there are some excellent bars in the major hotels, many of them mellow enough for conversation. Two of the best are the **Lobby Lounge** at the Ritz-Carlton Buckhead, 3434 Peachtree Rd. (© 404/237-2700; MARTA: Peachtree Center), and **Park 75 Lounge** at the Four Seasons Hotel, 75 14th St., in Midtown (© 404/253-3840; MARTA: Arts Center). The **Sun Dial Restaurant and Bar,** high atop the Westin Peachtree Plaza, 210 Peachtree St. (© 404/589-7506; MARTA: Peachtree Center), and **A Point of View at Nikolai's Roof,** at the Hilton Atlanta, 255 Courtland St. (© 404/221-6362; MARTA: Peachtree Center), have spectacular views of the city skyline. None of the places has a cover charge unless otherwise stated.

**Atkins Park**    This place hosts a mix of casually dressed regulars from the Virginia-Highland neighborhood and young crowds from other parts of town. The atmosphere is friendly and the ambience mellow and comfortable. Atkins Park began as a deli in 1922 (it holds the oldest existing tavern license in the city) and now includes a full-scale restaurant that stays open until 11pm (until midnight Fri–Sat). After that, better-than-average bar food is available until 2:30am. Atkins Park is known as *the* place to go for Jägermeister—it sells more than almost any other bar in Atlanta. Things get lively when the restaurant closes and the music (rock, blues, and jazz) is turned up. 794 N. Highland Ave. NE (at St. Charles Place, 1 block north of Ponce de Leon Ave.). © 404/876-7249. www.atkins park.com. Some free parking in lot off St. Charles; paid parking in nearby lots. MARTA: Five Points.

**Dark Horse Tavern**    This multiple-deck tavern is primarily a neighborhood hangout during the week, but it attracts a mix of young professionals and college students on the weekends. There's live entertainment in the performance area, called 10 High—mostly local bands, but occasionally a nationally known group. Trivia and comedy nights are

## (Tips) Martinis & IMAX, Anyone?

For a different kind of action, check out Martinis & IMAX, a Friday-night event for grown-ups that's held January through November at the **Fernbank Museum of Natural History.** From 5:30 to 10pm, enjoy a martini or other cocktail, have dinner, watch the films, and listen to a jazz group starting at 6:30pm. To reserve tickets, call ℭ **404/929-6400.** There is a $7 cover after 6:30pm for nonmembers who do not purchase IMAX or special-exhibition tickets. IMAX tickets are $15.

held weekly. Upstairs, there's a dining area serving American fare, where you can eat, drink, and socialize into the wee hours. For major sporting events, there's a big-screen TV. 816 N. Highland Ave. NE (2 blocks north of Ponce de Leon Ave.). ℭ **404/873-3607.** www. darkhorseatlanta.com. Cover $5–$7 for entertainment in High 10. Limited free parking in lot around back; paid lot across the street. MARTA: Five Points.

**Fadó** If you haven't had a good glass of Guinness since your last trip to Dublin, Fadó (Gaelic for "long ago") is the place to pause for a pint or two. The interior is divided into five pub areas, each one distinct from the next: a cottage pub with a peat-burning fireplace, a Victorian pub with dark wood and stained glass, and so on. As the night goes on and serious revelers invade, the pleasant, unhurried atmosphere of the early evening gives way to loud and crowded boisterousness. There's traditional Irish or Celtic music several days a week, and the Irish fare is good, especially the *boxty* (the Irish version of a potato pancake) and the fish and chips in Guinness batter. 3035 Peachtree Rd. NE (at the corner of Buckhead Ave., just south of E. Paces Ferry Rd.). ℭ **404/841-0066.** www.fadoirishpub.com. Limited parking on neighboring streets; paid valet parking out back. MARTA: Buckhead.

**Manuel's Tavern** (Finds) Not far from the yuppiness of Virginia Highland and the funkiness of Little Five Points is an authentic neighborhood bar that's been a gathering spot since 1956. Now operated by Brian Maloof, the tavern was opened by his father, the late Manuel Maloof, former DeKalb County chief executive officer (his ashes rest in an urn on a shelf behind the bar). It's the quintessential watering hole for journalists, politicos, cops, students, and writers. Former President Jimmy Carter often drops by with the Secret Service in tow. The main bar, with its dark wood and large booths, is the best spot in the building, but there are two larger rooms with tables to accommodate the considerable crowds. It's lots of fun to watch the Braves here if you can't get tickets to the game. There's a full bar with 26 beers on a rotating tap, plus dozens of beer blends and craft beers. Manuel's menu includes his famous meatloaf and lasagna entrees along with other stick-to-your-ribs home-cooked fare such as turkey and dressing, pork chops, and pecan trout. 602 N. Highland Ave. NE (at North Ave.). ℭ **404/525-3447.** www.manuelstavern. com. MARTA: Five Points.

**Park Tavern Brewery** This restaurant/bar on the edge of Piedmont Park has great views of the park and all its goings-on. There are two cozy, rustic bars inside, but the large patio is the best spot for sipping one of the brewery's handcrafted beers. 500 10th St. (at Monroe Dr.). ℭ **404/249-0001.** www.parktavern.com. Limited parking. MARTA: Midtown.

**Star Community Bar**   Housed in a former bank, this funky and cavernous club fea- tures the "Grace Vault"—a small shrine filled with Elvis posters, an all-Elvis jukebox, Elvis clocks, and other memorabilia. Primarily a Little Five Points neighborhood hangout, it's very low-key and offbeat. Live music Wednesday through Saturday nights runs the gamut from rockabilly to rock 'n' roll and R & B. Most of the performers are local and regional, but occasionally bigger names play here as well. It's closed on Sunday. 437 Moreland Ave. NE (btw. Euclid and Mansfield aves.). ℰ 404/681-9018. www.starbar.net. Cover $3–$10. MARTA: Five Points.

## SPORTS BARS

**ESPN Zone**   It's all TV all the time with 210 screens located throughout this 33,000-square-foot sports lover's paradise (you won't even miss the action when you go to the bathroom as there are televisions in there, too). In addition to a separate screening room, there is also a game room and a sports simulation area to keep the kids busy while mom and dad cheer their favorite team to victory. Special events bring athletes up close and personal for patrons to meet and greet. Voted the city's number one sports bar in 2008, ESPN Zone includes a retail store with all your favorite sports memorabilia. 3030 Peachtree Rd. ℰ 404/682-3776. www.espnzone.com. MARTA: Buckhead, then bus 23 or bus 110 southbound.

**High Velocity**   Formerly Champions, this popular spot underwent major renovation as well as a name change. Twenty-one plasma TVs air nonstop sporting events and are located everywhere you look, so catching your sporting event is easy here. Or grab a leather recliner in the Media Room and watch the featured game on a 40-foot matrix theatrical projection screen. Sports celebrities tend to stop by when they're in town. Visitors will find 24 beers on tap and a long list of appetizers and munchies. At the Marriott Marquis, 265 Peachtree Center Ave. (btw. Baker and Harris sts.). ℰ 404/586-6017. www. highvelocityatlanta.com. MARTA: Peachtree Center.

**Jocks & Jills**   This is the only branch of Jocks & Jills still left in the city, and it does attract some sports celebrities. If nobody famous shows up, you can still watch sporting events on one of the many televisions scattered around, or check out the sports memorabilia. 1 Galleria Pkwy. ℰ 770/952-8401. www.jocksandjills.com.

## GAY & LESBIAN BARS & CLUBS

Also see **HALO Lounge** (p. 213) and **Outwrite Bookstore & Coffeehouse** (p. 218).

**Blake's on the Park**   Not too far from Piedmont Park in Midtown, you'll find this landmark: a friendly, mostly gay bar that's popular with locals. A few doors away on Monroe Drive is Outwrite Bookstore & Coffeehouse, another pleasant gay and lesbian hangout. 227 10th St. (at Piedmont Ave.). ℰ 404/892-5786. Limited parking. MARTA: Midtown.

**Burkhart's**   Located in Midtown's Ansley Square Shopping Center, this two-level gay men's hotspot offers three bars, pool tables, and outdoor seating. Many come for the weekly drag shows officially held Friday through Sunday, but recent visits have proved that a show might happen at any time. Karaoke is also a favorite here, if you can squeeze in a tune before the queens hit the stage or wait until the show is over. 1482 Piedmont Ave. NE. ℰ 404/872-9060. MARTA: Midtown.

# 4 COFFEEHOUSES, CAFES & LATE-NIGHT BITES

Also see the box "I Scream for Ice Cream," on p. 198.

**Apres Diem**   This popular coffeehouse has an atmosphere that is laid-back and casual, and you can linger undisturbed over an espresso or glass of wine on the comfy couches inside or outdoors on the patio. This spot reinvents itself when the sun goes down—there's a full bar and live music several nights of the week. Apres Diem serves good desserts, a variety of French-style coffee drinks and teas, and an expanded menu if you want something more substantial. 931 Monroe Dr. (south of 10th St.). © 404/872-3333. www.apres diem.com. MARTA: Arts Center.

**Café Intermezzo**   Café Intermezzo, in South Buckhead, is a great place to stop after dinner or the theater, or if you just don't want the evening to end. In the tradition of a Vienna-style cafe, there's excellent coffee to go with the decadent desserts and pastries. Speaking of desserts, there are so many that each patron receives a private "tour" of the sweets cases to choose his or her poison. There's also free Wi-Fi here. 1845 Peachtree Rd. (just south of Collier Rd.). © 404/355-0411. www.cafeintermezzo.com. MARTA: Lenox.

**Majestic Food Shop**   Known simply as "the Majestic" to locals, this all-night restaurant has been serving up diner food and a slice of life since 1935. You'll find obnoxious drunks, middle-class regulars, working girls, cops, street people, couples on dates, you name it. Sooner or later, just about everybody comes to the Majestic for a late-night breakfast, a cup of coffee, or just to take in the scene. The late Nick Bitzis, a longtime owner who used to keep an aluminum baseball bat behind the register, once chased a group of customers with a butcher knife for smoking pot in one of the booths. Since the Majestic is open 24 hours, things invariably get more interesting as the night goes on. 1031 Ponce de Leon Ave. NE (west of N. Highland Ave.). © 404/875-0276. MARTA: Inman Park.

**Outwrite Bookstore & Coffeehouse**   This casual Midtown spot caters to the gay and lesbian community and is a sort of clearinghouse for information on local issues and activities. The coffee and pastries are good, and the atmosphere is comfortable. Open daily until 11pm. 991 Piedmont Ave. (at 10th St.). © 404/607-0082. www.outwritebooks.com. MARTA: Midtown.

**R. Thomas Deluxe Grill**  ★★   You won't find this menu available at any other round-the-clock restaurant in Atlanta. The grill serves up healthy, eclectic food with a large number of vegetarian dishes among the offerings. Open 24 hours a day, 7 days a week. 1812 Peachtree St. NW. © 404/872-2942. www.rthomasdeluxegrill.com. MARTA: Midtown.

**San Francisco Coffee**   It's hard to find a coffeehouse that's strictly local and not part of a national chain, but this is the real McCoy. A neighborhood spot that roasts its own coffee and bakes most of its own pastries, it has a lot of atmosphere and is a great place for just hanging out. 1192 N. Highland Ave. (at Amsterdam Ave.). © 404/876-8816. MARTA: Five Points or Arts Station.

# Appendix: Fast Facts, Toll-Free Numbers & Websites

## 1 FAST FACTS: ATLANTA

**AMERICAN EXPRESS** The Buckhead office, across from the Westin Buckhead near Lenox Square, provides travel services and currency exchange (© **404/262-7561**).

**AREA CODES** In metro Atlanta, you must dial the area code (404, 770, or 678) and the seven-digit telephone number, even if you are calling a number within the same area code. It is not necessary to dial "1" before the area code when calling between communities within the Atlanta local calling area, even if they have different area codes.

**ATM NETWORKS & CASHPOINTS** See "Money & Costs," in chapter 3.

**AUTOMOBILE ORGANIZATIONS** Motor clubs will supply maps, suggested routes, guidebooks, accident and bail-bond insurance, and emergency road service. The **American Automobile Association (AAA)** is the major auto club in the United States. If you belong to a motor club in your home country, inquire about AAA reciprocity before you leave. You may be able to join AAA even if you're not a member of a reciprocal club; to inquire, call AAA (© **800/222-4357**; www.aaa.com). AAA is actually an organization of regional motor clubs, so look under "AAA Automobile Club" in the White Pages of the telephone directory.

AAA has a nationwide emergency road service telephone number (© **800/AAA-HELP [222-4357]**).

**BABYSITTERS** Most hotels will arrange a babysitter for you. If yours doesn't, a highly recommended service is **A Friend of the Family** (© **770/725-2748**), which has been in business for 25 years. All of its sitters are carefully screened and are at least 21 years old. You can interview the sitter in advance on the phone. On request, the agency will send someone who is trained in CPR and first aid. Rates are about $12 per hour, with a 4-hour minimum, plus an agency fee of $30 to $45 per day. The agency fee must be paid by credit card; the sitters prefer cash. If you're staying in a hotel without free parking, you may be asked to pay for the sitter's parking cost as well. Advance notice of 24 hours is appreciated but not required. A Friend of the Family also provides pet care and companions for adults. Office hours are Monday through Sunday from 6am to 10pm.

**BUSINESS HOURS** Most stores are open until at least 6pm nightly, with extended hours at larger shopping centers and malls. Banks are typically open 9am to 5pm, with some open a half-day on Saturday.

**CAR RENTALS** See "Toll-Free Numbers & Websites," p. 227.

**DENTISTS** The **Georgia Dental Association of Atlanta** (© 404/636-7553) provides a free referral service. It will point you in the direction of a dentist close to your hotel or, if need be, one who can accommodate your special needs. It cannot, however, match patients with dentists who offer services through specific insurance companies. Call Monday through Friday between 8am and 5pm. At other times, inquire at your hotel desk.

**DRINKING LAWS** The legal age for purchase and consumption of alcoholic beverages is 21; proof of age is required and often requested at bars, nightclubs, and restaurants, so it's always a good idea to bring ID when you go out.

Beer and wine are sold in most grocery stores and all liquor stores. Some areas of the Atlanta region do not allow liquor sales on Sundays, but it can often be purchased by the drink after noon on Sundays in restaurants that serve alcohol. Closing times for bars and clubs in Atlanta vary and can be as late as 2, 3 or even 4am.

Do not carry open containers of alcohol in your car or any public area that isn't zoned for alcohol consumption. The police can fine you on the spot. And nothing will ruin your trip faster than getting a citation for DUI ("driving under the influence"), so don't even think about driving while intoxicated.

**DRIVING RULES** See "Getting There & Getting Around," in chapter 3.

**ELECTRICITY** Like Canada, the United States uses 110–120 volts AC (60 cycles), compared to 220–240 volts AC (50 cycles) in most of Europe, Australia, and New Zealand. Downward converters that change 220–240 volts to 110–120 volts are difficult to find in the United States, so bring one with you.

Wherever you go, bring a **connection kit** of the right power and phone adapters, a spare phone cord, and a spare Ethernet network cable—or find out whether your hotel supplies them to guests.

**EMBASSIES & CONSULATES** All embassies are located in the nation's capital, Washington, D.C. Some consulates are located in major U.S. cities, and most nations have a mission to the United Nations in New York City. If your country isn't listed below, call for directory information in Washington, D.C. (© 202/555-1212) or check **www.embassy.org/embassies**.

The embassy of **Australia** is at 1601 Massachusetts Ave. NW, Washington, DC 20036 (© **202/797-3000;** www.austemb.org). There are consulates in New York, Honolulu, Houston, Los Angeles, and San Francisco.

The embassy of **Canada** is at 501 Pennsylvania Ave. NW, Washington, DC 20001 (© **202/682-1740;** www.canadianembassy.org). Other Canadian consulates are in Buffalo (New York), Detroit, Los Angeles, New York, and Seattle.

The embassy of **Ireland** is at 2234 Massachusetts Ave. NW, Washington, DC 20008 (© **202/462-3939;** www.irelandemb.org). Irish consulates are in Boston, Chicago, New York, San Francisco, and other cities. See website for complete listing.

The embassy of **New Zealand** is at 37 Observatory Circle NW, Washington, DC 20008 (© **202/328-4800;** www.nzemb.org). New Zealand consulates are in Los Angeles, Salt Lake City, San Francisco, and Seattle.

The embassy of the **United Kingdom** is at 3100 Massachusetts Ave. NW, Washington, DC 20008 (© **202/588-6500;** www.britainusa.com). Other British consulates are in Atlanta, Boston, Chicago, Cleveland, Houston, Los Angeles, New York, San Francisco, and Seattle.

**EMERGENCIES** To report a fire, summon the police, or get an ambulance, simply dial © **911.** See also the listing for the **Travelers Aid Society of Metropolitan Atlanta** under "Visitor Information," in chapter 3.

**GASOLINE (PETROL)** At press time, in the U.S., the cost of gasoline (also known as gas, but never petrol), is abnormally low, with unleaded gas averaging $1.55 a gallon at most Atlanta stations. Taxes are already included in the printed price. One U.S. gallon equals 3.8 liters or .85 imperial gallons. Fill-up locations are known as gas or service stations.

**HOLIDAYS** Banks, government offices, post offices, and many stores, restaurants, and museums are closed on the following legal national holidays: January 1 (New Year's Day), the third Monday in January (Martin Luther King, Jr., Day), the third Monday in February (Presidents' Day), the last Monday in May (Memorial Day), July 4 (Independence Day), the first Monday in September (Labor Day), the second Monday in October (Columbus Day), November 11 (Veterans' Day/Armistice Day), the fourth Thursday in November (Thanksgiving Day), and December 25 (Christmas). The Tuesday after the first Monday in November is Election Day, a federal government holiday in presidential-election years.

For more information on holidays, see "Calendar of Events," in chapter 3.

**HOSPITALS** **Piedmont Hospital,** 1968 Peachtree Rd., just above Collier Road (© 404/605-3297), provides 24-hour full emergency-room service, as does **Grady Health Systems,** 35 Butler St., downtown (© 404/616-6200). For life-threatening medical emergencies, dial © **911.**

**INSURANCE** **Medical Insurance** Although it's not required of travelers, health insurance is highly recommended. Most health insurance policies cover you if you get sick away from home—but check your coverage before you leave.

International visitors to the U.S. should note that, unlike many European countries, the United States does not usually offer free or low-cost medical care to its citizens or visitors. Doctors and hospitals are expensive, and in most cases will require advance payment or proof of coverage before they render their services. Good policies will cover the costs of an accident, repatriation, or death. Packages such as **Europ Assistance's "Worldwide Healthcare Plan"** are sold by European automobile clubs and travel agencies at attractive rates. **Worldwide Assistance Services, Inc.** (© 800/777-8710; www.worldwideassistance.com) is the agent for Europ Assistance in the United States.

Though lack of health insurance may prevent you from being admitted to a hospital in non-emergencies, don't worry about being left on a street corner to die: The American way is to fix you now and bill the daylights out of you later.

If you're ever hospitalized more than 150 miles from home, **MedjetAssist** (© 800/527-7478; www.medjetassistance.com) will pick you up and fly you to the hospital of your choice in a medically equipped and staffed aircraft 24 hours day, 7 days a week. Annual memberships are $225 individual, $350 family; you can also purchase short-term memberships.

**Canadians** should check with their provincial health plan offices or call **Health Canada** (© 866/225-0709; www.hc-sc.gc.ca) to find out the extent of their coverage and what documentation and receipts they must take home in case they are treated in the United States.

Travelers from the U.K. should carry their European Health Insurance Card (EHIC), which replaced the E111 form as proof of entitlement to free/reduced-cost medical treatment abroad (© 0845 606 2030; www.ehic.org.uk). Note, however, that the EHIC only covers "necessary medical treatment," and for repatriation costs, lost money, baggage, or cancellation, travel insurance from a reputable company should always be sought (www.travelinsuranceweb.com).

**Travel Insurance** The cost of travel insurance varies widely, depending on the destination, the cost and length of your trip, your age and health, and the type of trip you're taking, but expect to pay between 5% and 8% of the vacation itself. You can get estimates from various providers through **InsureMyTrip.com**. Enter your trip cost and dates, your age, and other information, for prices from more than a dozen companies.

U.K. citizens and their families who make more than one trip abroad per year may find an annual travel insurance policy to be cheaper. Check **www.moneysupermarket. com**, which compares prices across a wide range of providers for single- and multi-trip policies.

Most big travel agents offer their own insurance and will probably try to sell you their package when you book a holiday. Think before you sign. **Britain's Consumers' Association** recommends that you insist on seeing the policy and reading the fine print before buying travel insurance. **The Association of British Insurers** (© 020/7600-3333; www.abi.org.uk) gives advice by phone and publishes Holiday Insurance, a free guide to policy provisions and prices. You might also shop around for better deals: Try **Columbus Direct** (© 0870/033-9988; www.columbusdirect. net).

**Trip Cancellation Insurance** Trip-cancellation insurance will help retrieve your money if you have to back out of a trip or depart early, or if your travel supplier goes bankrupt. Trip cancellation traditionally covers such events as sickness, natural disasters, and State Department advisories. The latest news in trip-cancellation insurance is the availability of **expanded hurricane coverage** and the **"any-reason"** cancellation coverage—which costs more, but covers cancellations made for any reason. You won't get back 100% of your pre-paid trip cost, but you'll be refunded a substantial portion. **TravelSafe** (© 888/ 885-7233; www.travelsafe.com) offers both types of coverage. Expedia also offers

any-reason cancellation coverage for its air-hotel packages. For details, contact one of the following recommended insurers: **Access America** (© 866/807-3982; www. accessamerica.com); **Travel Guard International** (© 800/826-4919; www.travel guard.com); **Travel Insured International** (© 800/243-3174; www.travelinsured. com); and **Travelex Insurance Services** (© 888/457-4602; www.travelex-insurance. com).

**INTERNET ACCESS** Internet access is easy to come by in Atlanta. In fact, sitting on a bench in a business area can typically result in any number of unsecured wireless connections from your laptop. In addition, nearly every coffee shop in town (and there are hundreds) offer free wireless access (Wi-Fi). If you aren't traveling with a computer, seek out any of the Atlanta public libraries as they offer free use of computers with Internet access. In addition, most large hotels provide computer access in the lobby or in the business center, though it is rarely free. If you get in a pinch, you can pay for Internet access at the Coffee Net, 931 Monroe Dr., Ste. C-103, where the fee is $3.50 per half-hour, or Maasty Computers Internet Café, 736-A Ponce De Leon Ave. NE, where it costs $2.50 for 15 minutes or $10 per hour. All Atlanta FedEx Office locations also have wireless Internet access.

**LAUNDROMATS** There are a number of self-serve and valet laundry facilities throughout the city. Among the most central locations are: **Poncey Cleaners and Laundry Mat,** 231 Ponce De Leon Ave. NE (© 404/817-0749); **Midtown Laundry,** 670 Myrtle St. NE (© 404/881-5872); and **Laundromax,** 1599 Memorial Dr. SE (© 404/373-2203).

**LEGAL AID** If you are "pulled over" for a minor infraction (such as speeding), never attempt to pay the fine directly to a police officer; this could be construed as attempted bribery, a much more serious crime. Pay fines by mail, or directly into the hands of the clerk of the court. If accused of a more serious offense, say and do nothing before consulting a lawyer. Here the burden is on the state to prove a person's guilt beyond a reasonable doubt, and everyone has the right to remain silent, whether he or she is suspected of a crime or actually arrested. Once arrested, a person can make one telephone call to a party of his or her choice. International visitors should call their embassy or consulate.

**LOST & FOUND**   Be sure to tell all of your credit card companies the minute you discover your wallet has been lost or stolen, and file a report at the nearest police precinct. Your credit card company or insurer may require a police report number or record of the loss. Most credit card companies have an emergency toll-free number to call if your card is lost or stolen; they may be able to wire you a cash advance immediately or deliver an emergency credit card in a day or two. Visa's U.S. emergency number is ℂ **800/847-2911** or 410/581-9994. American Express cardholders and traveler's check holders should call ℂ **800/221-7282.** Master-Card holders should call ℂ **800/307-7309** or 636/722-7111. For other credit cards, call the toll-free number directory at ℂ **800/555-1212.**

If you need emergency cash over the weekend when all banks and American Express offices are closed, you can have money wired to you via **Western Union** (ℂ **800/325-6000;** www.westernunion. com).

**MAIL**   Open 24 hours a day, Atlanta's main post office is located not in the downtown area, but close to Hartsfield-Jackson Atlanta International Airport at 3900 Crown Rd. (ℂ **800/ASK-USPS** [**275-8777**].

At press time, domestic postage rates were 27¢ for a postcard and 42¢ for a letter. For international mail, a first-class letter of up to 1 ounce costs 94¢ (72¢ to Canada and Mexico); a first-class postcard costs 94¢ (72¢ to Canada and Mexico); and a preprinted postal aerogramme costs 97¢. For more information, go to **www. usps.com** and click on "Calculate Postage."

If you aren't sure what your address will be in the United States, mail can be sent to you, in your name, c/o General Delivery at the main post office of the city or region where you expect to be. (Call ℂ **800/275-8777** for information on the nearest post office.) The addressee must pick up mail in person and must produce proof of identity (such as a driver's license or passport). Most post offices will hold your mail for up to 1 month, and are open Monday to Friday from 8am to 6pm, Saturday from 9am to 3pm.

Always include zip codes when mailing items in the U.S. If you don't know your zip code, visit www.usps.com/zip4.

**MEASUREMENTS**   The nonmetric system of measurement is used in the U.S. Conversions for nonmetric to metric, and vice versa, are available online at www. onlineconversion.com.

**MEDICAL CONDITIONS**   If you have a medical condition that requires **syringe-administered medications,** carry a valid signed prescription from your physician; syringes in carry-on baggage will be inspected. Insulin in any form should have the proper pharmaceutical documentation. If you have a disease that requires treatment with **narcotics,** you should also carry documented proof with you—smuggling narcotics aboard a plane carries severe penalties in the U.S.

For **HIV-positive visitors,** requirements for entering the United States are somewhat vague and change frequently. For up-to-the-minute information, contact **AIDSinfo** (ℂ **800/448-0440** or 301/519-6616 outside the U.S.; www.aidsinfo. nih.gov) or the **Gay Men's Health Crisis** (ℂ **212/367-1000;** www.gmhc.org).

**NEWSPAPERS & MAGAZINES** The major newspaper in town is the *Atlanta Journal-Constitution* (www.ajc.com). Its "Access Atlanta" section, published every Thursday, highlights plays, festivals, live music, gallery openings, and other happenings for the weekend and the week ahead. It includes restaurant and movie reviews as well. You'll also find it helpful to pick up a current issue of *Atlanta* magazine when you're in town. And keep an eye out for *Creative Loafing* (www.cln.com), an offbeat free publication available in shops, restaurants, and on the street; it has lots of interesting information, including excellent restaurant reviews.

**PASSPORTS** The websites listed provide downloadable passport applications as well as the current fees for processing applications. For an up-to-date, country-by-country listing of passport requirements around the world, go to the "International Travel" tab of the U.S. State Department at http://travel.state.gov. International visitors to the U.S. can obtain a visa application at the same website. *Note:* Children are required to present a passport when entering the United States at airports. More information on obtaining a passport for a minor can be found at http://travel.state.gov. Allow plenty of time before your trip to apply for a passport; processing normally takes 4–6 weeks (3 weeks for expedited service) but can take longer during busy periods (especially spring). And keep in mind that if you need a passport in a hurry, you'll pay a higher processing fee.

**For Residents of Australia** You can pick up an application from your local post office or any branch of Passports Australia, but you must schedule an interview at the passport office to present your application materials. Call the **Australian Passport Information Service** at ℂ **131-232,** or visit the government website at www. passports.gov.au.

**For Residents of Canada** Passport applications are available at travel agencies throughout Canada or from the central **Passport Office,** Dept. of Foreign Affairs and International Trade, Ottawa, ON K1A 0G3 (ℂ **800/567-6868;** www.ppt. gc.ca). *Note:* Canadian children who travel must have their own passport. However, if you hold a valid Canadian passport issued before December 11, 2001, that bears the name of your child, the passport remains valid for you and your child until it expires.

**For Residents of Ireland** You can apply for a 10-year passport at the **Passport Office,** Setanta Centre, Molesworth Street, Dublin 2 (ℂ **01/671-1633;** www.irlgov. ie/iveagh). Those 17 and under and seniors 66 and over must apply for a 3-year passport. You can also apply at 1A South Mall, Cork (ℂ **21/494-4700**) or at most main post offices.

**For Residents of New Zealand** You can pick up a passport application at any New Zealand Passports Office or download it from their website. Contact the **Passports Office** at ℂ **0800/225-050** in New Zealand or 04/474-8100, or log on to www. passports.govt.nz.

**For Residents of the United Kingdom** To pick up an application for a standard 10-year passport (5-yr. passport for children 15 and under,) visit your nearest passport office, major post office, or travel agency or contact the **United Kingdom Passport Service** at ℂ **0870/521-0410** or search its website at www.ukpa. gov.uk.

**POLICE** Call ℂ **911** in an emergency. Otherwise, call ℂ **404/853-3434.**

**SMOKING** While the city of Atlanta has yet to impose a smoking ban on the city, statewide "no smoking" efforts have drastically reduced the number of places that remain smoker-friendly. Smoking is still allowed in bars and some restaurants, and efforts to pass a more stringent code that would ban smoking in all bars, restaurants, and other public places have been unsuccessful to date. Designated smoking areas can be found in some public places, such as the airport and some sports/entertainment venues.

**TAXES** Sales tax in Atlanta is 7%. A total of 14% is paid by hotel and motel guests within the city of Atlanta and Fulton County. Of that tax, 7% is sales tax and 7% is room tax. Car rentals at Hartsfield-Jackson Atlantic International Airport are assessed 20% in taxes, but rentals in the metro area incur only the local sales tax. The United States has no value-added tax (VAT) or other indirect tax at the national level. Every state, county, and city may levy its own local tax on all purchases, including hotel and restaurant checks and airline tickets. These taxes will not appear on price tags.

**TELEPHONES** Many convenience groceries and packaging services sell **pre-paid calling cards** in denominations up to $50; for international visitors, these can be the least expensive way to call home. Many public pay phones at airports now accept American Express, MasterCard, and Visa credit cards. **Local calls** made from pay phones in most locales cost either 25¢ or 35¢ (no pennies, please). Most long-distance and international calls can be dialed directly from any phone. **For calls within the United States and to Canada,** dial 1 followed by the area code and the seven-digit number. **For other international calls,** dial 011 followed by the country code, city code, and the number you are calling.

Calls to area codes **800, 888, 877,** and **866** are toll-free. However, calls to area codes **700** and **900** (chat lines, bulletin boards, "dating" services, and so on) can be very expensive—usually a charge of 95¢ to $3 or more per minute, and they sometimes have minimum charges that can run as high as $15 or more.

For **reversed-charge** or **collect calls,** and for **person-to-person calls,** dial the number 0, then the area code and number; an operator will come on the line, and you should specify whether you are calling collect, person-to-person, or both. If your operator-assisted call is international, ask for the overseas operator.

For **local directory assistance** ("information"), dial © **411;** for long-distance information, dial 1, then the appropriate area code and 555-1212.

**TELEGRAPH, TELEX & FAX** Telegraph and telex services are provided primarily by **Western Union** (© **800/325-6000;** www.westernunion.com). You can telegraph (wire) money, or have it telegraphed to you, very quickly over the Western Union system, but this service can cost as much as 15% to 20% of the amount sent.

Most hotels have **fax machines** available for guest use (be sure to ask about the charge to use it). Many hotel rooms are wired for guests' fax machines. A less expensive way to send and receive faxes may be at stores such as the **UPS Store.**

**TIME** Atlanta is in the Eastern Standard Time Zone. The continental United States is divided into **four time zones:** Eastern Standard Time (EST), Central Standard Time (CST), Mountain Standard Time (MST), and Pacific Standard Time (PST). Alaska and Hawaii have their own zones. For example, when it's 9am in Los Angeles (PST), it's 7am in Honolulu (HST), 10am in Denver (MST), 11am in Chicago (CST), noon in New York City (EST), 5pm in London (GMT), and 2am the next day in Sydney.

**Daylight saving time** is in effect from 1am on the second Sunday in March to 1am on the first Sunday in November, except in Arizona, Hawaii, the U.S. Virgin Islands, and Puerto Rico. Daylight saving time moves the clock 1 hour ahead of standard time.

**TIPPING** Tips are a very important part of certain workers' income, and gratuities are the standard way of showing appreciation for services provided. (Tipping is certainly not compulsory if the service is poor!) In hotels, tip **bellhops** at least $1 per bag ($2–$3 if you have a lot of luggage) and tip the **chamber staff** $1 to $2 per day (more if you've left a disaster area for him or her to clean up). Tip the **doorman** or **concierge** only if he or she has provided you with some specific service (for example, calling a cab for you or obtaining difficult-to-get theater tickets). Tip the **valet-parking attendant** $1 every time you get your car.

In restaurants, bars, and nightclubs, tip **service staff** 15% to 20% of the check, tip **bartenders** 10% to 15%, tip **checkroom attendants** $1 per garment, and tip **valet-parking attendants** $1 per vehicle.

As for other service personnel, tip **cab drivers** 15% of the fare; tip **skycaps** at airports at least $1 per bag ($2–$3 if you have a lot of luggage); and tip **hairdressers** and **barbers** 15% to 20%.

**TOILETS** You won't find public toilets or "restrooms" on the streets in most U.S. cities, but they can be found in hotel lobbies, bars, restaurants, museums, department stores, railway and bus stations, and service stations. Large hotels and fast-food restaurants are often the best bets for clean facilities. Restaurants and bars in resorts or heavily visited areas may reserve their restrooms for patrons.

**USEFUL PHONE NUMBERS** U.S. Dept. of State Travel Advisory: ✆ 202/647-5225 (manned 24 hrs.).

U.S. Passport Agency: ✆ 202/647-0518.

U.S. Centers for Disease Control International Traveler's Hotline: ✆ 404/332-4559.

**VISAS** For information about U.S. Visas go to **http://travel.state.gov** and click on "Visas." Or go to one of the following websites:

**Australian** citizens can obtain up-to-date visa information from the **U.S. Embassy Canberra,** Moonah Place, Yarralumla, ACT 2600 (✆ 02/6214-5600) or by checking the U.S. Diplomatic Mission's website at **http://usembassy-australia.state.gov/consular**.

**British** subjects can obtain up-to-date visa information by calling the **U.S. Embassy Visa Information Line** (✆ 0891/200-290) or by visiting the "Visas to the U.S." section of the American Embassy London's website at **www.usembassy.org.uk**.

**Irish** citizens can obtain up-to-date visa information through the **Embassy of the USA Dublin,** 42 Elgin Rd., Dublin 4, Ireland (✆ 353/1-668-8777; or by checking the "Consular Services" section of the website at **http://dublin.usembassy.gov**.

Citizens of **New Zealand** can obtain up-to-date visa information by contacting the **U.S. Embassy New Zealand,** 29 Fitzherbert Terrace, Thorndon, Wellington (✆ 644/472-2068), or get the information directly from the website at **http://wellington.usembassy.gov**.

## MAJOR U.S. AIRLINES

(*flies internationally as well)

**American Airlines***
✆ 800/433-7300 (in U.S. or Canada)
✆ 020/7365-0777 (in U.K.)
www.aa.com

**Continental Airlines***
✆ 800/523-3273 (in U.S. or Canada)
✆ 084/5607-6760 (in U.K.)
www.continental.com

**Delta Air Lines***
✆ 800/221-1212 (in U.S. or Canada)
✆ 084/5600-0950 (in U.K.)
www.delta.com

**Frontier Airlines**
✆ 800/432-1359 (in U.S.)
www.frontierairlines.com

**Midwest Airlines** (in U.S.)
✆ 800/452-2022
www.midwestairlines.com

**Northwest Airlines***
✆ 800/225-2525 (in U.S.)
✆ 870/0507-4074 (in U.K.)
www.nwa.com

**United Airlines***
✆ 800/864-8331 (in U.S. or Canada)
✆ 084/5844-4777 (in U.K.)
www.united.com

**US Airways***
✆ 800/428-4322 (in U.S. or Canada)
✆ 084/5600-3300 (in U.K.)
www.usairways.com

## MAJOR INTERNATIONAL AIRLINES

**Aeroméxico**
✆ 800/237-6639 (in U.S.)
✆ 020/7801-6234 (in U.K., information only)
www.aeromexico.com

**Air France**
✆ 800/237-2747 (in U.S.)
✆ 800/375-8723 (in U.S. or Canada)
✆ 087/0142-4343 (in U.K.)
www.airfrance.com

**Air Jamaica**
✆ 800/523-5585 (in U.S. or Canada)
✆ 208/570-7999 (in Jamaica)
www.airjamaica.com

**American Airlines**
✆ 800/433-7300 (in U.S. or Canada)
✆ 020/7365-0777 (in U.K.)
www.aa.com

**British Airways**
✆ 800/247-9297 (in U.S. or Canada)
✆ 087/0850-9850 (in U.K.)
www.british-airways.com

**Continental Airlines**
✆ 800/523-3273 (in U.S. or Canada)
✆ 084/5607-6760 (in U.K.)
www.continental.com

**Delta Air Lines**
✆ 800/221-1212 (in U.S. or Canada)
✆ 084/5600-0950 (in U.K.)
www.delta.com

**Japan Airlines**
✆ 012/025-5931 (international)
www.jal.co.jp

**Korean Air**
✆ 800/438-5000 (in U.S. or Canada)
✆ 0800/413-000 (in U.K.)
www.koreanair.com

**Lufthansa**
✆ 800/399-5838 (in U.S.)
✆ 800/563-5954 (in Canada)
✆ 087/0837-7747 (in U.K.)
www.lufthansa.com

**United Airlines**
℗ 800/864-8331 (in U.S. or Canada)
℗ 084/5844-4777 (in U.K.)
www.united.com

**US Airways**
℗ 800/428-4322 (in U.S. or Canada)
℗ 084/5600-3300 (in U.K.)
www.usairways.com

## BUDGET AIRLINES

**AirTran Airways**
℗ 800/247-8726
www.airtran.com

**Frontier Airlines**
℗ 800/432-1359
www.frontierairlines.com

## CAR RENTAL AGENCIES

**Alamo**
℗ 800/GO-ALAMO (800/462-5266)
www.alamo.com

**Avis**
℗ 800/331-1212 (in U.S. or Canada)
℗ 084/4581-8181 (in U.K.)
www.avis.com

**Budget**
℗ 800/527-0700 (in U.S.)
℗ 087/0156-5656 (in U.K.)
℗ 800/268-8900 (in Canada)
www.budget.com

**Dollar**
℗ 800/800-4000 (in U.S.)
℗ 800/848-8268 (in Canada)
℗ 080/8234-7524 (in U.K.)
www.dollar.com

**Enterprise**
℗ 800/261-7331 (in U.S.)
℗ 514/355-4028 (in Canada)
℗ 012/9360-9090 (in U.K.)
www.enterprise.com

**Virgin America**
℗ 877/359-847446
www.virginamerica.com

**Spirit Airlines**
℗ 800/772-7117
www.spiritair.com

**Hertz**
℗ 800/645-3131 (in U.S.)
℗ 800/654-3001 (international
   reservations)
www.hertz.com

**National**
℗ 800/CAR-RENT (800/227-7368)
www.nationalcar.com

**Payless**
℗ 800/PAYLESS (800/729-5377)
www.paylesscarrental.com

**Rent-A-Wreck**
℗ 800/535-1391
www.rentawreck.com

**Thrifty**
℗ 800/367-2277
℗ 918/669-2168 (international)
www.thrifty.com

# MAJOR HOTEL & MOTEL CHAINS

## Best Western International
📞 800/780-7234 (in U.S. or Canada)
📞 0800/393-130 (in U.K.)
www.bestwestern.com

## Clarion Hotels
📞 800/CLARION or 877/424-6423 (in U.S. or Canada)
📞 0800/444-444 (in U.K.)
www.choicehotels.com

## Comfort Inns
📞 800/228-5150
📞 0800/444-444 (in U.K.)
www.comfortinn.com

## Courtyard by Marriott
📞 888/236-2427 (in U.S.)
📞 0800/221-222 (in U.K.)
www.marriott.com/courtyard

## Crowne Plaza Hotels
📞 888/303-1746
www.ichotelsgroup.com/crowneplaza

## Days Inn
📞 800/329-7466 (in U.S.)
📞 0800/280-400 (in U.K.)
www.daysinn.com

## Doubletree Hotels
📞 800/222-TREE (800/222-8733) (in U.S. or Canada)
📞 087/0590-9090 (in U.K.)
www.doubletree.com

## Econo Lodges
📞 800/55-ECONO (800/552-3666)
www.choicehotels.com

## Embassy Suites
📞 800/EMBASSY (800/362-2779)
www.embassysuites1.hilton.com

## Fairfield Inn by Marriott
📞 800/228-2800 (in U.S. or Canada)
📞 0800/221-222 (in U.K.)
www.marriott.com/fairfield-inn/travel.mi

## Four Seasons
📞 800/819-5053 (in U.S. or Canada)
📞 0800/6488-6488 (in U.K.)
www.fourseasons.com

## Hampton Inn
📞 800/HAMPTON (800/426-4766)
www.hamptoninn1.hilton.com

## Hilton Hotels
📞 800/HILTONS (800/445-8667) (in U.S. or Canada)
📞 087/0590-9090 (in U.K.)
www.hilton.com

## Holiday Inn
📞 800/315-2621 (in U.S. or Canada)
📞 0800/405-060 (in U.K.)
www.holidayinn.com

## Howard Johnson
📞 800/446-4656 (in U.S. or Canada)
www.hojo.com

## Hyatt
📞 888/591-1234 (in U.S. or Canada)
📞 084/5888-1234 (in U.K.)
www.hyatt.com

## InterContinental Hotels & Resorts
📞 800/424-6835 (in U.S. or Canada)
📞 0800/1800-1800 (in U.K.)
www.ichotelsgroup.com

## La Quinta Inns and Suites
📞 800/642-4271 (in U.S. or Canada)
www.lq.com

## Loews Hotels
📞 800/23LOEWS (800/235-6397)
www.loewshotels.com

## Marriott
📞 877/236-2427 (in U.S. or Canada)
📞 0800/221-222 (in U.K.)
www.marriott.com

## Motel 6
📞 800/4MOTEL6 (800/466-8356)
www.motel6.com

## Omni Hotels
📞 888/444-OMNI (888/444-6664)
www.omnihotels.com

## Quality Inn
📞 877/424-6423 (in U.S. or Canada)
📞 0800/444-444 (in U.K.)
www.qualityinn.com

**Radisson Hotels & Resorts**
© 888/201-1718 (in U.S. or Canada)
© 0800/374-411 (in U.K.)
www.radisson.com

**Ramada Worldwide**
© 888/2-RAMADA (888/272-6232)
  (in U.S. or Canada)
© 0800/8100-0783 (in U.K.)
www.ramada.com

**Red Carpet Inns**
© 800/251-1962
www.bookroomsnow.com

**Red Roof Inns**
© 866/686-4335 (in U.S. or Canada)
© 614/601-4075 (international)
www.redroof.com

**Renaissance**
© 888/236-2427
www.renaissance.com

**Residence Inn by Marriott**
© 800/331-3131 (in U.S. or Canada)
© 800/221-222 (in U.K.)
www.marriott.com/residenceinn

**Rodeway Inns**
© 877/424-6423
www.rodewayinn.com

**Sheraton Hotels & Resorts**
© 800/325-3535 (in U.S.)
© 800/543-4300 (in Canada)
© 0800/3253-5353 (in U.K.)
www.starwoodhotels.com/sheraton

**Super 8 Motels**
© 800/800-8000
www.super8.com

**Travelodge**
© 800/578-7878
www.travelodge.com

**Westin Hotels & Resorts**
© 800/937-8461 (in U.S. or Canada)
© 0800/3259-5959 (in U.K.)
www.starwoodhotels.com/westin

**Wyndham Hotels & Resorts**
© 877/999-3223 (in U.S. or Canada)
© 050/6638-4899 (in U.K.)
www.wyndham.com

# INDEX

See also Accommodations and Restaurant indexes, below

# A Guide for Every Type of Travele

## Frommer's Complete Guides

For those who value complete coverage, candid advice, and lots of choices in all price ranges.

## Pauline Frommer's Guides

For those who want to experien a culture, meet locals, and save money along the way.

## MTV Guides

For hip, youthful travelers who want a fresh perspective on today's hottest cities and destinations.

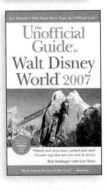

## Day by Day Guides

For leisure or busi ness travelers who want to organize their time to get th most out of a trip

## Frommer's With Kids Guides

For families traveling with children ages 2 to 14 seeking kid-friendly hotels, res-taurants, and activities.

## Unofficial Guides

For honeymoon families, busines travelers, and others who valu no-nonsense, *Consumer Reports*–style advice.

## For Dummies Travel Guides

For curious, inde-pendent travelers looking for a fun and easy way to plan a trip.

**Visit Frommers.com**

# ⊗ WILEY
## Now you know.

## FROMMER'S® PORTABLE GUIDES

Acapulco, Ixtapa & Zihuatanejo
Amsterdam
Aruba, Bonaire & Curacao
Australia's Great Barrier Reef
Bahamas
Big Island of Hawaii
Boston
California Wine Country
Cancún
Cayman Islands
Charleston
Chicago
Dominican Republic

Florence
Las Vegas
Las Vegas for Non-Gamblers
London
Maui
Nantucket & Martha's Vineyard
New Orleans
New York City
Paris
Portland
Puerto Rico
Puerto Vallarta, Manzanillo &
    Guadalajara

Rio de Janeiro
San Diego
San Francisco
Savannah
St. Martin, Sint Maarten, Anguilla
    St. Bart's
Turks & Caicos
Vancouver
Venice
Virgin Islands
Washington, D.C.
Whistler

## FROMMER'S® CRUISE GUIDES

Alaska Cruises & Ports of Call

Cruises & Ports of Call

European Cruises & Ports of Call

## FROMMER'S® NATIONAL PARK GUIDES

Algonquin Provincial Park
Banff & Jasper
Grand Canyon

National Parks of the American West
Rocky Mountain
Yellowstone & Grand Teton

Yosemite and Sequoia & Kings
    Canyon
Zion & Bryce Canyon

## FROMMER'S® WITH KIDS GUIDES

Chicago
Hawaii
Las Vegas
London

National Parks
New York City
San Francisco

Toronto
Walt Disney World® & Orlando
Washington, D.C.

## FROMMER'S® PHRASEFINDER DICTIONARY GUIDES

Chinese
French

German
Italian

Japanese
Spanish

## SUZY GERSHMAN'S BORN TO SHOP GUIDES

France
Hong Kong, Shanghai & Beijing
Italy

London
New York
Paris

San Francisco
Where to Buy the Best of Everyth

## FROMMER'S® BEST-LOVED DRIVING TOURS

Britain
California
France
Germany

Ireland
Italy
New England
Northern Italy

Scotland
Spain
Tuscany & Umbria

## THE UNOFFICIAL GUIDES®

Adventure Travel in Alaska
Beyond Disney
California with Kids
Central Italy
Chicago
Cruises
Disneyland®
England
Hawaii

Ireland
Las Vegas
London
Maui
Mexico's Best Beach Resorts
Mini Mickey
New Orleans
New York City
Paris

San Francisco
South Florida including Miami &
    the Keys
Walt Disney World®
Walt Disney World® for
    Grown-ups
Walt Disney World® with Kids
Washington, D.C.

## SPECIAL-INTEREST TITLES

Athens Past & Present
Best Places to Raise Your Family
Cities Ranked & Rated
500 Places to Take Your Kids Before They Grow Up
Frommer's Best Day Trips from London
Frommer's Best RV & Tent Campgrounds in the U.S.A.

Frommer's Exploring America by RV
Frommer's NYC Free & Dirt Cheap
Frommer's Road Atlas Europe
Frommer's Road Atlas Ireland
Retirement Places Rated